ALAN DAVIS'

THE FUN ALSO RISES
TRAVEL GUIDE NORTH AMERICA

The Most Fun Places To Be At The Right Time

Launched in early 1998 as a subsidiary of Capital Values, Inc., San Francisco-based Greenline Publications introduces a list of unique books in its FunGuide series with the 1999 release of *The Fun Also Rises Travel Guide North America: The Most Fun Places To Be at the Right Time*. The culmination of several years of exhaustive research and planning, *The Fun Also Rises* kicks-off a series of related titles, including *The Fun Also Rises Travel Guide International*. These companion editions together include initeraries and Hot Sheets for all events and destinations listed on *The FunGuide 100: The 100 Most Fun Places To Be in the World at the Right Time*.

For updated information on all Greenline books, visit the Greenline Publications Web site at www.TheFunGuides.com

The Fun Also Rises is an independent guide. We accept no payment of any kind from events or establishments for inclusion in this book. We welcome your views on our selections.

The information contained in this book was checked as rigorously as possible before going to press. The publisher accepts no responsibility for any changes that may have occurred since, or for any other variance of fact from that recorded here in good faith.

Front Cover Photo Credits: Hookers' Ball (left); Richard McMullin, Office of the City Representative, Philadelphia, Pa. (center); Ville de France (right)

Back Cover Photo Credits: Chuck Thompson (top); Shane East Photography (bottom)

100% recycled paper including not less than 20% postconsumer content

ISBN: 0-9666352-0-5

Library of Congress: Catalog Card Number 98-75474

Distributed in the United States and Canada by Publishers Group West (PGW), Berkeley, California

Printed in the United States of America

10 9 8 7 6 5 4 3 2 1

GREENLINE PUBLICATIONS

10 Lombard Street, Suite 200

San Francisco, California 94111

ALAN DAVIS'

THE Fun
ALSO RISES

TRAVEL GUIDE
NORTH AMERICA

The Most <u>Fun</u> Places To Be At The Right Time

Edited by Chuck Thompson

First Edition

Special thanks to brother James Marti, whose encouragement got me started on this adventure.

Special thanks to brother Mitch Rofsky, whose help and optimism got me through to the end.

As author, I acknowledge the hundreds of people who have contributed to this book. This includes friends, tourist-board and travel-industry representatives, event organizers, and all those people who help make these events fun. In particular, I'd like to thank Dr. Roger Brunswick (a psychiatrist who helped me develop The Mating Rating), Bob Chirlian (whose travel agency got me where I needed to go), Jeff, Bob, and Mark Ross, Air France, Carmen McCarty of American Airlines, Jane Watkins and Cheryl Andrews, Fred Farkouh and Richard Faccio, Ann Opara, David Cole, Richard Ross, Jim Weston, Jim and Gloria Hassan, Josh in Indianapolis, Eugene Yee, Jorge Guarro, Elaine Petrocelli, Donald George, and Raul Santiago.

As publisher, I thank Carole Bidnick, our marketing consultant, and our friends at PGW, who helped put our ideas onto bookshelves. I also want to single out Terrance Mark and Gerard Gleason for their extraordinary work—they were always there when needed.

As author and publisher, I thank Chuck Thompson—there could not have been a person more responsible, effective, and nicer to work with, or one from whom I could have learned so much about writing.

Alan Davis

To my parents,
with thanks for their support
and for passing on the travel bug

To Jaimee and Paul, who have lovingly accepted
their father's endeavors

And to Emile, whose love, companionship, and humor
have made this one terrific ride

Editor	Chuck Thompson
Contributing Editor, chapters	Heidi Craig
Contributing Editor, Junos	Susan Kinsella

Contributors

Barbara Fulton (Québec Winter Carnaval), Candace O'Connor (Big Muddy), David Swanson (Disney World), Douglas Lloyd (Juno: About Car Racing), George Murphy (Fantasy Fest), Heidi Craig (Bike Week, Black and White Ball, Carnaval South Beach, Concours d'Elegance, Detroit Auto Show, Hookers' Ball/Halloween), Janet Byron (Country Music Fan Fair), Janet Coutts (Montréal Jazz Festival), Judy Eisen (Great American Beer Festival), Leslie Harlib (Napa Valley Wine Auction), Lisa Meltzer (New Year's Eve New York), Margaret Laybourn (Cheyenne Frontier Days), Marty Olmstead (Memphis in May Barbecue, St. Patrick's Day), Mary Lou D'Auray (Bumbershoot), Michael Schiller (Guavaween), Michelle Medley (Kentucky Derby), Paris Permenter and John Bigley (Dickens on the Strand, Fiesta San Antonio), Richelle Thomson (Aloha Festival, Las Vegas Rodeo, Phoenix Open, Super Bowl Weekend), Robert Landon (Academy Awards, Fourth of July, Mardi Gras, New Orleans Jazz Festival, Skiing Tahoe, The Preakness), Shannon Jones (South by Southwest), Steve Jermanok (Boston Harborfest), Steven Saffold (Taste of DC), Stuart Mangrum (Burning Man), Susan Guyett (Indy 500), Susan Kinsella (Balloon Fiesta, Street Scene), Teri Orr (Sundance Film Festival), Theresa Schadeck (Calgary Stampede), Tim Harlow (Aquatennial), Todd Malensek (Chicago Blues Festival, Milwaukee Summerfest, Riverfest), Wendell Brock (Spoleto).

Book Design	Terrance Mark Studio
Illustrations	Maureen Radcliffe George
Research and Administration	Gerard Gleason

Eileen Gordon, Jaimee Davis, James Marti, JoAnn Caballo, Joyce Jones, Laurel Calsoni, Laurie Pantell, Leslie Jirsa, Michele Powers Glaze, Paul Davis, Robert Leone

The Fun Also Rises
Travel Guide North America

Table of Contents

(continued on next page)

Table of Contents
cont.

F our years ago, while hiking at Point Reyes, Calif., one of the world's most beautiful spots, I started thinking that I was ready for a change in my life. As much as I enjoyed natural beauty, and fine restaurants, theater, movies, and tennis, I was ready for a kind of fun that was markedly different from what I'd grown accustomed to. I realized that elegant dinners with fine wines often were not satisfying—I wanted to be in restaurants where the people and surroundings were attractive, animated, downright noisy. I wanted to find places where people came together to interact, where people were participators, not spectators.

That was the point at which the need for this book became apparent. Most travel publications virtually ignore the most fun part of the day—night! *Zagat* doesn't have a "fun" category. Call the Dutch tourist board and ask about the most fun time to go to Amsterdam—"We're not interested in promoting fun, we promote tulips." Despite the fact that there are millions of single people over 30, ask a concierge for advice on where to meet singles, and it's likely you'll be directed to a Hard Rock Cafe (or if you look as old as I do, to a strip club). The multitude of available lists of events make no distinctions between, say, a potato festival in North Dakota and *La Tomatina* (the incredible tomato-throwing festival in Spain). According to *Event Business News*, there are more than 45,000 annual events just in the United States! But how are you supposed to know which are the best?

Everybody has some idea of what constitutes fun. But ask them to define it or describe it and, as with pornography, you end up with a Supreme Court interpretation: You'll know it when you see it. Well, I did see it—fun, that is—at its best.

T he Fun Also Rises draws its title from Ernest Hemingway's *The Sun Also Rises*, which helped popularize what has become perhaps the most thrilling party on earth—Pamplona's *Fiestas de San Fermín*, also known as the Running of the Bulls. For years, I'd been hesitant to go, but armed with a mission, I knew my time had come. Like Don Erñesto, I didn't run with the bulls, but *I was there* and it was one of the greatest experiences of my life.

Since then, I've been to more than 90 annual events around the world. One thing I've learned in the process of doing this book is that I don't have to lose my Type A personality status just because my job happens to be the pursuit of fun. Say what you will—looking for fun is hard work. Showing up at a club in Madrid at 2 a.m. and being told to come back at 4 a.m. when it fills up isn't easy when you've got a museum scheduled for the morning. Attending the world's largest annual rock concert in freezing rain and sloshing through the mud may be OK for teenagers, but not for me.

If you get the impression I'm a wimp, you're right. And this book is especially useful for people who, like me, enjoy their comforts and who are not aficionados of anything. After all, if you're a tennis fan, going to Wimbledon would be your idea of fun heaven. But if your primary interest is fun, not tennis, would you rather watch two guys whacking a ball back and forth, or grind to calypso music with beautiful costumed people in Barbados?

If you answered Wimbledon, this book is definitely for you. That's because, like me with Pamplona, you're probably intimidated by some of these events. With tips; ticket information; detailed itineraries; and Hot Sheets that identify the right hotels, the most hip restaurants and night life, and must-see sights and attractions, this book does everything possible to remove the intimidation factors from attending big-time events.

Will you follow these itineraries? We hope so. We've spent thousands of hours researching the best ways to get the most out of our top events and destinations. We've packed each itinerary, often with more than 15 hours of activities a day. Yet even if you don't faithfully follow our plan, you can consult the Hot Sheet for recommendations for the best of each destination.

We also want you to have fun reading the book. To that end, we've made the itineraries concise, the information easy to find. But you won't meet our criteria for fun just by reading the book. You've got to participate, smile, laugh, and move some body parts—you've got to go.

Although everyone can probably pick 20 events from *The FunGuide 100* list that they would readily enjoy, experimenting with not-so-obvious choices can add to the fun. The contrast between events heightened my enjoyment. For example, the two top-rated events (five stars each for both event and city) are the Vienna Opera Ball and Carnaval Rio—two that could hardly be more different. Just preparing for events is also a lot of fun. My companion and I took Viennese waltz lessons to get ready for the Vienna Opera Ball. We outfitted ourselves in Wrangler jeans and Stetsons and learned the two-step for the Las Vegas Rodeo. And we did what we could to prepare for the Hookers' Ball in San Francisco.

Mostly, though, this book is about being with people, meeting people, connecting with people. I was thrilled to find travelers like Paul Walton (see page 56), who focus their journeys on finding the world's fun spots. Of course, as Paul says, it's whom you're with or whom you meet that determines how good a trip you'll have.

My job has simply been to improve your chances of having fun and experiencing the world in the sensuous flash of color, light, sound, flavor, and motion that describes some of the best moments of life. It's up to you to break out of the ordinary, ignore the accepted, reject the expected. From Homer to Aerosmith, philosophers have pondered the metaphor of travel and place, and have summed up things pretty much the way *The New York Times* did recently: "For many people, life draws meaning from its journeys, not its destinations." This book proves that there are exceptions (100 of them) to every rule.

—Alan Davis
San Francisco, December 1998

ABOUT THE FUNGUIDE 100

Our goal is to create a list of a broad range of the world's most fun events and destinations for every week of the year. Here are our rules, exceptions, and results.

SELECTION CRITERIA FOR EVENTS

Rule: Events in this book must take place every year in the same location.

Exception: San Francisco's biennial Black and White Ball.

Rule: Events in this book must have a total attendance of at least 10,000.

Exceptions: The smallest event is the Napa Valley Wine Auction (2,000), followed by the Vienna Opera Ball (5,000).

The total attendance at all 92 events (eight of our chapters are destinations without events) is more than 62 million. More than two-thirds of the events have an attendance greater than 50,000. The three most attended events are: Carnaval Rio (10 million), Munich's Oktoberfest (6 million), and Stuttgart's Volkfest (5 million). The most attended events in North America are Fiesta San Antonio and Mardi Gras (both 3.5 million).

Rule: We cannot visit a city twice.

Exceptions: San Francisco, New Orleans, Las Vegas, London, Edinburgh. These world-class cities (★★★★★ or ★★★★) have two world-class events and warrant second visits. For other cities, alternative world-class events are listed in the Alternatives section of each itinerary.

Individual events are judged on:

Participation (The outrageous parties of Mardi Gras are a great example.)

Transformation (During Calgary's Stampede, the entire city gets a Western makeover.)

People-watching (From celebrities in Los Angeles during the Academy Awards to bikers at Daytona's Bike Week, this is always rewarding.)

Uniqueness (There's nothing like the Hookers' Ball in San Francisco.)

Spectacle (New Year's Eve in Times Square is tough to beat.)

Gorgeous surroundings (Hawaii's Aloha Festival comes to mind.)

Gorgeous surroundings of a more human variety

Personal release (Events like Key West's Fantasy Fest coax people into being a little more crazy and daring than they normally would be.)

WHAT EVENT RATINGS MEAN

★★★★★ and ★★★★

Must do. These events are worth making a special trip for, even planning your life around.

★★★ and ★★

Should do. These are events you should attend if you're already planning to visit the region, or if you are just looking for something fun to do on a given weekend.

★

These events, though not worth a special trip, are the times when it is most fun to be at the destination.

THE WORLD'S TOP EVENTS

★★★★★

Carnaval Rio	Trinidad Carnival
Mardi Gras	Venice Carnival
Munich's Oktoberfest	Vienna Opera Ball
Running of the Bulls	

NORTH AMERICA'S TOP EVENTS

★★★★★

Mardi Gras

★★★★

Bike Week	Fiesta San Antonio
Burning Man	Hookers' Ball/Halloween
Calgary Stampede	St. Patrick's Day
Fantasy Fest	Sundance Film Festival

DISTRIBUTION OF EVENT RATINGS

	★5	★4	★3	★2	★1	N/A*	Total
NA	1	8	23	9	6	3	50
EUR	4	9	10	3	1	3	30
LAC	2	1	3	2	1	2	11
AASP	—	3	1	4	1	—	9
Total	7	21	37	18	9	8	100

NA—North America (US and Canada); EUR—Europe; LAC—Latin America, Caribbean; AASP—Africa, Asia, South Pacific

*Eight destinations are not tied to specific events.

Cities are evaluated for the quality and quantity of their night life, restaurants, attractions, and hotels. We also consider a city's overall aesthetic.

CITY RATINGS

★★★★★ or ★★★★

These world-class fun cities are worth a visit any time, but are most fun during the recommended event.

★★★ or ★★

These are nice places to visit, but only worth a special trip during the event.

★

Save going here for the event.

Included in *The FunGuide 100* are eight destinations that are not tied to specific events, but must be included on any list of the world's most fun places to be: Acapulco, Athens, Ibiza/Majorca, Lake Tahoe, Zermatt, Hedonism II, the *Carnival Destiny* cruise ship, and Disney World.

NORTH AMERICA'S TOP CITIES

★★★★★

Boston	Miami
Chicago	New York City
Las Vegas	Philadelphia
Los Angeles	San Francisco

★★★★

Montréal	Toronto
New Orleans	Washington, DC

DISTRIBUTION OF CITY RATINGS

	5	4	3	2	1	N/A	Total
NA	8	4	22	9	1	3	47
EUR	10	4	4	5	2	3	28
LAC	1	1	4	2	1	2	11
AASP	4	1	1	2	1	—	9
Total	23	10	31	18	5	8	95**

**Five cities with two events are counted once

TOTAL RATINGS

Two events/destinations scored a perfect 10: Carnaval Rio in Rio de Janeiro, Brazil, and the Vienna Opera Ball, in Vienna, Austria. The events with the highest total rating (combined event and city rating) in North America were the Hookers' Ball/Halloween in San Francisco and Mardi Gras in New Orleans (nine stars each).

DISTRIBUTION OF TOTAL (EVENT + CITY) RATINGS

	10	9	8	7	6	5	4	N/A	Total
NA	—	2	8	6	13	11	7	3	50
EUR	1	7	4	4	5	6	—	3	30
LAC	1		1	1	—	5	1	2	11
AASP	—	1	1	2	2	0	3	—	9
Total	2	10	14	13	20	22	11	8	100

SELECTION CRITERIA FOR THE ITINERARY

Itineraries usually run Thursday through Saturday (when destinations are most lively) unless the high points of an event justify being there on a different day.

Rule: We spend only three days at any event/destination. **Exception**: We spend a week aboard the *Carnival Destiny*.

Hotels—When available, we choose only first-class hotels. Selected hotels should, in priority order: fit in with the events (convenient location to recommended events is important); be hip or classy but not stuffy; and capture the character of each city.

Restaurants—The food must be good, but ambience is as important as the meal. Otherwise, the criteria are the same as for hotels.

Night life—We cover the hottest places for the over-30 crowd. Our bias is toward Scotch over beer, classy over funky. We generally don't include performing arts.

Sightseeing—We include the best each destination has to offer, but we shy away from zoos, natural-history museums, botanical gardens, and shopping destinations (there's no time for shopping), unless they are unique.

Itineraries—We typically begin after breakfast on Day One and end when nightclubs close on Day Three.

Juno (short for "Did you know?"):

Every week of the year there's a fun place to be. And every fun place to be has a best time to be there.

Each event in this book involves a lot of people coming together for a good time. Especially for people over 30, some events are better than others for meeting someone with whom you can develop a relationship, even if just for a three-day visit. The key ingredients are sexual energy, the number of singles attending, and an opportunity to interact. Regrettably, there's no such thing as a sure thing, but here are our ratings for the chances of finding a mate at each event. (Medications optional)

HOPE (VIAGRA)

Phoenix Open	Phoenix	Arizona	Carnaval South Beach	Miami Beach	Florida
Skiing Tahoe	Lake Tahoe	California	St. Patrick's Day	Savannah	Georgia
Academy Awards	Los Angeles	California	Mardi Gras	New Orleans	Louisiana
Great American Beer Festival	Denver	Colorado	Sundance Film Festival	Park City	Utah
Fantasy Fest	Key West	Florida	Carnival Destiny	Miami	Florida

HOPE, NO CHANCE (PROZAC)

Concours d'Elegance	Carmel/Monterey	California	Burning Man	Reno	Nevada
Street Scene	San Diego	California	New Year's Eve New York	New York	New York
Hookers' Ball/Halloween	San Francisco	California	Fourth of July	Philadelphia	Pennsylvania
Black and White Ball	San Francisco	California	Spoleto	Charleston	South Carolina
Bike Week	Daytona Beach/		Country Music Fan Fair	Nashville	Tennessee
	Orlando	Florida	South by Southwest	Austin/Dallas/	
Guavaween	Tampa	Florida		Fort Worth	Texas
Aloha Festival	Honolulu	Hawaii	Dickens on the Strand	Houston/Galveston	Texas
Chicago Blues Festival	Chicago	Illinois	Fiesta San Antonio	San Antonio	Texas
Indy 500	Indianapolis	Indiana	Bumbershoot	Seattle	Washington
Kentucky Derby	Louisville	Kentucky	Summerfest	Milwaukee	Wisconsin
New Orleans Jazz Festival	New Orleans	Louisiana	Montréal Jazz Festival	Montréal	Québec
Boston Harborfest	Boston	Massachusetts	Québec Winter Carnaval	Québec City	Québec
Aquatennial	Minneapolis	Minnesota	Caribana	Toronto	Ontario
Big Muddy	St. Louis	Missouri			

NO CHANCE (HEMLOCK)

The remainder of the events and destinations are fun, really, but they don't exactly lend themselves to mating opportunities.

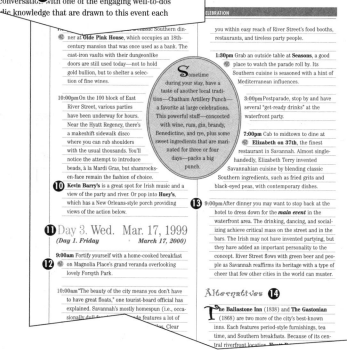

1. Destination location (If the event location is different from the city destination, it will be indicated in parentheses.)

2. Popular name of event

3. Official or secondary name, if applicable

4. Calendars for 1999 and 2000 (Light shading indicates duration of event. Dark shading indicates the recommended three days to spend at each event. These three days correspond with the daily itineraries.)

5. First year of event

6. One- to five-star event rating

7. One- to five-star city rating

8. Most recent attendance figures

9. Explanation of event and overview of event city

10. Bold-faced recommendations for where to stay, where to eat, or what to do (More detailed information, such as phone numbers, addresses, and price guides, can be found in the Hot Sheet at the end of each chapter.)

11. Recommended dates of travel for 1999 and 2000 (In some cases, the best three days to attend an event are not the same each year. For example, in 1999, we recommend visiting Savannah Monday-Wednesday, March 15-17; in 2000, Friday-Sunday, March 17-19.)

12. 🍽 indicating restaurant or eating option

13. Colored time entries and bold-faced, italicized entries, indicating an official activity connected to the event

14. Other significant events or subevents in the area occurring outside the recommended travel dates, and alternative hotels, restaurants, and activities

15. Numbers indicating the day on which a corresponding description can be found in the itinerary (*Alt* indicates the Alternatives section. A star indicates our top hotel pick.)

16. Prices for each hotel's best nonsuite double room during each event

$	Up to $100
$$	$100-$200
$$$	$200-$300
$$$$	$300-$400
$$$$+	More than $400

17. *Rms,* indicating number of rooms in each hotel

18. *Best Rooms,* indicating rooms to request when making reservations

19. Restaurant prices indicating average cost of one entree for the recommended meal (*Cover* and *Entry Fee* indicates prices at nightspots and attractions.)

$	Up to $10
$$	$10-$20
$$$	$20-$30
$$$$	$30-$40
$$$$+	More than $40

20. *Rec,* indicating the recommended meal in the itinerary at each restaurant with a / followed by other suggested meals, if applicable

B	Breakfast
L	Lunch
D	Dinner
T	High tea or snack

21. *Dress,* indicating the atmosphere at each establishment

Kazh	Casual, somewhat elegant, hip
Euro	A more continental take on Kazh, lots of attitude
Dressy	Men in suits, women in cocktail or evening wear
Yuppie	Khakis, button-downs, Ralph Lauren, Gap
FABs	Fraternity-alumni boys (think baseball caps)
Local	What locals wear (varies broadly between places like Los Angeles and Cheyenne, Wyoming)

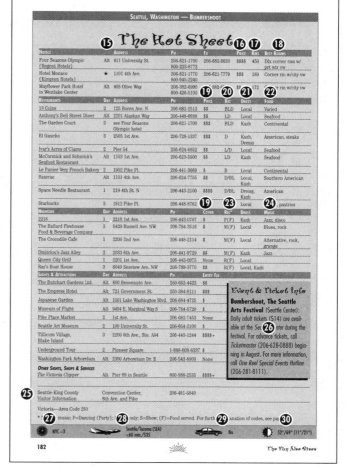

22. *Food,* indicating each restaurants' cuisine

23. *Rec,* indicating the scene at nightspots

M	Live music
P	Party atmosphere or dancing
S	Show
R	Bar only
(F)	Food available

24. Type of music featured at nightspot

25. Convention and Visitors Bureau (CVB) information

26. Detailed information, such as phone numbers, addresses, and prices (CD indicates a charitable donation included) for main events (bold-faced) and subevents (bold-faced, italic) (Contact phone numbers are provided only for alternative events.)

27. Local time zone relative to New York City

28. Local airport name, three-letter airport code, and approximate time and taxi fare from the airport to our recommended hotel, rounded up to nearest $5

29. Recommendation on whether or not to rent a car: Yes, No, or Yes/No (could go either way)

30. Average high and low temperatures during event in Fahrenheit (and Celsius)

31. (Not shown) All prices expressed in US dollars with $ followed by the value of US$1 in foreign currency

The FunGuide 100

INAUGURAL LIST 1999

	Travel Date	Event Date	Event / Offical Name (if different)	City, State, Country / Host City (if different)	Event/City Rating / Origin/Attendance	Pg / ✓
Week 1 1999	Jan. 1	Dec. 26-Jan. 1	Junkanoo	Nassau, Bahamas	★★★★★★★	Intl
2000	Jan. 1	Dec. 26-Jan. 1			c. 1800/10,000	
1999	Jan. 1	Jan. 1-30	Cape Minstrel Festival	Cape Town, South Africa	★★★★★★★	Intl
2000	Jan. 1	Jan. 1-30			1898/50,000	
Week 2 1999	Jan. 7	Jan. 8-18	Detroit Auto Show	Detroit, Michigan, USA	★★★★★	37
2000	Jan. 6	Jan. 7-17	North American International Auto Show, NAIAS		1907/790,000	
Week 3 1999	Jan. 15	Jan. 11-17	Ati Atihan	Manila, Phillipines	★★★★★	Intl
2000	Jan. 14	Jan. 10-16		(Kalibo)	1212/200,000	
1999	Jan. 15	Jan. 15-17	Calle San Sebastián	San Juan, Puerto Rico	★★★★★	Intl
2000	Jan. 14	Jan. 14-16			1970/50,000	
Week 4 1999	Jan. 21	Jan. 21-30	Sundance Film Festival	Park City, Utah, USA	★★★★★★★	43
2000	Jan. 20	Jan. 20-29			1978/18,000	
Week 5 1999	Jan. 27	Jan. 25-31	Phoenix Open	Phoenix, Arizona, USA	★★★★★★	47
2000	Jan. 26	Jan. 24-30		(Scottsdale)	1932/470,000	
1999	Jan. 29	Jan. 29-31	Super Bowl Weekend	Las Vegas, Nevada, USA	★★★★★★★	51
2000	Jan. 28	Jan. 28-30			1967/200,000	
Week 6 1999	Feb. 5	Jan. 29-Feb. 14	Québec Winter Carnaval	Québec City, Québec, Canada	★★★★★★	57
2000	Feb. 4	Jan. 28-Feb. 13	Carnaval de Québec		1894/1,000,000	
1999	Feb. 9	Feb. 11	Vienna Opera Ball	Vienna, Austria	★★★★★★★★★	Intl
2000	Feb. 29	Mar. 2			1877/5,000	
1999	Feb. 11	Feb. 10-15	Viña del Mar Song Festival	Santiago, Chile	★★★★★	Intl
2000	Feb. 12	Feb. 9-14	International Song Festival of Viña del Mar	(Viña del Mar)	1959/110,000	
Week 7 1999	Feb. 12	Feb. 6-16	Venice Carnival	Venice, Italy	★★★★★★★★	Intl
2000	Mar. 3	Feb. 26-Mar. 7	Carnevale di Venezia		1979/500,000	
1999	Feb. 13	Feb. 12-16	Karneval	Köln, Germany	★★★★★★★	Intl
2000	Mar. 4	Mar. 3-7			1823/100,000	
1999	Feb. 14	Feb. 6-16	Mardi Gras	New Orleans, Louisiana, USA	★★★★★★★★	61
2000	Mar. 5	Feb. 26-Mar. 7			1837/3,500,000	
1999	Feb. 14	Feb. 13-16	Carnaval Rio	Rio de Janeiro, Brazil	★★★★★★★★★	Intl
2000	Mar. 5	Mar. 4-7			1930/10,000,000	
Week 8 1999	Feb. 14	Feb. 15-16	Trinidad Carnival	Trinidad, Trinidad	★★★★★★★	Intl
2000	Mar. 5	Mar. 6-7			c. 1750/100,000	
1999	Feb. 15	Feb. 16-18	Chinese New Year	Hong Kong, China	★★★★★★	Intl
2000	Feb. 4	Feb. 5-7	New World Telephone Chinese New Year Fiesta		1996/25,000	
Week 9 1999	Feb. 25	Feb. 5-27	Sydney Gay and Lesbian Mardi Gras	Sydney, Australia	★★★★★★★★	Intl
2000	Feb. 24	Feb. 4-26			1978/100,000	

Events are listed according to the week in which the 1999 travel date takes place. Subsequent to January 1, weeks begin on Monday.

Intl = Itinerary in companion edition *The Fun Also Rises Travel Guide International*
Readers' ✓: Been there, Done that, or Plan to

The Fun Also Rises

THE 100 MOST FUN PLACES TO BE IN THE WORLD AT THE RIGHT TIME

January

Junkanoo	Kick off the new year at 2 a.m with a parade of elaborately costumed dancers, Caribbean music, and enthusiastic crowds that keep the party spirit alive past the break of dawn.
Cape Minstrel Festival	High-energy minstrels begin the year by taking over the streets and coaxing crowds to join them in singing, dancing, and marching in one of the world's most gorgeous and under-appreciated cities.
Detroit Auto Show	Detroit? Dead of winter? The city synonymous with cars revs up for a great weekend during North America's premier auto show (complete with a black-tie preview).
Ati Atihan	Filipinos take to the streets of Kalibo in a wildly costumed religious festival that celebrates dancing, shaking, foot-stomping, and noise-making.
Calle San Sebastián	Wall-to-wall people mingle, dance, and drink together along the closed-off streets of San Juan at Puerto Rico's biggest fiesta.
Sundance Film Festival	The glitterati schmooze, party, ski, and even watch the world's best new films being unveiled at the hottest film festival in the US.
Phoenix Open	Phoenix is golf heaven and no pro-golf tournament is more associated with fun, sun, and action than this one. You don't need to be a golfer to enjoy the highlight of Phoenix's social season.
Super Bowl Weekend	Hotels and casinos unfurl red carpets for players who know that the football game is just a sidelight during the world's quintessential gambling weekend.

February

Québec Winter Carnaval	This three-week samba in parkas is fueled by happy throngs and ubiquitous sticks filled with Caribou (a wicked libation made of port and grain alcohol).
Vienna Opera Ball	The best formal party in the world—the unparalleled Vienna Opera House is the setting for gorgeous debutantes, ties and tails, and the most elegant evening of the year.
Viña del Mar Song Festival	A music festival that coincides with Carnaval Rio—the late-night crowd warms up here with beaches and top-name Latin acts before proceeding to Rio.
Venice Carnival	The world's most beautiful city is transformed into a Fellini-esque world of masked paraders and costumed street performers by day, and a land of elegant balls by night.
Karneval	Not everyone in Köln is dressed like a clown, it just seems like it. One of the world's great pre-Lenten events, this surreal three-day gathering of clowns is about as organized as debauchery gets.
Mardi Gras	The event that's inspired 1,000 imitations could take place only in New Orleans—Mardi Gras launches into a separate universe of costumes, music, and uninhibited revelry.
Carnaval Rio	The world's *numero uno* biggest party features (almost) naked people, outrageous costumes, the best dance music on the planet, and more fun than some continents have in an entire year.
Trinidad Carnival	Steel drums, wild costumes, calypso bands, no sleep, and a 3 a.m. kickoff party that covers participants (there are no spectators here) with mud and music.
Chinese New Year	The biggest holiday in China is the most fun in Hong Kong, where a samba party and other Western twists are added to traditional fireworks and dragon dances.
Sydney Gay and Lesbian Mardi Gras	Boas, leather, glitter, G-strings, rubber, and Saran Wrap—lots of people (straights and gays) call one of the world's largest gay-and-lesbian-pride events the best human spectacle on earth.

		Travel Date	Event Date	Event / Offical Name (if different)	City, State, Country / Host City (if different)	Event/City Rating / Origin/Attendance	Pg ✓
Week 10	1999	Mar. 4	Feb. 26-Mar. 7	Bike Week	Daytona Beach/Orlando, Florida, USA	★★★★★★	67
	2000	Mar. 9	Mar. 3-12			1937/500,000	
	1999	Mar. 4	Mar. 5-7	Vendimia	Buenos Aires, Argentina	★★★★★	Intl
	2000	Mar. 2	Mar. 3-5		(Mendoza)	1936/30,000	
	1999	Mar. 5	Mar. 5-7	Carnaval South Beach	Miami Beach, Florida, USA	★★★★★★★★	71
	2000	Mar. 3	Mar. 3-5	Carnaval Miami		1978/1,000,000	
Week 11	1999	Mar. 5	—	Skiing Tahoe	Lake Tahoe, California, USA	—	75
	2000	Feb. 17	—	The Most Fun Place To Ski : North America		—	
	1999	Mar. 12	Mar. 4-14	Moomba	Melbourne, Australia	★★★★★★★	Intl
	2000	Mar. 17	Mar. 9-19	The Melbourne Moomba Festival		1955/1,500,000	
	1999	Mar. 15	Mar. 12-17	St. Patrick's Day Celebration	Savannah, Georgia, USA	★★★★★★	79
	2000	Mar. 17	Mar. 16-19			1813/300,000	
Week 12	1999	Mar. 17	Mar. 12-19	Las Fallas	Valencia, Spain	★★★★★★	Intl
	2000	Mar. 17	Mar. 12-19			1497/500,000	
	1999	Mar. 17	Mar. 13-17	St. Patrick's Festival	Dublin, Ireland	★★★★★★	Intl
	2000	Mar. 17	Mar. 11-17			1996/850,000	
	1999	Mar. 18	Mar. 17-21	South by Southwest	Austin/Dallas/Ft. Worth, Texas, USA	★★★★★	83
	2000	Mar. 16	Mar. 15-19	South by Southwest Music and Media Conference, SXSW		1987/25,000	
	1999	Mar. 19	Mar. 21	Academy Awards	Los Angeles, California, USA	★★★★★★★★	87
	2000	Mar. 17	Mar. 19			1929/n/a	
Week 13	1999	Mar. 28	—	Carnival Destiny	Miami, Florida, USA	—	91
	2000	Mar. 26	—	The Most Fun Cruise		—	
Week 15	1999	Apr. 9	Apr. 10-11	Fertility Festival	Tokyo, Japan	★★★★★★	Intl
	2000	Apr. 7	Apr. 8-9	Kanamara Matsuri	(Kawasaki)	c. 1750/10,000	
Week 16	1999	Apr. 12	Apr. 12-14	Songkran Water Festival	Chiang Mai, Thailand	★★★★	Intl
	2000	Apr. 12	Apr. 12-14	Songkran		c. 1300/200,000	
	1999	Apr. 18	Apr. 16-25	Fiesta San Antonio	San Antonio, Texas, USA	★★★★★★★	95
	2000	Apr. 23	Apr. 22-30			1891/3,500,000	
Week 17	1999	Apr. 23	Apr. 9-May 2	Feria de San Marcos	Aguascalientes, Mexico	★★★★	Intl
	2000	Apr. 25	Apr. 14-May 7	Feria Nacional de San Marcos		1848/3,500,000	
	1999	Apr. 25	Apr. 25-May 1	Sailing Week	Antigua, Antigua	★★★★★★	Intl
	2000	Apr. 23	Apr. 23-29	Annual Antigua Sailing Week		1967/10,000	
Week 18	1999	Apr. 28	Apr. 30	Queen's Day	Amsterdam, Netherlands	★★★★★★★	Intl
	2000	Apr. 28	Apr. 30	Koninginnedag		1948/720,000	
	1999	Apr. 29	Apr. 16-May 2	Kentucky Derby	Louisville, Kentucky, USA	★★★★★★	99
	2000	May 4	Apr. 21-May 7	Kentucky Derby Festival		1875/140,000	
	1999	Apr. 29	Apr. 23-May 2	New Orleans Jazz & Heritage Festival	New Orleans, Louisiana, USA	★★★★★★	103
	2000	May 4	Apr. 28-May 7			1970/480,000	

Events are listed according to the week in which the 1999 travel date takes place. Subsequent to January 1, weeks begin on Monday.

Intl = Itinerary in companion edition *The Fun Also Rises Travel Guide International*
Readers' ✓: Been there, Done that, or Plan to

March

Bike Week
Thousands of bikers thunder into Florida, and Daytona becomes Harley heaven during an extraordinary week of motorcycle worshiping and partying.

Vendimia
Unlike most wine festivals, this one is not a laid-back taste test—it turns the town into a party and makes a most convincing argument for the South American wine industry.

Carnaval South Beach
While other carnivals are moving into Lent, Miami's is cranking up two weeks of Latin music and dancing in the streets of North America's (still) hottest destination.

Skiing Tahoe
The skiing may be fantastic, but it's extraordinary night life and scenery that make Lake Tahoe North America's most fun ski resort for skiers and nonskiers alike.

Moomba
More than 1.5 million attend Australia's largest outdoor festival, which combines cultural and sporting events with out-of-this-world native-arts displays and performances.

St. Patrick's Day Celebration
An improbable mix of Southern hospitality and Irish moxie makes this two-centuries-old party one of the world's biggest and best St. Patrick's Day celebrations.

Las Fallas
Europe's fireworks capital hosts an incredible spectacle—gorgeous papier-mâché tableaux are constructed, then burned simultaneously while firefighters nervously stand by and fireworks explode overhead.

St. Patrick's Festival
Inspired by the Irish-American celebrations, Dubliners throw the most entertaining parade in the world and follow it up with visits to—what else?—Irish pubs.

South by Southwest
The world's hippest music festival features 900 bands playing in a city that proudly claims that it has more bars and restaurants per capita than any other US city.

Academy Awards
Los Angeles is the North American destination for glitz and glamour, but with film-biz luminaries, screen superstars, and major media clamoring about, the buzz is deafening.

Carnival Destiny
There are sailboats, motorboats, lifeboats, and love boats—but when 2,600 fun-seekers have a week-long party in Caribbean waters, this one becomes the Fun Boat.

April

Fertility Festival
They're not shooting *Attack of the Giant Phallus* in the streets of Kawasaki, it just looks that way when 10,000 people fill the streets to celebrate the biggest game in town.

Songkran Water Festival
This wild-and-wet festival commemorates the end of the dry season by staging a monsoon that soaks everybody in sight with pails of flying water.

Fiesta San Antonio
How have the 3.5 million people who annually attend this event kept secret one of the nation's best festivals of music, food, parades, and street parties?

Feria de San Marcos
Hardly a tourist destination, Aguascalientes draws top-name musicians and bullfighters to Mexico's biggest national fair for a nonstop fiesta.

Sailing Week
The premier Caribbean race-and-party week is always ranked among the top-five regattas, but it also has the number-one set of beaches.

Queen's Day
The world's largest flea market turns into a party for 750,000 at night—fireworks and Amsterdam's infamous pleasures are the calling cards of this unusual event.

Kentucky Derby
Forget about the 20 horses—it's the 70-event festival, 80,000 mint juleps, and the city that's the crown jewel of Southern style that make the Derby a winner.

New Orleans Jazz & Heritage Festival
Some people consider this the world's best jazz festival because of the daylong talent lineup, but it's the backdrop of New Orleans night life that really makes it stand out.

		Travel Date	Event Date	Event / Offical Name (if different)	City, State, Country / Host City (if different)	Event/City Rating / Origin/Attendance	Pg / ✓
Week 19	1999	May 7	May 6-9	Monaco Grand Prix	Monte Carlo, Monaco	★★★★★★★	Intl
	2000	May 26	May 25-28	Grand Prix Automobile de Monaco		1942/75,000	
Week 20	1999	May 13	May 7-15	The Preakness	Baltimore, Maryland, USA	★★★★	105
	2000	May 18	May 12-20	Preakness Celebration		1873/90,000	
	1999	May 14	May 7-16	Fiestas de San Isidro	Madrid, Spain	★★★★★★	Intl
	2000	May 13	May 12-21			1622/25,000	
	1999	May 20	May 20-22	Memphis in May Barbecue	Memphis, Tennessee, USA	★★★★★★	109
	2000	May 18	May 18-20	Memphis in May World Championship Barbecue Cooking Contest		1976/80,000	
Week 21	1999	May 20	May 12-23	Cannes Film Festival	Cannes, France	★★★★★★★★	Intl
	2000	May 18	May 10-21	Festival International du Film		1939/31,000	
	1999	May 21	May 20-24	Feria de Nimes	Nimes, France	★★★★★	Intl
	2000	Jun. 9	Jun. 8-12	Feria de Pentecote		1952/50,000	
Week 22	1999	May 27	May 1-May 30	Indy 500	Indianapolis, Indiana, USA	★★★★★	115
	2000	May 25	May 6-May 28	The 500 Festival		1911/400,000	
Week 23	1999	Jun. 3	Jun. 5	Black and White Ball	San Francisco, California, USA	★★★★★★★	121
	2000	none	none			1956/12,000	
	1999	Jun. 3	Jun. 3-6	Chicago Blues Festival	Chicago, Illinois, USA	★★★★★★★	125
	2000	Jun. 8	Jun. 8-11			1984/650,000	
	1999	Jun. 3	Jun. 3-5	Napa Valley Wine Auction	Napa Valley, California, USA	★★★★★	129
	2000	Jun. 1	Jun. 1-3		(St. Helena)	1981/2,000	
	1999	Jun. 3	May 28-Jun. 13	Spoleto	Charleston, South Carolina, USA	★★★★★	133
	2000	Jun. 1	May 26-Jun. 11	Spoleto Festival USA/Piccolo Spoleto		1977/72,000	
Week 24	1999	Jun. 10	Jun. 2-13	Feast of St. Anthony	Lisbon, Portugal	★★★★★	Intl
	2000	Jun. 10	Jun. 2-13	Festas de Lisboa		1232/300,000	
Week 25	1999	Jun. 16	Jun. 14-19	Country Music Fan Fair	Nashville, Tennessee, USA	★★★★★	137
	2000	Jun. 14	Jun. 12-17	International Country Music Fan Fair		1972/24,000	
	1999	Jun. 16	Jun. 15-18	Royal Ascot	London, England	★★★★★★★★	Intl
	2000	Jun. 21	Jun. 20-23	The Royal Meeting at Ascot Racecourse	(Ascot)	1711/230,000	
Week 26	1999	Jun. 24	Jun. 24-Jul. 4	Summerfest	Milwaukee, Wisconsin, USA	★★★★	141
	2000	Jun. 29	Jun. 29-Jul. 9			1968/940,000	

Events are listed according to the week in which the 1999 travel date takes place.
Subsequent to January 1, weeks begin on Monday.

Intl = Itinerary in companion edition *The Fun Also Rises Travel Guide International*
Readers' ✓: Been there, Done that, or Plan to

The Fun Also Rises

May

Monaco Grand Prix	Monte Carlo's streets are so tightly packed that spectators—many of them part of Europe's beautiful-people crowd—can almost touch the racing cars.
The Preakness	The second jewel in horse racing's Triple Crown is really an excuse for Mardi Gras-style fun that combines let-it-all-hang-out revelry with quaint traditions.
Fiestas de San Isidro	The fiesta is celebrated with music and bullfighting, but this really just makes it the best time of year to visit one of the world's great cities.
Memphis in May Barbecue	When disciples of blues, beer, and barbecue invade Memphis, how could the result be anything less than the world's greatest marriage of down-home food and fun?
Cannes Film Festival	The world's most important film festival transforms this Mediterranean resort into one big, nonstop cast party, where glamour and attention-getting stunts reign supreme.
Feria de Nimes	A completely packed town throws a street party that puts a French twist on everything Spanish, from bullfighting to paella.
Indy 500	The actual race may be "the greatest spectacle in racing," but the days leading up to the main event are geared as much to party fans as to racing fans.

June

Black and White Ball	Highlighting the city's refined side, this biennial event turns the streets of San Francisco into a set from a glamorous black-and-white movie and the world's largest indoor-outdoor black-tie ball.
Chicago Blues Festival	Featuring 60 mind-blowing acts on four stages set against the shores of Lake Michigan, the world's largest blues festival amplifies Chicago's musical heritage.
Napa Valley Wine Auction	Great food, great wine, great food, great wine, great food, great wine, great food, great wine— the nation's largest charity wine auction.
Spoleto	One of the world's best interdisciplinary arts festivals—neither drunken bacchanal nor hoity-toity gathering— has as its backdrop one of the nation's most beautiful cities.
Feast of St. Anthony	In every nook and cranny of Lisbon's Old Town, someone is barbecuing sardines, while crowds of people (packed like sardines) dance shoulder-to-shoulder at outdoor concerts.
Country Music Fan Fair	This five-day orgy of fan appreciation pulls in more than 20,000 die-hards for 35 hours of performances and face time with their beloved stars.
Royal Ascot	The premier event of London's social season isn't just about horse racing—it's about royalty, outrageous fashions, and a demonstration that the upper crust can get down.
Summerfest	With 11 stages, more than 2,500 local, regional, and international acts, and about a million spectators, The Big Gig is arguably the world's largest music festival.

		Travel Date	Event Date	Event	City, State, Country	Event/City Rating	Pg
				Offical Name (if different)	Host City (if different)	Origin/Attendance	✓
Week 27	1999	Jul. 1	Jul. 1-4	Roskilde Rock Festival	Copenhagen, Denmark	★★★★★★★	Intl
	2000	Jun. 29	Jun. 29-Jul. 2	Roskilde Festival	(Roskilde)	1971/90,000	
	1999	Jul. 2	Jun. 25-Jul. 4	Fourth of July	Philadelphia, Pennsylvania, USA	★★★★★★★★	147
	2000	Jul. 3	Jun. 23-Jul. 4	Sunoco Welcome America		1993/1,000,000	
	1999	Jul. 2	Jun. 29-Jul. 5	Boston Harborfest	Boston, Massachusetts, USA	★★★★★★★	151
	2000	Jul. 2	Jun. 28-Jul. 4			1982/2,500,000	
Week 28	1999	Jul. 6	Jul. 1-11	Montréal Jazz Festival	Montréal, Québec, Canada	★★★★★★	155
	2000	Jul. 4	Jun. 28-Jul. 9	Festival International de Jazz de Montréal		1979/1,500,000	
	1999	Jul. 6	Jul. 6-14	Running of the Bulls	Pamplona, Spain	★★★★★★	Intl
	2000	Jul. 6	Jul. 6-14	Los San Fermines		c. 1600/100,000	
Week 29	1999	Jul. 13	Jul. 13-14	Bastille Day	Paris, France	★★★★★★★★	Intl
	2000	Jul. 13	Jul. 13-14			1789/na	
	1999	Jul. 15	Jul. 10-17	Nice Jazz Festival	Nice, France	★★★★★★	Intl
	2000	Jul. 14	Jul. 9-16			1948/49,000	
	1999	Jul. 16	Jul. 16-25	Aquatennial	Minneapolis, Minnesota, USA	★★★★	159
	2000	Jul. 14	Jul. 14-23	Minneapolis Aquatennial Festival		1940/800,000	
	1999	Jul. 16	Jul. 9-18	Calgary Stampede	Calgary, Alberta, Canada	★★★★★★	163
	2000	Jul. 14	Jul. 7-16			1912/1,100,000	
Week 30	1999	Jul. 16	Jul. 2-17	Montreux Jazz Festival	Montreux, Switzerland	★★★★★	Intl
	2000	Jul. 21	Jul. 6-23			1967/170,000	
	1999	Jul. 22	—	Fun Destination: Ibiza/Majorca	Ibiza/Majorca, Spain	—	Intl
	2000	Aug. 10	—			—	
Week 31	1999	Jul. 29	Jul. 16-Aug. 2	Caribana	Toronto, Ontario, Canada	★★★★★★	167
	2000	Aug. 3	Jul. 21-Aug. 7			1967/1,500,000	
	1999	Jul. 29	Jul. 23-Aug. 1	Cheyenne Frontier Days	Cheyenne, Wyoming, USA	★★★★	171
	2000	Jul. 27	Jul. 21-30			1897/400,000	
	1999	Jul. 31	Jul. 23-Aug. 2	Crop Over Festival	Bridgetown, Barbados	★★★★★	Intl
	2000	Aug. 5	Jul. 2-Aug. 7			c. 1790/100,000	
Week 32	1999	Aug. 5	Jul. 31-Aug. 7	Cowes Week	Isle of Wight, England	★★★★★	Intl
	2000	Aug. 3	Jul. 29-Aug. 5			1812/30,000	
Week 33	1999	Aug. 12	Aug. 6-14	Stockholm Water Festival	Stockholm, Sweden	★★★★★★★★★	Intl
	2000	Aug. 17	Aug. 11-19			1991/1,100,000	
Week 34	1999	Aug. 14	Aug. 13-17	Palio	Siena, Italy	★★★★★	Intl
	2000	Aug. 14	Aug. 13-17	Palio di Siena		c. 1600/30,000	
	1999	Aug. 19	Aug. 8-31	Edinburgh Fringe Festival	Edinburgh, Scotland	★★★★★★★★	Intl
	2000	Aug. 17	Aug. 6-29			1947/410,000	
Week 35	1999	Aug. 23	Aug. 25	La Tomatina	Barcelona, Spain	★★★★★★★	Intl
	2000	Aug. 28	Aug. 30		(Bunol)	1957/25,000	
	1999	Aug. 27	Aug. 29	Concours d'Elegance	Carmel/Monterey, California, USA	★★★★★	175
	2000	Aug. 18	Aug. 20	Pebble Beach Concours d'Elegance	(Pebble Beach)	1950/12,000	
	1999	Aug. 28	Aug. 29-30	Notting Hill Carnival	London, England	★★★★★★★	Intl
	2000	Aug. 26	Aug. 27-28			1965/1,500,000	

Events are listed according to the week in which the 1999 travel date takes place.
Subsequent to January 1, weeks begin on Monday.

Intl = Itinerary in companion edition *The Fun Also Rises Travel Guide International*
Readers' ✓: Been there, Done that, or Plan to

The Fun Also Rises

July

Roskilde Rock Festival
Europe's largest annual rock festival is distinguished by precision organization, hearty audiences who brave consistently poor weather, and, of course, lots of music.

Fourth of July
The first and last words on Independence Day celebrations have always belonged to the City of Brotherly Love—food fests, parades, concerts, and fireworks keep 2 million patriots coming back each year.

Boston Harborfest
Bostonians commemorate their city's first party (something about tea being thrown in a harbor) with a celebration that blends history with spectacle.

Montréal Jazz Festival
Often called the best jazz festival in the world—2,000 musicians from 25 countries get crowds moving at 400 shows—this event rates as one of Canada's best annual shindigs.

Running of the Bulls
This is it—the world's greatest party! You don't have to run with the bulls to feel the spirit of the crowds, who all come together for the same purpose: fiesta, fiesta, fiesta!

Bastille Day
French Independence Day is celebrated with a dramatic parade down the Champs-Elysées and two nights of solid revelry in the most romantic city in the world.

Nice Jazz Festival
The world's top jazz acts probably come for the same reason the crowds do—nothing beats the French Riviera in summer.

Aquatennial
It's time to come out from the cold—800,000 warm-weather lovers celebrate The 10 Best Days of Summer with food, music, and games.

Calgary Stampede
Calgary, the home of wild chuck-wagon races, becomes one of the world's biggest and best country-style party towns, with a world-class rodeo as its centerpiece.

Montreux Jazz Festival
Still the world's premier jazz event, the festival transforms the already beautiful town into one of the most hip spots in the universe.

Fun Destination: Ibiza/Majorca
The Spanish islands are the pick for the world's top beach destinations—fashionable crowds tan on beaches by day and hit the world's best discos by night.

Caribana
One of North America's largest and most exuberant street parties—a million revelers celebrate Toronto's Caribbean and Latin populations with dance, music, and food.

Cheyenne Frontier Days
Real cowboys and cowgirls still exist and nearly every last one of 'em rides into town for this century-old rodeo, Wild West show, and summertime hoedown.

Crop Over Festival
The highlight of the Barbados year, this *Carnaval*-style event is an all-island jubilee that celebrates the end of the sugar-cane harvest with great music and molten energy.

August

Cowes Week
The world's largest international yacht regatta transforms the small town of Cowes into a wild gathering of sailors and a frenzied meet market.

Stockholm Water Festival
The beautiful setting and constant surprises by street performers contribute to one of the world's best street fairs and music festivals, which takes place in Europe's most underrated city.

Palio
The tension leading up to and at the world's most incredible horse race—the animals and jockeys speed around the small town square—is released in a centuries-old tradition.

Edinburgh Fringe Festival
You'd have to see it to believe it, but you can't see it all. The world's largest arts festival has hundreds of daily performances of theater, music, opera, dance, and comedy from around the world.

La Tomatina
The world's largest food fight lasts just 60 minutes, but where else can you join 10,000 people throwing tomatoes at each other on a hot summer day?

Concours d'Elegance
Champagne flows at the "Super Bowl of auto shows," as prestigious Pebble Beach Golf Course turns into a spectacle of vintage autos and period costumes.

Notting Hill Carnival
Europe's biggest street party, this *Carnaval*-style parade showcases an ethnic side of London that, as a bookend to Royal Ascot, rounds out the picture of one of the world's most happening cities.

	Travel Date	Event Date	Event / Offical Name (if different)	City, State, Country / Host City (if different)	Event/City Rating / Origin/Attendance	Pg / ✓
Week 36 1999	Sep. 3	Sep. 3-6	Bumbershoot	Seattle, Washington, USA	★★★★★	179
2000	Sep. 1	Sep. 1-4	Bumbershoot, The Seattle Arts Festival		1971/250,000	
1999	Sep. 3	Aug. 30-Sep. 6	Burning Man	Reno, Nevada, USA	★★★★★★★	183
2000	Sep. 1	Aug. 28-Sep. 4		(Black Rock City)	1986/10,000	
1999	Sep. 3	Sep. 4-5	Big Muddy	St. Louis, Missouri, USA	★★★★	187
2000	Sep. 1	Sep. 2-3	Big Muddy Blues & Roots Music Festival		1992/50,000	
1999	Sep. 3	Sep. 5	Riverfest	Cincinnati, Ohio, USA	★★★★	191
2000	Sep. 1	Sep. 3			1977/500,000	
Week 37 1999	Sep. 9	Sep. 10-12	Street Scene	San Diego, California, USA	★★★★★	195
2000	Sep. 7	Sep. 8-10			1984/85,000	
1999	Sep. 10	Sep. 10-19	Aloha Festival	Honolulu, Hawaii, USA	★★★★★	199
2000	Sep. 15	Sep. 15-24			1947/300,000	
1999	Sep. 10	Sep. 9-12	Fiesta de Santa Fe	Santa Fe, New Mexico, USA	★★★★	203
2000	Sep. 8	Sep. 7-10			1712/75,000	
Week 38 1999	Sep. 18	Sep. 18-Oct. 3	Oktoberfest	Munich, Germany	★★★★★★★★★	Intl
2000	Sep. 16	Sep. 16-Oct. 1			1810/6,000,000	
Week 39 1999	Sep. 24	Sep. 23-26	Galway Oyster Festival	Galway, Ireland	★★★★★★	Intl
2000	Sep. 22	Sep. 21-24	Galway International Oyster Festival		1955/10,000	
Week 40 1999	Oct. 1	Sep. 25-Oct.10	Stuttgart's Volksfest	Stuttgart, Germany	★★★★★	Intl
2000	Sep. 29	Sep. 23-Oct. 8			1818/5,000,000	
Week 41 1999	Oct. 7	Oct. 2-10	Balloon Fiesta	Albuquerque, New Mexico, USA	★★★★★★	207
2000	Oct. 12	Oct. 7-15	Kodak Albuquerque International Balloon Fiesta		1972/1,500,000	
1999	Oct. 7	Oct. 7-9	Great American Beer Festival	Denver, Colorado, USA	★★★★★	211
2000	Oct. 5	Oct. 5-7			1982/35,000	
1999	Oct. 8	Oct. 9-11	Taste of DC	Washington, DC, USA	★★★★★	215
2000	Oct. 6	Oct. 7-9			1990/1,200,000	
Week 42 1999	Oct. 14	—	Disney World	Orlando, Florida, USA	—	223
2000	Oct. 19	—	Walt Disney World	(Lake Buena Vista)	—	
Week 43 1999	Oct. 21	—	Fun Destination: Athens	Athens, Greece	—	Intl
2000	Nov. 2	—			—	
1999	Oct. 28	Oct. 22-31	Fantasy Fest	Key West, Florida, USA	★★★★★★★	227
	Oct. 26	Oct. 20-29			1979/100,000	
Week 44 1999	Oct. 28	Oct. 30	Guavaween	Tampa, Florida, USA	★★★★★★	231
2000	Oct. 26	Oct. 28			1984/100,000	
1999	Oct. 29	Oct. 30-31	Hookers' Ball/Halloween	San Francisco, California, USA	★★★★★★★★★	235
2000	Oct. 27	Oct. 28-31			1978/50,000	

Events are listed according to the week in which the 1999 travel date takes place. Subsequent to January 1, weeks begin on Monday.

Intl = Itinerary in companion edition *The Fun Also Rises Travel Guide International*
Readers' ✓ : Been there, Done that, or Plan to

September

Bumbershoot
One of the largest music-and-arts festivals in the US attracts top international talent to this beautiful city known for its cutting-edge music (and coffee and computers).

Burning Man
The world's latest attempt at utopia is a mix of offbeat art and cultural experimentation—free spirits create a perfect (and wild) temporary city in the Nevada desert.

Big Muddy
St. Louis knows the blues—this mix of music and food, set on the banks of the Mississippi River, provides the best reason to explore this often-overlooked city.

Riverfest
America's biggest farewell-to-summer event includes games, music, food, sun, and one of the world's most outrageous fireworks displays.

Street Scene
Tans, tacos, tequila, and tank tops—at this giant street party, you won't find a shortage of any of the local specialties.

Aloha Festival
Honolulu is where Hawaiians party and the city rolls out all its (greatest) clichés—hula girls, mai tais, perfect beaches, tropical breezes—for this celebration of island culture.

Fiesta de Santa Fe
The festival begins when a 40-foot-tall puppet is burned to banish gloom from the lives of 75,000 assembled partyers—the food, music, and dancing that follow guarantee success.

Oktoberfest
The massive scale of the world's largest beer blowout is stunning—and so is the city—but it's the camaraderie in the huge beer tents that makes this one special.

Galway Oyster Festival
Oysters are simply the excuse for drinking lots of Guinness, which is simply the excuse for starting a party (not ending it) by dancing on the tables.

October

Stuttgart's Volkfest
Not as famous, but almost as large as Munich's Oktoberfest, this beer bash pours the best of German cheer and proves that being number two can still be one heck of a good time.

Balloon Fiesta
With nearly 1,000 multicolored balloons ascending into the clear Southwestern sky, the world's largest ballooning event transforms Albuquerque into one big fiesta.

Great American Beer Festival
The opportunity to taste 1,700 different brews gives *mile-high city* new meaning and makes this event the must-do pilgrimage for malt worship and good times.

Taste of DC
One of the world's most important cities shows off with one of the nation's best *Taste* events—more than a million people fill Pennsylvania Avenue for food and music.

Disney World
The world's best theme park and ... party place for adults? Fuzzy cartoon characters may never completely lose their appeal, but often overlooked is this park's grown-up good time.

Fun Destination: Athens
Mykonos is great, but Greeks know that the action is in Athens, where the clubs are among the best in the world and dance floors give way to table tops.

Fantasy Fest
Relaxing Key West transforms itself for one of the world's most extravagant and wild costume balls, complete with legendary Florida weather and sunsets.

Guavaween
Guavaween is a combination of Halloween and a tribute to Tampa's nickname, The Big Guava— a wild street celebration fills the historic district of Ybor City.

Hookers' Ball/Halloween
San Francisco confirms its liberal reputation when tens of thousands make Halloween night the highlight of their year—the Hookers' Ball and Castro street party blow away any haunted house.

		Travel Date	Event Date	Event	City, State, Country	Event/City Rating	Pg
				Offical Name (if different)	Host City (if different)	Origin/Attendance	✓
Week 45	1999			(No FunGuide 100 events this week)			
	2000						
Week 46	1999			(No FunGuide 100 events this week)			
	2000						
Week 47	1999	Nov. 19	Nov. 20-21	Macau Grand Prix	Macau, Macau	★★★★	Intl
	2000	Nov. 17	Nov. 18-19			1954/20,000	
	1999	Nov. 21	Nov. 20-23	Pushkar Camel Fair	Pushkar, India	★★★★	Intl
	2000	Nov. 9	Nov. 9-11	Pushkar Mela		1976/200,000	
Week 48	1999	Nov. 25	—	Fun Destination: Acapulco	Acapulco, Mexico	—	Intl
	2000	Nov. 23	—			—	
Week 49	1999	Dec. 2	Dec. 4-5	Dickens on the Strand	Houston/Galveston, Texas, USA	★★★★★	239
	2000	Nov. 30	Dec. 2-3			1974/50,000	
Week 50	1999	Dec. 10	Dec. 3-12	Las Vegas Rodeo	Las Vegas, Nevada, USA	★★★★★★★★	244
	2000	Dec. 8	Dec. 1-10	National Finals Rodeo		1985/140,000	
Week 51	1999	Dec. 17	—	Skiing Zermatt	Zermatt, Switzerland	—	Intl
	2000	Dec. 15	—	The Most Fun Place To Ski: Europe		—	
Week 52	1999	Dec. 24	—	Hedonism II	Negril, Jamaica	—	Intl
	2000	Dec. 22	—	The Most Fun Resort		—	
Week 53	1999	Dec. 29	Dec. 31	New Year's Eve New York	New York, New York, USA	★★★★★★★★	247
	2000	Dec. 29	Dec. 31			1904/500,000	
	1999	Dec. 30	Dec. 29-Jan. 1	Hogmanay	Edinburgh, Scotland	★★★★★★★★★	Intl
	2000	Dec. 30	Dec. 29-Jan. 1	Edinburgh's Hogmanay		1993/200,000	

Events are listed according to the week in which the 1999 travel date takes place.
Subsequent to January 1, weeks begin on Monday.

Intl = Itinerary in companion edition *The Fun Also Rises Travel Guide International*
Readers' ✓: Been there, Done that, or Plan to

November

Macau Grand Prix	Macau is a let-your-hair-down town for the Chinese—probably even after the Portuguese give it back to China in December 1999—and this formula-racing event is the largest of its kind.
Pushkar Camel Fair	One of the most enthralling and exotic spectacles anywhere—the sight of thousands-strong caravans arriving from across the desert to the world's largest camel fair defies description.
Fun Destination: Acapulco	Cancún and Cabo are charging hard, but this is still Mexico's number-one party destination for adults. Great beaches, strolling mariachis, and wild, warm nights.

December

Dickens on the Strand	Revelers don period clothes and hoist cups of cheer to the literature and culture of 19th-century Britain in one of the nation's top yuletide parties.
Las Vegas Rodeo	The Western side of Las Vegas takes over the town during the world championship National Finals Rodeo, where the hootin' and hollerin' is as big as the $4 million purse.
Skiing Zermatt	Zermatt takes the European title for best ski-party town, adding its special touch of Swiss hospitality and gorgeous scenery (the Alps aren't the only things worth looking at).
Hedonism II	This activity-filled Jamaican resort is divided by a walkway that separates the nude side from the prude side—as close to an anything-goes environment as a hotel gets.
New Year's Eve New York	New York has just about the best of everything—restaurants, night life, things to do—but the city never gets closer to being the center of the universe than on New Year's Eve.
Hogmanay	Despite the cold, this is New Year's Eve the way you'd like it to be. Europe's largest organized year-end celebration closes off its streets for musical entertainment and partying.

The FunGuide 100

GEOGRAPHICAL INDEX AND WORLD MAPS

Map Locator	State	City / Host City	Event / Official Name (if different)	Travel Date	Event Date	Event/City Ranking / Origin/Attendance	Pg ✓
					1999		
	North America—United States				2000		
1	Arizona	Phoenix (Scottsdale)	Phoenix Open	Jan. 27 Jan. 26	Jan. 25-31 Jan. 24–30	★★★ ★★★★ 1932/470,000	47
2	California	Carmel/Monterey (Pebble Beach)	Concours d'Elegance Pebble Beach Concours d'Elegance	Aug. 27 Aug. 18	Aug. 29 Aug. 20	★★★ ★★ 1950/12,000	175
3	California	Lake Tahoe	Skiing Tahoe The Most Fun Place To Ski: North America	Mar. 5 Feb. 17	— —	— —	75
4	California	Los Angeles	Academy Awards	Mar. 19 Mar. 17	Mar. 21 Mar. 19	★★★ ★★★★★ 1929/na	87
5	California	Napa Valley (St. Helena)	Napa Valley Wine Auction	Jun. 3 Jun. 1	Jun. 3-5 Jun. 1-3	★★★ ★★★ 1981/2,000	129
6	California	San Diego	Street Scene	Sep. 9 Sep. 7	Sep. 10-12 Sep. 8-10	★★★ ★★★ 1984/85,000	195
7	California	San Francisco	Hookers' Ball/Halloween	Oct. 29 Oct. 27	Oct. 30-31 Oct. 28-31	★★★★ ★★★★★ 1978/50,000	235
7	California	San Francisco	Black and White Ball	Jun. 3 none	Jun. 5 none	★★★ ★★★★★ 1956/12,000	121
8	Colorado	Denver	Great American Beer Festival	Oct. 7 Oct. 5	Oct. 7-9 Oct. 5-7	★★ ★★★ 1982/35,000	211
9		Washington, DC	Taste of DC	Oct. 8 Oct. 6	Oct. 9-11 Oct. 7-9	★ ★★★★ 1990/1,200,000	215
10	Florida	Daytona Beach/ Orlando	Bike Week	Mar. 4 Mar. 9	Feb. 26-Mar. 7 Mar. 3-12	★★★★ ★★ 1937/500,000	67
11	Florida	Key West	Fantasy Fest	Oct. 28 Oct. 26	Oct. 22-31 Oct. 20-29	★★★★ ★★★ 1979/100,000	227
12	Florida	Miami	Carnival Destiny The Most Fun Cruise	Mar. 28 Mar. 26	— —	— —	91
13	Florida	Miami Beach	Carnaval South Beach Carnaval Miami	Mar. 5 Mar. 3	Mar. 5-7 Mar. 3-5	★★★ ★★★★★ 1978/1,000,000	71
14	Florida	Orlando (Lake Buena Vista)	Disney World Walt Disney World	Oct. 14 Oct. 19	— —	— —	223
15	Florida	Tampa	Guavaween	Oct. 28 Oct. 26	Oct. 30 Oct. 28	★★★ ★★ 1984/100,000	231
16	Georgia	Savannah	St. Patrick's Day Celebration	Mar. 15 Mar. 17	Mar. 12-17 Mar. 16-19	★★★★★ ★★ 1813/300,000	79
17	Hawaii	Honolulu	Aloha Festival	Sep. 10 Sep. 15	Sep. 10-19 Sep. 15-24	★★ ★★★ 1947/300,000	199
18	Illinois	Chicago	Chicago Blues Festival	Jun. 3 Jun. 8	Jun. 3-6 Jun. 8-11	★★★ ★★★★★ 1984/650,000	125
19	Indiana	Indianapolis	Indy 500 The 500 Festival	May 27 May 25	May 1-May 30 May 6-May 28	★★★ ★★ 1911/400,000	115
20	Kentucky	Louisville	Kentucky Derby Kentucky Derby Festival	Apr. 29 May 4	Apr. 16-May 2 Apr. 21-May 7	★★★ ★★★★ 1875/140,000	99

Index continued on page 30

Readers' ✓: Been there, Done that, or Plan to

The Fun Also Rises

GEOGRAPHICAL INDEX

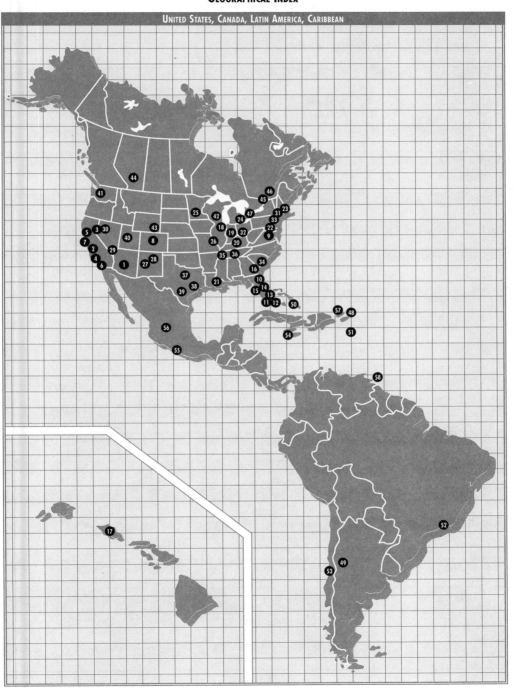

Map Locator	State	City / Host City	Event / Official Name (if different)	Travel Date	Event Date	Event/City Ranking / Origin/Attendance	pg ✓
					1999 / 2000		
21	Louisiana	New Orleans	Mardi Gras	Feb. 14 / Mar. 5	Feb. 6-16 / Feb. 26-Mar. 7	★★★★★★★★★ / 1837/3,500,000	61
21	Louisiana	New Orleans	New Orleans Jazz & Heritage Festival	Apr. 29 / May 4	Apr. 23-May 2 / Apr. 28-May 7	★★★★★ / 1970/480,000	103
22	Maryland	Baltimore	The Preakness / Preakness Celebration	May 13 / May 18	May 7-15 / May 12-20	★★★ / 1873/90,000	105
23	Massachusetts	Boston	Boston Harborfest	Jul. 2 / Jul. 2	Jun. 29-Jul 5 / Jun. 28-Jul 4	★ ★★★★ / 1982/2,500,000	151
24	Michigan	Detroit	Detroit Auto Show / North American International Auto Show, NAIAS	Jan. 7 / Jan. 6	Jan. 8-18 / Jan. 7-17	★★★★ / 1907/790,000	37
25	Minnesota	Minneapolis	Aquatennial / Minneapolis Aquatennial Festival	Jul. 16 / Jul. 14	Jul. 16-25 / Jul. 14-23	★★★ / 1940/800,000	159
26	Missouri	St. Louis	Big Muddy / Big Muddy Blues & Roots Music Festival	Sep. 3 / Sep. 1	Sep. 4-5 / Sep. 2-3	★★★ / 1992/50,000	187
27	New Mexico	Albuquerque	Balloon Fiesta / Kodak Albuquerque International Balloon Fiesta	Oct. 7 / Oct. 12	Oct. 2-10 / Oct. 7-15	★★★★★ / 1972/1,500,000	207
28	New Mexico	Santa Fe	Fiesta de Santa Fe	Sep. 10 / Sep. 8	Sep. 9-12 / Sep. 7-10	★★★ / 1712/75,000	203
29	Nevada	Las Vegas	Las Vegas Rodeo / National Finals Rodeo	Dec. 10 / Dec. 8	Dec. 3-12 / Dec. 1-10	★★★★★★★ / 1985/140,000	244
29	Nevada	Las Vegas	Super Bowl Weekend	Jan. 29 / Jan. 28	Jan. 29-31 / Jan. 28-30	★★★★★★★ / 1967/200,000	51
30	Nevada	Reno (Black Rock City)	Burning Man	Sep. 3 / Sep. 1	Aug. 30-Sep. 6 / Aug. 28-Sep. 4	★★★★★★ / 1986/10,000	183
31	New York	New York	New Year's Eve New York	Dec. 29 / Dec. 29	Dec. 31 / Dec. 31	★★★★★★★ / 1904/500,000	247
32	Ohio	Cincinnati	Riverfest	Sep. 3 / Sep. 1	Sep. 5 / Sep. 3	★★★ / 1977/500,000	191
33	Pennsylvania	Philadelphia	Fourth of July / Sunoco Welcome America	Jul. 2 / Jul. 3	Jun. 25-Jul. 4 / Jun. 23-Jul. 4	★★★★★★★ / 1993/1,000,000	147
34	South Carolina	Charleston	Spoleto / Spoleto Festival USA/Piccolo Spoleto	Jun. 3 / Jun. 1	May 28-Jun. 13 / May 26-Jun. 11	★★★★★ / 1977/72,000	133
35	Tennessee	Memphis	Memphis in May Barbecue / Memphis in May World Championship Barbecue Cooking Contest	May 20 / May 18	May 20-22 / May 18-20	★★★★★ / 1976/80,000	109
36	Tennessee	Nashville	Country Music Fan Fair / International Country Music Fan Fair	Jun. 16 / Jun. 14	Jun. 14-19 / Jun. 12-17	★★★★★ / 1972/24,000	137
37	Texas	Austin/Dallas/ Fort Worth	South by Southwest / South by Southwest Music and Media Conference, SXSW	Mar. 18 / Mar. 16	Mar. 17-21 / Mar. 15-19	★★★★★ / 1987/25,000	83
38	Texas	Houston/Galveston	Dickens on the Strand	Dec. 2 / Nov. 30	Dec. 4-5 / Dec. 2-3	★★★★★ / 1974/50,000	239

Readers' ✓: Been there, Done that, or Plan to

Map Locator	State	City / Host City	Event / Official Name (if different)	Travel Date	Event Date	Event/City Ranking / Origin/Attendance	Pg ✓
					1999		
					2000		
39	Texas	San Antonio	Fiesta San Antonio	Apr. 18 / Apr. 23	Apr. 16-25 / Apr. 22-30	★★★★★★★ / 1891/3,500,000	95
40	Utah	Park City	Sundance Film Festival	Jan. 21 / Jan. 20	Jan. 21-30 / Jan. 20-29	★★★★★★★ / 1978/18,000	43
41	Washington	Seattle	Bumbershoot / Bumbershoot, The Seattle Arts Festival	Sep. 3 / Sep. 1	Sep. 3-6 / Sep. 1-4	★★★★ / 1971/250,000	179
42	Wisconsin	Milwaukee	Summerfest	Jun. 24 / Jun. 29	Jun. 24-Jul. 4 / Jun. 29-Jul. 9	★★★★ / 1968/940,000	141
43	Wyoming	Cheyenne	Cheyenne Frontier Days	Jul. 29 / Jul. 27	Jul. 23-Aug. 1 / Jul. 21-30	★★★★ / 1897/400,000	171

North America—Canada

Map Locator	Province	City	Event / Official Name (if different)	Travel Date	Event Date	Event/City Ranking / Origin/Attendance	Pg ✓
44	Alberta	Calgary	Calgary Stampede	Jul. 16 / Jul. 14	Jul. 9-18 / Jul. 7-16	★★★★★★ / 1912/1,100,000	163
45	Québec	Montréal	Montréal Jazz Festival / Festival International de Jazz de Montréal	Jul. 6 / Jul. 4	Jul. 1-11 / Jun. 28-Jul. 9	★★★★★★★ / 1979/1,500,000	155
46	Québec	Québec City	Québec Winter Carnaval / Carnaval de Québec	Feb. 5 / Feb. 4	Jan. 29-Feb. 14 / Jan. 28-Feb. 13	★★★★★★ / 1894/1,000,000	57
47	Ontario	Toronto	Caribana	Jul. 29 / Aug. 3	Jul. 16-Aug. 2 / Jul. 21-Aug. 7	★★★★★★ / 1967/1,500,000	167

Latin America and the Caribbean

Map Locator	Country	City	Event / Official Name (if different)	Travel Date	Event Date	Event/City Ranking / Origin/Attendance	Pg ✓
48	Antigua	Antigua	Sailing Week / Annual Antigua Sailing Week	Apr. 25 / Apr. 23	Apr. 25-May 1 / Apr. 23-29	★★★★★ / 1967/10,000	
49	Argentina	Buenos Aires (Mendoza)	Vendimia	Mar. 4 / Mar. 2	Mar. 5-7 / Mar. 3-5	★★★★★ / 1936/30,000	
50	Bahamas	Nassau	Junkanoo	Jan. 1 / Jan. 1	Dec. 26-Jan. 1 / Dec. 26-Jan. 1	★★★★★★★ / c. 1800/10,000	
51	Barbados	Bridgetown	Crop Over Festival	Jul. 31 / Aug. 5	Jun. 23-Aug. 2 / Jun. 28-Aug. 7	★★★★★ / c. 1790/100,000	
52	Brazil	Rio de Janeiro	Carnaval Rio	Feb. 14 / Mar. 5	Feb. 13-16 / Mar. 4-7	★★★★★★★★★★ / 1930/10,000,000	
53	Chile	Santiago (Viña del Mar)	Viña del Mar Song Festival / International Song Festival of Viña del Mar	Feb. 11 / Dec. 12	Feb. 10-15 / Feb. 9-14	★★★★★ / 1959/110,000	
54	Jamaica	Negril	Hedonism II / The Most Fun Resort	Dec. 24 / Dec. 22	— / —	— / —	
55	Mexico	Acapulco	Fun Destination: Acapulco	Nov. 25 / Nov. 23	— / —	— / —	
56	Mexico	Aguascalientes	Feria de San Marcos / Feria Nacional de San Marcos	Apr. 23 / Apr. 25	Apr. 9-May 2 / Apr. 14-May 7	★★★★ / 1848/3,500,000	
57	Puerto Rico	San Juan	Calle San Sebastián	Jan. 15 / Jan. 14	Jan. 15-17 / Jan. 14-16	★★★★★ / 1970/50,000	
58	Trinidad	Trinidad	Trinidad Carnival	Feb. 14 / Mar. 5	Feb. 15-16 / Mar. 6-7	★★★★★★★★ / c. 1750/100,000	

Readers' ✓: Been there, Done that, or Plan to

Map Locator	Country	City Host City	Event Official Name (if different)	Travel Date	Event Date	Event/City Ranking Origin/Attendance	✓
					1999		
	Europe				2000		
59	Austria	Vienna	Vienna Opera Ball	Feb. 9	Feb. 11	★★★★★ ★★★★★	
				Feb. 29	Mar. 2	1877/5,000	
60	Denmark	Copenhagen (Roskilde)	Roskilde Rock Festival Roskilde Festival	Jul. 1 Jun. 29	Jul. 1-4 Jun. 29-Jul. 2	★★★ ★★★★ 1971/90,000	
61	England	Isle of Wight	Cowes Week	Aug. 5 Aug. 3	Jul. 31-Aug. 7 Jul. 29-Aug. 5	★★★★ ★ 1812/30,000	
62	England	London (Ascot)	Royal Ascot The Royal Meeting at Ascot Racecourse	Jun. 16 Jun. 21	Jun. 15-18 Jun. 20-23	★★★★ ★★★★★ 1711/230,000	
62	England	London	Notting Hill Carnival	Aug. 28 Aug. 26	Aug. 29-30 Aug. 27-28	★★★ ★★★★ 1965/1,500,000	
63	France	Cannes	Cannes Film Festival Festival International du Film	May 20 May 18	May 12-23 May 10-21	★★★★ ★★★★ 1939/31,000	
64	France	Nice	Nice Jazz Festival	Jul. 15 Jul. 14	Jul. 10-17 Jul. 9-16	★★ ★★★★ 1948/49,000	
65	France	Nimes	Feria de Nimes Feria de Pentecote	May 21 Jun. 9	May 20-24 Jun. 8-12	★★ ★★★ 1952/50,000	
66	France	Paris	Bastille Day	Jul. 13 Jul. 13	Jul. 13-14 Jul. 13-14	★★★ ★★★★ 1789/na	
67	Germany	Köln	Karneval	Feb. 13 Mar. 4	Feb.12-16 Mar. 3-7	★★★★ ★★★ 1823/100,000	
68	Germany	Munich	Oktoberfest	Sep. 18 Sep. 16	Sep. 18-Oct. 3 Sep. 16-Oct. 1	★★★★★ ★★★★ 1810/6,000,000	
69	Germany	Stuttgart	Stuttgart's Volkfest	Oct. 1 Sep. 29	Sep. 25-Oct. 10 Sep. 23-Oct. 8	★★★ ★★ 1818/5,000,000	
70	Greece	Athens	Fun Destination: Athens	Oct. 21 Nov. 2	— —	— —	
71	Ireland	Dublin	St. Patrick's Festival	Mar. 17 Mar. 17	Mar. 13-17 Mar. 11-17	★★★ ★★★ 1996/850,000	
72	Ireland	Galway	Galway Oyster Festival Galway International Oyster Festival	Sep. 24 Sep. 22	Sep. 23-26 Sep. 21-24	★★★★ ★★ 1955/10,000	
73	Italy	Siena	Palio Palio di Siena	Aug. 14 Aug. 14	Aug. 13-17 Aug. 13-17	★★★ ★★ c. 1600/30,000	
74	Italy	Venice	Venice Carnival Carnevale di Venezia	Feb. 12 Mar. 3	Feb. 6-16 Feb. 26-Mar. 7	★★★★★ ★★★★ 1979/500,000	
75	Monaco	Monte Carlo	Monaco Grand Prix Grand Prix Automobile de Monaco	May 7 May 26	May 6-9 May 25-28	★★★ ★★★★ 1942/75,000	
76	Netherlands	Amsterdam	Queen's Day Koninginnedag	Apr. 28 Apr. 28	Apr. 30 Apr. 30	★★★ ★★★★ 1948/720,000	
77	Portugal	Lisbon	Feast of St. Anthony Festas de Lisboa	Jun. 10 Jun. 10	Jun. 2-13 Jun. 2-13	★★ ★★★ 1232/300,000	
78	Scotland	Edinburgh	Edinburgh Fringe Festival	Aug. 19 Aug. 17	Aug. 8-31 Aug. 6-29	★★★★ ★★★★★ 1947/410,000	
78	Scotland	Edinburgh	Hogmanay Edinburgh's Hogmanay	Dec. 30 Dec. 30	Dec. 29-Jan. 1 Dec. 29-Jan. 1	★★★★ ★★★★★ 1993/200,000	

Readers' ✓: Been there, Done that, or Plan to

The Fun Also Rises

GEOGRAPHICAL INDEX

Map Locator	Country	City / Host City	Event / Official Name (if different)	Travel Date	Event Date	Event/City Ranking / Origin/Attendance	✓
					1999 / 2000		
79	Spain	Barcelona (Buñol)	La Tomatina	Aug. 23 / Aug. 28	Aug. 25 / Aug. 30	★★★★★★★★ 1957/25,000	
80	Spain	Ibiza/Majorca	Fun Destination: Ibiza/Majorca	Jul. 22 / Aug. 10	— / —	— / —	
81	Spain	Madrid	Fiestas de San Isidro	May 14 / May 13	May 7-16 / May 12-21	★★★★★★ 1622/25,000	
82	Spain	Pamplona	Running of the Bulls / Los San Fermines	Jul. 6 / Jul. 6	Jul. 6-14 / Jul. 6-14	★★★★★★ c. 1600/100,000	
83	Spain	Valencia	Las Fallas	Mar. 17 / Mar. 17	Mar. 12-19 / Mar. 12-19	★★★★★★ 1497/500,000	
84	Sweden	Stockholm	Stockholm Water Festival	Aug. 12 / Aug. 17	Aug. 6-14 / Aug. 11-19	★★★★★★★★★ 1991/1,100,000	
85	Switzerland	Montreux	Montreux Jazz Festival	Jul. 16 / Jul. 21	Jul. 2-17 / Jul. 6-23	★★★★★ 1967/170,000	
86	Switzerland	Zermatt	Skiing Zermatt / The Most Fun Place To Ski: Europe	Dec. 17 / Dec. 15	— / —	— / —	

Readers' ✓: Been there, Done that, or Plan to

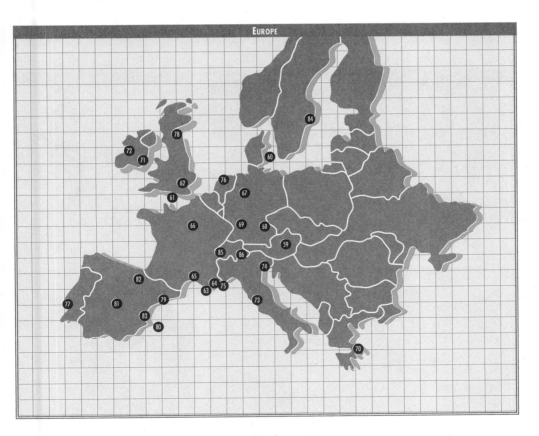

EUROPE

GEOGRAPHICAL INDEX

Map Locator	Country	City / Host City	Event / Official Name (if different)	Travel Date	Event Date	Event/City Ranking / Origin/Attendance	✓
	Asia, Africa, South Pacific			▭ 1999			
				▭ 2000			
87	Australia	Melbourne	Moomba	Mar. 12	Mar. 4-14	★★★★★★★★	
			The Melbourne Moomba Festival	Mar. 17	Mar. 9-19	1955/1,500,000	
88	Australia	Sydney	Sydney Gay and Lesbian Mardi Gras	Feb. 25	Feb. 5-27	★★★★★★★★★	
				Feb. 24	Feb. 4-26	1978/100,000	
89	China	Hong Kong	Chinese New Year	Feb. 15	Feb. 16-18	★★★★★	
			New World Telephone Chinese New Year Fiesta	Feb. 4	Feb. 5-7	1996/25,000	
90	India	Pushkar	Pushkar Camel Fair	Nov. 21	Nov. 20-23	★★★★	
			Pushkar Mela	Nov. 9	Nov. 9-11	1976/200,000	
91	Japan	Tokyo (Kawasaki)	Fertility Festival	Apr. 9	Apr. 10-11	★★★★★★	
			Kanamara Matsuri	Apr. 7	Apr. 8-9	c. 1750/10,000	
92	Macau	Macau	Macau Grand Prix	Nov. 19	Nov. 20-21	★★★★	
				Nov. 17	Nov. 18-19	1954/20,000	
93	Phillipines	Manila (Kalibo)	Ati Atihan	Jan. 15	Jan. 11-17	★★★★★	
				Jan. 14	Jan. 10-16	1212/200,000	
94	South Africa	Cape Town	Cape Minstrel Festival	Jan. 1	Jan. 1-30	★★★★★★	
				Jan. 1	Jan. 1-30	1898/50,000	
95	Thailand	Chiang Mai	Songkran Water Festival	Apr. 12	Apr. 12-14	★★★★	
			Songkran	Apr. 12	Apr. 12-14	c. 1300/200,000	

Readers' ✓: Been there, Done that, or Plan to

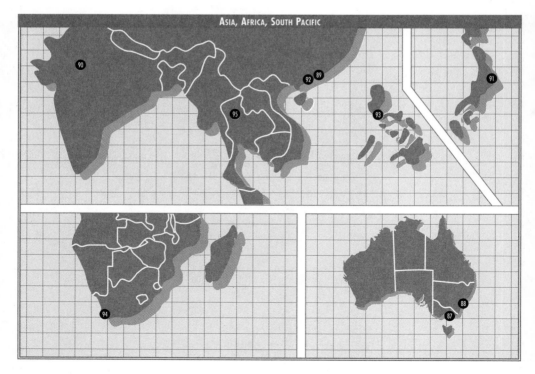

ASIA, AFRICA, SOUTH PACIFIC

The Fun Also Rises

The Fun Also Rises

North American Events & Destinations

Detroit Auto Show

(North American International Auto Show, NAIAS)

Origin: 1907   Event ★ ★ ★ ★ ★ City   Attendance: 790,000

Detroit in the dead of winter may not sound like an inviting proposition for fun-seeking travelers. Hearty souls, however, can spend a stellar weekend during the first three days of the *North American International Auto Show*—the United States' most prestigious event for auto lovers. It's the only event in North America that features the finest international exhibits, and it commands the worldwide acclaim necessary to place it among the top five international auto shows, along with shows in Frankfurt, Geneva, Paris, and Tokyo.

The action kicks off Friday night with the black-tie *Charity Preview*. Raising nearly $4 million, it's the most profitable, annual, single-night fund-raising event in the world, and its 15,000 well-dressed VIPs and schmoozing make it the social highlight of the city's season. All the following week, a more casual crowd of car enthusiasts will step through the doors of the Cobo Center to ogle hundreds of cars and trucks that international automakers unveil throughout 700,000 square feet of floor space. Not surprisingly, 5,900 media representatives come from across the globe to cover this 10-day event.

Detroit's history makes it a natural choice for *NAIAS* host city. Founded in 1701 by a French trader named Cadillac, Detroit was the first site of the mass-production car industry, earning the nickname "Motortown" on the way to launching a worldwide auto boom of unforeseen proportions. Since the 1960s, oil crises and foreign competition have forced industry closures in the region. Still, the auto industry's legacy endures in the city's site and street names, industrial zones, and industry-related attractions.

Motortown comes through for *NAIAS* attendees, topping off this tanked-up weekend with high-octane night life, great dining options, famous blues venues, and plenty else to do and see. New businesses and more than $1 billion have gone into reviving Detroit's downtown area and the city's entertainment offerings draw increasing numbers of out-of-towners. Especially in the heart of winter, "Motown" offers mo' than most visitors expect.

Detroit Auto Show

Day 1. Thu. Jan. 7, 1999
(Day 1. Thursday   January 6, 2000)

10:30am Occupying a converted 19th-century warehouse, your hotel, **The River Place**, offers luxury accommodations and proximity to night life. It sits on the river away from the downtown hub.

Noon After the obligatory walk through Greektown, stop for lunch at **Fishbone's Rhythm Kitchen Cafe**. Connected to the Atheneum, it's a fun spot for cocktails, oyster-slurping, and Cajun cuisine, including smoked whiskey ribs and crispy fried catfish. Check out the world's tallest indoor waterfall.

1:30pm Take a cab up the nation's fifth-longest thoroughfare, Woodward Avenue, to visit the **Detroit Institute of Arts**. Sample some of more than 100 galleries that bring together famous and obscure works of the past five millennia. Especially significant to *NAIAS* pilgrims are Diego Rivera's *The Detroit Industry* frescoes that cover all four walls of the institute's colorful courtyard.

3:30pm Walk to the nearby **Detroit Historical Museum**. Stroll through displays, city-scene reproductions, and an automotive exhibit that relates the century-long story of our four-wheeled friends.

6:00pm Touch base back at the hotel, then take its shuttle to **The Summit Lounge** to toast a stunning 73rd-floor view from the crown of the Westin—the world's tallest hotel.

8:00pm Shuttle back to the tremendously popular **Rattlesnake Club**. Enjoy Detroit River views and the creative menu of world-renowned chef Jimmy Schmidt.

10:00pm Rivertown, the surrounding four-block area, is rich with night life. Although billed as "Detroit's

home of the blues," the ever-popular **Soup Kitchen Saloon** has big-band music on Thursday nights. The brick-lined **Rhinoceros** has funky live music.

Day 2. Fri. Jan. 8, 1999
(Day 2. Friday   January 7, 2000)

10:30am Have room-service breakfast with your river view before taking a short drive to the handsome new **Charles H. Wright Museum of African American History**. Local African-American artists designed the museum's building and contributed the mosaics, sculptures, and detailing that adorn the structure and its grounds. The museum includes exhibits created by Ralph Applebaum, known for his poignant displays at the Holocaust Museum in Washington, DC.

1:00pm By now you ought to have built an appetite worthy of the **Majestic Cafe**'s Middle Eastern favorites and other more inventive dishes, such as strudel with chicken, apple, and Gorgonzola.

2:30pm Visit the **Motown Historical Museum**, where Barry Gordy Jr. set up the original Motown studios using guts, gumption, and $800 in 1959. Now a bit rundown, the former site of "Hitsville, USA" is still a 20th-century music mecca.

5:30pm Cab to the Cobo Center for the ***Charity Preview*** or avoid traffic by taking Detroit's clean, elevated monorail, the **People Mover**. Arrive at Cobo's concourse in time to see industry executives launch the event with a ribbon-cutting ceremony, a spectacle of music, indoor fireworks, and fuel-injected fanfare.

6:00pm (to 9 p.m.) About 15,000 attendees get an auto-show sneak peak on the carpeted show floor. You can talk catalytic converters and design over champagne and hors d'oeuvres with other dapper show-goers, from moto-zealots to celebrities to pleasure-seekers who mourn the passing of the days when 6' 2" blond babes decorated displays. (The ladies were gone once research revealed that women make the final decision on 80 percent of all new-car purchases.)

9:00pm The Whitney's exquisitely prepared American cuisine is served in a 19th-century mansion that once belonged to lumber baron David Whitney. The experience is well worth the planning and effort required to secure a table for *Charity Preview* night.

11:00pm Move into The Whitney's lounge for after-dinner drinks and live music until past midnight. The crowd will be dominated by others who have come from the *Charity Preview*.

Midnight Cab to **Coyote Cantina** in the Crowne Plaza Pontchartrain Hotel. *Charity Preview* guests and employees show up until well after the excitement ends at Cobo, keeping this funky hangout busy until its 2 a.m. closing.

Day 3. Sat. Jan. 9, 1999
(Day 3. Saturday   January 8, 2000)

9:30am Stop at **The Clique**, where word-of-mouth and the *Detroit Free Press* have made their breakfasts famous.

10:30am A short drive southwest takes you to the **Henry Ford Museum & Greenfield Village**, which claims to be the world's largest indoor-outdoor museum. The Henry Ford Museum displays more than a century's worth of cars, along with exhibits on just about everything made in America. Work spaces of innovative Americans have been relocated to Greenfield Village, where you can see (only exteriors during winter season) the Wright brothers' workshop, portions of Thomas Edison's laboratory, and much more.

1:30pm Back in Detroit's Greektown, **Pegasus Taverna** serves Greek food in a bustling atmosphere. Start with a fiery *saganaki*—Greek *kasseri* cheese with flaming brandy.

3:00pm Head back to Cobo, where you'll see last night's cars and displays, but without the fanfare. Don't miss presentations of new and experimental vehicles, as well as special exhibitions from automakers and ad-campaign debuts.

7:30pm In a wide-open space of brick and bare wood, **Intermezzo** is an appropriately boisterous setting for a hearty Italian meal. The place sometimes gets as loud as the abstract art hung on its walls.

10:00pm Laugh off your lasagna at **The Second City**, the first copy of the Chicago original, where live comedy sketches mix down-home humor with timely political and social satire.

Midnight On your way back to the River Place, stop back at **Intermezzo** for a goodbye drink in the lounge, with live music, an upscale crowd, and a year's worth of car fantasies.

Alternatives

Detroit's preferred hotel is the **Atheneum Suite Hotel**, but it's reserved this week for Auto Show bigwigs. You can still check out its grand lobby, with Greek-style murals, and for this week only, a gleaming car parked in the middle of the lobby's marble-and-granite floor. At **The Westin Hotel Renaissance Center**, views, amenities, and a convenient location compensate for the blah rooms.

If you stay over Saturday night, reserve a cozy nook for Sunday brunch at **O'Leary's Tea Room**, which features homemade soda bread and scones.

High rollers can head south into Canada—yes, due *south*—to get lucky at the **Casino Windsor** or the **Northern Belle Casino**. But if all goes according to plan, by the time you get to Detroit it should have three new casinos in town, the "Avenue of Fun" on Columbia Street, and even more to rev up your visit.

The Fun Also Rises   **39**

The Hot Sheet

HOTELS		ADDRESS	PH	FX	PRICE	RMS	BEST ROOMS
Atheneum Suite Hotel	Alt	1000 Brush St.	313-962-2323 800-772-2323	313-962-2424	$$$	174	Suite w/bedside whirlpool bath
The River Place	★	1000 River Pl.	313-259-9500 800-890-9505	313-259-0657	$$	108	Deluxe rms w/full river vw
The Westin Hotel Renaissance Center	Alt	100 Renaissance Ctr.	313-568-8000 800-228-3000	313-568-8146	$$	1414	Upper flrs w/city vw

RESTAURANTS	DAY	ADDRESS	PH	PRICE	REC	DRESS	FOOD
The Clique	3	1326 E. Jefferson St.	313-259-0922	$	B/LD	Local	American
Fishbone's Rhythm Kitchen Cafe	1	400 Monroe St.	313-965-4600	$$	L/BD	Local	Cajun
Intermezzo	3	1435 Randolph Ave.	313-961-0707	$$$	D/L	Kazh	Italian
Majestic Cafe	2	4140 Woodward Ave.	313-833-0120	$	L/D	Kazh	Middle Eastern
O'Leary's Tea Room	Alt	1411 Brooklyn Ave.	313-964-0936	$$	BLD	Kazh	Irish, American
Pegasus Taverna	3	558 Monroe St.	313-964-6800	$	L/D	Local	Greek
Rattlesnake Club	1	300 River Pl. Dr.	313-567-4400	$$$	D/L	Kazh	Contemporary American
The Whitney	2	4421 Woodward Ave.	313-832-5700	$$$	D/L	Dressy, Kazh	Contemporary American

NIGHTLIFE	DAY	ADDRESS	PH	COVER	REC*	DRESS	MUSIC
Coyote Cantina	2	2 Washington Blvd.	313-965-0200	None	R	Kazh	
Rhinoceros	1	265 Riopelle St.	313-259-2208	$	M	Kazh	Jazz, top 40
The Second City	3	2301 Woodward Ave.	313-965-2222	$$	S	Local	
Soup Kitchen Saloon	1	1585 Franklin St.	313-259-2643	$	M(F)	Kazh, Local	Blues, big band
The Summit Lounge	1	see The Westin Hotel	313-832-5700	$$	R	Kazh	

SIGHTS & ATTRACTIONS	DAY	ADDRESS	PH	ENTRY FEE
Casino Windsor	Alt	445 Riverside Dr. W	519-258-7878	None
Charles H. Wright Museum of African American History	2	315 E. Warren Ave.	313-494-5800	$
Detroit Historical Museum	1	5401 Woodward Ave.	313-833-1805	$
Detroit Institute of Arts	1	5200 Woodward Ave.	313-833-7900	$
Henry Ford Museum & Greenfield Village	3	20900 Oakwood Blvd.	313-271-1620	$$
Motown Historical Museum	2	2648 W. Grand Blvd.	313-875-2264	$
Northern Belle Casino	Alt	350 Riverside Dr. E	519-258-2141	None
People Mover	2		313-961-6446	$
Detroit CVB		211 W. Fort St.	800-338-7648	

Event & Ticket Info

The North American International Auto Show (Cobo Center and Exhibition Hall, 1 Washington Blvd.): Tickets ($8) are available in advance from *Ticketmaster* (248-645-6666) or from the *Cobo Center* (313-877-8111) during the show. For more information, contact the *Detroit Auto Dealers Association* (248-643-0250).

Charity Preview (Cobo Center and Exhibition Hall): The 15,000 tickets ($250 CD) usually sell out two months in advance. To request an invitation, contact *Detroit Institute for Children* (313-832-1100 ext. 202).

* M=Live music; P=Dancing (Party); R=Bar only; S=Show; (F)=Food served. For further explanation of codes, see page 14.

 NYC Detroit Metropolitan Wayne County (DTW) <60 min./$30 Yes/No 19°/32° (-7°/0°)

Running of the Bowls

The great thing about football is you no longer have to know a fullback from a hole in the ground to enjoy the party atmosphere that has grown up around this most American of pastimes.

Once second fiddle to major league baseball, professional and college football now dominate the American sports scene from the National Football League's preseason in August to its top-rated Super Bowl finale on the last Sunday of January, a game that draws more than 100 million television viewers worldwide.

In between there's the weekly *Monday Night Football* ritual—a 1970s invention that has single-handedly recast once-quiet Monday nights into big business in the bar and tavern world—and Thanksgiving, a day now associated with professional football as well as turkey and American history. On the amateur level, Americans devote an entire autumn of Saturdays to watching the best collegiate players in the nation. The last two weekends in November are usually saved for intense intrastate "Civil War" weekends—Washington and Washington State, for example, play for state pride and the Apple Cup each year—and settling legendary regional and national rivalries for another year. Georgia and Tennessee universities' Battle Between the Hedges is always one of the most anticipated games of the year, as are matchups between Auburn and Alabama, Ohio State and Michigan, Army and Navy, Notre Dame and the University of Southern California, Stanford and the University of California at Berkeley, and dozens of other games.

College football's biggest day has traditionally been New Year's Day, when top teams vie for the national championship by competing in major bowls attended and watched by millions. Since college football's inaugural year in 1869 (Princeton University was the national champ just four years after the real Civil War), the system for determining the national champion has been inexact and protean. Traditional bowl games are still important—the Rose Bowl and Rose Parade are New Year's Day fixtures—but the big games are currently being restructured and attention may start shifting away from New Year's Day (the 1999 championship game will likely be played on January 4).

One thing the pro and college games have in common is the tailgater, a ritual that's now a fixture at virtually every college and professional football stadium. How do eager fans build entire weekends around games that last only a few hours? Simple. They bring their parties to the stadiums—in cars, trucks, vans, and rented RVs—set up camp in the parking lot, and start cracking cold ones. For dedicated tailgaters, the outcome of the game is never as important as the outcome of the party.

To the uninitiated, a football tailgater might appear to exude all the charm and subtlety of a village raid by Viking berserkers. And it's true, having fun at a tailgater depends on participants' willingness to suspend certain standards of normal behavior. Liberate yourself from your prejudices and you'll soon understand the joy of tailgating: Where else but a tailgater is it acceptable to hang around a parking lot drinking Southern Comfort from a flask at 10:30 in the morning? Where else is it OK to, just for the hell of it, cut loose with a rebel yell in front of 2,000 strangers (not counting a Metallica concert)? Where else is one at complete liberty to verbally abuse any passerby who happens to be wearing the logo of an opposing team?

OK, getting away with crazy behavior isn't all that tailgaters are about. In fact, it's best to think of football parties—whether indoor or outdoor—as autumn's answer to the summer picnic. The props are the same—chips, dip, burgers, dogs, and beer—but more important are the surrounding faces of friends and family who gather in increasing numbers each year to laugh, eat, drink, and cheer together in a distinctly American tradition poised to enter the arena for its third century of play.

See and Be Seen

Whenever someone says, "They don't make 'em like they used to," you can be certain they're not talking about parades. In recent years, parades have become so extravagant that people spend entire years preparing for them.

For millions of people around the world, New Year's Day is synonymous with parades, the most extraordinary being The Tournament of Roses Parade in Pasadena, Calif.—a typical Rose Parade float includes more flowers than the average florist uses in five years. Balloons in New York City's Macy's Thanksgiving Day parade dwarf even the skyscrapers of Manhattan. Tens of thousands of devotees swear that New Orleans' infamous Mardi Gras parade is the single most fun event of any kind in the world.

From military might to flower power, parades cover hundreds of different themes, but the best ones have a single element common to virtually every event in this book: participation. While there are no parades without spectators, shared experience is the key. Whether in the streets or on the sidewalk sidelines, the parade atmosphere prevails as communities join together to sing, dance, eat, drink, and smile together as the spectacle passes by.

Today's parades are descendants of religious processions, holiday festivals, and military parades. Marching bands have replaced fife-and-drum corps and civic groups, police, and fire fighters have replaced soldiers. But even today, parades are often shows of patriotism and strength. One of the best all-marching-unit parades is New York City's St. Patrick's Day Parade, where two million spectators cheer on fire fighters, police, and other might-and-muscle units.

Most parades have moving mechanical parts—floats—that fall into one of three categories for judging (in order of prestige): floral, motorized disguising what propels the float, and visible-motorized. The Tournament of Roses Parade, which showcases Southern California's mild winter with flowers and fruit, is the world's most famous parade. One million curbside spectators are joined by 425 million television viewers in more than 100 countries. Every inch of every phenomenal float is covered with flowers or other natural materials.

Philadelphia starts the New Year with its Mummers Parade, complete with comic brigades in sequins and ostrich plumes, and marching string bands. The Fourth of July is parade day in towns across the United States—Philadelphia turns the whole city into a patriotic celebration (see page 147). Milwaukee's Great Circus Parade relives old-time, promotional circus street processions, complete with circus wagons and wild animals. Dancing dragons herald Chinese New Year's parades in San Francisco, New York, and other cities. New York's ethnic communities parade in a different language every week during summer. San Francisco's Lesbian, Gay, Bisexual, Transgender Pride Parade is the largest annual lesbian/gay event in the world. New York's Greenwich Village Halloween Parade invites everybody in costume to join thousands of wild dancers, artists, and bands. Pasadena's silly Doodah Parade—celebrated around Thanksgiving—includes witty parodies and marching units such as The BBQ and Hibachi Marching Grill Team and the Synchronized Precision Briefcase Drill Team.

No matter what kind of parade, where you stand makes a difference. Units perform before judging stands and cameras, so be nearby those for the best views. Walking a parade route backward makes the parade go by faster. If crowds are too large, bring a footstool to raise yourself above the crowd for a good view—at least until everybody else takes our advice.

January 1999

January 2000

Park City, Utah, USA

Sundance Film Festival

Origin: 1978   Event ★ ★ ★ ★ ★ ★ ★ City   Attendance: 18,000

You'll be at the hottest film festival in the country and the coolest spot in the West when you land at Robert Redford's *Sundance Film Festival*. Be sure not to miss the opening three days, when Park City's population (6,000) doubles with independent directors, producers, agents, and actors trying to start, revive, or expand their careers.

Think of your favorite independent film from recent years and chances are it premièred at *Sundance—sex, lies and videotape, Four Weddings and a Funeral, Breaking the Waves, The Big Lebowski, The Full Monty*—they're all *Sundance* originals. Directors have broken out from here, too. Quentin Tarantino, Michael Moore, and Steven Soderbergh got their starts at the world-class festival. Foreign films, American originals, plays from the Sundance Institute theater project, and sightings of Ordinary Bob (Redford won his Oscar for directing *Ordinary People*, ergo the nickname) are all part of the action.

Make sure to leave time for the town. There's good gallery browsing—art, jewelry, and clothes are the mainstays—and some fun pubs in the not quite sober Beehive State. But "the greatest snow on earth" is what the winter is all about here. Catch the Town Lift and ride up the former silver-mine tram route. Or take the new gondola up the backside of Deer Valley Resort and ski in knee-deep powder among native deer.

The worst thing you can do in any movie town—and Park City definitely becomes a movie town each January—is not dress the part. Fortunately, dressing right is pretty easy: jeans, turtlenecks, parkas, hats, gloves, and warm footwear. This is not a place where you need to make any huge fashion statements, but shivering people are immediately spotted as outsiders and nobody comes to this insider event to be an outsider.

Park City consistently ranks among the world's top ski destinations, and during the festival, the fun is notched up to even higher levels. With cutting-edge films, incredible snow, and celebrities at every turn, *Sundance* is the place to star in your own fun vacation.

Sundance Film Festival

Day 1. Thu. Jan. 21, 1999
(Day 1. Thursday   January 20, 2000)

10:00am Stop first in Salt Lake City, which has the closest major airport to Park City. Long blocks make Salt Lake a tough walking city, so head to **Temple Square**, which houses the headquarters of the Church of Jesus Christ of the Latter-day Saints and the Mormon Tabernacle Choir. There are daily tours on the hour of the gorgeous temple.

Noon With an art-deco interior, linen cloths, black and white tiles, big mirrors, and award-winning food, lunch at **The New Yorker** is a must. Their fresh desserts are worth saving room for.

1:30pm Head for Park City and check in at the **Stein Eriksen Lodge**. Named for the Norwegian Olympic-gold-medal skier who lives in town, it's considered one of the most elegant ski lodges in North America, with awards for exquisite design, comfort, and gourmet food and wine.

2:30pm Grab a film guide at the hotel and decide which movies you want to see. If a film is sold out, get in the waiting line, anyway. Almost everybody who waits gets in. Your best chance any day or time is at the 1,300-seat George S. and Dolores Dore Eccles Center for the Performing Arts. Other venues seat between 100 and 400, so tickets can be harder to come by.

5:00pm Catch the shuttle (45 minutes) from The Kimball Art Center for the ***Opening Night Gala*** in Salt Lake City. Festival directors have a flair for picking a great yet-to-be-discovered film to première at the event. Afterward, cruise the party, where you can't throw a popcorn kernel without hitting an industry biggie. There are lots of bright lights, rolling cameras, and energetic dancers at this gathering, which always begins the festival on a high note.

12:30am Avant-garde people and projects tend to show up for midnight screenings at several venues. But you may want to have a drink at **Lakota**. Back at the hotel, you can enjoy brandy and the fireplace in the bar. Nicolas Cage, Madonna, Keifer Sutherland, and other celebrities have been known to hang out here.

Day 2. Fri. Jan. 22, 1999
(Day 2. Friday   January 21, 2000)

9:00am If you can tear yourself away from your down comforter, head back to Main Street for breakfast at **The Eating Establishment**, known as the Double E to locals. The Miner's Delight is an eggs-fries-and-cheese dish served in a cast-iron skillet.

10:00am Head to the Town Lift to ride up Treasure Mountain at **Park City Mountain Resort**. Ski where Olympians will race in 2002. Park City is generally blessed with great weather and what the ski magazines love to call "champagne powder" snow.

1:00pm Lunch at the historic **Mid Mountain Lodge**, where beef dominates the menu. Or ski at the **Deer Valley Resort**, also Olympic terrain, where runs are groomed like putting greens. You can valet-check your skis when you lunch at **Silver Lake Lodge**, which has some of the finest food of any North American ski resort.

6:00pm Craving another cutting-edge film? At almost any hour in this schedule, you can insert a movie. But you've gotta eat sometime. For an Old Tuscan dinner experience, get a table at **Grappa**, complete with hand-thrown pottery dishes, hand-painted walls, and an ebullient staff who love to cook and serve. Don't miss the ravioli-and-butternut-squash winter soup.

10:00pm The late première screening at the Eccles Center includes the directors, writers, producers, and stars of the film, who show up for a question-and-answer session afterward. Attending means you'll have to miss some of the partying hosted by movie companies and producers. Don't worry, the parties won't finish up too early. The one you go to will depend on whom you've met in the last 24 hours and whether or not your **Sundance** ticket gets you in the door.

12:30am Head up Main Street to **Cisero's**, where live music—usually dance-type rock—is always featured.

Day 3. Sat.   Jan. 23, 1999
(Day 3. Saturday   January 22, 2000)

9:00am Morning Ray Cafe and Bakery is a good way to start the day, if you don't mind waiting in line. Afterward, grab a (very fast) bobsled ride at the **Winter Sports Park**. Bobsledding is not for the timid, so if you prefer a slower pace, visit **Park City Silver Mine Adventure**, an interesting exhibit about all things silver mining.

Noon Enjoy the cozy charm of **Zoom** (Ordinary Bob's place) at the bottom of Main Street. Roaring fireplaces and wooden floors inside this historic train depot are offset by photos of festival winners and celebs. The open grill allows you to watch the stylish chefs at work. The greatest number of sightings of the rich and famous take place here—most of them come for the legendary garlic mashed potatoes.

3:00pm Look at the movie schedule and pick the most off-the-wall documentary. Odds are good it will grab a fistful of awards come Oscar time. Filmmakers and casts hang out with their movies and they want to talk about them. Find a question-and-answer session and become part of the experience. You're likely to learn more about movies than you thought possible at an industry schmooze fest.

6:00pm Bundle up under blankets and let the huge Clydesdale horses at the Victorian **Snowed Inn** take you through nearby meadows, where you may see moose, elk, and golden eagles. Back at the barn, you can choose a Western beef-and-beans dinner or head inside to the **Juniper** restaurant, where the lobster ravioli is accompanied by an

excellent wine list and topped off by something called chocolate dragon delight.

10:00pm Main Street is hopping at this time and if you wander into local favorite **The Cozy**, you can catch live music. Across the street, dance upstairs at **The Club** (Butch Cassidy used to hang out here) or do drinks downstairs. Next door at **The Alamo**, chalk up a stick and pick a pocket or two. This is the kind of Old West hangout that inspires set designers, as well as fans of the Duke.

Midnight It's Saturday night in one of the world's best ski towns during a festival where the second most important reason for being is to have fun—you shouldn't need cue cards for this one.

Alternatives

Shadow Ridge Hotel and **The Yarrow Resort Hotel** are two good, centrally located accommodation options. Both are full-service hotels with all the amenities you'd expect from a top-draw ski resort. The best chain stay is the **Radisson Inn Park City**.

Former Swiss ski racer Adolph Imboden serves cosmopolitan fare, from veal to *escargot*, at his restaurant, **Adolph's**. His flaming desserts are legendary. The sushi chefs know their fish at **Mikado Restaurant** on lower Main. Ask for Krys the waitress, and you could hear a great blues song with your fish eggs. The **Riverhorse Cafe** is a hip restaurant that gets booked up by major players, but if there's an opening, try their new-American fare. Fresh game is the name of the game at **Gamekeeper's Grille**. At the top of Main Street, sample beers at the best microbrewery around, **Wasatch Brew Pub**. **Texas Red's** has the best ribs in town.

You can visit one of the few remaining territorial jails in the basement of the **Park City Museum**. Local buzz has it that the secluded cell below street level offers enough privacy for adventuresome paramours to engage in at least misdemeanor behavior (handcuffs not included).

The Hot Sheet

HOTELS		ADDRESS	PH	FX	PRICE	RMS	BEST ROOMS
Radisson Inn Park City	Alt	2121 Park Ave.	435-649-5000 800-649-5012	435-649-2122	$$	131	Mtn vw
Shadow Ridge Hotel	Alt	50 Shadow Ridge Rd.	435-649-4300 800-451-3031	435-645-9132	$$	150	Dlx Park City vw
Stein Eriksen Lodge	★	7700 Stein Way	435-649-3700 800-453-1302	435-649-5825	$$$$+	130	Lux rm w/everything
The Yarrow Resort Hotel	Alt	1800 Park Ave.	435-649-7000 800-327-2332	435-645-7007	$$$	181	Mtn vw

RESTAURANTS	DAY	ADDRESS	PH	PRICE	REC	DRESS	FOOD
Adolph's	Alt	1500 Kearns Blvd.	435-649-7177	$$$	D	Local	European, American
The Eating Establishment	2	317 Main St.	435-649-8284	$$	B/LD	Local	American
Gamekeeper's Grille	Alt	508 Main St.	435-647-0327	$$$	D	Kazh	American
Grappa	2	151 Main St.	435-645-0636	$$$	D	Kazh	Northern Italian
Juniper at Snowed Inn	3	3770 N. Hwy. 224	435-647-3311	$$	D	Local	American
Mid Mountain Lodge	2	Park City Mountain Resort	435-649-8111	$$	L	Local	American
Mikado Restaurant	Alt	738 Main St.	435-655-7100	$$	D	Local	Japanese
Morning Ray Cafe and Bakery	3	268 Main St.	435-649-5686	$	B/L	Local	American eclectic
The New Yorker	1	60 W. Market St.	801-363-0166	$$	L/D	Kazh	American
Riverhorse Cafe	Alt	540 Main St.	435-649-3536	$$	D	Yuppie	American
Silver Lake Lodge	2	Deer Valley Resort	435-649-1000	$$	L	Local	American
Texas Red's	Alt	440 Main St.	435-649-7337	$$	LD	Local	Barbecue
Zoom	3	660 Main St.	435-649-9108	$$	L/D	Kazh	American eclectic

NIGHTLIFE	DAY	ADDRESS	PH	COVER	REC*	DRESS	MUSIC
The Alamo	3	447 Main St.	435-649-2380	$	MP(F)	Local	Rock, blues
Cisero's	2	306 Main St.	435-649-5044	$	MP(F)	Kazh	Rock
The Club	3	449 Main St.	435-649-6693	$	MP(F)	Local	Various
The Cozy	3	435 Main St.	435-649-6038	$	P(F)	Local	Various
Lakota	1	751 Main St.	435-658-3400	$	R(F)	Kazh	
Wasatch Brew Pub	Alt	250 Main St.	435-649-0900	None	R(F)	Local	

SIGHTS & ATTRACTIONS	DAY	ADDRESS	PH	ENTRY FEE
Park City Silver Mine Adventure	3	Hwy. 224, 1.5 mi. south of Park City	435-655-7444	$$
Temple Square	1	50 W. North Temple St., Salt Lake City	801-240-2534	None

OTHER SIGHTS, SHOPS & SERVICES

	DAY	ADDRESS	PH	ENTRY FEE
Deer Valley Resort	2	Deer Valley Dr. S	435-649-1000	
Park City Mountain Resort	2	345 Lowell Ave.	435-649-8111	
Park City Museum	Alt	528 Main St.	435-649-6104	None
Snowed Inn Sleigh Company	3	3770 N Hwy. 224	435-647-3310	$$$$+
Winter Sports Park	3	3000 Bear Hollow Dr.	435-658-4200	$$$$+
Park City CVB		528 Main St.	800-453-1360	

Salt Lake City—Area Code 801

Event & Ticket Info

Sundance Film Festival: All ticket packages are obtained via mail. The best option for Film Festival Opening Parties is Festival Package A ($650). Daily screening tickets are available each morning. For information, call the *Sundance Institute* (801-328-3456). For registration information, call *Sundance Film Festival Customer Service* (801-322-4033).

* M=Live music; P=Dancing (Party); R=Bar only; S=Show; (F)=Food served. For further explanation of codes, see page 14.

 NYC –2   Salt Lake City (SLC) <60 min./$45   Yes/No   19°/40° (–7°/4°)

Phoenix Open

Origin: 1932   **Event** ★ ★ ★ ★ ★ ★ **City**   **Attendance:** 470,000

66 "They had a party—and a golf tourney broke out!" That's how the organizers of the world's most well-attended golf tournament, the **Phoenix Open**, explain its origins. You don't need to know your way around a 9-iron at this seven-day fiesta, because the **Phoenix Open**'s main appeal is its status as the best party this side of a golf course. It's the only Professional Golf Association (PGA) tournament big enough to compete with the Super Bowl for an audience.

Golf isn't the only game being played at the Stadium Course of the Tournament Player's Club of Scottsdale. The PGA circuit's VIP and party tents are infamous for their "meet market" appeal, conducive to both sightseers and more interactive thrill seekers. The best places to watch and be watched are the 16th hole, where up to 20,000 fans gather daily, and the Bird's Nest, a party tent with a capacity of 9,000, plentiful beverages, and live music.

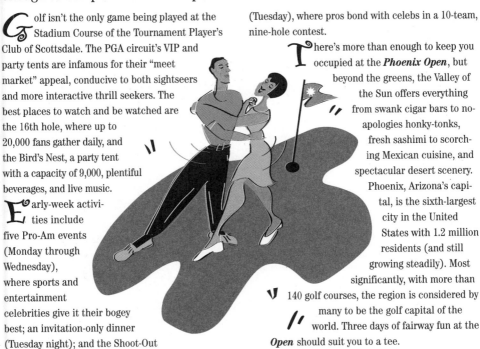

Early-week activities include five Pro-Am events (Monday through Wednesday), where sports and entertainment celebrities give it their bogey best; an invitation-only dinner (Tuesday night); and the Shoot-Out (Tuesday), where pros bond with celebs in a 10-team, nine-hole contest.

There's more than enough to keep you occupied at the **Phoenix Open**, but beyond the greens, the Valley of the Sun offers everything from swank cigar bars to no-apologies honky-tonks, fresh sashimi to scorching Mexican cuisine, and spectacular desert scenery. Phoenix, Arizona's capital, is the sixth-largest city in the United States with 1.2 million residents (and still growing steadily). Most significantly, with more than 140 golf courses, the region is considered by many to be the golf capital of the world. Three days of fairway fun at the **Open** should suit you to a tee.

Excluding some shopping and restaurant areas, attractions in the Phoenix area are spread out and blocks are long. Unless otherwise noted, plan to drive between each itinerary destination.

Day 1. Wed. Jan. 27, 1999
Day 1. Wednesday   *January 26, 2000*

8:30am Check into the **Scottsdale Princess Resort**. In the heart of the action—it's the official home to the **Phoenix Open**'s Stadium Course—it offers luxurious accommodations amid breathtaking desert surroundings.

9:00am Mimi's Cafe serves casual cafe fare in an atmosphere reminiscent of the New Orleans French Quarter. Try the Mediterranean vegetable omelet or the *oeufs et pain perdu*—eggs with French toast stuffed with orange marmalade and cream cheese.

10:00am Get acquainted with the magnificent Sonoran Desert with a visit to Papago Park's **Desert Botanical Garden**, the world's most extensive collection of arid-land plants with beautiful displays of cactus, wildflowers, and desert trees.

Noon Drive to the Royal Palms Resort for lunch at **T. Cooks**. Request one of the tables at the back of the restaurant for gorgeous views of the Camelback Mountains. Keep an eye out for celebrity diners while you enjoy the ambience of Old World elegance and New World sophistication.

1:30pm The pros teed off long before breakfast, but afternoon is the best time to catch golf action on the course and extracurricular action in the beer tents. The largest party is around the 16th hole, a short par-3 where thousands hang around the huge grandstand waiting for holes-in-one. (Tiger Woods hit one here in the 1996 *Phoenix Open*.) The highly animated crowd is not what you'd usually expect to see at a professional golf tournament, but most of the tour players enjoy the enthusiasm as much as the spectators.

5:00pm Choose one: Party on at the course's very crowded **Bird's Nest** tent or relax with a massage at your hotel.

7:30pm Enjoy a leisurely dinner at the Scottsdale Princess' **La Hacienda**, an elegant ranchero with all the charms of Old Mexico—even strolling mariachis.

9:00pm Head out on the town for a night of Arizona culture. In Scottsdale, stop at the **Handlebar J** for a high-end honky-tonk with a fun-loving Western atmosphere before heading to **The Rockin' Horse** for live country music.

Day 2. Thu. Jan. 28, 1999
Day 2. Thursday   *January 27, 2000*

7:00am For the ideal perspective of the Sonoran landscape, enjoy the Valley of the Sun's perfect winter weather with a sunrise balloon ride with **Hot Air Expeditions Inc.** Coming back down to earth means a ceremony of induction into the ballooning society and a champagne breakfast created by the renowned chef Vincent Guerithault, acclaimed for applying French cooking techniques to Southwestern ingredients. Or ...

8:30am If 7 a.m. is too early for you, make a reservation with **Cave Creek Outfitters** for an early-morning horseback ride through nearby canyons and mountains. Relive the legends of cowboys and Indians and soldiers and outlaws as your guide recounts the history of the desert. Have room service send up a hearty breakfast before you go.

Noon Drive to Phoenix for lunch at **RoxSand**, which has a hip environment with transcontinental flair. Or check into **Harris' Steak House**. Although part of a chain, it consistently receives superb reviews and breaks steakhouse conventions with fashionable art and alternative menu choices.

2:00pm The galleries and courtyards of the **Heard Museum** feature dramatic collections of prehistoric, ancient, and contemporary Hohokam, Apache, Hopi, and Navajo art. Be sure to see the world-famous Kachina Doll Gallery.

3:30pm The **Phoenix Art Museum** displays Asian, European, and Latin American art, as well as an excellent collection of Western art. The nearby sports arenas and new buildings are part of a 1990s downtown reclamation project that has been one of the most successful in the country.

5:00pm Unwind with a cocktail at **The MercBar**, a sophisticated retreat where the beautiful people go to be with each other.

7:30pm Return to Scottsdale for dinner at **P.F. Chang's China Bistro**, a popular spot that almost always has a line out the door. Call an hour in advance to avoid a long wait for their elegant Chinese cuisine accompanied by a comprehensive wine list and specially blended teas.

9:00pm Continue your evening on the town at **Axis**, where jazz is served in a supper-club atmosphere. **The Famous Door** provides live music and vintage supper-club ambience, while **Marco Polo Supper Club** puts a twist on swank, as Italy meets the Orient.

Day 3. Fri.   Jan. 29, 1999
Day 3. Friday   *January 28, 2000*

9:00am After breakfast, visit Frank Lloyd Wright's famous architecture school, **Taliesin West**.

11:00am Be back in Scottsdale in time for a stroll through Old Town, where you may get sidetracked by the extensive up-market shopping available.

Noon At **Old Town Tortilla Factory**, get a head start on margaritas—choose from more than 50 tequilas— and great Mexican food.

1:30pm Head back to the TPC Stadium Course. Several spots allow you to view driving tees and putting greens simultaneously, but most spectators hang out in beer tents or on the lawns, soaking in liquids, sunshine, and intoxicating views of the opposite sex sporting desert tans in midwinter. It's the second day of the tournament, with two more days to go, so most of the excitement centers around the desperation of the still-dateless denizens.

6:00pm Be sure to get to the **Bird's Nest** by this time. Otherwise, it may be too crowded to gain admission. Drinks, conversation, and lots of golfing stories and jokes flow until 11 p.m., so snack food will have to suffice for dinner.

10:00pm Leave the tourney for additional nourishment and partying. The hefty cover is worth the experience at the huge **Cajun House** in Old Town Scottsdale. You'll feel as if you've been transported to New Orleans' Bourbon Street, complete with theme bars and live music on the stage at the end of the "street." If you'd rather take it easy, leave the tournament early and drive 15 minutes to the **Top of the Rock** at the Buttes. Grab a late dinner and enjoy the 360-degree view of the valley that's the best in the area.

Alternatives

They're not as close to the Stadium Course, but other hotel possibilities include the desert-chic **Boulders Resort and Club**, on the route to Cave Creek, and the **Hyatt Regency Scottsdale at Gainey Ranch**, with ten interconnecting pools, golf, and a spa. It's worth a visit to the lobby lounge to hear Estevan playing Spanish guitar.

You'll want to find time to take advantage of the resort amenities, perhaps including golf. The concierge can assist you in reserving tee times up to a year in advance. In the Phoenix area, you could golf twice a week for a year and never play the same course twice.

The Hot Sheet

HOTELS		ADDRESS	PH	FX	PRICE	RMS	BEST ROOMS
The Boulders Resort and Club Grand Bay Luxury Division	Alt	36431 N. Tom Darlington Dr.	602-488-9009 800-553-1717	602-488-4118	$$$$+	201	Vw of boulder formations
Hyatt Regency Scottsdale at Gainey Ranch	Alt	7500 E. Doubletree Ranch Rd.	602-991-3388 800-223-1234	602-483-5550	$$$$+	493	Back of hotel w/vw of resort or mtns
Scottsdale Princess Resort	★	7575 E. Princess Dr.	602-585-4848 800-223-1818	602-585-9895	$$$$+	650	A casita

RESTAURANTS	DAY	ADDRESS	PH	PRICE	REC	DRESS	FOOD
La Hacienda	1	see Scottsdale Princess Resort	602-585-4848	$$$	D	Kazh	Mexican
Harris' Steak House	2	3101 E. Camelback Rd.	602-508-8888	$$	L	Kazh	Steakhouse, continental
Mimi's Cafe	1	8980 E. Shea Blvd.	602-451-6763	$	B	Kazh	Cafe French
Old Town Tortilla Factory	3	6910 E. Main St.	602-945-4567	$	L	Local	Mexican, Native American
P.F. Chang's China Bistro	2	7014 E. Camelback Rd.	602-949-2610	$$	D	Kazh	Chinese
RoxSand	2	2594 E. Camelback Rd.	602-381-0444	$$	L	Kazh	Transcontinental, fusion
T. Cooks	1	5200 E. Camelback Rd.	602-808-0766	$	L	Kazh	Rustic Mediterranean
Top of the Rock	3	1000 Westcourt Way	602-225-9000	$$$	D	Kazh	American w/ Southwestern accent

NIGHTLIFE	DAY	ADDRESS	PH	COVER	REC*	DRESS	MUSIC
Axis	2	7340 E. Indian Plaza	602-970-1112	None	M(F)	Kazh	Jazz, swing, '80s
Cajun House	3	7117 E. 3rd Ave.	602-945-5150	Varies	MP(F)	Local	Varies
The Famous Door	2	7419 E. Indian Plaza	602-970-1945	None	M	Kazh	Jazz
Handlebar J	1	7116 E. Becker Lane	602-948-0110	$	MP(F)	Local	Country, rock
Marco Polo Supper Club	2	8608 E. Shea Blvd.	602-483-1900	None	M(F)	Kazh, Dressy	Classics, oldies
The MercBar	2	2525 E. Camelback Rd.	602-508-9449	None	R(F)	Kazh	
The Rockin' Horse	1	7316 E. Stetson Dr.	602-949-0992	$	M	Local	Country

SIGHTS & ATTRACTIONS	DAY	ADDRESS	PH	ENTRY FEE
Desert Botanical Garden	1	1201 N. Galvin Pky.	602-941-1217	$
Heard Museum	2	22 Monte Vista Rd.	602-252-8840	$
Phoenix Art Museum	2	1625 N. Central Ave.	602-257-1222	$
Taliesin West	3	12621 N. Frank Lloyd Wright Blvd.	602-860-8810	$$
Cave Creek Outfitters	2	31313 N. 144th St.	602-471-4635	$$$$+
Hot Air Expeditions Inc.	2	7500 E. Butherus Dr., Ste. F	602-502-6999	$$$$+
Phoenix and Valley of the Sun CVB		2476 E. Camelback Rd.	602-254-6500	

Event & Ticket Info

Phoenix Open (Tournament Players Club, Scottsdale Princess Resort): The tournament is never sold out, and tickets ($20) are available at the *TPC* (602-585-3939), or may be purchased in advance from *Dillard's Box Office* (602-503-5555). Golf enthusiasts may prefer more elaborate packages (starting at $150). For more information, contact the *Thunderbirds* (602-870-4431).

* M=Live music; P=Dancing (Party); R=Bar only; S=Show; (F)=Food served. For further explanation of codes, see page 14.

 NYC –2   Phoenix Sky Harbor (PHX) <30 min./$20   Yes   38°/65° (3°/19°)

 The Fun Also Rises

January 1999 — Las Vegas, Nevada, USA — January 2000

Super Bowl Weekend

Origin: 1967   Event ★ ★ ★ ★ ★ ★ ★ ★ City   Attendance: 200,000

O n the last Sunday in January, everyone wants to be in the town that hosts the **Super Bowl**, right? Well, not really. That's because the best **Super Bowl** action takes place in Las Vegas, where casinos unfurl red carpets for high rollers, hot players, and party veterans who know that the actual game is just a sidelight during one of the best weekends of the year.

M ore people head to Las Vegas for **Super Bowl weekend** than to the site of the game (Miami in 1999, Atlanta in 2000). By the tens of thousands, they hit the sports books, pick a team, place a bet, then cruise the inescapable array of football parties and gatherings.

J ust arriving in Las Vegas by plane is a unique experience. Slot machines jam the terminal. Screens in the baggage area tout shows, hotels, and anything else good-looking showgirls can sell. Outside, a battalion of limousines await privileged guests.

T his is the showiest weekend of the year in a town that defines America's obsession with big-time glitz. (For another side of Las Vegas, see page 244.) In years past, the famous lights of the Strip simply amazed out-of-towners. Now,

coming into Vegas is like entering a neon dreamscape. In recent years, Las Vegas has attempted to rebuild itself as a family destination, but this 24-hour city still caters mostly to adults. World-class attractions offered by most casinos remain mere diversions from the serious business at hand—gambling.

T he combination of gaming and entertainment is paying off. The new $1.7 billion Bellagio The Resort hotel, for example, can afford to transport northern Italy to the middle of the desert. Its art collection, which includes works by Van Gogh, Cezanne, and Picasso, makes this hotel the most well-hung, artfully speaking, on the Strip.

T he macho allusion isn't out of place during this weekend that celebrates the most watched annual sporting event in the world. **Super Sunday** can almost be considered America's first holiday after New Year's Day and no place rings it in like Vegas.

Super Bowl Weekend

We've abandoned our itinerary formula for this chapter in favor of a more general overview of options built around the Super Bowl.

Hotel

For the **Super Bowl**, pick a hotel that has top-end accommodations and caters to high rollers. **Caesars Palace** holds the heavyweight title as the first and best theme hotel and casino in Las Vegas. At the heart of the Strip, Caesars was completed in 1966 in ageless Greco-Roman style. The four-acre Garden of the Gods outdoor area was completed in 1998. With a 90-foot atrium filled with exotic palms and tropical foliage, **The Mirage** evokes a Polynesian paradise. The erupting volcano and Siegfried and Roy's rare white tigers complete the set. **Bellagio The Resort** is the new deluxe hotel, catering to upper-crust patrons with gardens, waterfalls, and the world-renowned Cirque du Soleil performing above and below the surface of a large fresh-water pool. **The Desert Inn Resort**, the only Strip hotel with an on-site golf course, is a smaller, quieter choice. For something different, the avant-garde suites at **The Rio Suite Hotel & Casino**—close to the Strip—cater to a somewhat hipper crowd.

Casinos

Each recommended hotel has a terrific casino, but part of the fun in Vegas is making the rounds. Although the games of chance are all the same, each casino has a different ambience and attracts a different crowd. Despite the fact that minimum betting amounts are higher all over town this weekend, you'll find an unusual number of people crowding around tables, waiting for an opening to play. Get close enough and you'll see more people betting more money than you thought possible.

Breakfast and lunch

Assigning names like breakfast and lunch to meal times will have no meaning to you or your body this weekend. The casinos and their coffee shops operate 24 hours. All major hotels have coffee shops that are particularly useful from midnight until dinner time. Many casinos also serve elaborate buffet breakfasts.

Area attractions

Daytime attractions in Glitter Gulch run the gamut. Arrive early for a good vantage point of **Treasure Island Buccaneer Bay Show** to watch pirates battle the British Navy every 90 minutes starting at 4 p.m. Spend your winnings at **The Forum Shops at Caesars**; take a break with the fountain show when Roman statues come to life for eight splashy minutes on the hour. Visit the Mirage shark tank and dolphin exhibit; return at night for the **Mirage Volcano** eruption every 15 minutes. **New York, New York** has the Statue of Liberty West outside and more Big Apple nostalgia inside, including a Coney Island roller coaster, Manhattan Express. Billing itself as the Gen X Casino, the **Hard Rock Hotel and Casino** doubles as a museum of popular culture, with a $2 million collection of rock-and-roll memorabilia. Jimi Hendrix's Flying V guitar resides regally near a fleet of vintage Harleys atop a bank of Sid Vicious slot machines, an irony that must have the deceased anti-everything punk rocker rolling in his grave.

The Super Bowl

The major hotels fill their rooms with "invited" guests who attend private parties on **Super Bowl Sunday**. However, "party" is just a hook used to gather a lot of people into a room to watch a big-screen television. If you don't go to a party, just watch the game on giant screens along with a crowd of people in any of the major casinos. It's fun and usually easy to pick out the white-knuckled gamblers who have backed the team that is winning or losing.

Wherever you go, you can be sure there'll be plenty of *Super Bowl* paraphernalia, hot dogs, and beer. In between tackles, cheers, and drinks, several casinos will have ex-NFL stars and current-day cheerleaders on hand to keep things interesting in case the score of the game gets (typically) out of hand. The game itself may sometimes be called the Super Bore, but nobody ever accused Las Vegas of falling asleep while there was still a player on the field or a bet to be made.

Super Bowl betting

The gigantic electronic display boards at The Race and Sports Book at Caesars Palace offer continuous computer wagering information, including odds changes and player-injury reports. Funky bets are *de rigueur*. Will the quarterback fumble the ball in the third quarter? How many times will the fullback run up the middle? Will the towel boy accidentally spill the Gatorade bucket, thereby ruining the traditional postgame Gatorade celebration? OK, you can't bet on that last one, but you can wager money on just about any other game situation you can think of.

Dinner

In the old days, major casino hotels used a standard formula—offer guests a choice of a gourmet restaurant, a steakhouse, and Italian and Asian eateries. Results were often bland. But resorts have been busy in recent years, plucking the nation's most famous restaurateurs from hometown nests, transplanting them to the desert and turning Vegas into a great eating town.

For nouvelle done à la West Coast, including an extraordinary wine list, check out **Napa**. Try the crab cakes or tuna sashimi, followed by a creamy risotto. Los Angeles moves east with **Spago**, where cuisines from around the world combine seamlessly; try the fried catfish with ginger-miso aioli and spicy bok choy. Other fine choices are **Mark Miller's Coyote Cafe** for Southwestern-influenced food; Wolfgang Puck's **Chinois** for fusion; and **Emeril's New Orleans Fish House**.

Entertainment

Major casinos have enough entertainment to keep you busy for weeks. Lounge shows are typically free, allowing you to drop in for a drink and listen to top-notch club entertainers. Picking a show is a matter of personal taste, but the must-see for everyone is Cirque du Soleil's **Mystère** (or any other show by this amazing French Canadian troupe), which is housed in a theater at Treasure Island built especially for this show.

Late night

While there's no such thing as being too late in this city, there are postdinner hot spots where the action makes the Super Bowl look like training camp. The Rio has two top-shelf choices: **Club Rio**, a raging disco with a very long line to get in, and **VooDoo Cafe & Lounge**, where you can check out acts such as Boogie Knights and Dr. Funkenstein from the comfort of an animal-print booth. Luxor's **Club Ra**, with an Egyptian motif, is another popular disco. **Studio 54** may be the most striking disco, with a backstage film-lot décor. If you're into music memorabilia, **The Joint** at the Hard Rock is also worth a stop, though more for the energetic crowd than the ambience. Try **Cleopatra's Barge** at Caesars for live music.

For clubs not in a hotel, **The Beach** and **Drink and Eat Too** are lower-tech and generally have less attitude. And remember, if you've had too much dancing and need to sit down, the slot machines have been known to sing a few tunes.

The Hot Sheet

HOTELS	ADDRESS	PH	FX	PRICE	RMS	BEST ROOMS
Bellagio The Resort	3600 Las Vegas Blvd. S	702-693-7111 888-987-6667	702-693-8965	$$$$+	3005	Strip vw
Caesars Palace	3570 Las Vegas Blvd.	702-731-7110 800-634-6001	702-731-6636	$$$	4,000	Palace tower
The Desert Inn Resort	3145 Las Vegas Blvd.	702-733-4444 800-634-6906	702-733-4774	$$$$	715	Mtn vw
The Mirage	3400 Las Vegas Blvd.	702-791-7111 800-627-6667	702-791-7446	$$$	3,044	Strip vw
The Rio Suite Hotel & Casino	3700 W. Flamingo Rd.	702-252-7777 800-752-9746	702-253-6090	$$	2,500	Las Vegas valley vw

RESTAURANTS	ADDRESS	PH	PRICE	REC	DRESS	FOOD
Chinois	see The Forum Shops at Caesars	702-737-9700	$$	LD	Kazh	Chinese, fusion
Emeril's New Orleans Fish House	3799 Las Vegas Blvd. S, in MGM Grand	702-891-7374	$$$$	LD	Yuppie	Creole, Cajun
Mark Miller's Coyote Cafe	3799 Las Vegas Blvd. S, in MGM Grand	702-891-7349	$$	BLD	Kazh	Southwestern
Napa	see The Rio Suite Hotel	702-252-7777	$$$	D	Yuppie	Country French
Spago	see The Forum Shops at Caesars	702-369-6300	$$$$	LD	Yuppie	Continental

NIGHTLIFE	ADDRESS	PH	COVER	REC*	DRESS	MUSIC
The Beach	365 Convention Center Dr.	702-731-1925	$	P(F)	Kazh	Top 40
Cleopatra's Barge	see Caesars Palace hotel	702-731-7110	None	MP(F)	Kazh	Top 40
Club Ra	3900 Las Vegas Blvd. S	702-262-4000	$	P(F)	Kazh	Disco
Club Rio	see The Rio Suite Hotel	702-252-7777	$	P	Yuppie	Top 40
Drink and Eat Too	200 E. Harmon Ave.	702-796-5519	$	MP(F)	Kazh	'70s disco
The Joint	4455 Paradise Rd. Hard Rock hotel	702-693-5000	$	MP	Kazh, Local	Rock
Mystère	3300 Las Vegas Blvd. S, Treasure Island Hotel	702-894-7722	$$$$+	S	Yuppie	Nuvo Circus
Studio 54	3799 Las Vegas Blvd. S	702-891-7915	$$	P	Kazh	House
VooDoo Cafe & Lounge	3700 W. Flamingo Rd.	702-252-7777	$	MP	Yuppie	Jazz

SIGHTS & ATTRACTIONS	ADDRESS	PH	ENTRY FEE
Hard Rock Hotel and Casino	4455 Paradise Rd.	702-693-5000	None
Mirage Volcano	see The Mirage hotel	702-791-7111	None
New York, New York	3790 Las Vegas Blvd. S	702-740-6969	None
Treasure Island Buccaneer Bay Show	3300 Las Vegas Blvd. S, Treasure Island Hotel	702-894-7111	None

OTHER SIGHTS, SHOPS & SERVICES

The Forum Shops at Caesars	see Caesars Palace hotel	702-893-4800	None
Las Vegas CVB	3150 Paradise Rd.	800-332-5333	

* M=Live music; P=Dancing (Party); R=Bar only; S=Show; (F)=Food served. For further explanation of codes, see page 14.

 NYC −3   McCarran (LAS) <30 min./$15   No   33°/56° (1°/13°)

The Fun Also Rises

A Whale of a Good Time

Whales are beloved creatures, but nowhere more beloved than in Las Vegas. Las Vegas? Yep, in Las Vegas, a whale is someone who gambles more than $1 million per visit, with lines of credit up to $20 million. Casinos love them.

If you don't happen to be one of the world's 250 players in this league, perhaps you're one of the thousands who wager more than $100,000 per visit. These are the people you see filling casinos during Super Bowl weekend, betting green ($25), black ($100), and pink ($500) chips on the turn of every card or the toss of the dice. These players help create a buzz in casinos and attract the attention of other gamblers, dealers, good-looking "escorts," and chip hustlers.

Apparently, there's something enjoyable about losing money. More than 30 million people come to Las Vegas each year to drop money on a variety of games—slot machines, Keno, roulette, baccarat, blackjack, poker, and pai gow are a few favorites. But for most aficionados of fun, the only worthwhile thrill is craps. When conditions are right, craps evolves beyond being a simple game and becomes a party. Anyone who can get near the table is invited.

Craps, whether played in the garages of the Runyonesque *Guys and Dolls*, or in billion-dollar resorts, is the fastest and liveliest casino game. Money moves quickly—it's fun for novices to simply watch dealers move the chips around—and it takes a fair amount of familiarity and comfort to play it well. Many books have been written about playing and winning at craps. To have fun, however, you only need to understand the language of the game. Start by learning how to count in crapsese:

Get the counting down and you'll soon understand terms such as *Two rolls, no coffee! Hands high, they fly! Too tall to call!* and *Pause is the cause!* Pretty soon you'll be kissing the dice (or letting the good-looking gamer next to you kiss them) and shouting "C'mon, dice, baby needs a new pair of shoes!" or the ever-popular "Rent money!" as you throw the bones across the felt. After that, you're just a slippery slope away from calling out bets like "Section eight press and a high/low with the cheese!" When you want to roll an eight, you'll call out "How do you spell relief?" and get the response "Roll eight!" When you win, you'll hear the stickman say, "Winner, winner, chicken dinner" and get high-fives all around. This sure beats pushing buttons and waiting for a bunch of cherries.

Two: *aces* or *low*	**Eight**: *eighter from Decatur*
Three: *ace-deuce*	**Nine**: *Nina from Pasadena*
Four: *little Joe*	**Ten**: *ten on the end* or *Big Ben*
Five: *fever*	
Six: *sex*	**Eleven**: *yo* or *yo-lev*
Seven: *seven, seven out,* or *lucky seven*	**Twelve**: *boxcars* or *high*

TABLE TALK

Whatever game you play, start with a rudimentary understanding of casino terminology and you can swim with the sharks, if not the whales.

Boxman: a craps dealer who sits over the drop box and supervises bets and payoffs
Casino boss: a person who oversees the entire casino
Comp: short for *complimentary* or *free*
Drop box: a locked box on tables where dealers deposit paper money
Eye in the sky: surveillance equipment, usually ceiling mirrors that conceal people assigned to watch the action to prevent cheating by players or dealers
Limit: the minimum or maximum bet accepted at a gambling table
Marker: an IOU owed the casino by a gambler allowed by the hotel to play on credit
Pit boss: a person who oversees table dealers
RFB comp: free room, food, and beverage
Shooter: a gambler who is rolling the dice on a craps table
Stickman (Stick chick): a dealer who moves the dice around on a craps table with a hooked stick

Living by the Book

What's it like to live this book, go to the best parties in the world, experience the most fun events? Ask Paul Walton. He's spent more than a decade reading about a party or event in the morning, getting on a plane in the afternoon, and being there that night.

The best event, according to Walton, is Mardi Gras in New Orleans. "It's the only time I can get away with being as completely spontaneous as a child."

A close runner-up is St. Patrick's Day in Savannah. With the river running green and the waterfront pulsing with thousands of people, there's magic in Savannah's Southern sense of hospitality and trust. " 'Fun' is interaction, meeting people and talking to them," Walton says. "It's a good feeling to be a stranger and be welcomed, a beautiful feeling that doesn't happen often."

But events can't "give" you fun, he adds. Even the best party or event won't change an unhappy person. "You have to be open, go to a place that receives you, that welcomes you, and mix it up with other people." That's when the crowd's energy becomes infectious. "I need the crowd and I like to think the crowd needs me," he says. "I become a catalyst for fun. I know I make a difference." Even in a crowd of 100,000 people? "One person can make a difference," says the well-traveled Walton.

66 I look at life as a journey," he continues. "It doesn't matter where you are along the way, you have to be having fun. But I also have an interest in what's going on in the world. I want to be a witness

> The best event, according to Walton, is Mardi Gras in New Orleans.
>
> A close runner-up is St. Patrick's Day in Savannah.

to history." Even a serious goal such as "witnessing" becomes fun with Walton's focus on 50th- and 100th-anniversary events.

He admits that a lot of his traveling is motivated by "the chance that I will meet the girl of my dreams." So it's not surprising that he thinks that events and parties are "absolutely more fun with a companion. The ultimate fun is sharing it with another." In fact, he's come up with a hierarchy of the best traveling companions: someone you're in love with, a good buddy, your sister or brother, a platonic friend.

66 The absolute worst," Walton cautions, again drawing on his vast experience, "is to go with someone you wish you weren't with."

Québec Winter Carnaval
(Carnaval de Québec)

Origin: 1894	Event ★★★★★★ City	Attendance: 1,000,000

It's one of the world's biggest carnivals, but with one big difference that separates it from the pack: snow. You won't see anyone sporting a bikini, except for a few nuts taking snow baths. And instead of dazzling clouds of tinsel, the streets more often swirl with sparkling snow. It's the *Québec Winter Carnaval*, a three-week samba in padded parkas.

Deep in the heart of winter, the oldest walled city north of Mexico defies hypothermia by becoming a pulsing conga line, with parades, balls, snow sports, and parties. Lit by millions of pinpoint lights stretching from the snow-banked suburbs to the heart of Old Québec, the celebration is fueled by 18,000 liters of local Caribou (a wicked libation made of port and grain alcohol). Presiding over the festivities is Bonhomme, a seven-foot walking, talking snowman in red toque. He's the city's ambassador of bonhomie and his massive ice palace—with fortified defense walls, crowded medieval alleys, huge ancient monasteries, burghers' stone homes, and reminders of battles lost and won—is a Québec legend.

Although *Québec's Winter Carnaval* wasn't officially established until 1894, it originated 390 years ago, when French explorer Samuel de Champlain threw a party for settlers. During the bitter January of 1608, they were hungry, sick with scurvy, freezing, and depressed. Champlain decreed the "Order of Good Times" and a festival filled with wine, food, and dancing. Suicidal spirits soared. From a celebration born of despair, *Carnaval* has become a lusty salut to *joie de vivre* and the world's biggest blast in the snow.

With its beautifully preserved historic buildings, Québec City is a UNESCO World Heritage site—one of only two in North America. Such a distinction hasn't fossilized the vibrancy of a populace proud to celebrate its roots, culture, art, gastronomy, sports, snow, and even, ice. During the carnival, Québec demonstrates its exuberance with endless rounds of *Carnaval*'s signature song: "*Car-na-val ... Mardi Gras ... Car-na-val!*" It's a refrain that will echo through your sleep—if you're lucky enough to get any.

Québec Winter Carnaval

Day 1. Fri.   Feb. 5, 1999
(Day 1. Friday   February 4, 2000)

9:00am The romantic and elegant **Château Frontenac** bases you close to *Carnaval* action. This turreted, copper-topped castle towers above the walled city and is the world's most photographed hotel. Your room may have hosted Churchill, Roosevelt, De Gaulle, Princess Grace, or any of 18 monarchs.

9:30am In the lobby souvenir boutique, purchase a Bonhomme figurine, your pass for outdoor *Carnaval* venues. Another must-buy is a hollow Bonhomme walking cane to fill with Caribou. If your cane should run empty, shots are sold at makeshift bars everywhere. Also pick up multicolored, traditional *ceinture fléchées* (sashes) from weavers working their looms in the lobby.

10:00am Breakfast at the hotel's **Café de la Terrasse** while watching strollers on the historic Dufferin Terrace boardwalk.

11:00am Walk two minutes to **rue du Trésor**. In this picturesque, open-air gallery, local artists display and sell their paintings—snow or shine.

Noon The **Québec Experience**, a 3-D sound-and-light show, gives an overview of the city's some 400-year history.

1:30pm Stroll three minutes to lunch at the fabled site of North America's first French kiss, across from your hotel. Built in 1679, **Auberge du Trésor** claims to be the continent's oldest continuously inhabited dwelling. Specialties include beef Wellington and rabbit in mustard sauce.

4:00pm Walk five minutes and take a one-horse open-sleigh ride across the Plains of Abraham, adjacent to the château.

6:00pm Dressed in evening finery, descend to the resplendent château ballroom for the **Bal de Bonhomme**. You and 300 others in fancy gowns or suits dine on five gourmet courses and dance to a full orchestra.

11:30pm Cap the night in the oak-paneled **Le Bar Saint-Laurent** for one last whirl on its tiny dance floor.

Day 2. Sat.   Feb. 6, 1999
(Day 2. Saturday   February 5, 2000)

10:00am Walk 15 minutes to a hearty, outdoor *flapjack breakfast*. Canada's cowboy city, Calgary, hosts 5,000 appetites on Place Loto-Québec in front of the Parliament building.

11:00am Nearby is **Bonhomme's Palace**, a glittering fantasy of 6,000 ice blocks weighing 225 tons. Visit rooms with ice furniture and mementos from Bonhomme's world tours, and meet some Knuks—merry dancers and pranksters from the Arctic Circle.

Noon Nearby, lunch on authentic Québecois cuisine—pea soup, *tourtière,* and maple-syrup pie—at the historic **Aux Anciens Canadiens**.

1:00pm Head to Place Desjardins for the **canoe race preliminaries**; competitors practice on snow for tomorrow's treacherous river crossing on the ice floes. If athletically inspired, you can tube down a glissade, climb a 40-foot ice mountain, play minigolf *en glace,* or snowboard. Laid-back pleasures include a dog-sled ride and an igloo village, with igloo-building lessons. On Côte de la Fabrique, 15-minutes away, watch the fast and colorful **Normandin Soapbox Derby**.

2:30pm Meander to the **Bain de Neige** in Place Loto-Québec, where 75 lunatics doff their duds for bracing rolls in the snow.

3:30pm Order a bowl of French onion soup or *moules et frites* (mussels and fries) at one of the Old City's many bistros. Or choose hearty German fare from the stone vaults of **Le Falstaff** or one of **Portofino**'s charcoal-baked pizzas.

4:30pm Head to your room for even warmer clothes for the night's outdoor activities.

7:00pm Cane reloaded, take the hotel shuttle to Charlesbourg and join the *Night Parade* throng. Floats and bands wend their way through snowy streets, while about 180,000 chant *"Car-na-val ... Mardi Gras ... Car-na-val,"* until it's forever imbedded in your head.

8:30pm Back on Grande Allée—the Champs-Elysées of North America—bistros and nightclubs shimmer with ice sculptures and tiny white lights. Dine at the award-winning French restaurant **Bonaparte**, as fine an establishment as you'll find with mitts, toques, and boots steaming by the fire. The specialty is local lobster from Sept-Îles.

10:00pm Stroll along crowded Grande Allée. Two happening spots are **Chez Dagobert**, where 1,500 people pulsate on a stainless-steel floor, and **Le Charlotte Lounge**, a more mellow nightclub. **Maurice Salon-Bar** has cognac, cigars, and pool tables.

2:00am Stop by Place Desjardins to watch *The Night of the Long Knives*—sculptors stay up all night carving massive blocks of snow into art for tomorrow's 9 a.m. judging.

Day 3. Sun.   Feb. 7, 1999
(Day 3. Sunday   February 6, 2000)

9:00am Take the funicular from Dufferin Terrace to the Quartier Petit-Champlain. The oldest commercial district in North America, it bustles with one-of-a-kind craft shops. Brunch at **Le Lapin Sauté**, a country-style nook warmed by a fireplace.

1:30pm About 30,000 turn out for the *canoe race final* at the Old Port's Bassin-Louise. Go to the pier across from Musée de la Civilisation by 12:30 p.m. for the best vantage.

3:30pm Visit **Musée de la Civilisation**. Exhibits range from Chinese civilization to "Mad about Hockey."

5:00pm Stop into **Pub Thomas Dunn** for a choice of more than 150 brews and 50 brands of single-malt Scotch.

8:00pm Cross to the Gare du Palais, a train station resembling a small castle, which holds two local hot spots. Dine at the hip **L'Aviatic Club**. Its menu includes sushi and Tex-Mex. Then ...

10:00pm Drop in next door at **Le Pavillon**, where late-night dancing heats the climax to a cold but dazzling weekend.

Alternatives

On Friday and Saturday of *Winter Carnaval*, a large crowd dances outdoors during the *Soirée Carnavalesque* at the Place Loto-Québec.

The second week of July, *du Maurier Québec Summer Festival* brings 1,000 artists from 20 countries for 800 mostly free performances.

Loews Le Concorde is a modern hotel popular partly for its revolving restaurant and central location. In historic Quartier Petit-Champlain are **Hôtel Dominion 1912**, a cozy boutique hotel, and **Auberge Saint-Antoine**, a charming small hotel.

The city's top maitre d's listed these eating spots among the best: **Laurie Raphaël** for tartares and desserts; **Marie Clarisse** for seafood dishes; **Louis-Hébert** for French cuisine; and **a la Bastille chez Bahuaud** for unique appetizers and entrees such as sting ray. **Café du Monde** is a lively hangout and a good brunch spot on Sunday.

Jules et Jim nightclub has an intimate French ambience. Call before catching a packed dinner show at **Le Capitole de Québec**. Have a *digestif* at the trendy **Ristorante Il Teatro**. Montmorency Falls is 114 feet higher than Niagara Falls. Cable car to the top for lunch at opulent **Manoir Montmorency**.

The Hot Sheet

HOTELS		ADDRESS	PH	FX	PRICE	RMS	BEST ROOMS
Auberge Saint-Antoine	Alt	10 rue St-Antoine	418-647-4433 800-263-1471	418-692-1177	$$	30	St. Lawrence River vw
Château Frontenac Canadian Pacific Hotels	★	1 rue des Carrières	418-692-3861 800-441-1414	418-698-1751	$$$	637	St. Lawrence River vw
Hôtel Dominion 1912	Alt	126 rue St-Pierre	418-692-2224 888-833-5253	418-692-4403	$$$	40	Old Town vw
Loews Le Concorde	Alt	1225 place Montcalm	418-647-2222 800-463-5256	418-647-4710	$$	409	City vw

RESTAURANTS	DAY	ADDRESS	PH	PRICE	REC	DRESS	FOOD
Auberge du Trésor	1	20 rue Ste-Anne	418-694-1876	$$	L/BD	Kazh	French
Aux Anciens Canadiens	2	34 rue St-Louis	418-692-1627	$$	L/D	Kazh	Québecois
L'Aviatic Club	3	450 Gare du Palais	418-522-3555	$$	D	Euro	International
a la Bastille chez Bahuaud	Alt	47 av. Ste-Geneviève	418-692-2544	$$$	LD	Euro	French
Bonaparte	2	680 Grande Allée	418-647-4747	$$$$	D/L	Euro	French
Café de la Terrasse	1	1 rue des Carrières	418-692-3861	$$	B/LD	Kazh	Continental
Café du Monde	Alt	57 rue Dalhousie	418-692-4455	$$	L/BD	Kazh	French bistro
Le Falstaff	2	45 rue Couillard	418-694-3090	$	L/BD	Kazh	Québecois
Le Lapin Sauté	3	52 Petit Champlain	418-692-5325	$$	B/LD	Kazh	French
Laurie Raphaél	Alt	117 rue Dalhousie	418-692-4555	$$$	LD	Euro	French
Louis-Hébert	Alt	668 Grande Allée	418-525-7812	$$	BLD	Local	French, seafood
Manoir Montmorency	Alt	490 av. Royale	418-663-3330	$$$	L	Kazh	Québecois
Marie Clarisse	Alt	12 Petit Champlain	418-692-0857	$$$$	LD	Euro	Seafood
Portofino	2	84 rue Couillard	418-692-8888	$$	L/D	Kazh	French
Ristorante Il Teatro	Alt	972 rue St-Jean	418-694-9930	$$	BLD	Kazh	Italian

NIGHTLIFE	DAY	ADDRESS	PH	COVER	REC*	DRESS	MUSIC
Le Bar Saint-Laurent	1	see Château Frontenac	418-692-3861	None	R	Dressy	
Le Charlotte Lounge	2	575 Grande Allée	418-640-0711	$	P	Kazh	Rock, Latin
Chez Dagobert	2	600 Grande Allée	418-522-0393	$	MP	Kazh	Alternative
Jules et Jim	Alt	1060 av. Cartier	418-524-9570	None	R	Local	
Maurice Salon-Bar	2	575 Grande Allée E 300	418-640-0711	None	R	Kazh	
Le Pavillon	3	450 de la Gare-du-Palais	418-522-0133	None	P(F)	Euro	Contemporary
Pub Thomas Dunn	3	369 rue St-Paul	418-692-4693	None	R(F)	Local	
Le Capitole de Québec	Alt	972 rue St-Jean	418-694-9930	$$$	S	Euro	

SIGHTS & ATTRACTIONS	DAY	ADDRESS	PH	ENTRY FEE
Montmorency Falls	Alt	2490 av. Royale	418-663-3330	None
Musée de Civilisation	3	85 rue Dalhousie	418-643-2158	$
Québec Experience	1	8 rue du Trésor	418-694-4000	$
Québec City Tourism		835 av. Wilfrid Leurier	418-649-2608	

Event & Ticket Info

Québec Winter Carnaval: A Bonhomme figurine ($5) is your pass for outdoor Carnaval venues. Some events have an additional, minimal fee. **Bal de Bonhomme** ($50) tickets sell out and should be purchased before Christmas. For tickets and a program, contact Carnaval de Québec (418-626-3716).

Alternative Event

du Maurier Québec City Summer Festival: Québec City Summer Festival, 418-692-5200

* M=Live music; P=Dancing (Party); R=Bar only; S=Show; (F)=Food served. For further explanation of codes, see page 14.

 NYC Jean-Lesage (YBQ) <30 min./$20   No 04°/20° (-16°/-7°) 1.51 Canadian Dollars

February 1999 — New Orleans, Louisiana, USA — February/March 2000

Mardi Gras

Origin: 1837	Event ★★★★★★★★★ City	Attendance: 3,500,000

There are parties, and then there are—PARTIES! During the days leading to Ash Wednesday and Lenten abstentions, New Orleans blasts off beyond our humble universe and enters an entirely superior galaxy, a world where parties transport you into a kind of unrestrained bliss you never knew you were capable of.

A citywide, unabashed bash of epic proportions, *Mardi Gras* (don't be fooled by hometown imitations that criminally borrow the name) is by far North America's most raging party and, by many accounts, the best annual event in the world. Day and night, crowds of exhibitionists and masked revelers pack Bourbon Street, taking full advantage of the city's liberal alcohol policies. A more select audience spends its evenings at a series of fancy-dress balls thrown by legendary "krewes"—social clubs dedicated to *Mardi Gras* week festivities. Stately mansions are draped with purple, green, and gold—official colors of *Mardi Gras*—and extravagant floats take over the streets, catapulting millions of beads into huge crowds during a series of colorful, musical parades.

The city's unofficial motto—*Laissez les bons temps rouler*—means "Let the good times roll." Mostly, they roll out of control during *Mardi Gras*. Highlights include Sunday's spirited *Bacchus Parade and Ball*; the classy *Orpheus Parade and Ball* held on Monday (Lundi Gras); and Fat Tuesday's (*Mardi Gras*) street partying and parades, starring the *Zulu* and *Rex parades*.

New Orleans' combination of French, African, Spanish, and Caribbean cultures has lent *Mardi Gras* celebrations a distinctive flair in a city that often seems like an exotic, foreign place, even to visiting Americans. You could easily occupy all your time partying and recovering from Mardi Gras festivities, but make a point of exploring the city's French Quarter, with its French-Creole buildings and flower-laden iron balconies. And don't miss the Garden District, known for rambling mansions and turn-of-the-century streetcars.

The music, food, and spirit of the people—locals and visitors—make New Orleans one of the world's favorite destinations. The wild days of *Mardi Gras* are when the city is at its most alive, colorful, and joyful.

Day-By-Day Plan For

Mardi Gras

Day 1. Sun. Feb. 14, 1999
(Day 1. Sunday   March 5, 2000)

9:00am The glamorous **Le Méridien New Orleans** situates you by the French Quarter in the midst of the *Mardi Gras* hubbub. An international clientele prefers the luxurious hotel for its contemporary design and rooms with views of Canal Street (the parade route) and downtown skyscrapers.

9:30am The nearby Windsor Court Hotel's classy **Grill Room** serves a wide selection of first-rate breakfasts in a clubby, English-style dining room.

10:30am Cab to the **New Orleans Museum of Art** on the grounds of City Park. One of the top museums in the South, it showcases European, African, pre-Columbian, and local arts. This time of year, some exhibits focus on *Mardi Gras* and New Orleans culture.

12:30pm Return to the French Quarter by taxi. In the thick of things is the **Desire Oyster Bar**, where you can have great oysters and jambalaya while watching the festivities outside on Bourbon Street.

2:00pm Get up to speed with one of the smaller parades this afternoon. Your hotel will have schedules—Le Méridien's concierge staff is among the best in the business and can help you with just about everything, including tickets to the balls.

5:00pm Get some rest before partaking of the night's high-intensity revelry. You might want to have a light meal at the hotel, but save room for street foods and drinks.

7:15pm *Bacchus Parade* floats pass Le Méridien, along Canal Street, carrying celebrities and masqueraders, who toss doubloons, coasters, medallions, and beads to wall-to-wall crowds. The parade ends at the Ernest N. Morial Convention Center (often called the New Orleans Convention Center), where the Bacchus Krewe holds the night's biggest ball.

The Roman god of wine and partying would be proud to lend his name to this wild party.

8:30pm Make a quick stop in your room to dress formally for the night, but don't forget to bring your beads.

9:00pm With luck, you can get a cab (the walk isn't too bad, if you don't mind hiking in formal wear) to the enormous Morial Convention Center, where the *Bacchus Ball* moves into high gear. The cream of New Orleans society, plus a smattering of Hollywood types, turn out for a night of dance, drink, (food is available, but useful only to allow you to continue drinking), and music by top-name performers.

Midnight Head to the French Quarter, where you'll experience a scene like nowhere else. Costume-clad crowds cram the streets and clubs and hoot themselves hoarse. Both ladies and gentlemen expose every bit of their anatomy. Bare breasts abound. New Orleans has no last call, so most of these people are used to staying out until all hours. For many, this evening/morning is the high point of *Mardi Gras*.

Day 2. Mon. Feb. 15, 1999
(Day 2. Monday   March 6, 2000)

9:30am A few blocks away, in a grand French Quarter home, brunch beside a semitropical courtyard at **Brennan's**. This New Orleans institution overwhelms even the fiercest hangover.

10:30am Explore the charming French Quarter, where wisteria hangs gracefully from iron balconies. Begin at the magnolia-filled epicenter, Jackson Square. Aristocratic 19th-century town houses line three sides of the square. Standing guard at the northern end is the 18th-century St. Louis Cathedral. A few blocks east of Jackson Square, tour the Old Ursuline Convent, an elegant French-colonial structure from the 1730s. Across the street, look inside the antebellum Beauregard-Keyes House.

1:30pm In a historic French Quarter town house, chef Emeril Lagasse's festive **NOLA Restaurant** serves updates of classic Creole recipes to a trend-conscious crowd.

2:30pm Walk to the nearby French Market. A former Indian trading post, it's been a lively social and commercial center since the 18th century. Today, this covered market is famous for fruit and vegetable merchants, fishmongers, oyster shuckers, butchers, and knickknack sellers, as well as a number of popular cafes. Jazz bands serenade the crowds.

3:00pm Meander toward New Orleans' largest shopping district, Riverwalk, at the foot of Canal Street. Take in views of the New Orleans skyline and Mississippi during the 20-minute **Canal Street Ferry** ride to Algiers Point, across the Mississippi River. There, a shuttle whisks you to **Mardi Gras World**, which includes Mardi Gras float workshops and exhibits detailing *Mardi Gras'* history.

5:30pm Back at Riverwalk, more than 200 shops and food stalls are housed in a series of refurbished warehouses. Enjoy the riverfront promenade and permanent New Orleans exhibits.

6:00pm At Riverwalk, Rex the King proclaims the beginning of *Mardi Gras* and asks the mayor to make the day an official holiday so that people can take off work. The mock ceremony is followed by fireworks and rock music.

7:00pm By now, the *Orpheus Parade* will be rolling along Canal Street, hailing doubloons, medallions, beads, cups, and sports bottles onto the crowds. Founded by local boy Harry Connick Jr., the Orpheus Krewe's ball and parade emphasize music. The floats take Canal Street to the Morial Convention Center for Monday's grandest gala, which you'll join later.

> ## Unbeadable salutations
>
> At Mardi Gras, the exchange of typical greetings—"Hello, how are you?" "Fine, how are you?"—is replaced by "Throw me something, Mister" and "Show me your (desired body part)." Members of Endymion and Bacchus krewes alone toss more than two million strings of beads during their parades!

8:00pm It's dress-up time again. Don fancy duds and weave your way from the hotel to ultratrendy **Emeril's Restaurant**. Another Emeril Lagasse venture, this up-market, nouveau-Creole restaurant occupies a refurbished warehouse and serves a heavenly crawfish over jambalaya cakes.

10:00pm One of *Mardi Gras'* major balls, the *Orpheuscapade* attracts local and national celebrities for the music, dancing, and carefree schmoozing that are the hallmarks of New Orleans social events. *Mardi Gras* partying will reach a fever pitch tonight.

1:30am New Orleans always comes alive after dark, but during *Mardi Gras*, the fun approaches frenzy. Head to the French Quarter, where the bars and clubs fuel wild times on Bourbon Street until dawn—at least. Duck into the **House of Blues** for a dose of live music at one of New Orleans' premier venues.

4:00am Stop at the city's party-people pit-stop, 24-hour **Café du Monde**. Find a seat on the covered patio, facing Jackson Square, and order the house specialties: beignets coated with powdered sugar and hickory-flavored coffee.

Day 3. Tue. Feb. 16, 1999
(Day 3. Tuesday   March 7, 2000)

10:00am Sure, you didn't get much sleep, but nobody said this would be easy. The *Zulu Parade* passes on enormous, tree-lined St. Charles Avenue, the Garden District's main drag. In addition to showering street celebrants with the usual *Mardi Gras* swag, the roughly 1,500 parade members toss hand-decorated coconut shells. The regally themed *Rex Parade* follows a similar path.

1:00pm Go to **Commander's Palace** in the Garden District. In an upstairs room with a courtyard view, enjoy outstanding French-Creole cuisine.

2:30pm Venture into the surrounding Garden District, which still serves as home to the New Orleans elite. The neighborhood is packed with graceful old mansions that are distinctly New Orleans.

4:30pm Return to the French Quarter madness, then head back to your hotel for a nap. Then throw on your most outrageous get-up for the final throes of *Mardi Gras*.

7:00pm Build an appetite by searching the French Quarter for a krewe, perhaps the Krewe of Mystic Debris, who lead a march that you can join.

8:30pm You're not too far from where Paul Prud'homme has set up his famous bistro, **K-Paul's Louisiana Kitchen**. The place is always bustling and the classic-to-contemporary Louisiana fare gives overindulgence a good name.

10:30pm A stunning concoction of brass, marble, and beveled glass, the French-run **Jazz Méridien** allows for a relatively calm after-dinner drink where talented jazz bands perform for a fashionable clientele.

Midnight Just as Jazz Méridien winds down, Bourbon Street moves into overdrive. At this point, Bourbon is a bit of a wreck, but still a ton of fun. Don't pass up the party at the trendy **Cat's Meow**, which sports the street's liveliest balcony. A New Orleans classic, **Pat O'Brien's Bar** has an old-fashioned bar, attractive patio, and piano lounge that gets very rowdy. The young, preppy crowd knocks back enough drinks to make Pat O'Brien's legendary for reputedly selling more liquor than any other bar in the world. The house specialty, Skylab, has vodka, peach brandy, pineapple juice, and grenadine. Stumbling around Bourbon Street is the appropriate way to wrap up *Mardi Gras* in the city that takes fun more seriously than any other on the continent.

Alternatives

If you're in New Orleans on Saturday, you'll have the chance to join the gigantic love fest known as the *Endymion Parade and Ball*. Named after a race-horse named after the Greek god of youth and fertility, Endymion's 40 bands and 28 double-decker floats (each carries about 1,600 people) travel down Canal Street. They end up at the Louisiana Superdome for *Mardi Gras'* single biggest party (15,000 people), which features top-name entertainers, celebrity guests, and fireworks. The fact that women are required to wear long gowns at this black-tie affair doesn't stop them from climbing on tables and jumping for beads.

The elegant **Windsor Court Hotel**'s canopy beds, plush carpets, and marble bathrooms envelope you in luxury. The **Royal Sonesta Hotel** could not be any closer to the madness. A few blocks off the French Quarter, **The Lafayette Hotel** is a charming and comfortable alternative.

For a century, one of New Orleans' favorite bistros has been **Galatoire's**. Its brass fittings, ornate chandeliers, and beveled mirrors recall *fin-de-siècle* Paris, and its classic Creole dishes have been refined to perfection. The chic bar and cafe at **Napoleon House Bar & Cafe** cater to the colorful and affluent. Local dishes are elegantly prepared and served in an 1814 town house allegedly built for Napoleon. The more hip version of Commander's Palace is **Palace Cafe**, which serves New Creole cuisine in a grand cafe setting. For action with your cup o' joe, try **Poppy's Grill**, a '50s-style diner and the most popular brunch place in town. **Bayona** does up Louisiana recipes in a charming French Quarter cottage, and the busy **Acme Oyster House** specializes in shellfish straight from the gulf waters. The **French Market Restaurant and Bar** makes a good stop for fresh seafood on a charming outdoor patio.

In the Garden District, venerable **Tipitina's** nightclub, home base for the Neville Brothers, draws a mixed crowd for live jazz. **Snug Harbor Jazz Bistro** features top jazz musicians—including regular Ellis Marsalis, father of Wynton and Branford. **Lon Bon Temps Roule** is another great music venue, especially during the Jazz Festival, as are the **Maple Leaf Bar** and **Mid-City Lanes Rock-n-Bowl**.

The Hot Sheet

HOTELS		ADDRESS	PH	FX	PRICE	RMS	BEST ROOMS
The Lafayette Hotel	Alt	600 St. Charles Ave.	504-524-4441 800-733-4754	504-523-7327	$$	44	2nd fl balc
Le Méridien New Orleans	★	614 Canal St.	504-525-6500 800-543-3000	504-525-8068	$$$	496	Dlx corner rm w/city vw
Royal Sonesta Hotel	Alt	300 Bourbon St.	504-586-0300	504-586-0335	$$$	484	Balc on Bourbon
Windsor Court Hotel (Orient Express Hotel)	Alt	300 Gravier St.	504-523-6000 800-262-2662	504-596-4513	$$$	235	River city vw

RESTAURANTS	DAY	ADDRESS	PH	PRICE	REC	DRESS	FOOD
Acme Oyster House	Alt	724 Iberville St.	504-522-5973	$$	LD	Local	Seafood
Bayona	Alt	430 Dauphine St.	504-525-4455	$$$	LD	Dressy, Kazh	Mediterranean
Brennan's	2	417 Royal St.	504-525-9711	$$$	B/LD	Yuppie	French-Creole
Café duMonde	2	800 Decatur St.	504-525-4544	$	T/B	Local	French doghnut
Commander's Palace	3	1403 Washington Ave.	504-899-8221	$$$$	L/D	Dressy	Creole
Desire Oyster Bar	1	see Royal Sonesta Hotel	504-586-0300	$$	L/D	Kazh	Oysters, Creole
Emeril's Restaurant	2	800 Tchoupitoulas St.	504-528-9393	$$$	D/L	Dressy	Creole
French Market Restaurant and Bar	Alt	1001 Decatur St.	504-525-7879	$$	LD	Local	Seafood
Galatoire's	Alt	209 Bourbon St.	504-525-2021	$$$$	LD	Dressy	French, Creole
The Grill Room	1	see Windsor Court Hotel	504-522-1992	$$$	B/LD	Kazh	Continental
K-Paul's Louisiana Kitchen	3	416 Chartres St.	504-524-7394	$$	D/L	Dressy	Cajun, Creole
Napoleon House Bar & Cafe	Alt	500 Chartres St.	504-524-9752	$	LD	Kazh	Mediterranean
NOLA Restaurant	2	534 St. Louis St.	504-522-6652	$$	L/D	Kazh	New American, Creole
Palace Cafe	Alt	605 Canal St.	504-523-1661	$$	LD	Kazh	Seafood, Creole
Poppy's Grill	Alt	717 St. Peter St.	504-524-3287	$	BLD	Local	American

NIGHTLIFE	DAY	ADDRESS	PH	COVER	REC*	DRESS	MUSIC
Cat's Meow	3	701 Bourbon St.	504-523-1157	$	P	Yuppie	Karaoke
House of Blues	2	225 Decatur St.	504-529-2583	$	M(F)	Kazh	Blues, rock, reggae
Jazz Méridien	3	see Le Méridien hotel	504-525-6500	$	M(F)	Kazh	Jazz
Lon Bon Temps Route	Alt	4801 Magazine St.	504-895-8117	$	M(F)	Local	Zydeco, blues, rock
Maple Leaf Bar	Alt	8316 Oak St.	504-866-9359	$	MP(F)	Local	Zydeco, blues, rock
Mid-City Lanes Rock-n-Bowl	Alt	4133 S. Carrollton	504-482-3133	$	MP(F)	Kazh	Zydeco, blues, rock
Pat O'Brien's Bar	3	718 St. Peter St.	504-525-4823	None	M	Kazh	Jazz, R&B
Snug Harbor Jazz Bistro	Alt	626 Frenchmen St.	504-949-0696	$$	M(F)	Kazh	Modern jazz, blues
Tipitina's	Alt	501 Napoleon Ave.	504-895-8477	$	M(F)	Kazh	Blues, zydeco, rock

SIGHTS & ATTRACTIONS	DAY	ADDRESS	PH	ENTRY FEE
Mardi Gras World	2	233 Newton St.	504-361-7821	$
New Orleans Museum of Art	1	1 Collins Diboll, Carrollton and Esplanade aves.	504-488-2631	$

OTHER SIGHTS, SHOPS & SERVICES

Canal Street Ferry	2	Canal Street Wharf	504-364-8100	$
New Orleans Welcome Center		529 St. Ann St.	504-566-5005	

Event & Ticket Info

Bacchus Ball (Ernest N. Morial Convention Center, 900 Convention Center Blvd.): Arrange tickets (generally $100) through area hotels or travel agents. For more information, contact Krewe of Bacchus: (504-525-0231).

Orpheuscapade (Ernest N. Morial Convention Center, 900 Convention Center Blvd.): For tickets ($100), contact Krewe of Orpheus (504-822-7200).

Endymion Ball (The Superdome): Tickets ($110) go on sale after November 1. Contact Krewe of Endymion (504-736-0160).

For a listing of parades, krewes, and events, call Arthur Hardy Enterprises (504-838-6111).

* M=Live music; P=Dancing (Party); R=Bar only; S=Show; (F)=Food served. For further explanation of codes, see page 14.

 NYC −1   New Orleans (MSY) <30 min./$25   No   46°/75° (8°/24°)

Beautiful People

Supermodel hasn't made it into *Webster's Dictionary* yet, but, as a cultural reference point, few of us are unaware of the weighty (and not so weighty) impact this group of beautiful people has had on modern society. We talk about them. We track their careers. We buy the clothes they wear. Mostly, though, we just want to look at them.

Most supermodels have unpredictable schedules, but there are times of the year when many are guaranteed to be in the right place at the right time. If you know the pattern, it's possible to schedule a lunch with Cindy, Elle, Christie, or Kate. Well, at least at the same cafe or restaurant.

Paris and Rome present most of the womens couture showings, with winter and fall designs on the runways in January, and spring designs in July. These are the times to book into grand hotels such as The Ritz that host the luxurious shows. In Paris, you're likely to spot models in Marais-district restaurants in the evenings, especially after a big show. (Supermodels prepare by skipping food for days before the shows.)

Designers follow the couture made-to-order extravaganzas with separate shows for ready-to-wear clothes. These start with March Fashion Week in London, followed by showings in Milan, Paris, and New York, then make the rounds again for spring ready-to-wear fashions from late September through early November. There are more ready-to-wear shows than couture shows, so Paris supermodel sightings toward the end of March are even more likely than in January.

Not all beautiful models have "supermodel" status. Catch glimpses of up-and-coming beauties at high-fashion catalog photo shoots—Miami in February is the favorite backdrop. Miami shines with models in April, too, when photographers shoot designer campaigns and fall magazine layouts. Cuba and Cape Town, South Africa, are fast gaining April favor as well.

Male models congregate in Paris for January shows following the womens couture collections, then move on to Milan for the Italian menswear shows. They return to Paris in July for the spring menswear collections.

So, since only the fashion elite are invited to see the runway shows that make headlines, where do you find supermodels when they're not on the job? Paris is a decent spot year-round, but New York is the best bet. Even if they hail from Australia, Germany, London, or Los Angeles, most models have homes in the Big Apple. They want proximity to the larger magazines and advertising firms, as well as designers like Calvin Klein and Donna Karan in the garment district on Sixth Avenue.

Models generally take vacations in August, but in only the most glamorous and exclusive locales: Majorca, Monte Carlo, and obscure islands in the Caribbean. Good bets in the Caribbean are St. Martin, Virgin Gorda, and Mustique.

Following supermodels' schedules gives you a good chance of sighting one. And even if you don't get lucky, there are worse places to hang around waiting than Paris, London, and New York.

Jan.: Paris couture, Paris menswear, Rome couture, Milan menswear

Feb.: Miami catalogs

Mar.: London Fashion Week, Milan ready-to-wear, Paris ready-to-wear

Apr.: New York ready-to-wear, Miami, Cape Town, Cuba designer campaigns, magazine photo shoots

Jul.: Paris couture, Paris menswear, Rome couture

Aug.: Holidays: Caribbean, Monte Carlo, Majorca

Sep.: London ready-to-wear

Oct.: Milan ready-to-wear, Paris ready-to-wear, New York ready-to-wear

Nov.: New York ready-to-wear

All year: New York, Paris

Bike Week

| Origin: 1937 | Event ★ ★ ★ ★ ★ ★ ★ City | Attendance: 500,000 |

Leave your Schwinns at home—we're talking Harleys! Unless you're already a tattooed hog-rider, **Bike Week** provides one of the most incredible scenes you're likely to encounter. Even if you weren't born to bike, herds of renegade wild ones in leather, constant roaring engines, and high levels of biker camaraderie at **Daytona Bike Week** will make you feel like one of the gang.

Thousands of bikers thunder their iron horses into Daytona for this annual week of motorcycle worship amid a down-'n'-dirty schedule of events. The "Miss" contests are a big draw—Miss Jägermeister, Miss Florida Biker, Miss Jack Daniels, etc.—as are the "ladies" arm-wrestling championships, tattoo contests, and wet T-shirt contests. Some bars pit wrestlers in coleslaw or stage fashion shows featuring the latest in road-hog couture. You can always attend a motorcycle show or derby.

Even the meek can get a thrill watching the perpetual parade of *Mad Max* refugees cruising through town on motorcycle and foot. Especially toward the end of *Bike Week*, Daytona becomes Harley heaven (or hell, depending on your perspective) when hordes of windburned Hell's Angels and other moto-clubbers slowly rumble and belch their bikes along Main Street, reinventing traffic laws and triggering a chorus of car alarms.

Your bases for the weekend, Daytona Beach and Orlando, are separated by 60 miles of highway and light years of attitude. Daytona's freewheeling spring-breaklike atmosphere features the world-famous Daytona International Speedway and a car-friendly, 500-foot-wide, 20-mile-long beach. By comparison, Orlando is Type A, a planned city where people are more carefully groomed, and lodging and dining are available for even the most fastidious customer. You could spend more time in either place, but the contrast between the two cities over a three-day vacation heightens the fun.

For details on a visit to an entirely different world (a make-believe world) near Orlando, read the chapter on **Walt Disney World** (see page 233). For the adventurous, however, **Bike Week** should prove that reality is often more bizarre than fantasy.

Bike Week

Day 1. Thu.   Mar. 4, 1999
(Day 1. Thursday   March 8, 2000)

9:00am Your vacation begins in Orlando at the **Hyatt Regency Grand Cypress,** with its 1,500 tropical acres. Breakfast outside in the hotel's **Palm Cafe.** Then spend the morning enjoying the hotel's trails, equestrian center, sports facilities, and huge grotto pool with waterfalls and slides.

1:30pm The Crab House stands out among dozens of tourist restaurants on nearby International Drive. Fresh fish is served in a casual atmosphere.

3:00pm At leviathan theme park **SeaWorld of Florida,** visit Shamu, the splash-happy killer whale. Worth scheduling are the people-drenching mammals in the Dolphin Pool; a ride on the water coaster, Wild Atlantis; and the exhibit of endangered manatees. Most park food is better left to the sharks, but have a snack so that you can stay for the "Red, Bright and Blue Spectacular" fireworks, laser, and water show.

9:00pm Located in a 1928 building and illuminated by wall candles, the **Sapphire Supper Club** is the best jazz venue in town. Piece together a meal of bar fare and a drink from Sapphire's specialty list—maybe a Fris Super Dag Daddy or a Luscious Lushes.

10:30pm Take a three-block walk south to the 19th-century-themed **Church Street Station,** where one ticket gets you into Rosie O'Grady's Dixieland Revue, the Orchid Garden for rock-and-roll, Phineas Fogg's Dance Club for disco dancing, and the Cheyenne Saloon and Opera House for a live Western show and dancing. It's touristy, but the period re-creations are outstanding.

Day 2. Fri.   Mar. 5, 1999
(Day 2. Friday   March 9, 2000)

8:30am Have a traditional American breakfast beside a 35-foot waterfall at **Cascade,** the Grand Cypress' restaurant.

10:00am A short drive north, **Universal Studios Florida** is the country's second most popular theme park (Walt Disney World is first). In addition to rides and attractions, the 400-acre sprawl includes television and movie studios. By the time you leave the park, you'll have survived a movie earthquake, ghostbusting, extraterrestrial contact, a tornado, time travel, and a cartoon chase.

1:30pm In Universal Studios' area reproducing San Francisco, grab an outdoor table with a view of the lagoon at **Lombard's Landing**. Lunch on specialties such as the Foggy City cioppino or freshly caught fish.

4:30pm As you approach Daytona, an hour away, the spectacle of droves of motorcycles and choppers will inspire you to shift gears. Pick up a *Bike Week* schedule at the ***Official Bike Week Welcome Center***. Have fun getting ready with biker-wear and tattoo decals at **Easyriders.**

7:30pm Check into the modern beachside **Adam's Mark Daytona Beach Resort**. Avoid the incessant street rumble by requesting a room high-up and facing the beach.

8:30pm A couple miles north, **Billy's Tap Room** has been wetting whistles since 1922. At one time, it served mere pub food, but now the menu lists *escargot,* burgers, and espresso.

10:00pm A mile north, Ormond Beach's two main biker bars roll with Southern rock. Choppers are parked in rows out front of the **Iron Horse** and **Jackson Hole**

Saloon—chances are you'll see an arm-wrestling match, a tattoo contest, and at least one wet T-shirt contest. Be out front at midnight when one unfortunate motorcycle is exploded, just for fun.

Day 3. Sat.   Mar. 6, 1999
(Day 3. Saturday   March 10, 2000)

10:00am After a hotel breakfast, make a pit stop at ® **Daytona USA**. Added in 1996 to Daytona International Speedway—"the birthplace of speed"—it features interactive car-racing exhibits.

12:30pm At the **Highlander Cafe**, ® savor an Angus steak on the shady deck while listening to local country or rock bands.

2:00pm Hit every wet T-shirt, arm-wrestling, and tattoo contest in Daytona. Stop by the Ocean Center to view Big Daddy Rat's *Rat's Hole Custom Chopper Show* and the *Harley-Davidson Traveling Museum*. Check out the *Boardwalk Ride-In Bike Show* on the Main Street Boardwalk, where attendees proudly showcase their gleaming hogs.

*O*verheard between two bikers as they cruised Daytona's beach: One says to the other, "Hey, man, chicks at 9 o'clock." His buddy stretches his neck around to the right, but can't see anything. The first guy says, "No, man, the *other* 9 o'clock!"

3:30pm At any of Daytona's beach entrances, pay a small fee, then take your sports utility vehicle where it's supposed to go—off the road. Cruise the beach, park—watch high tide!—and catch some final rays.

6:00pm Join *Bike Week* partyers taking over Main Street. Walk to Oceanfront Park where you're likely to find a rock group playing. At the Adam's Mark beachside pool bar, **Splash Bar & Grill**, listen to live music and knock back tropical drinks.

8:00pm Head to the airy **St. Regis** restaurant, four ® blocks away. Housed in an 1886 Victorian, it serves American-Continental cuisine on a garden patio.

9:30pm Tonight it's "last chance" partying. The crowd is extra rowdy and pubs pump enough beer to threaten world reserves. Go to **Froggy's Saloon**, a *Bike Week* favorite, and **Boot Hill Saloon**, which has live music and a beer garden. Or retreat to the **Clocktower Lounge** at the Adam's Mark.

2:00am With your leather lust stirred and wild side uncaged, vow to return to next year's *Bike Week* on the wings of an iron eagle.

Alternatives

*O*n the last Sunday of **Bike Week**, a couple hundred motorcycles are blessed at 7 a.m. by a priest at St. Paul's Catholic Church in Daytona. At 9 a.m., fans gather to cheer 4,000 bikers parading from Bellair Plaza to Daytona International Speedway. Stay for the *Daytona 200* and watch motorcycles buzz around extreme grades that make the racecourse arguably the fastest in the world.

*W*hile many of Orlando's hotels are strictly cookie-cutter, the **Peabody Orlando** is distinguished by marble floors and fountains. Just outside the *Bike Week* action, the **Daytona Beach Hilton Oceanfront Resort** is a place to relax near the beach.

*A*t Orlando's Church Street Station, the touristy **Lili Marlene's Aviator Club** serves traditional, American dinners. In Daytona, **Aunt Catfish's on the River** does down-home dishes such as fried catfish fingerlings. A linen-and-flowers retreat from Daytona's biker brouhaha, **Anna's Trattoria** is run by a Sicilian family who make Old Country specialties. Ormond Beach's upscale **Frappes North** combines fresh and unusual ingredients in its dishes.

*T*ake Highway 1 south from Ormond Beach, then go east on Route 44 to **Gilly's Pub 44**, where live rock bands play until 2 a.m. The **Daytona Opry** puts on country dance and music performances.

*Y*ou could spend Saturday at the **Kennedy Space Center Visitor Complex** touring Space Shuttle launch sites. Stop at Spaceport USA to see capsules, the Viking spacecraft, and other far-out stuff.

The Hot Sheet

Hotels		Address	Ph	Fx	Price	Rms	Best Rooms
Adam's Mark Daytona Beach Resort	★	100 N. Atlantic Ave.	904-254-8200 800-872-9269	904-253-8841	$$$	437	Ocean front
Daytona Beach Hilton Oceanfront Resort	Alt	2637 S. Atlantic Ave.	904-767-7350 800-221-2424	904-760-3651	$$$	214	Ocean front
Hyatt Regency Grand Cypress	★	1 Grand Cypress Blvd.	407-239-1234 800-233-1234	407-239-3800	$$$$	750	Pool or lake vw
Peabody Orlando	Alt	9801 International Dr.	407-352-4000 800-732-2639	407-351-9177	$$$	891	Pool side

Restaurants	Day	Address	Ph	Price	Rec	Dress	Food
Anna's Trattoria	Alt	304 Seabreeze Blvd.	904-239-9624	$$	D	Local	Italian
Aunt Catfish's on the River	Alt	4009 Halifax Dr.	904-767-4768	$$	LD	Local	Seafood
Billy's Tap Room	2	58 E. Granada Blvd.	904-672-1910	$$	D/L	Local	American
Cascade	2	see Hyatt Regency hotel	407-239-1234	$$	B/LD	Local	American
The Crab House	1	8291 International Dr.	407-352-6140	$$	L/D	Local	Fish, seafood
Frappes North	Alt	123 W. Granada Blvd.	904-615-4888	$$	LD	Local	New American
Highlander Cafe	3	1821 S. Ridgewood Ave.	904-322-0320	$	L/D	Local	American
Lili Marlene's Aviator Club	Alt	see Church St. Station	407-422-2434	$$	LD	Local	American
Lombard's Landing	2	see Universal Studios Florida	407-363-8000	$$	L/D	Local	Seafood
Palm Cafe	1	see Hyatt Regency hotel	407-239-1234	$$	B/LD	Local	American buffet
Sapphire Supper Club	1	54 N. Orange Ave.	407-246-1419	$	D	Local	American
St. Regis	3	509 Seabreeze Blvd.	904-252-8743	$$	D	Kazh	American, continental

Nightlife	Day	Address	Ph	Cover	Rec*	Dress	Music
Boot Hill Saloon	3	310 Main St.	904-258-9506	None	MP(F)	Local	Blues, rock
Church Street Station	1	129 W. Church St.	407-422-2434	$$	MPS(F)	Local	Rock, country
Clocktower Lounge	3	see Adam's Mark Daytona Beach Resort	904-254-8200	None	MP(F)	Kazh	Jazz
Daytona Opry	Alt	2400 S. Ridgewood Ave.	904-756-6779	$$	S	Local	Country
Froggy's Saloon	3	800 Main St.	904-253-0330	None	MP(F)	Local	Blues, rock
Gilly's Pub 44	Alt	1889 State Rd. 44	904-428-6523	None	MP(F)	Local	Rock
Iron Horse	2	1068 N. US Hwy. 1	904-677-1550	None	M	Local	Southern rock
Jackson Hole Saloon	2	1081 N. US Hwy. 1	904-673-6996	None	M(F)	Local	Southern rock
Splash Bar & Grill	3	see Adam's Mark Daytona Beach Resort	904-254-8200	None	M(F)	Local	Reggae, rock

Sights & Attractions	Day	Address	Ph	Entry Fee
Daytona USA	3	1801 International Speedway Dr.	904-253-7223	$$
Kennedy Space Center Visitor Complex	Alt	State Road 405 at Kennedy Space Center	407-452-2121	None
SeaWorld of Florida	1	7007 SeaWorld Dr.	407-363-2613	$$$
Universal Studios Florida	2	1000 Universal Studios Plaza	407-363-8000	$$$

Other Sights, Shops & Services				
Easyriders	2	605 Main St.	904-238-1645	None
Daytona Beach Area CVB		126 E. Orange Ave.	800-854-1234	
Orlando Orange County CVB		8723 International Dr.	407-363-5871	

Event & Ticket Info

Bike Week: For more information, contact Official Bike Week Welcome Center (904-255-0981).

The Boardwalk Ride-In Show (Boardwalk at Main St.): Free. For more information, contact Boardwalk Merchant's Association (904-253-2054).

Harley-Davidson Traveling Museum (Ocean Center, 101 N. Atlantic Ave.): Free. For more information, contact 904-254-4500.

Rat's Hole Custom Chopper Show (Ocean Center, 101 N. Atlantic Ave.): Free. For more information, contact 904-254-4500.

Alternative Event
Daytona 200: Daytona International Speedway, 904-253-7223

Daytona Beach—Area Code 904   Orlando—Area Code 407

* M=Live music; P=Dancing (Party); R=Bar only; S=Show; (F)=Food served. For further explanation of codes, see page 14.

 NYC Orlando (MCO) <30 min./$15
Daytona Beach (DAB) <30 min./$10 Yes   53°/75° (12°/24°)

The Fun Also Rises

Carnaval South Beach

(Carnaval Miami)

Origin: 1978 Event ★ ★ ★ ★ ★ ★ ★ ★ City **Attendance:** 1,000,000

At the same time most of the world's great carnivals are moving into 40 days of Lenten restraint, **Carnaval Miami** is cranking up two weekends filled with the flavors, sounds, and exuberance of a Latin American fiesta. Dancing in the streets, raucous music, thinly clad revellers, and high energy are its hallmarks, making it one of the world's best and friendliest parties.

The first Saturday night of **Carnaval Miami** (also called *Fiesta de las Americas*) revolves around a concert attracting about 12,000 spectators and featuring some of the most famous musicians of the Latin world. The next day, **Carnaval South Beach** sends waves of sexually charged motion through fashionable Ocean Drive and its adjacent shoreline. Happy hordes of partyers dance and sing to Latin music, many of them waving flags from their native Latin American and Caribbean countries. Bands, floats, street dancers, and performers entertain while tens of thousands of **Carnaval**-goers are rallied in the annual attempt to break the world record for mass-dancing. One year, 119,000 dancers formed history's longest conga line. More recently, 65,000 joined in for the *macarena*. Nights are surreal when fireworks and neon light up a scene filled with people already colored by sun and alcohol.

No other place in the United States can capture the spirit of a Latin carnival like the Miami area. South Beach (the hot spot of Miami Beach) and nearby Miami, with its well-deserved reputation for hedonism and beautiful people, provide ready-made **Carnaval** allure. Sultry weather relaxes inhibitions and demands skimpy clothing. The region's ethnic populations infuse the event with authenticity.

A less intense party might get lost amid South Beach's art-deco chic, gorgeous people, and white-sand beaches—you'll quickly see why the area attracts an international collection of jet-setters who display fame and affluence as conspicuously as models and wannabes flaunt their deep tans and gym-toned, silicone-shaped bodies. Any given weekend night of the November-to-March carnival season, however, shows South Beach at its passionate and musical best.

Carnaval South Beach

Day 1. Fri. Mar. 5, 1999
(Day 1. Friday *March 3, 2000)*

9:00am Check into one of the nicest of South Beach's many renovated art-deco hotels, **The Raleigh**. It's away from the noise, but within walking distance of just about everything in South Beach.

10:00am In South Beach's Art Deco District, nearly a thousand buildings have been restored to their original elegance. Grab a map from the **Art Deco District Welcome Center** and walk through this zone of pastel beauty.

12:30pm Madonna co-owns the **Blue Door** in the Delano Hotel, so you may have a celebrity sighting while lunching on a New World mélange of eclectic flavors. The Delano itself is a tourist attraction (staying there requires too much attitude).

2:30pm Tote your megatowel to South Beach's ample white-sand beach and enjoy the Atlantic's warm waves. You might recognize this famed strip of sand from a number of movies and television shows.

4:30pm Built in 1940, The Raleigh Hotel's pool remains indisputably the most beautiful in Florida. Lounge poolside and try Miami's best martini at the art-deco bar.

7:30pm Walk along Ocean Avenue to the trendy **Mezzanotte**. The kitchen turns out good fresh pastas and desserts, but the party atmosphere is the draw.

9:30pm Break from the scene for laid-back jazz at a local favorite, **Van Dyke**. Later, drive 10 minutes to plush **Jimmy'z**, where you can dance to modern music and select a bottle of wine from an $8 million cellar. Madonna and other upscale customers rent humidors here, where they stash their favorite smuggled stogies.

Day 2. Sat. Mar. 6, 1999
(Day 2. Saturday *March 4, 2000)*

9:00am Drive to Coconut Grove for a casual, sidewalk breakfast at **Green Street Cafe**. For a taste of the tropics, have the Jamaican-jerk scrambled eggs.

11:00am Industrialist James Deering built **Vizcaya** in 1916 as his palatial winter residence, but you can stroll through its stately gardens, 34 rooms, and displays of European antiques.

1:30pm From the hotel, walk to Michael Caine's airy **South Beach Brasserie**. Choose a traditional European dish or a more inventive concoction, such as *escargot* won tons.

3:00pm Browse the shops and art galleries on pedestrian-only Lincoln Road, which is second only to Ocean Drive for people-watching. The **Bass Museum of Art** has fine examples of old European and new Latin American art. Or browse the human artwork tanning around The Raleigh's pool and on the beach.

6:00pm Practice your Spanish by ordering from an array of appetizers on the authentic Cuban menu at Gloria Estefan's **Larios on the Beach**, in the middle of Ocean Drive's bustle.

8:00pm Drive to Orange Bowl Stadium for *Noche de Carnaval*, a colorful Latin variety show and concert that opens *Carnaval* with dancers, elaborate stage sets, balloons, and superstars of the Latin world. Prepare to dance in the aisles and on chairs, but try to leave by 10:30 p.m. to avoid the 11 p.m. parking-lot rush.

11:00pm For world-modern cuisine in a happening setting, try **Nemo**. There's also **Red Square**, where hammer-and-sickle decorations emphasize the restaurant's Russian opulence. The stylish crowd—pumped up by caviar, cream, and a selection of 100 vodkas—dances and socializes to a variety of DJ music until 2 a.m.

1:00am Quit Stalin, and hit one of the many clubs in South Beach. The enormous tropical-theme club **Amnesia**, with an open-air courtyard, swings in every sexual direction. **Chaos** and **Liquid** are also hot.

Day 3. Sun. Mar. 7, 1999
(Day 3. Sunday March 5, 2000)

11:00am Grab a curbside table at **News Cafe**. The food is passable, but this quintessential South Beach spot is *the* place to hang during the day. Along with great-looking models and wannabes sitting and passing by, you'll see the embodiment of the tourist board's statistics: About half of South Beach visitors are international, with nearly 40 percent coming from South America, 20 percent from Central America and the Caribbean, and 25 percent from Europe.

1:00pm Where 10th Street meets the beach, popular bands give the ***Superbands Concert***. It's always packed with crowds doing the full-on Latin grind—an easy participatory event, even for the inhibited.

2:00pm Stop into **Wet Willy's** for drinks and snacks at the balcony bar. You'll have a clear view of the parade and, more importantly, the crowd on Ocean Drive.

2:30pm *Comparsas* (street dancers) and floats, which are usually more interesting for their sounds than for their decorations, proceed along Ocean Drive. After the official parade, join the unofficial one in which *Carnaval*-goers strut through the streets and beach-side promenade.

6:00pm Join the massive crowd on Ocean Drive trying to break the world's record for most people dancing in unison. Each year, the trendiest Latin dance is chosen, and everyone dances to a current blockbuster song.

8:00pm Although a fireworks show explodes above the beach, most people on Ocean Drive will be more interested in pickup techniques than pyrotechnics.

9:30pm **China Grill** is as much a nightclub as a restaurant. The Asian-inspired menu encourages diners to nibble together from several shared plates.

Midnight A couple of blocks away, show up at **The Living Room** (it adjoins the posh Strand restaurant) in time for the nightly switch from jazz to DJ grooves. Models, Europeans, and other fashion-forward types lounge at the 60-foot bar and crowd the dance floor.

4:00am A rumba back to The Raleigh ends your Latin-carnival weekend—and you didn't even need a visa.

Alternatives

Time permitting, hit one of the world's largest block parties, ***Calle Ocho*** (Eighth Street), on the closing Sunday of ***Carnaval***. More than half a million revellers spread over 23 blocks in Little Havana enjoying food, dancing, and Latin American and Caribbean entertainment. Another option in South Beach is ***Art Deco Weekend***. On the second full weekend of January, 350,000 people come to the Art Deco District for a parade, a street festival, concerts, and a film festival.

You don't have to stay at The Raleigh to be stylish in South Beach. The art-deco-style **Tides** provides all the essentials right on Ocean Drive. **The Casa Grande Suite Hotel** is a classy, subdued spot in the center of the action.

Since 1913, natives have been waiting in long lines to wield a mallet and clobber through stacks of clawed critters at **Joe's Stone Crab**. Too violent? Try **Yuca**'s superb nouvelle-Cuban cuisine —they have live salsa or Cuban music on weekends. Another popular restaurant on Lincoln Road is **Pacific Time**.

The Hot Sheet

HOTELS		ADDRESS	PH	FX	PRICE	RMS	BEST ROOMS
The Casa Grande Suite Hotel	Alt	834 Ocean Dr.	305-672-7003 800-688-7678	305-673-3669	$$$$	208	Ocean front
The Raleigh Hotel	★	1775 Collins Ave.	305-534-6300 800-848-1775	305-538-8140	$$$$	107	Ocean vw
The Tides	Alt	1220 Ocean Dr.	305-604-5000 800-688-7678	305-604-5180	$$$$	45	Ocean vw

RESTAURANTS	DAY	ADDRESS	PH	PRICE	REC	DRESS	FOOD
Blue Door	1	1685 Collins Ave.	305-674-6400	$$$	L/BD	Euro, Kazh	American, Brazilian
China Grill	3	404 Washington Ave.	305-534-2211	$$$$	D/L	Yuppie	Asian, World
Green Street Cafe	2	3110 Commodore Plaza	305-444-0244	$$	B/LD	Local	American
Joe's Stone Crab	Alt	227 Biscayne St.	305-673-0365	$$	LD	Kazh	Stone crab
Larios on the Beach	2	820 Ocean Dr.	305-532-9577	$	D/L	Local	Cuban
Mezzanotte	1	1200 Washington Ave.	305-673-4343	$$$	D	Kazh	Italian
Nemo	2	100 Collins Ave.	305-532-4550	$$$	LD	Kazh	Nuvo American
News Cafe	3	800 Ocean Dr.	305-538-6397	$	B/LD	Local	American
Pacific Time	Alt	915 Lincoln Rd.	305-534-5979	$$$	LD	Kazh	Nuvo Asian
Red Square	2	411 Washington Ave.	305-672-0200	$$	D	Kazh	Nuvo Russian
South Beach Brasserie	2	910 Lincoln Rd.	305-534-5511	$$$	L/BD	Kazh	Nuvo American
Yuca	Alt	501 Lincoln Rd.	305-532-9822	$$$	LD	Kazh	Cuban

NIGHTLIFE	DAY	ADDRESS	PH	COVER	REC*	DRESS	MUSIC
Amnesia	2	136 Collins Ave.	305-531-5535	$	P	Local	Hip-hop, rap
Chaos	2	743 Washington Ave.	305-674-7350	$	P	Local	House
Jimmy'z	1	432 41st St.	305-604-9798	$$	P(F)	Dressy, Kazh	Dance
Liquid	2	1439 Washington Ave.	305-532-9154	$$	P	Kazh	Hip-hop, jazz, rock
The Living Room	3	671 Washington Ave.	305-532-2340	$$	P	Dressy, Kazh	Contemporary
Van Dyke	1	846 Lincoln Rd.	305-534-3600	$	M(F)	Kazh	Jazz
Wet Willy's	3	760 Ocean Dr.	305-532-5650	None	R(F)	Local	

SIGHTS & ATTRACTIONS	DAY	ADDRESS	PH	ENTRY FEE
Bass Museum of Art	2	2121 Park Ave.	305-673-7530	$
Vizcaya Museum and Gardens	2	3251 S. Miami Ave.	305-250-9133	$
Art Deco District Welcome Center	1	1001 Ocean Dr.	305-672-2014	None
Miami CVB		701 Brickell Ave.	305-539-3000	

Event & Ticket Info

Carnaval South Beach: Most activities, including the **Superbands Concert**, are free. For more information, contact *The Kiwanis* (305-644-8888).

Noche de Carnaval (Orange Bowl): Tickets ($19 for reserved seats) should be purchased in advance from *Ticketmaster* (305-358-5885).

Calle Ocho: *The Kiwanis* (305-644-8888)

Alternative Event
Art Deco Weekend: *Miami Design Preservation League*, 305-672-2014

* M=Live music; P=Dancing (Party); R=Bar only; S=Show; (F)=Food served. For further explanation of codes, see page 14.

 NYC Miami (MIA) <60 min./$40   Yes/No 63°/80° (17°/27°)

March 1999

M	T	W	T	F	S	S
1	2	3	4	5	6	7
8	9	10	11	12	13	14
15	16	17	18	19	20	21
22	23	24	25	26	27	28
29	30	31				

February 2000

M	T	W	T	F	S	S
	1	2	3	4	5	6
7	8	9	10	11	12	13
14	15	16	17	18	19	20
21	22	23	24	25	26	27
28	29					

Lake Tahoe, California, USA

Skiing Tahoe

(The Most Fun Place To Ski: North America)

A FunGuide 100 Destination

A lift moves briskly toward the top of the mountain. Dotted with the colorful traces of skiers in motion, a blanket of glistening snow stretches for hundreds of miles. This could describe the view from the top of most major ski areas, but at Lake Tahoe, the Sierra Nevada mountain views are just as fine from the turquoise waters of the lake below as they are from the craggy peaks above. That's because Tahoe is North America's most fun ski resort for skiers and nonskiers alike.

Tahoe has everything you'd expect from a superior ski resort—scenery, charm, restaurants, night life, first-class ski facilities and accommodations—but it also offers something no other ski destination can: gambling. Whether it be Crystal Bay or Incline Village on the north shore, or Stateline on the south shore, casinos guarantee action all night.

Though it's an all-season resort, Lake Tahoe is most beautiful in winter, when snow blankets the land and turns steep mountainsides into some of the most exciting ski slopes in the country. The ski season usually lasts from Thanksgiving until early April, but off-slope activity peaks in early March with the arrival of *Snowfest*, the biggest winter carnival in the West.

By day, you can ski, snowshoe, or take boat rides around the lake. As dusk gathers, parties begin with string concerts, dances, and martini tastings, and conclude with fireworks and a torchlight ski parade.

Along with its natural beauty, the Tahoe area lures strangers with its Old West legacy, from Truckee's Old Town to the small but fascinating Donner Museum, which recounts the history of the entire region. You can also pay your respects to the Olympic torch that still burns at Squaw Valley, one of the area's biggest and most popular resorts, where skiers brave the slopes that played host to the 1960 Winter Olympic Games.

In return for cheap drinks, lavish buffets, and variety shows featuring top names directly from Las Vegas, glitzy resorts will happily relieve you of any sum of money you're willing to wager. The only sure bet is that Tahoe in winter is a great place to be.

Skiing Tahoe

We've abandoned our itinerary formula for this chapter in favor of a more general overview of options built around skiing and area attractions.

Hotels

The north shore is the more rustic of the two shores, with two outstanding ski resorts that allow you to step out of your hotel right onto the slopes. For a deluxe experience, try the **Resort at Squaw Creek**, which has the nicest accommodations in the Tahoe area. The resort offers everything you need for a complete winter vacation. **PlumpJack Squaw Valley Inn** is another good choice. Jacuzzis and king-size rooms (many rooms have Shakespearean themes) are part of the royal treatment. The **Hyatt Regency Lake Tahoe** offers comfortable rooms and the best casino on the north shore. If you want Vegas-type action, however, try Stateline's **Caesars Tahoe** or **Harrah's Lake Tahoe** hotels. Both offer rooms with great lake views and large casinos with showrooms.

Restaurants

For excellent cuisine coupled with romantic lakeside views, try one of three local hot spots. **Christy Hill** serves upscale California cuisine in a chic, contemporary setting. The old-fashioned **Lone Eagle Grille on the Lake** specializes in gourmet versions of hearty surf-and-turf cuisine; the spit-roasted duckling is a house specialty. **Le Petit Pier** offers the region's most elegant dining experience, serving fine wines and French cuisine right on the shimmering waters of Lake Tahoe.

The Squaw Valley resort complex features two of the area's best restaurants, including **Glissandi**, which serves creative versions of classic French and continental dishes in a semiformal atmosphere, and the more casual **PlumpJack Cafe**, sister restaurant to the critically acclaimed PlumpJack in

San Francisco. Built on the winding banks of the Truckee River, the **River Ranch Restaurant** serves steak, seafood, and wild game in a dining room that recalls an old-fashioned English inn. The south-shore casino hotels have gourmet dining rooms as well as good coffee shops. **The Summit**, with mountain views, is the gourmet restaurant at Harrah's Lake Tahoe.

Snowfest

Snowfest kicks off on a Friday night with opening ceremonies that include drinking, dancing, and a fireworks-and-laser show that lights up the slopes of Squaw Valley. On Saturday, events include the *Wild Things Parade* along the snow-lined streets of Tahoe City. On Sunday, the *Great Ski Race* attracts hundreds of colorfully clad cross-country skiers who dash madly from the shores of Lake Tahoe all the way to Truckee, some 19 miles away. When skiers arrive in Truckee, they usually head to the *Wild West Fest*, an event recalling Truckee's glory days as a mining town. There are also ski races and demonstrations by day, dances and concerts by night, and fun events for non-skiers such as the *Naughty Dawg Monster Dawg Pull*, which pits pooch against pooch. Dogs are harnessed to kegs (empty or full, depending on the size of the dog) and speed to the end of a 100-foot-long raceway where their masters beckon them from behind the finish line.

Nonskiers can amuse themselves during the day with a series of lighthearted events. Human polar bears test their nerve, endurance, and sanity by swimming in frigid lake waters and more local dogs compete in a festive variation of a sled race. Other events include a pancake breakfast inside the Tahoe City firehouse, a costume ball where guests come as Jack Frost and Old Man Winter, the *Wild West Fest* in Truckee's Old Town, and the coronation of the Snowfest Queen.

Nighttime entertainment

Lake Tahoe has plenty of places for après-ski schmoozing. You can join the under-35 crowd at **Borderhouse Brewery**, which makes its own tasty brew and serves decent sandwiches and finger foods. If your muscles aren't too sore for dancing, head to the nearby **Pierce Street Annex**, which has a crowded and fun dance floor seven nights a week.

For a quiet drink, try the classy **River Ranch Bar**, which has lovely bowed windows that look onto the swift-moving waters of the Truckee River. **Garwoods** is a popular hangout with a guitar duo playing most of the time. **Cottonwood** has jazz on the weekends. The Hyatt at Lake Tahoe has a lounge, but if you can manage the 30-minute drive (weather and traffic permitting), you'll get more variety in Reno. If you're on the south shore, **Nero's 2000** in Caesars Tahoe is an all-night dance club. There are also shows at each of the casino hotels, many with the same big-name entertainers that you'll find in the best Las Vegas casinos.

Ski resorts

Ask a dozen skiers what their favorite Tahoe resort is and you're likely to get a dozen different answers. Three of Lake Tahoe's dozen or so resorts are located along the south shore. Because of its fantastic runs and proximity to the town of Stateline, the best place to ski (and hang out at the lodge) is at **Heavenly**. On the north shore, **Northstar-at-Tahoe** is the most beginner-friendly of the big resorts, with open tracked areas. **Squaw Valley USA** is the area's largest resort, has the cachet of having hosted the Olympics, and also boasts some of the area's most challenging runs, making it great for experienced skiers. Nearby **Alpine Meadows** is an excellent choice for intermediate as well as advanced skiers, and like all Lake Tahoe resorts, puts skiers in the midst of spectacular scenery.

Area attractions

Along with natural beauty, the north-Tahoe area offers intriguing reminders of the Old West. Old Town Truckee has the storefronts and wooden sidewalks that recall the days when a brand-new railroad brought food and supplies to California's early settlers and returned east with gold panned from the nearby Truckee River. For a complete survey of the region's history, visit the **Donner Museum**, which documents the travails of early settlers as well as the history of the Central Pacific Railroad, which changed the region forever.

The Top Five Fun Ski Destinations, North America

If your primary interest is skiing, you may well have a different list of favorite places to go. But if your interest is the après-ski culture, certain destinations stand out. Whether you read *Skiing* or *Travel and Leisure* magazine, you'll find there's a general consensus regarding the five most fun ski resorts in North America.

The most significant challenger to Tahoe's rank as the most fun place to ski is **Aspen**. It's more exclusive than Tahoe and stands out for celebrity sightings. The people in Aspen know how to throw a party, whether it be the Sneaker Ball (black tie and—what else?—sneakers) or New Year's Eve at one of the area's exclusive clubs.

Killington is on the East Coast and many of its visitors are high-intensity New Yorkers. **Breckenridge** livens up things with a series of festivals and **Park City** (see page 43) visitors compensate for being in antiparty Utah by being intensely dedicated to the late-night arts.

General Information Numbers:
Aspen, Colo.: 800-525-6200
Breckenridge, Colo.: 800-789-7669
Killington, Vt.: 800-621-6867
Lake Tahoe, Nev.: 800-824-6348
Park City, Utah: 800-227-2754

The Hot Sheet

HOTELS	ADDRESS	PH	FX	PRICE	RMS	BEST ROOMS
Caesars Tahoe	55 Hwy. 50	702-588-3515 800-648-3353	702-586-2056	$$	440	Lake vw
Harrah's Lake Tahoe	219 N. Center St.	702-588-6611 800-427-7247	702-586-6607	$$	532	Lake and mtn vw
Hyatt Regency Lake Tahoe	Lakeshore and Country Club drs.	720-832-1234 800-233-1234	720-831-7508	$$	458	Mtn vw
PlumpJack Squaw Valley Inn	1920 Squaw Valley Rd.	530-583-1576 800-824-6348	530-583-1734	$$	61	Mtn vw
Resort at Squaw Creek	400 Squaw Creek Rd.	530-581-6637 800-327-3353	530-581-6647	$$$	404	Squaw Valley vw

RESTAURANTS	DAY	ADDRESS	PH	PRICE	REC	DRESS	FOOD
Christy Hill		115 Grove St.	530-583-8551	$$	D	Kazh	California
Glissandi		see Resort at Squaw Creek	530-583-6300	$$$	D	Kazh	California
Le Petit Pier		7238 N. Lake Blvd.	530-546-4464	$$	D	Kazh	French
Lone Eagle Grille on the Lake		Country Club Dr.	702-832-1234	$$$	LD	Kazh	California
PlumpJack Cafe		see PlumpJack Squaw Valley Inn	530-583-1576	$$	LD	Kazh	American
River Ranch Restaurant		Hwy. 89 near Alpine Meadows Rd.	530-583-4264	$$	LD	Kazh	California
The Summit		see Harrah's Lake Tahoe	702-588-6611	$$$	D	Kazh	American, continental

NIGHTLIFE	DAY	ADDRESS	PH	COVER	REC*	DRESS	MUSIC
Borderhouse Brewery		24 Stateline Rd.	702-832-2739	None	R(F)	Local	
Cottonwood		Brew Hilltop Rd.	530-587-5711	None	M(F)	Local	Jazz
Garwoods		5000 N. Lake Blvd.	800-298-2463	None	M(F)	Kazh	'70s, '80s
Nero's 2000		see Caesars Tahoe	702-588-3515 800-648-3353	$	P	Kazh	Top 40
Pierce Street Annex		N. Lake Blvd.	530-583-5800	$	P(F)	Local	'70s
River Ranch Bar		see River Ranch Restaurant	530-583-4264	None	R(F)	Kazh	

SIGHTS & ATTRACTIONS	DAY	ADDRESS	PH	ENTRY FEE
Donner Museum		West of Truckee on Donner Pass Rd.	530-582-7892	$

OTHER SIGHTS, SHOPS & SERVICES

Alpine Meadows	Hwy. 89, 6 miles north of Tahoe City	800-441-4423	$
Heavenly	140 S. Benjamin	702-586-7000	$
Northstar-at-Tahoe	Hwy. 267, 6 miles south of Truckee	800-466-6784	$
Squaw Valley USA	1960 Squaw Valley Rd.	800-545-4350	$
North Lake Tahoe Resort Association	245 N. Lake Blvd.	800-824-6348	

Event & Ticket Info

Snowfest (North Lake Tahoe area): Most events, including the opening ceremonies and parade, are free. For more information, contact *Snowfest* (702-832-7625).

North Lake Tahoe—Area Code 530   South Lake Tahoe—Area Code 702

* M=Live music; P=Dancing (Party); R=Bar only; S=Show; (F)=Food served. For further explanation of codes, see page 14.

 NYC –3   Reno-Tahoe (RNO) <60 min./$30   Yes   22°/43° (-6°/6°)

March 1999

March 2000

St. Patrick's Day Celebration

Savannah, Georgia, USA

| Origin: 1813 | Event ★ ★ ★ ★ ★ ★ ★ City | Attendance: 300,000 |

St. Patrick's Day in Georgia? Other cities may have more Irish blood than Savannah, but for nearly two centuries this city has hosted one of the country's biggest *St. Patrick's Day* celebrations. If the South's proud Irish legacy (ever heard of Scarlett O'Hara?) doesn't convince you this is the best place to celebrate the day, then a few hundred-thousand indefatigable partyers probably will. The improbable mix of Southern hospitality and Irish moxie make this a party like no other in the world.

As many as one-third of Southern settlers emigrated from Ireland. By the 19th century, Savannah had built a reputation for hospitality, welcoming many different groups of new Americans. Now, "Irish" revelers from across the nation—largely college age up to mid-30s—descend on moss-draped Savannah each year, swelling its population from 140,000 to about 450,000. The Savannah Waterfront Association sponsors the week-long event that creates an infectious party atmosphere and, in the best of American tradition, allows everyone to be Irish, at least for a day or two.

Although most days the celebratory siege officially lasts until 11 p.m., many inspired partyers cram local streets and pubs until at least 3 a.m. Crowds are so thick along the 100 block of East River Street that movement is often restricted to slow shuffling and desperate guarding of filled beer cups. Bands, dancing, souvenir stands, food tents, and beer stands attract so many people that some are nearly forced into the Savannah River. Few seem to mind. And when *St. Patrick's Day* falls on a Friday in the year 2000, larger and more boisterous crowds are anticipated.

Just a few blocks from the riverfront's wild party, Savannah remains incredibly calm and lush, providing an appropriately green backdrop for a more relaxed *St. Patrick's Day* that is rich with sights and history. Take time for some old-fashioned touring and find out why *Walking* magazine called Savannah one of the country's top-ten walking cities. Savannah's seasonably hospitable weather enhances the on-foot experience and adds the return of spring to your excuses for either remembering or pretending you're Irish.

St. Patrick's Day Celebration

The travel dates and sequence reflect the best three days for each year. Depending on which day of the week St. Patrick's Day falls, the best partying either leads up to March 17 (1999) or follows it (2000).

Day 1. Mon. Mar. 15, 1999
(Day 2. Saturday   March 18, 2000)

9:00am Check into the **Magnolia Place Inn**. It was built in 1878, but Jacuzzis and gas fireplaces in selected rooms lend a modern touch. Not that you'll need a fire—you'll be enjoying the warmest climate of all major *St. Patrick's Day* celebrations.

11:00am Walk to a late breakfast at **Clary's**. You may recognize the modest diner from John Berendt's bestseller, *Midnight in the Garden of Good and Evil*. There will be a line, but the food is fresh and the staff is friendly. Afterward, head over to River Street.

2:00pm Reflect on the craziness you see taking place on the waterfront as you relax on the **River Street Riverboat Company**'s one-hour cruise.

3:30pm Meander around City Market, a four-block area of shops, galleries, and restaurants that provides live music throughout the afternoon and evening during this holiday. The crowd is a little calmer and older than on River Street.

7:00pm In the midst of party central, **River House Seafood** is an oasis of calm, providing views of the chaos outside. Its lengthy menu features local fish, crab, and shrimp.

9:00pm The riverfront party is raging on, but a short walk away you can cap off the night with drinks or dessert at **Hannah's East**

(another *Midnight* landmark), the premier place to hear live jazz.

Day 2. Tues. Mar. 16, 1999
(Day 3. Sunday   March 19, 2000)

8:30am Start your day with Southern cooking at **Mrs. Wilkes Dining Room**. The set-menu monster breakfasts are served family style at big tables.

10:30am It's a pleasant walk to the **Telfair Mansion and Art Museum**. Its collection includes works by American impressionists and European artists. (The museum doesn't open until 2 p.m. on Sundays.)

12:15pm Nearby, you can lunch on **The Lady & Sons'** Southern buffet. It's known for bargain prices, crab burgers, and asparagus salad.

1:30pm If you'd prefer to ride through the historic district, reserve a trip with **Carriage Tours of Savannah**. Otherwise, walking is the best way to acquaint yourself with Savannah's charm. Mosey four blocks west to the **Owens-Thomas Museum House**—designed by famed English architect William Jay—considered the finest example of English Regency architecture in the United States. Five blocks south is the **Juliette Gordon Low Birthplace**, a gorgeous Regency-style house that was home to the founder of the Girl Scouts of America. At the **Green-Meldrim Mansion**, General Sherman set up headquarters during the Civil War. To see the interior, go on Tuesday, Thursday, or Saturday.

5:00pm Gear up for your evening with a glass of sherry. Savannahians always have what they call a get-ready drink.

Who has the biggest parade?					
	Irish Pop.	Spectators*	In Parade	Date Held	Hrs.	Miles
Savannah	10%	300,000	10,000	17th	3	3.2
New York	7%	2,000,000	150,000	17th	4	1.5
Boston	22%	1,000,000	10,000	Sun. before 17th	2	3.2
Chicago	8%	400,000	15,000	Sat. before 17th	2	1
Dublin	95%	500,000	5,000	17th	1	1

*Approximate, dependent on weather

7:00pm Take a cab or trolley for a classic Southern dinner at the **Olde Pink House**, which occupies an 18th-century mansion that was once used as a bank. The cast-iron vaults with their dungeonlike doors are still used today—not to hold gold bullion, but to shelter a selection of fine wines.

10:00pm On the 100 block of East River Street, various parties have been underway for hours. Near the Hyatt Regency, there's a makeshift sidewalk disco where you can rub shoulders with the usual thousands. You'll notice the attempt to introduce beads, à la Mardi Gras, but shamrocks-en-face remain the fashion of choice.

Kevin Barry's is a great spot for Irish music and a view of the party and river. Or pop into **Huey's**, which has a New Orleans-style porch providing views of the action below.

Sometime during your stay, have a taste of another local tradition—Chatham Artillery Punch—a favorite at large celebrations. This powerful stuff—concocted with wine, rum, gin, brandy, Benedictine, and rye, plus some sweet ingredients that are marinated for three or four days—packs a big punch.

Day 3. Wed. Mar. 17, 1999
(Day 1. Friday   March 17, 2000)

9:00am Fortify yourself with a home-cooked breakfast on Magnolia Place's grand veranda overlooking lovely Forsyth Park.

10:00am "The beauty of the city means you don't have to have great floats," one tourist-board official has explained. Savannah's mostly homespun (i.e., occasionally dull for visitors) parade features a lot of local dignitaries waving from automobiles. Clear paths and not-too-deep crowds allow for walking the parade route in reverse to see the whole show in less than half the time it would take if you sat still—which in the case of this parade is a major advantage. It's also a great way to see the city. Begin at the parade terminus, Madison Square, just south of Liberty Street. Follow the blocked-off streets (parade-route maps are also available at the tourist-board office). A good place to stop for a look at parade spectators is on the 600 block of Abercorn Street, or along Bay Street. This also puts you within easy reach of River Street's food booths, restaurants, and tireless party people.

1:30pm Grab an outside table at **Seasons**, a good place to watch the parade roll by. Its Southern cuisine is seasoned with a hint of Mediterranean influences.

3:00pm Postparade, stop by and have several get-ready drinks at the waterfront party.

7:00pm Cab to midtown to dine at **Elizabeth on 37th**, the finest restaurant in Savannah. Almost single-handedly, Elizabeth Terry invented Savannahian cuisine by blending classic Southern ingredients, such as fried grits and black-eyed peas, with contemporary dishes.

9:00pm After dinner you may want to stop back at the hotel to dress down for the *main event* in the waterfront area. The drinking, dancing, and socializing achieve critical mass on the street and in the bars. The Irish may not have invented partying, but they have added an important personality to the concept. River Street flows with green beer and people as Savannah reaffirms its heritage with a type of cheer that few other cities in the world can muster.

Alternatives

The Ballastone Inn (1838) and **The Gastonian** (1868) are two more of the city's best-known inns. Each features period-style furnishings, tea time, and Southern breakfasts. Because of its central riverfront location, **Hyatt Regency Savannah** is probably the best of Savannah's chain hotels.

For a dinner alternative, try the sautéed shrimp or crisp pecan chicken at **Bistro Savannah**. **Wet Willie's** and **Spanky's River Street** are popular nightspots on the riverfront. Both serve food. Another is the **Exchange Tavern & Restaurant**, a longtime local favorite for meaty meals, bar snacks, stiff drinks, and socializing.

The Hot Sheet

HOTELS		ADDRESS	PH	FX	PRICE	RMS	BEST ROOMS
The Ballastone Inn	Alt	14 E. Oglethorpe St.	912-236-1484 800-822-4553	912-236-4626	$$$$	18	Scarborough Fair w/access to balc
The Gastonian	Alt	220 E. Gaston St.	912-232-2869 800-322-6603	912-232-0710	$$$	17	Scarborough w/access to whirlpool, balc
Hyatt Regency Savannah	Alt	2 W. Bay St.	912-238-1234 800-233-1234	912-944-3678	$$$	346	River vw
Magnolia Place Inn	★	503 Whitaker St.	912-236-7674 800-238-7674	912-236-1145	$$$	15	3rd fl rms w/vw and verandah

RESTAURANTS	DAY	ADDRESS	PH	PRICE	REC	DRESS	FOOD
Bistro Savannah	Alt	309 W. Congress St.	912-233-6266	$$	D	Local	Southern
Clary's	1	404 Abercorn St.	912-233-0402	$	B	Local	Diner
Elizabeth on 37th	3	105 E. 37th St.	912-236-5547	$$	D	Kazh	Nuvo Southern
The Lady & Sons	2	311 W. Congress St.	912-233-2600	$$	L	Local	Southern
Mrs. Wilkes Dining Room	2	107 W. Jones St.	912-232-5997	$	B	Local	Southern
Olde Pink House	2	23 Abercorn St.	912-232-4286	$$	D	Kazh	Classic
River House Seafood	1	125 W. River St.	912-234-1900	$$$	D	Local	Seafood
Seasons	3	315 W. St. Julian St.	912-233-2626	$$	L/D	Local	Southern

NIGHTLIFE	DAY	ADDRESS	PH	COVER	REC⁺	DRESS	MUSIC
Exchange Tavern & Restaurant	Alt	201 E. River St.	912-232-7088	None	R(F)	Local	
Hannah's East	1	20 E. Broad St.	912-233-2225	$	M(F)	Local	Jazz
Huey's	2	115 E. River St.	912-234-7385	None	M(F)	Local	Guitar mix
Kevin Barry's	2	117 W. River St.	912-233-9626	$	M(F)	Local	Irish
Spanky's River Street	Alt	317 E. River St.	912-236-3009	None	R(F)	Local	
Wet Willie's	Alt	101 E. River St.	912-233-5650	None	P(F)	Local	Lite rock

SIGHTS & ATTRACTIONS	DAY	ADDRESS	PH	ENTRY FEE
Carriage Tours of Savannah	2	St Julian & Jefferson sts.	912-236-6756	$$
Green-Meldrim Mansion	2	1 W. Macon St., Bull St. at Madison Sq.	912-232-1251	$
Juliette Gordon Low Birthplace	2	142 Bull St.	912-233-4501	$
Owens-Thomas Museum House	2	124 Abercorn St.	912-233-9743	$
River Street Riverboat Company	1	9 E. River St.	912-232-6404	$$
Telfair Mansion and Art Museum	2	121 Barnard St.	912-232-1177	$
Savannah Visitor Information		101 Bay St.	800-444-2427	

Event & Ticket Info

St. Patrick's Day: Events are free. For more information, contact *The Savannah Waterfront Association* (912-234-0295).

* M=Live music; P=Dancing (Party); R=Bar only; S=Show; (F)=Food served. For further explanation of codes, see page 14.

 NYC   Savannah (SAV) <30 min./$20   No 47°/70° (8°/21°)

March 1999 — Austin/Dallas/Fort Worth, Texas, USA — March 2000

South by Southwest

(South by Southwest Music and Media Conference, SXSW)

Origin: 1987	Event ★ ★ ★ ★ ★ City	Attendance: 25,000

The ***South by Southwest Music and Media Conference*** proves that Austin ain't just whistlin' Dixie when proclaiming itself "live-music capital of the world." All you need is an ***SXSW*** admission wristband to get free rein on scores of citywide music events, highlighted by dynamic crowds at nightly performances by some 900 bands from all over the world, from Austin to Australia.

Many fans and industry types consider ***SXSW*** the pop-music world's most important gathering. While shopping around for favorite artists playing in 40 bars and clubs downtown (as well as alternative locations such as record shops, art galleries, and garages), you might stumble upon rare, small-venue performances by well-known artists such as Johnny Cash, the Fugees, or Blues Traveler.

Once University of Texas students drain out of Austin for spring break, ***SXSW*** participants flood the city to attend seminars, panels, and a trade show, in addition to live performances. Most important for industry people, ***SXSW*** offers the chance to make connections and sign contracts. Musicians, hoping to be discovered, perform with special vigor. Off-stage, Austin is charged with intense networking and the conspicuous presence of celebrity entertainers.

The state capital, with a population of just more than 500,000, Austin is the "misfit" of Texas, defined more by openness, university culture, and creativity than by oil rigs and cattle ranches. Per capita, it has more artists than any other Texas city, and more bars and restaurants than any other American city (many Austin clubs feature live music throughout the year). Its live-music scene centers around Sixth Street. There, more than 70 venues, restaurants, and shops occupy the Victorian buildings that play host to all types of music, from hip-hop to tears-in-your-beer country.

To make the most of a three-day itinerary, visitors can combine two nights at ***SXSW*** with a visit to nearby San Antonio (see page 95), Houston (see page 239) or as in this chapter, Dallas/Fort Worth. The Dallas metroplex is known primarily as a commercial center, but a day there makes for a great beginning to a musical weekend.

South by Southwest

Day 1. Thu. Mar. 18, 1999
(Day 1. Thursday   March 16, 2000)

10:00am Start your journey through the Old West, or what's left of it, in Fort Worth's **Stockyards National Historic District** (although it's more fun at night when the clubs are open). Then head downtown to Sundance Square for a look at its array of architectural styles, from art-deco to glass-and-steel.

Noon On top of the Bank One Tower, have lunch at **Reata**. The "cowboy cuisine," such as chicken-fried steak, is as great as the view. A street-level alternative is **Mi Cocina** for well-prepared Mexican food.

1:30pm Drive to the cultural district and spend a few hours at two small but wonderful museums. The **Kimbell Art Museum** has a range of painting masterpieces. Across a pretty park, **The Amon Carter Museum** has a good collection of American art.

3:30pm Cap off the one-hour drive to Dallas with a cocktail and another tower view from the 50th floor of **Reunion Tower**.

5:30pm Check into the magnificent **Hotel Crescent Court**. It has a limestone façade and beautifully appointed rooms and lobby. Then stop at its **Beau Nash Bar**, an upscale meeting place.

8:30pm Sipango is a trendy-crowd restaurant with Italian-inspired dishes, a lively bar scene, music, and a downstairs disco, the Rio Room (open only on Fridays and Saturdays).

11:30pm Drive to Deep Ellum, Dallas' popular area for funky shops, galleries, restaurants, and music venues. Try **Sambuca** for jazz.

1:00am On the opposite end of downtown, finish the night at **Starck**, a two-level Euro disco.

Day 2. Fri. Mar. 19, 1999
(Day 2. Friday   March 17, 2000)

9:30am After a hotel breakfast, head downtown to **The Sixth Floor Museum**, the site where Lee Harvey Oswald supposedly fired the shots that killed President John F. Kennedy. It's now a powerful exhibit about the president, the times, and the assassination, including film clips and memorabilia.

11:30am Drive through downtown Dallas, notable for architecture and sculptures that dot the landscape, especially Robert Summer's longhorns in Pioneer Plaza.

12:30pm Lunch at **Arcodoro**—it serves contemporary Italian dishes for the casually elegant crowd— before leaving for Austin (a 30-minute flight or a three-hour drive).

4:30pm You're part of the action at the modern Southwest-style **Four Seasons Hotel Austin**. It's the unofficial *SXSW* headquarters, popular with conference participants and performers who meet up and hang around the lobby. Pick up the special edition of the *Austin American-Statesman*. It has a complete list of bands and venues for the week.

5:00pm Walk along Auditorium Shore to the memorial statue of guitar legend Stevie Ray Vaughan. No blues or rock fan should miss this one.

6:00pm Enjoy an outdoor concert on Sixth Street. You'll be a few hours early for the incredible sea of people that fill this area.

7:00pm The **Cafe at the Four Seasons** serves New Texas cuisine in the city's only four-star restaurant. Make reservations in advance to get a view of Town Lake at sunset, and you may see more than a million bats emerge from under the Congress Avenue bridge.

8:30pm If you can't decide which band to see, walk to **Antone's** for what promises to be one of the best *SXSW* lineups. Willie Nelson celebrated his 60th birthday here, Stevie Ray Vaughan was a regular, and major blues acts frequently play at this diverse and popular venue.

11:00pm For a change of scenery, walk to **Top of the Marc** for live jazz with a sophisticated crowd. It's not affiliated with *SXSW*, but always books talented jazz musicians. After dancing, have a late-night Reuben sandwich from **Katz's Deli**, which serves in Top of the Marc or in their 24-hour diner below the club.

Day 3. Sat. Mar. 20, 1999
(Day 3. Saturday   March 18, 2000)

9:30am Stroll nine blocks to the modern Southwestern-style **Little City Cafe** for light, home-baked blueberry or espresso muffins.

11:00am Walking up Congress Avenue, you can't miss the distinctive **State Capitol**—it's the country's tallest. After the original limestone version burned down in 1881, it was rebuilt with Texas' own red granite. Take a free guided tour, and don't miss the awesome rotunda.

1:00pm Lunch at nearby **Cafe Serranos at Symphony Square** for good Tex-Mex food with a view that takes advantage of its location in the historic square.

2:30pm Continue north to **The University of Texas at Austin** visitor information center to get a map of the campus. Since it's Saturday and spring break, you'll see few students as you explore the grounds and its 19th-century Texas architecture. Visit the **Lyndon B. Johnson Library and Museum**.

7:00pm Have dinner at **Mezzaluna**. It's known for Italian cuisine and a fun bar scene.

9:00pm Jump into the scene at the 2,900-capacity **Austin Music Hall**, *SXSW*'s largest venue. Long lines might lead you a block away to the brightly painted **La Zona Rosa**, a renovated garage that always hops with cutting-edge sounds from alternative country to punk polka.

11:00pm Try **Cedar Street Courtyard**, an upscale martini bar with a '40s-style band on the patio. Or stomp around the wood-plank dance floor at the **Broken Spoke**, a honky-tonk with solid *SXSW* lineups.

12:30am Stay a little bit country at the **Continental Club**, a small, smoky Austin classic. Or head to **Maggie Mae's**, a club with a great lineup of rock bands and beer, two things that *SXSW* is all about.

2:00am Stroll down Sixth Street for a final hit of musical energy, ignited by *SXSW*'s collision of the music industry's art, business, and fun.

Alternatives

The **Four Seasons Austin** fills up a year in advance. You might try the **Driskill Hotel**. It's located in a renovated 19th-century building located right in the action on Sixth Street. The **Omni Austin,** part of a large office complex, is a more modern alternative. In Dallas, **The Mansion on Turtle Creek** is beautiful and refined. The **Worthington** is the place to stay in Fort Worth.

Threadgill's was the first live-music club to open in Austin after the repeal of Prohibition in 1933 and where Janis Joplin got her start. Their chicken-fried steak is good. In Dallas, **Star Canyon**, which serves upscale Southwestern cuisine, attracts a people-watching crowd.

A cocktail-hour alternative in Dallas is **Cedar Street**—an attractive martini bar with jazz music. For a different type of evening, try multi-clubbed **Dallas Alley** in Dallas' West End Historic District. The main draw is its Alley Cats dueling-pianos venue. A night in Fort Worth means **Billy Bob's Texas**—the world's largest honky-tonk (100,000 square feet), complete with an indoor rodeo arena, dance floor, and concert stage.

The Hot Sheet

HOTELS		ADDRESS	PH	FX	PRICE	RMS	BEST ROOMS
Driskill Hotel	Alt	604 Brazos St.	512-474-5911 800-252-9367	512-474-2188	$$$	179	Senate rms
Four Seasons Austin	★	98 San Jacinto Blvd.	512-478-4500 800-332-3442	512-478-3117	$$$	296	Town or lake vw
Hotel Crescent Court	★	400 Crescent Court	214-871-3200		$$$	216	
The Mansion on Turtle Creek Rosewood Hotels & Resorts	Alt	2821 Turtle Creek Blvd.	214-559-2100 800-527-5432	214-528-4187	$$$$	141	Courtyard vw
Omni Austin	Alt	700 San Jacinto Blvd.	512-476-3700 800-843-6664	512-320-5882	$$	320	Atrium vw
Worthington	Alt	200 Main St.	817-870-1000 800-433-5677		$$$	504	Downtown vw

RESTAURANTS	DAY	ADDRESS	PH	PRICE	REC	DRESS	FOOD
Arcodoro	2	2520 Cedar Springs Rd.	214-871-1924	$$	L/D	Yuppie	Italian
Cafe at the Four Seasons	2	see Four Seasons hotel	512-685-8300	$$$	D/BL	Yuppie	Nuvo Texas
Cafe Serranos at Symphony Square	3	1111 Red River St.	512-322-9080	$$	L	Kazh	Tex-Mex
Katz's Deli	2	618 W. 6th St.	512-472-2037	$	T/BLD	Local	Deli
Little City Cafe	3	916 Congress Ave.	512-476-2489	$	B/LD	Local	American
Mezzaluna	3	310 Colorado St.	512-472-6770	$$	D/L	Kazh	Italian
Mi Cocina	1	509 Main St.	817-877-3600	$	L/D	Local	Mexican
Reata	1	500 Throckmorton	817-336-1009	$	L/D	Kazh	American
Sipango	1	4513 Travis St.	214-522-2411	$$$	D	Yuppie, Kazh	Italian
Star Canyon	Alt	3102 Oaklawn Ave.	214-520-7827	$$$	D	Yuppie, Kazh	Southwestern
Threadgill's	Alt	6416 N. Lamar Blvd.	512-451-5440	$$	LD	Local	Southern

NIGHTLIFE	DAY	ADDRESS	PH	COVER	REC*	DRESS	MUSIC
Antone's	2	213 W. 5th St.	512-474-5314	$$	MP	Kazh	Blues
Austin Music Hall	3	208 Nueces St.	512-495-9962	$$$	M	Local	Blues, jazz, swing, rock
Beau Nash Bar	1	see Hotel Crescent Court	214-871-3240	None	R(F)	Yuppie	Jazz
Billy Bob's Texas	Alt	2520 Rodeo Plaza	817-624-7117	$	MP	Local	Country
Broken Spoke	3	3201 S. Lamar Blvd.	512-442-6189	$	MP(F)	Local	Country
Cedar Street	Alt	2708 Routh St.	214-871-2232	$	M(F)	Kazh	Jazz, blues
Cedar Street Courtyard	3	208 4th St.	512-495-9669	$	MP	Kazh	Jazz
Continental Club	3	1315 S. Congress Ave.	512-441-2444	$	MP	Local	Country, blues, rock
Dallas Alley	Alt	Dallas Alley	214-720-0170	$	MP(F)	Local	Sing-a-long, country
La Zona Rosa	3	612 W. 4th St.	512-472-2293	$$	M	Kazh	Blues, jazz, rock
Maggie Mae's	3	325 E. 6th St.	512-478-8541	$	MP(F)	Local	Rock
Sambuca	1	2618 Elm St.	214-744-0820	None	R(F)	Kazh	Jazz
Starck	1	703 McKinney St.	214-922-9677	$	MP	Euro	R&B, Top 40
Top of the Marc	2	618 W. 6th St.	512-472-9849	None	M(F)	Yuppie	Jazz

SIGHTS & ATTRACTIONS	DAY	ADDRESS	PH	ENTRY FEE
The Amon Carter Museum	1	3501 Camp Bowie Blvd.	817-738-1933	None
Kimbell Art Museum	1	3333 Camp Bowie Blvd.	817-332-8451	None
Lyndon B. Johnson Library and Museum	3	2313 Red River St.	512-478-0098	None
Reunion Tower	1	300 Reunion Blvd.	214-651-1234	None
Sixth Floor Museum	2	411 Elm St.	214-747-6660	$
State Capitol	3	11th St. & Congress Ave.	512-463-0063	None
Stockyards National Historic District	1	Main and Exchange sts.	817-624-4741	None
University of Texas at Austin	3	2300 Red River St.	512-471-1655	None
Austin CVB		201 E. 2nd St.	800-888-8287	
Dallas CVB		1303 Commerce St.	800-232-5527	
Fort Worth CVB		415 Throckmorton	800-433-5747	

Austin—Area Code 512   Dallas—Area Code 214   Fort Worth—Area Code 817

Event & Ticket Info

South by Southwest: A festival wristband ($100) gives you second-priority (after convention-goers, before pay-at-door) admission to all SXSW-sponsored performances. You may have to wait in line at some venues. Wristbands, which sell out by Friday morning, must be picked up in person in Austin. For information, contact *SXSW Headquarters* (512-467-7979).

* M=Live music; P=Dancing (Party); R=Bar only; S=Show; (F)=Food served. For further explanation of codes, see page 14.

 NYC –1   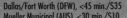 Dallas/Fort Worth (DFW), <45 min./$35 Mueller Municipal (AUS), <30 min./$10   Yes   48°/71° (9°/21°)

Academy Awards

Los Angeles, California, USA

Origin: 1929	Event ★★★★★★★★ City	Attendance: n/a

Whether you consider action, romance, comedy, or adventure the most fun, you can always count on Hollywood to deliver a damn good show. And the show it puts on for itself—the *Academy Awards*—grabs the attention of the entire world. With film-industry luminaries, screen superstars, and major media clamoring about, Hollywood in springtime is the destination for glitzy partying and world-class glamour.

Even celebrities who normally avoid Los Angeles like the plague swarm into town for the late-March ceremonies. Star sightings are never more frequent—you may find one sitting next to you at lunch or strolling on Rodeo Drive, the shopping street that epitomizes luxury. Everyone within six degrees of separation from Tinseltown dons their finest, making the weekend a celebration of beauty and fashion, as well as cinema. The *Oscars*-night parade of stars—a two-hour procession of filmdom's biggest names arriving at the show—rivals the Milky Way for sheer star power. And though getting into after-show parties such as the *Vanity Fair* bash or Elton John's annual shindig requires extraordinary finesse, the surrounding scene is still a first-class tourist attraction.

Los Angeles is a city, county, and geopolitically confusing place. Beverly Hills, Burbank, and Santa Monica, places that people associate with LA, are independent cities within the vast county. But along with the smog and road rage of the valley, they help create its indelible image.

Musts among the city's movie-related attractions include the campy Mann's Chinese Theatre and Universal Studios, where you can tour movie sets. Beyond Hollywood glitter, the billion-dollar Getty Museum is the brightest star in the cultural firmament, with its vast holdings housed in a hilltop complex. The area boasts the largest collection of ultrahip restaurants and night life in the world. Though tickets to the *Academy Awards* come by invitation only and the cost of scalped seats runs into the thousands of dollars, March is still a blockbuster time to be in Southern California to celebrate the magic of cinema and its celluloid Eden of Hollywood.

Academy Awards

Day 1. Fri.   Mar. 19, 1999
(Day 1. Friday   March 17, 2000)

9:30am On Sunset Boulevard, the cozy, art-deco **Argyle** makes a glamorous base. You might share the elevator with a nominee. From your room, enjoy a wonderful room-service breakfast with views of Hollywood, Beverly Hills, and downtown Los Angeles.

11:00am Drive 20 minutes to Rodeo Drive, shopping mecca to America's filthy rich. Sports and luxury cars fill the streets and dressy crowds fill the sidewalks, toting shopping bags from the showcase boutiques.

1:00pm Backtrack a bit to the **Ivy** for lunch. This pioneer of California cuisine is a meeting place for film-industry insiders.

3:00pm Drive 30 minutes on Santa Monica Boulevard to Santa Monica and the **Santa Monica Pier**. The pier offers sweeping views of the coast, as well as cotton candy and a giant carousel. Continue north on the legendary Pacific Coast Highway to Malibu, where the Santa Monica Mountains meet the Pacific Ocean in a series of dramatic bluffs and many Hollywood types seek weekend refuge.

6:00pm Stop at the gorgeous **Shutters Hotel**, just blocks south of the Santa Monica Pier. The lobby bar is perfect for cocktails and views of the sunset over the Pacific.

7:30pm Santa Monica's ultrachic **Chinois-on-Main** is a blend of East and West, with a Sino-French menu and décor combining European and Asian elements.

9:30pm Third Street Promenade is a great people-watching hangout. Plant yourself at any one of a number of restaurant/bars within its pedestrian zone.

11:30pm Join celebrities back in Beverly Hills. **The Coconut Club** at the Beverly Hilton Hotel, one of the city's trendiest nightclubs, usually features swing music. Farther down Wilshire, the popular **Conga Room** showcases big-name Latin acts for a slightly younger crowd.

Day 2. Sat.   Mar. 20, 1999
(Day 2. Saturday   March 18, 2000)

8:30am For brunch and star-gazing, you can't beat the chic **Campanile**. Friendly servers bring wonderful pastries in a covered courtyard with Moroccan accents.

10:00am Thirty minutes away, the pristine **J. Paul Getty Museum** contains a huge collection of master paintings, but the main attractions are the architecture and grounds. To park, you need reservations six months in advance. Take a cab and get there early.

1:00pm Drive 15 minutes for Mediterranean-influenced cuisine on the large patio at **Le Petit Four**, where pretty people and young starlets gather.

2:30pm Ten minutes away, **Mann's Chinese Theatre** is an essential stop. The theater resembles an opulent Asian palace and its famed courtyard preserves in cement the handprints and footprints of celebrities from Sharon Stone to Jimmy Stewart. The sidewalk out front, known as the Hollywood Walk of Fame, is covered with plaques commemorating hundreds of entertainment-biz greats. Squeeze in a visit to the **Frederick's of Hollywood** flagship store, which includes a fun museum of bras and other intimate apparel.

7:00pm Dress stylishly and drive to **Spago Beverly Hills**. The original one rocketed chef Wolfgang Puck to stardom and put California cuisine on the epicurean palette, but the real reason to go is the Hollywood A-list clientele.

9:30pm After dinner, stroll to **Le Dome**. The round bar has served many celebrities at post-*Oscars* parties.

11:00pm By now the **Garden of Eden**, one block from Mann's Chinese Theatre, should be packed with beautiful creatures. You won't see the Tree of Knowledge, but there's plenty of forbidden fruit on display, especially on the crowded dance floor that thumps with house music.

Day 3. Sun. Mar. 21, 1999
(Day 3. Sunday   March 19, 2000)

9:00am Breakfast on The Argyle's terrace before driving to **Universal Studios**. Take the tram tour of some of Hollywood's artful illusions. You'll pass the miniature lagoon where Jaws attacks a fisherman. Don't miss the exploding boiler room from *Backdraft* or the *Back to the Future* cyber-ride.

Noon Have lunch in one of Universal Studio's outdoor cafes, then take in live shows. Favorites are the *Waterworld* scene reenactment and Old West stunt show.

4:00pm Allow an hour to reach the Dorothy Chandler Pavillion (in 1999) or the Shrine Auditorium (in 2000), park, and claim standing space across the street in time for celebrity arrivals to the *Academy Awards*. The excitement makes it worth the hassle. Along with a huge crowd of gawkers, you'll see a two-hour parade of limousines and stars dressed in outrageous and classy fashions.

5:30pm Return to the hotel to dress for the big night. Flick on the television to see the first award-winners on stage.

7:00pm The hip crowd watching the ceremonies on television at the casual **Barfly** makes being there more fun than being at the show. With industry types all around, you'll hear exclamations such as "I did her hair!" and "He always mumbles—we had to get him a special mike!"

9:00pm Join a classy crowd for dinner at **Drai's**, where elegance and intimacy share top billing with a good combo playing for dancers.

11:00pm Cruise the post-*Oscars* parties. Locations vary, but your hotel concierge should know where this year's are.

1:00am Either because you're staying at the right hotel, or you have connections, script yourself a happy ending to the weekend by checking out the talent at **SkyBar** or **The Whiskey**.

Alternatives

With easy access to Rodeo Drive, the **Regent Beverly Wilshire** combines Old World grandeur with Beverly Hills glamour. The exclusive **Sunset Marquis Hotel** is a favorite of celebrities, who enjoy the private garden and excellent room service (and admission to The Whiskey). Similarly, many people stay at the ultrahip **Mondrian** just to get into its SkyBar.

Dinner at the Mondrian's **Coco Pazzo** also gets you into SkyBar next door, but the food and chic surroundings are enough of a draw. The ultracool **Pinot Hollywood** serves creative California cuisine. On the other side of attitude, the **Farmers Market** is a series of food shops and small restaurants in a pleasantly old-fashioned building.

You might take in a comedy show at the famous **Improv**. The **Crush Bar** features fun tunes from the '60s and '70s, plus lots of dancing and flirting.

The **Los Angeles County Museum of Art** has a fine collection of masterpieces and contemporary works. The **Museum of Contemporary Art** also houses a first-rate collection. For more celebrity-hunting, buy a map to the stars' homes and drive the lush streets of Beverly Hills and Bel-Air.

The Hot Sheet

HOTELS		ADDRESS	PH	FX	PRICE	RMS	BEST ROOMS
The Argyle	★	8358 Sunset Blvd.	323-654-7100 800-225-2637	213-654-9287	$$$	64	City vw
Mondrian	Alt	8440 Sunset Blvd.	213-650-8999 800-525-8029	213-650-5215	$$$	238	Balcony suite city vw
Regent Beverly Wilshire	Alt	9500 Wilshire Blvd.	310-275-5200 800-427-4354	310-274-2851	$$$$	395	Wilshire wing, Rodeo Dr vw
Sunset Marquis Hotel	Alt	1200 N. Alta Loma Rd.	310-657-1333 800-858-9758	310-652-5300	$$$	114	Garden villas

RESTAURANTS	DAY	ADDRESS	PH	PRICE	REC	DRESS	FOOD
Campanile	2	624 S. La Brea Blvd.	213-938-1447	$$$	B/LD	Dressy, Kazh	California, Mediterranean
Chinois-on-Main	1	2709 Main St.	310-392-9025	$$$$+	D/L	Dressy, Kazh	Asian, French
Coco Pazzo	Alt	see the Mondrian hotel	213-650-8999	$$	BLD	Kazh	Italian, American
Drai's	3	730 N. La Cienega Blvd.	310-358-8585	$$$	D	Dressy, Kazh	French
Ivy	1	113 N. Robertson Blvd.	310-274-8303	$$$	L/D	Kazh	American
Le Petit Four	2	8654 Sunset Blvd.	310-652-3863	$$	L/BD	Kazh	Mediterranean
Pinot Hollywood	Alt	1448 N. Cower St.	323-461-8800	$$	LD	Kazh	California
Spago Beverly Hills	2	176 N. Canon Dr.	310-385-0880	$$$	D/L	Dressy, Kazh	California

NIGHTLIFE	DAY	ADDRESS	PH	COVER	REC*	DRESS	MUSIC
Barfly	3	8730 W. Hollywood Blvd.	310-360-9490	None	R(F)	Yuppie	
The Coconut Club	1	9876 Wilshire Blvd. at the Beverly Hilton	310-274-7777	$$	MP(F)	Dressy, Kazh	Swing
Conga Room	1	5364 Wilshire Blvd.	213-938-1696	$$	M(F)	Euro	Latin
Crush Bar	Alt	1735 N. Cahuenga Blvd.	213-461-9017	$	P	Kazh	DJ, disco
Garden of Eden	2	7080 Hollywood Blvd.	213-465-3336	$$	P(F)	Kazh	Hip-hop
The Improv	Alt	8162 Melrose Ave.	213-651-2583	$$	S(F)	Kazh	
Le Dome	2	8720 Sunset Blvd.	310-659-6919	None	R(F)	Yuppie	
Shutters Hotel	1	1 Pico Blvd.	310-458-0030	None	R(F)	Kazh	
SkyBar	3	see the Mondrian hotel	213-650-8999	None	R	Kazh	
The Whiskey	3	see the Sunset Marquis Hotel	310-657-0611	None	R	Kazh	

SIGHTS & ATTRACTIONS	DAY	ADDRESS	PH	ENTRY FEE
Farmers Market	Alt	Fairfax and 3rd St.	213-624-7300	None
The J. Paul Getty Museum	2	1200 Getty Center Dr.	310-440-7300	None
Los Angeles County Museum of Art	Alt	5905 Wilshire Blvd.	323-857-6000	$
Mann's Chinese Theatre	2	6925 Hollywood Blvd.	323-464-8186	None
Museum of Contemporary Art	Alt	250 S. Grand Ave.	213-621-2766	$
Santa Monica Pier	1	at end of Olympic Blvd.	213-624-7300	None
Universal Studios	3	100 Universal City Plaza	818-622-3801	$$$$
Frederick's of Hollywood	2	6608 Hollywood Blvd.	323-466-5151	None
Los Angeles CVB		685 S. Figueroa St.	213-624-7300	

Event & Ticket Info

Academy Awards (1999: Dorothy Chandler Pavilion, 135 N. Grand Ave.; 2000: Shrine Auditorium, 649 W. Jefferson Blvd.): It's nearly impossible to get invitations to the ceremony or post-*Oscars* parties without fame or serious connections, but you can call *The Academy of Motion Picture Arts and Sciences* (310-247-3000) for *Oscars*-night details.

* M=Live music; P=Dancing (Party); R=Bar only; S=Show; (F)=Food served. For further explanation of codes, see page 14.

 NYC −3   **Los Angeles (LAX)** <60 min./$40   Yes   49°/69° (9°/21°)

Carnival Destiny

(The Most Fun Cruise)

A FunGuide 100 Destination

The recipe is simple. Take 2,600 fun-loving people, put them in a first-class hotel where the scenery changes daily, provide warm weather, food, drink, and music galore. Spice things up with a high-tech disco. Add water and you've got one hell of a party—and that's exactly what you'll find on the *Carnival Destiny*.

The cruise industry is booming, with the latest surge prompted by the cinematic sinking of the *Titanic* (go figure). This is good news, because it means a wide range of choices among destinations, ship sizes, cruise lines, and cabin prices.

While you can sail into any of the seven seas—it takes a harder-than-ice hull to navigate the Arctic and Antarctic—the most popular destinations include Mexico, Alaska, the Mediterranean, and the most popular year-round cruise destination, the Caribbean. The combination of climate and island ambience—no heavy sightseeing here—also makes the Caribbean the most fun.

The cruise line to check out is *Carnival*, which takes fun so seriously they've registered the term *fun ship* for more than a dozen vessels decorated in what they call entertainment architecture. The quintessential fun ship, *Carnival Destiny*, sails every Sunday afternoon from Miami into the Caribbean and some of the fabled ports of paradise. You can sail eastward for San Juan, St. Croix, and St. Thomas, or as detailed here, head west toward Cozumel to tour the Maya ruins of the Yucatán, sunbathe on Grand Cayman's Seven Mile Beach, and make a splashy climb up Dunn's River Falls in Ocho Rios.

One of the biggest cruise ships ever built, the 101,000-ton *Carnival Destiny* carries not only 2,600 fun-seeking people, but also the largest waterslide ever built on a cruise ship (214 feet), two outdoor pools, a swim-up bar, an indoor pool, seven Jacuzzis, a high-tech disco with 567 video monitors, a 15,000-square-foot fitness facility, and a 9,000-square-foot casino. But who's counting? The idea is just to kick back and have fun.

Carnival Destiny

Day 1. Sun. Mar. 28, 1999
(Day 1. Sunday   March 26, 2000)

12:30pm When you arrive at the Port of Miami, the first thing you'll notice is how the **Destiny** dwarfs the other ships docked in port. Take the obligatory boarding photo. You'll soon pass through the incredible nine-story Rotunda atrium on the way to your cabin.

1:15pm Settle into your comfortable suite with a veranda. Other than the ship's library, this is about the only place to get away from it all. Head to the *Sea & Sun Restaurant* and get oriented with the extensive buffet and salad bar, complete with ice cream. Although plentiful, the food at all but dinner leaves much to be desired.

2:00pm Report to the *Nautica Spa* for first dibs on booking a massage, manicure, haircut, or beauty treatment—appointments fill up quickly. You'll get a tour of the giant coed hot tubs and his-and-hers saunas and steam rooms.

3:00pm Partyers will already be on the Lido Deck dancing to calypso music, but you may want to use this time to explore the ship. You can watch videos about shore excursions, rent tuxedos or snorkeling equipment, or buy anything you may have forgotten.

4:30pm Stay on deck after the mandatory (the only thing that is) lifeboat drill to watch the ship sail from port. You'll get good views of Miami Beach from the port (left) side of the upper decks. Explore *Destiny Way*, the entertainment area that includes some of the ship's 17 bars and lounges.

7:30pm Drop by the casino for a complimentary rum swizzle and sit in the off-the-wall *Downbeat Lounge*, with its bigger-than-life musical instruments filling in as stools, tables, and wall decorations.

8:15pm Late seating begins in the two attractive dining rooms. You'll be seated at the dinner table that will be yours for the rest of the cruise (although you can ask to be moved). A table for four is intimate, one for eight more fun. Every meal will have a version of pasta, fish, veal, pork, and beef, along with appetizers, soup, salad, cheese, and dessert. If you can't decide between two menu items, your waiter will cheerfully deliver both.

10:00pm Singles over 18 are invited to the singles party in the *Point After Dance Club* for "getting to know you" games. With more than 200 people showing up, about a quarter of whom are over 30, it's a great way to check out opportunities for the week.

Size Matters

Any list of the largest cruise ships changes several times a year as new vessels come on-line. As of this writing, the biggest is Princess' *Grand Princess* (109,000 tons), followed by the soon-to-appear *Carnival Triumph* (102,353 tons), and the *Carnival Destiny* (101,353 tons). Eclipsing these and their upcoming sister ships (*Carnival Victory* and two more *Grand Princess* sisters), is Royal Caribbean International's *Voyager of the Seas* (136,000 tons), due in November 1999, to be followed by two more that size. Not so coincidentally, all these giants are built by the Big Three cruise companies, Carnival Corporation (the biggest, and parent of Carnival, Holland America, Seabourn, Cunard, Costa, and Windstar ships), Royal Caribbean, and Princess.

Top cruise ships	Tons (000)	Passengers	Rank By Passengers
Grand Princess (Princess Cruises)	109	2,600	5
Carnival Destiny (Carnival Cruise Lines)	101	3,400	1
Disney Magic (Disney Cruise Lines)	85	2,400	
Disney Wonder (Disney Cruise Lines)	85	2,400	
Rhapsody of the Seas (Royal Caribbean)	78	2,435	
Majesty of the Seas (Royal Caribbean)	74	2,744	3
Monarch of the Seas (Royal Caribbean)	74	2,744	3
Sovereign of the Seas (Royal Caribbean)	73	2,852	2
Fantasy (Carnival Cruise Lines)	70	2,600	5

10:30pm You may want to check out the *Welcome Aboard* show in the 1,500-seat *Palladium*. The audience-participation games are a bit goofy, but fun.

Midnight Each of the six cruise nights offers a similar choice of activities. A band plays dance music each night in the *Criterion Lounge*. You can sing along with a piano player in the *Apollo Bar*, with karaoke microphones at each table. *The All-Star Bar* has TVs for sporting events. The *Point After Dance Club* will help you build an appetite for the midnight buffet. Below the disco is the attractive but under-utilized *Onyx Bar*. And, of course, there's always the *casino*.

Days 2, 4, and 7.

These are "days at sea," which means the ship is cruising between ports and everything from deck games to the casino, shops, and spa are running full blast. There's something to do every minute—check Carnival Capers, the daily program placed in your cabin.

8:00am Have a leisurely breakfast in the dining room. You don't have to return to the table where you dined last night. Show up at either restaurant and you'll meet more fellow passengers.

10:00am There will be a choice of shipboard activities, but this is a great time to use your veranda.

Noon Choose from the ship's lunch venues—outdoor buffet, Asian, Italian, and American restaurants. Eat outside in a lounge chair. A deck steward will fetch you a cold drink while you listen to a calypso band.

2:00pm Check out the mens hairy-chest contest on Day Two; bring a partner to the massage demonstration on Day Four; take a line-dancing class on Day Seven.

7:15pm This is the cocktail hour. Day Two is the formal *Captain's Welcome*. For a ship that attracts bargain-seeking travelers, passengers look mighty fine tonight.

8:15pm If you're sitting with new acquaintances at dinner, it will be much more enjoyable if you can master the art of cruise conversation—what you did today and what you plan to do tomorrow are stalwart topics.

10:30pm See the sexy Parisian revue show, "Formidable," in the *Palladium* on Day Two; watch a magic show in the *Palladium* or enjoy country-Western night in the *Criterion Lounge* on Day Four; the infamous, X-rated male nightgown contest in the *Palladium* closes out the last night on board on Day Seven.

Day 3. Tue.   Mar. 30, 1999
(Day 3. Tuesday   March 28, 2000)

7:00am Head for the *Sun & Sea Restaurant* for the express breakfast of scrambled eggs, bacon, and toast.

Choosing a cruise ship

In the right situation small is beautiful, but partyers know that with size comes choice in on-board activities. Ship size is a good indicator of the kind of experience to expect. As a general rule, there's a direct relationship between the size of the ship (larger) and the cost of a cruise (cheaper), the quality of the food (poorer), and the average age of the passengers (younger). Unfortunately, there's also a direct relationship between the average age of the passengers and the let-your-hair-down partying on board. Here's a rough guide for what you can expect:

	Mega-ships (>1500 pass.) mass market	Midsize ships (500-1500 pass.) popular	Small ships (<500 pass.) deluxe
PRICE	$	$$	$$$$
Avg. age	35	45	55
Food	passable	acceptable	excellent
Range of activities	extraordinary	good	limited
Drink of choice	beer	Bahama mama	champagne
Excursions	party boats	sports activities	sightseeing

There are **two notable exceptions** to the size rule.

Crystal Cruises—although midsize (but pricier than most in the category), the *Crystal Harmony* and *Crystal Symphony* consistently rate among the top ships for food and service, and offer a surprisingly wide range of activities. Maybe the best for combining sophistication with fun.

Windstar Cruises—these small, tall-sail ships, the *Wind Song*, *Wind Spirit*, and *Wind Star*, attract an upscale but younger, sports-minded clientele looking for laid-back good times.

7:40am Meet at the *Palladium* and get a boat to *Playa del Carmen*. A 40-minute drive along the Yucatán coast in an air-conditioned bus takes you to the Maya ruins of Tulum while the ship moves to Cozumel. You'll return to Cozumel by ferry around noon.

1:00pm Have a delicious Mexican lunch at *Palmero's* on the main square across from the ferry pier.

2:00pm Head for the beach or enjoy some of the best diving in the Caribbean at *Playa San Francisco*.

6:00pm Don't expect an authentic Mexican experience— Cozumel exists for cruise-ship tourists. Nonetheless, rather than going back on ship, share stories and tequila shots with passengers from other ships at *Carlos 'n' Charlie's*. It's one of a chain of eating (pretty good) and drinking (great) joints, conveniently located near the pier.

Midnight Be on the Lido Deck for a balmy evening sail from Cozumel, with food, drink, and games into the early hours. The casino and dance club open after the ship sails and you can sleep in tomorrow because it's a day at sea.

Day 5. Thu.   Apr. 1, 1999
(Day 5. Thursday   *March 30, 2000)*

7:30am The ship arrives in Grand Cayman, but if you're lucky, you'll still be asleep. At dinner, you may hear stories about two of the more popular excursions here. *Atlantis Submarine* is an air-conditioned sub that dives to depths of 150 feet for looks at the incredible marine life on the reefs around Grand Cayman. The *Stingray City* tour allows you to snorkel beside divers feeding the stingray. Or ...

11:45am Catch the party boat for drinking and dancing as you sail to *Seven Mile Beach*, or simply do the beach on your own.

4:00pm Hang around the Lido Deck to watch the *Miss Carnival Destiny* contest as the ship sails from Grand Cayman. The routine for the rest of the evening should be familiar by this time.

Day 6. Fri.   Apr. 2, 1999
(Day 6. Friday   *March 31, 2000)*

7:00am Hit the breakfast buffet in the *Sun & Sea Restaurant* and take your tray on deck to watch as the ship sails into Ocho Rios.

8:30am Meet the *Cool Runnings and Dunn's River Falls* tour on the pier. With bathing suit, climbing shoes, and waterproof camera, you'll experience one of the Caribbean's highlights as you climb alongside the 600-foot waterfall.

1:00pm For genuine Jamaican jerk pork or chicken, walk a couple blocks from the pier to the *Jerk Center* (the ship's staff can direct you).

2:30pm Join in the reggae at the *Jamaica Sailaway Party* on the Lido Deck. There'll be plenty of the island's Red Stripe Beer and live music.

7:15pm Dressed in your fanciest get-up, make your way to the *Captain's Farewell* cocktail party in the *Criterion Lounge*. Then move on to your table for a gala dinner.

10:30pm Head to the *Palladium* for the Las Vegas-style musical show, "Nightclub Express." Later, if you're in a raunchy mood, take in the adult-comedy show.

1:00am The casino, disco, and a few of the lounges are still open. But you still have to pack—Miami comes at 8 a.m.—so take a final stroll on deck and, like the moon on the water, reflect on an extraordinary week.

Event & Ticket Info
Prices for a week aboard the **Carnival Destiny**, which vary depending on season and cabin category, range from $1,709 to $2,819 per person, double occupancy for a room with a veranda (an essential upgrade). Discounting is prevalent policy, typically 50 percent off for a second person.

Request the second (or "late") seating for dinner. This will give you more time ashore or around the ship in the late-day sunshine. For a free color brochure or to book a tour, call *Carnival Cruise Lines* (800-227-64825) or a travel agent.

The Fun Also Rises

Fiesta San Antonio

Origin: 1891　　　　Event ★ ★ ★ ★ ★ ★ ★ City　　　　Attendance: 3,500,000

Throw together a whopping dose of Texas pride, the partying spirit of Old Mexico, plenty of *cerveza* and tequila, and what have you got? Nothing less than *Fiesta San Antonio*, the annual fete that wakes up this South Texas city and draws party lovers from across the United States and Mexico.

While the event may have been founded for the purpose of commemorating Texas heroes and April 21, the anniversary of the Battle of San Jacinto (which won Texas independence from Mexico), today, the emphasis is on Texas-size fun and the recognition of San Antonio's entire cultural heritage. Events begin at about 10 every morning, although most of the dedicated partying takes place much later in the day.

Music festivals, elaborate parades, and serious noshing with everything from Tex-Mex to German to Cajun offerings appeal to cowboys and *caballeros*, ranch hands and city slickers. The food and music reflect the cultural pride of the more than one million people living in metropolitan San Antonio. While most events wrap up by midnight, the party continues at crowded nightclubs along the River Walk until about 2 a.m. Mariachi music floats through the air, often punctuated with the kinds of hoots and hollers Texas made famous.

Crowds are thickest along the River Walk, or *Paseo del Rio*, the meandering arm of the San Antonio River that winds through downtown. Located below street level, this is ground zero for out-of-towners, a shady walkway lined with hotels, sidewalk cafes, bars, and colorful night life. During *Fiesta*, the busiest stretch lies between La Mansion del Rio hotel at Navarro Street and around the horseshoe-shaped stretch of the river to La Villita historic area at Presa.

The River Walk stretches for two and a half miles, so, away from the partying crowds, there's plenty of opportunity for touring, walking, or relaxing beneath a riverside cypress tree enjoying the perfect antidote to a fiesta—a siesta. This will give you a chance to ponder how San Antonio has managed to keep one of America's greatest parties a secret for so long.

Day-By-Day Plan For

Fiesta San Antonio

Day 1. Sun. Apr. 18, 1999
(Day 1. Sunday   April 23, 2000)

9:30am Check into **La Mansion del Rio**. With south-of-the-border elegance and north-of-the-border comfort, this historic hotel is within walking distance of much of the action, as well as good dining.

10:30am Head to **The Alamo**, a mission that became the scene of a bloody battle in the fight for Texas independence. Walk through what's called the cradle of Texas liberty, a quiet attraction tucked in a bustling commercial district.

Noon Cab to the Mission Trail and the **Mission San José**, once called the Queen of the Missions. Attend a San Antonio tradition: Mariachi Mass.

1:30pm Cab to the River Walk and stroll to **Rio Rio Cantina** for Tex-Mex favorites and some of the best margaritas in town. Snag an outdoor table with a view of the river and passing tourist barges.

3:00pm Tour the River Walk by barge. Hop aboard near the kiosk at Rivercenter Mall or across from the Hilton Palacio del Rio.

7:00pm Bus to the Sunken Gardens in Brackenridge Park for *A Taste of New Orleans*. Gumbo and beignets top the menu. Jazz, salsa, and big bands keep things hopping.

11:00pm End the evening with Dixieland jazz at **Jim Cullum's Landing** at the Hyatt.

Day 2. Mon. Apr. 19, 1999
(Day 2. Monday   April 24, 2000)

9:00am Walk to the King William District for breakfast at the **Guenther House**. Built in 1860, the restaurant

> **D**uring *Fiesta*, there's no escape from *cascarones*, dyed eggshells filled with confetti and covered with tissue paper. Sold in many stores, everyone's a target for these little bombs.

serves breakfast favorites plus a Texas standby—biscuits and gravy.

10:30am Stroll through the King William District, home of stately mansions built during the 19th century. You can tour the most opulent one, the **Steves Homestead**, which boasts a natatorium (or "swimming pool" to the less well-bred).

1:00pm Head to the River Walk for lunch at **Zuni Grill**. Selections start with blue-corn nachos and progress to roasted poblano peppers filled with shrimp and mozzarella.

3:30pm See the story of the Alamo at the **IMAX Theatre** at **Rivercenter**. From a rolling thunderstorm over the rugged Texas landscape to the daybreak siege by Santa Ana's troops, this 45-minute movie makes you feel as though you're witnessing the fateful battle.

4:45pm Do as visitors have done since 1925 and make the pilgrimage to *The Alamo*, a tribute to the heroes of that battle. A special ceremony today includes costumed participants walking up to the former mission where the name of each of the Alamo defenders is called out.

5:30pm Try **Boudro's**, many San Antonians' favorite River Walk eatery. Arrive early for a good chance at a riverside table. Start with a cactus margarita, a frozen concoction with a jolt of red-cactus liqueur. Follow with an appetizer of crab-and-shrimp tamales. Save room for the specialties—coconut shrimp, pecan-grilled fish fillet, or blackened prime rib.

6:00pm Thousands pack the river bank, but you can beat the madness by enjoying the parade from your table. *The Texas Cavaliers' River Parade* features more than 40 floats, each with musicians, singers, and celebrities.

The Fun Also Rises

10:30pm On a Monday night, **The Cypress Club** may be the best place to dance or just hang out. Another jazzy, sophisticated club is the **Rhino Room**.

12:30am Get a nightcap at **Dick's Last Resort**, one of the rowdiest places on the river. The wait staff likes to crack jokes and toss out matchbooks decorated with old photos of topless women. Ladies can check out restroom walls decorated with more photos of scantily clad hunks.

Day 3. Tue. Apr. 20, 1999
(Day 3. Tuesday   April 25, 2000)

8:00am Breakfast at **Schilo's Delicatessen**, which opened as a saloon in 1917, but became a deli with the coming of Prohibition.

9:00am Head to the **Institute of Texan Cultures** to explore the 30-plus ethnic cultures that settled Texas. Costumed docents mosey through the museum, ready to explain the role of a chuck-wagon cook on a cattle drive or the rigors of life as a frontier woman.

11:00am Walk to the **Tower of the Americas**, the symbol of the 1968 HemisFair world's fair and a landmark of San Antonio. The tower soars 750 feet, but visitors view the city from the observation deck at 579 feet.

12:30pm Head to **Mi Tierra**, the restaurant that never sleeps. Twenty-four hours a day, 365 days a year, this San Antonio institution serves some of the city's best Tex-Mex in a festive eatery garnished with Christmas decorations. Strolling troubadours take requests for Mexican ballads.

2:00pm Start partying at *Fiesta del Mercado*, where five stages showcase mariachi, Tejano, jazz, and rock. Pop inside El Mercado, the largest Mexican marketplace in the United States.

5:30pm Party away the evening at the biggest *Fiesta* event. *A Night in Old San Antonio* is better known by its nickname, NIOSA (*nie-o-sa*). The

party, featuring 15 elaborate cultural areas, takes place in La Villita, a restored 18th-century village on the River Walk. Dance to Western, *conjunto*, oompah, or mariachi music. Dine on-the-fly at food booths that sell everything from *escargot* to German sausage to tacos.

8:00pm Walk to the *Mariachi Festival*, one of the oldest in the country. Amateurs and pros battle for the spotlight.

10:30pm Follow the River Walk to **Howl at the Moon**, a sing-along bar that features dueling pianos. Not for quiet types, the bar is filled with folks singing to show tunes and classic-rock songs. Next door, finish the evening with jazz and cocktails at **Swig**.

Alternatives

The *Fiesta* continues through the following weekend, when there is a *Battle of Flowers* street parade instead of the river parade.

The **Fairmount** hotel is a small property that pampers guests with personal attention amid turn-of-the-century elegance. The recently opened **Havana Riverwalk Inn** is housed in a historic building. The **Hyatt Regency on the River** is perfectly located with great views.

Biga is an innovative restaurant in a century-old house. Menu offerings include oak-roasted antelope and barbecued lamb on couscous. For Italian fare, check out **Paesano's** for steak Florentine with spaghetti or the house specialty, buttery shrimp Paesano's. **Presidio** provides a Sunday dinner alternative, combining good food with a happening ambience.

In addition to Dick's, you might try **Acapulco Sam's** for last call.

The **McNay Museum** has unusual 19th- and 20th-century European and American paintings housed in a beautiful mansion.

The Hot Sheet

HOTELS		ADDRESS	PH	FX	PRICE	RMS	BEST ROOMS
The Fairmount	Alt	401 S. Alamo	210-224-8800	210-475-0082	$$$	37	City vw
Havana Riverwalk Inn	Alt	1015 Navarro St.	210-222-2008 888-224-2008	210-222-2717	$$	27	River vw
Hyatt Regency on the River	Alt	123 Losoya St.	210-222-1234 800-233-1234	210-227-4925	$$$$	632	Alamo vw
La Mansion del Rio	★	112 College St.	210-225-2581 800-292-7300	210-226-0389	$$$	337	River vw

RESTAURANTS	DAY	ADDRESS	PH	PRICE	REC	DRESS	FOOD
Biga	Alt	206 E. Locust St.	210-225-0722	$$$	D	Dressy, Kazh	American fusion
Boudro's	2	421 E. Commerce St.	210-224-8484	$$	D/L	Kazh	Southwestern, Tex-Mex
Guenther House	2	205 E. Guenther St.	210-227-1061	$	B/L	Kazh	Texas breakfast
Mi Tierra	3	218 Produce Row	210-225-1262	$	L/BD	Local	Tex-Mex
Paesano's	Alt	555 E. Basse St.	210-828-5191	$$$	L/D	Kazh	Italian
Presidio	Alt	245 E. Commerce St.	210-472-2265	$$	LD	Kazh	Mediterranean
Rio Rio Cantina	1	421 E. Commerce St.	210-226-8462	$$	L/D	Local	Tex-Mex
Schilo's Delicatessen	3	424 E. Commerce St.	210-223-6692	$	B/LD	Local	Deli
Zuni Grill	2	511 River Walk	210-227-0864	$$	L/BD	Kazh	Southwestern

NIGHTLIFE	DAY	ADDRESS	PH	COVER	REC*	DRESS	MUSIC
Acapulco Sam's	Alt	212 College St.	210-212-7267	$	MP	Local	Top 40
The Cypress Club	2	140 E. Houston St.	210-476-8661	None	MP	Local	Jazz
Dick's Last Resort	2	406 Navarro St.	210-224-0026	None	MP(F)	Kazh	R&B, Motown
Howl at the Moon	3	111 W. Crockett St.	210-212-4695	$	M	Local	Piano sing-along
Jim Cullum's Landing	1	see Hyatt Regency hotel	210-223-7266	$	MP(F)	Kazh	Jazz
Rhino Room	2	245 Commerce St.	210-281-1410	$	MP	Kazh	Swing, rockabilly
Swig	3	111 W. Crockett St.	210-476-0005	None	M	Kazh	Jazz

SIGHTS & ATTRACTIONS	DAY	ADDRESS	PH	ENTRY FEE
The Alamo	1	300 Alamo Plaza	210-225-1391	None
IMAX Theatre at Rivercenter	2	849 E. Commerce St.	210-225-4629	$
Institute of Texan Cultures	3	801 S. Bowie St.	210-458-2300	$
McNay Museum	Alt	6000 New Braunfels Ave.	210-824-5368	$
Mission San José	1	6539 San José Dr.	210-932-1001	None
Steves Homestead	2	509 King William	210-225-5924	$
Tower of the Americas	3	600 HemisFair Park	210-207-8615	$
San Antonio CVB		317 Alamo Plaza	210-207-8700	

Event & Ticket Info

Fiesta San Antonio: Many events, including **Fiesta del Mercado**, **Mariachi Festival**, and **The Alamo** ceremony are free. For more information, contact *Fiesta San Antonio Commission* (877-723-4378).

Texas Cavaliers' River Parade (River Walk): Tickets for riverside viewing ($8-$20) sell out and are available after January 1 (you don't need a ticket if you have dinner at a riverside restaurant). Contact *Texas Cavaliers' River Parade* (210-227-4837).

Night in Old San Antonio (La Villita, Alamo and Nueva streets): Tickets ($8) are available at the gate. Contact *NIOSA* (210-226-5188).

A Taste of New Orleans (Sunken Garden Theater, Brackenridge Park): Tickets ($5) available at the gate. For information, contact *San Antonio Zulu Association* (210-225-2331).

* M=Live music; P=Dancing (Party); R=Bar only; S=Show; (F)=Food served. For further explanation of codes, see page 14.

 NYC −1   San Antonio (SAT) <30 min./$15   No   59°/79° (15°/26°)

The Fun Also Rises

Kentucky Derby
(Kentucky Derby Festival)

Origin: 1875	Event ★ ★ ★ ★ ★ ★ City	Attendance: 140,000

Twenty horses, 600 roses, 80,000 mint juleps. On the first Saturday in May, America's best three-year-old Thoroughbreds race for glory (and lots of money) in the *Kentucky Derby*. With steel in their teeth and mud in their eyes, horses with legs become horses with wings in the first jewel of the Triple Crown, held each year in Louisville. The odds on owning the winner are 30,000 to 1. The odds on getting a reserved seat under the famed Twin Spires of Churchill Downs are slightly better, but box seats are generally handed down with the family silver.

At one of the oldest sporting facilities in the United States still in use, a $2 bet buys a million thrills. It's tough to ignore the pressure to wager at this next-largest sporting event for betting after the Super Bowl ($10 million is wagered at the track, five times that, nationally). A bugler plays the "Call to Post" and everyone sings "My Old Kentucky Home." Red-coated out-riders escort horses to the starting gate, binoculars go up, the bell sounds, and the gate flies open.

The *Derby* is called the most exciting two minutes in sports, but the days leading up to the race might be the most exhausting two weeks in sports. The *Kentucky Derby Festival* hosts more than 70 events. "Thunder over Louisville," the nation's largest fireworks show, ignites two weeks of revelry. The *Pegasus Parade* and *Kentucky Oaks* race mark the final approach to Derby Day. Celebrities descend on Louisville for elaborate balls, and everyone, it seems, has a house full of guests. Think Mardi Gras, Super Bowl, and New Year's Eve mixed with the Great Balloon Race, Great Steamboat Race (both are *Derby Festival* events), and great local bourbon.

Although Louisville's metro-area population is about a million, for visiting urbanites the pace may feel like syrup coursing through a julep's crushed ice. The visitor's biggest challenge is pronouncing the name correctly: *Loo ah vull*. Come spring, though, the pace quickens as more than a million people arrive for the *Derby Festival*, the *Run for the Roses* (arguably the world's greatest race), and an unforgettable three-day trifecta.

Kentucky Derby

Day 1. Thu. Apr. 29, 1999
(Day 1. Thursday   May 4, 2000)

10:00am The hotel situation this weekend is bleak—you may not know where you're staying until a waiting list clears (see Alternatives section), and you'll be paying two to three times the normal rate for a room you won't spend much time in. Wherever you wind up, unpack the formal wear and consider sending out for roses. Then trot over to the **Louisville Slugger Museum and Bat Factory** for highlights of the great game and a tour of the bat factory.

1:00pm Walk toward the river to Waterfront Park and the *Derby Festival Downtown Chow Wagon*. There should be live music coming from the bandstand, a good crowd, cheap eats from food stands, and an opportunity to be ridiculed for your mispronunciation of the city's name.

2:30pm Drive to the **Speed Art Museum** and its collection of Rembrandt, Monet, and contemporary works.

5:30pm Head to Broadway for the *Pegasus Parade* (6–7:15 p.m.), the granddaddy of all *Derby Festival* events. You can easily walk the 13-block parade route in reverse for a quick review of the spectacle.

8:00pm Retrieve the car and proceed to **Azalea** for trendy blends of New American cuisine.

10:00pm Sip a martini and hear jazz at **Bobby J's**, a bistro and nightclub with a balcony and separate bar for the cigar set. If you prefer the blues, **Stevie Ray's** is the place. It has warm brick walls and a hot dance floor.

Midnight Change the pace with a visit to **O'Malley's**, one of Louisville's two popular multiclub venues. This one has four clubs within its building: disco, rock, country (the dancing here is not for amateurs), and dueling pianos (sheer fun).

Day 2. Fri. April 30, 1999
(Day 2. Friday   May 5, 2000)

8:00am Slip on the feed bag at **Lynn's Paradise Cafe**. It's a short drive to this kitschy, '40s-style diner that serves country ham, biscuits, and comfort food. Go early to beat the herd.

10:30am Follow your concierge-assisted transportation plan to the **Kentucky Derby Museum**. The displays and exhibits celebrate every *Derby*, every day. Lay off the pace and grab a bite in its **Derby Cafe**, a local institution.

2:00pm Walk to Churchill Downs for the *Kentucky Oaks* (11:30 a.m.–6:30 p.m.) race. Locals say the *"Run for the Lilies"* is a good bet for avoiding *Derby* crowds. Head to the infield where a band starts playing after the fifth race. You can see the whole track from there and also watch the races on large-screen video monitors.

7:30pm Attend one of the legendary *Derby*'s-eve parties. The wild *Anita Madden party* for 2,500 close friends—an hour's drive away in Lexington—is everything you'd want a party to be. The new kids on the block (actor Matt Battaglia and Chris and Tom Thieneman) host the official *Mint Jubilee* in Louisville. Both are star-studded charity events (dress is black-tie or costume), with cocktails, dinner, dancing, and entertainment.

When you arrive at the airport, just past the Tobacco Leaf Lounge—which has recently been turned into a nonsmoking area—you'll be handed bourbon bonbons by gracious Derby Belles to set the mood for three glorious days of Southern tradition.

Midnight Savor the bourbon and jazz at the **Old Seelbach Bar**, one of the South's premier jewels among watering holes. Or go to local favorite **Rick's Square Piano** to listen to jazzy ballads or dance to disco music.

Day 3. Sat.   May 1, 1999
(Day 3. Saturday   May 6, 2000)

9:00am Drive to the ***Derby Day Breakfast*** (9 a.m.–ñoon) at Farmington Historic Home (it'll be at Locust Grove in 2000). It's a great way to meet people (about 1,000, including the Derby Queen and her court), listen to jazz, and have a traditional Derby breakfast. You can also tour the historic house.

Noon A limo is the preferred way to arrive at Churchill Downs for the ***Kentucky Derby*** (11:30 a.m.–7 p.m.). Hitching a ride with a new friend is also acceptable. Once inside, go to the infield where, weather permitting—the weather can be as fickle as the outcome of the race; temperatures range from the 40s to the 90s and rain is not unusual—a party atmosphere prevails. Snack on excellent barbecue-beef, pork, or turkey sandwiches. Try a Bones of Beer—18 inches and 28 ounces of beer in a green glass with a bulbous bottom. It's slightly less traditional but, for many, slightly more tasty than the bourbon, water, sugar, and mint leaves that go into the ubiquitous mint julep.

5:45pm High-tail it after the *Derby* race (the eighth of ten races) to beat the crowd. Return to your stall and collapse, briefly.

7:30pm Drive to **Brasserie Dietrich** for a classic meal in a stunning dining room, a restored movie theater.

11:00pm Louisville's second multiclub venue is **Jim Porter's**, where you can choose between blues, '70s disco, '90s rock, and a swingin' (literally, above the bar) singer. If you feel the need for food or quiet, stop in at the **Bristol Bar & Grille** for a good late-night snack. You may need the down time, because, whether you've won or lost this weekend, the smart money says it was the wildest time you've ever had hanging around a bunch of three-year-olds.

Alternatives

There's little hope of getting a room at **The Camberley Brown Hotel**, a restored 1923 jewel. You may clear a wait list at **The Seelbach Hilton Hotel**, another downtown gem. Another option is **The Galt House** and **Galt House East** complex with 1,300 rooms. The best bet for getting a downtown room is the **Club Hotel by Doubletree Louisville Downtown**.

Louisville has three major restaurant strips: Bardstown Road, Frankfort Avenue, and Hurstborne Parkway. For ethnic influences, **Asiatique** offers Pacific Rim fare. **Ermin's French Bistro** will pack you a Derby Day box lunch. **Club Grotto** and **Zephyr Cove** are two other recently popular spots in town. Or consider a dining cruise on the ***Star of Louisville***, a yacht-style cruiser with dancing and live music.

*On your last legs, but still staying through Sunday? Drive to the **Melrose Inn** for breakfast. Derby Pie was born here and is a fiercely protected trademark. You'll find it elsewhere as Bluegrass Pie, Museum Winner's Pie, Run for the Roses, or Louisville Pie, but if you haven't had Derby Pie, you haven't had the original chocolate-chip-and-nut creation.*

(continued from next page)

For information on these and other activities, contact *Kentucky Derby Festival* (502-584-6383).

Pegasus Parade (Broadway, from Campbell to Ninth streets): Bleacher and chair tickets ($8-$10) are available (although standing is preferred) at *Kentucky Center for the Arts* ticket service outlets (502-584-7777).

Derby Day Breakfast (1999 in Farmington at 3033 Bardstown Rd.; 2000 in Locust Grove at 561 Blankenbaker Ln.): For information and tickets (reserved $95 CD, open seating $80), which sell out a few weeks before the event, contact (starting in January) *Historic Homes Foundation* (502-899-5079).

Mint Jubilee (University Club, University of Louisville): For information and tickets ($275 CD), contact *Mint Jubilee* (502-326-7513).

Madden Party (Hamburg Place Farm, Lexington): $300 CD. Request an invitation (in January) in writing from Anita Madden, PO Box 12128, Lexington, KY 40580.

The Hot Sheet

HOTELS		ADDRESS	PH	FX	PRICE	RMS	BEST ROOMS
The Chamberley Brown Hotel	Alt	335 Broadway	502-583-1234 800-866-7666	502-587-7006	$$$$+	302	
Club Hotel by Doubletree Louisville Downtown	Alt	101 E. Jefferson St.	502-585-2200 888-444-2582	502-584-5657	$$$$	182	
The Galt House and Galt House East	Alt	Riverfront at 4th Ave.	502-589-5200 800-626-1814	502-589-3444	$$$	1300	River vw
The Seelbach Hilton Hotel	Alt	500 4th St.	502-585-3200 800-333-3399	502-585-9240	$$$$+	321	Dlx (larger)

RESTAURANTS	DAY	ADDRESS	PH	PRICE	REC	DRESS	FOOD
Asiatique	Alt	106 Sears Ave.	502-899-3578	$$	D	Yuppie	Seafood
Azalea	1	3612 Brownsboro Rd.	502-895-5493	$$$	D/L	Kazh	New American
Brasserie Dietrich	3	2862 Frankfort Ave.	502-897-6076	$$	D	Kazh	American bistro
Bristol Bar & Grille	3	1321 Bardstown Rd.	502-456-1702	$$	T/LD	Kazh	New American
Club Grotto	Alt	2116 Bardstown Rd.	502-459-5275	$$$	D	Kazh	American bistro
Derby Cafe	2	see Kentucky Derby Museum	502-637-7097	$$	L	Kazh	American
Ermin's French Bistro	Alt	1538 Bardstown Rd.	502-485-9755	$$	LD	Kazh	French, American
Lynn's Paradise Cafe	2	984 Barret Ave.	502-583-3447	$	B/LD	Kazh	American
Zephyr Cove	Alt	2330 Frankfort Ave.	502-897-1030	$$	LD	Kazh	American bistro

NIGHTLIFE	DAY	ADDRESS	PH	COVER	REC*	DRESS	MUSIC
Bobby J's	1	1314 Bardstown Rd.	502-452-2665	None	MP(F)	Kazh	Jazz
Jim Porter's	3	2345 Lexington Rd.	502-452-9531	$	MP	Kazh	Rock, blues
O'Malley's	1	133 W. Liberty St.	502-589-3866	$	MP	Kazh	New rock, alternative
Old Seelbach Bar	2	500 4th St.	502-585-3200	None	MP(F)	Kazh	Jazz, R&B
Rick's Square Piano	2	20 Theater Sq.	502-583-6090	None	MP	Yuppie	Jazz, '70s
Stevie Ray's	1	230 E. Main St.	502-582-9945	$	M	Local	Blues

SIGHTS & ATTRACTIONS	DAY	ADDRESS	PH	ENTRY FEE
Kentucky Derby Museum	2	704 Central Ave.	502-637-7097	$
Louisville Slugger Museum and Bat Factory	1	800 Main St.	502-588-7228	$
Speed Art Museum	1	2035 S. 3rd St.	502-634-2700	None
Star of Louisville	Alt	151 W. River Rd.	502-589-7827	$$$$+
Louisville and Jefferson County CVB		400 S. 1st St.	502-584-2121	

Event & Ticket Info

Kentucky Derby (Churchill Downs, 700 Central Ave.): Churchill Downs requires written requests (beginning the day after the Derby) for the few available reserved seats to the Derby and Oaks (combined tickets): clubhouse ($175-$550), grandstand ($42-$160), or infield bleachers ($70). General admission tickets ($30 for Derby/$15 for Oaks) are sold on race day for standing only, including the infield. Send request to Consumer Sales Department, Churchill Downs, 700 Central Ave., Louisville, KY 40208. Contact *Churchill Downs* (502-636-4400).

Derby Festival Downtown Chow Wagon (Waterfront Park): $5

(continued on previous page)

* M=Live music; P=Dancing (Party); R=Bar only; S=Show; (F)=Food served. For further explanation of codes, see page 14.

 NYC   Louisville/Standiford (SDF) <30 min./$15   Yes   54°/76° (12°/24°)

New Orleans, Louisiana, USA

New Orleans Jazz & Heritage Festival

Origin: 1970 **Event** ★★★★★ **City** **Attendance:** 480,000

Born in the "clubs" of New Orleans' red-light district, the fame of jazz and ragtime are inseparable from the city. New Orleans celebrates its musical heritage 365 days a year, but without doubt, the party is best during the last weekend in April, when the *New Orleans Jazz & Heritage Festival* brings in hundreds of top musicians for 10 days of music, food, and Nawlins fun.

Jazz Fest is more like three giant festivals in one. First and foremost, it highlights music. The largest music festival in the United States, it books top names in jazz, ragtime, funk, R&B, zydeco, gospel, Latin, Caribbean, blues, rock, and country music. After music, New Orleans' passion is food, and you can relish savory local cuisine—from crawfish to andouille gumbo to alligator pie—at the festival grounds. Finally, the festival acts as a giant crafts show, with special emphasis on the folk art of old Louisiana. Some artisans craft their wares on the spot.

The music stages, tents, food stands, and crafts stalls dress up the otherwise drab Fairgrounds Race Course setting. But the combination of top-flight talent and the New Orleans backdrop makes this one of America's top events.

The *Jazz Fest* is the more quiet and sophisticated of New Orleans' two world-class events, but, really, what event isn't quieter than Mardi Gras? The festival runs 11 a.m.-7 p.m. each day. The typical daily routine is brunch or lunch, festival, "disco nap," dinner, and nightclubbing until 3 or 4 a.m. Regulars say that the last weekend is best, when the partying is most intense. Closing Sunday starts with a stirring gospel concert and ends with hometown favorites, the Neville Brothers. For all that's best to do in the city, refer to the itinerary and New Orleans Hot Sheet in the Mardi Gras chapter (see page 61).

Event & Ticket Info

New Orleans Jazz & Heritage Festival (Fairgrounds Race Course, 1751 Gentilly Blvd.): Tickets ($16) are available at the gate. The *Jazz Festival* never sells out, except in the late evening. Advance tickets ($12) are available from Ticketmaster (800-488-5252). For more information, contact *New Orleans Jazz and Heritage Foundation* (504-941-5100).

 NYC −1 New Orleans (MSY) <30 min./$25 No 65°/85° (18°/29°)

Meet Me at the Fair

The thrill of the midway, blue-ribbon competitions, stellar entertainment, and remnants of "grandfather's farm"—these still draw 120 million people to more than 2,700 county, state, and regional fairs in the United States. Because nearly every community has a fair appealing to local interests, we haven't covered them in this book. But lots of people consider them a great place to have fun.

The York (Pa.) Fair, one of the oldest in the country, started in 1765, eleven years before the Declaration of Independence. Back then, neighboring farmers got together once a year to show off their best livestock and skills and everyone went home with tips to improve their farms. Today's fairs still center on agriculture, even though 98 percent of the country's population is now urban.

But fairs also have adapted to city interests. Now there may be ostriches, llamas, and angora goats as well as cows, pigs, and rabbits. The Orange County (Calif.) Fair's "sheep to shawl" exhibit connects farm animals to modern couture, the Ozark Empire (Mo.) Fair's highly popular Birthing Center welcomes dozens of calves into the world to audience acclaim, and excitement runs high as competitors bet on powerful frog legs at the Calaveras County (Calif.) Fair and Jumping Frog Jubilee. Not content with only apple-pie contests, the Utah State Fair adds chili cook-offs and salsa competitions, and the Del Mar (Calif.) Fair rates the best home-brew in its beer-making contest. Multimedia computer exhibits, complete with virtual-reality games, are just as likely now as livestock exhibits.

Fairs increasingly feature top entertainment. Country stars such as John Michael Montgomery, Patty Loveless, and Alabama join old rock stars such as the Doobie Brothers, Pat Benatar, Huey Lewis and the News, and The Neville Brothers. Rodeos, big-top circuses, stock-car races, horse and harness racing, and boxing add to the excitement.

The midway, with its games and Ferris wheels, adds daring thrill rides. The Minnesota State Fair has featured the 125-foot-high Ejection Seat towers, while California State Fair-goers have thrilled to the Skyscraper, two 16-story towers positioned like airplane propeller blades that perform dive-bomb spins, accelerating riders at the end of each tower to speeds of up to 70 mph.

Fairs reflect local cultures. The Los Angeles County Fair meets a particularly complex challenge by including the usual butter-churning and husband-calling contests, then adding the Chinese Moon Festival, the Latino Independence Parade, Halau Kau Ike O Lani, Mo Better Blues, Trinidad Steel Drum Band, and Mariachi Sol de Mexico. Even the Arizona State Fair reflects its region—its UFO Encounters puts participants through an interactive re-creation of four types of alien abductions.

Why do fairs have such staying power? One reason is money. Minnesota estimates the total economic impact of its state fair at $80 million annually. That's quite an increase from the first Hopkinton (NH) State Fair in 1915, which reported net profits of less than five dollars. Fairs make history, too. In 1955, a vendor distributed flying disks at the Los Angeles County Fair. These days, who doesn't own a Frisbee?

Top Ten Best-Attended US Fairs

1. State Fair of Texas, Dallas - 3,479,425
2. Houston Livestock Show and Rodeo, Houston, Texas - 1,788,437
3. State Fair of Oklahoma, Oklahoma City - 1,741,515
4. Minnesota State Fair, Minneapolis-St. Paul - 1,683,454
5. Los Angeles County Fair, Pomona, Calif. - 1,277,250
6. Western Washington Fair, Puyallup, Wash. - 1,265,171
7. Eastern States Exposition, West Springfield, Mass. - 1,226,069
8. Tulsa State Fair, Oklahoma - 1,165,789
9. Del Mar (Calif.) Fair - 1,085,000
10. Erie County Fair and Exposition, Hamburg, NY - 965,822

The Preakness
(Preakness Celebration)

Origin: 1873	Event ★ ★ ★ City	Attendance 90,000

For the hard-core horse-racing crowd, the world-renowned ***Preakness*** is the high-stakes follow-up to the Kentucky Derby. But for the 150,000 partyers in Baltimore, the second jewel in horse racing's Triple Crown is really just an excuse for a Mardi Gras-style celebration, complete with a black-tie ball. You can be part of the pomp that surrounds the sport of kings in the Pimlico Race Course's grandstand, which rivals Ascot's Royal Enclosure for fancy dress and refined manners.

Or cruise the infield, where wet T-shirts and cheap beer carry the day. If your breeding wasn't good enough to get you an invitation to the former, or too good for the latter, there's always a great party in the corporate-hospitality Preakness village.

Race fever is at a critical level by the Thursday night before the race, when the black-tie ***Triple Crown Ball*** attracts a Who's Who of Baltimore —from politicians and corporate bigwigs to the region's horse-happy gentry. Other events include a parade, crab race, and week-long block party. All this is mere warm-up, however, for a raucous day at the races on the third Saturday of May, which combines a series of quaint traditions with let-it-all-hang-out revelry.

Baltimore, with a population of more than 700,000, was once the butt of unkind jokes. In the last 20 years, though, what was once an ugly duckling of a city has grown into a savvy swan. Downtown has gotten a makeover, especially the revitalized harbor. Once-decaying factories and warehouses are now occupied by chic restaurants and boutiques. Hidden within the shiny new city are remnants of a rich past that began in the early 18th century when forward-looking settlers saw the potential of Chesapeake Bay (which harbors the country's third-largest port). The city's cuisine is built on the Chesapeake's shellfish, an object of local love and obsession. Eating, clubbing, and sightseeing for three days among the world's equestrian elite in one of America's best "new" cities will erase any doubts you may have had about Baltimore's resurgence.

The Preakness

Day 1. Thu. May 13, 1999
(Day 1. Thursday   May 18, 2000)

10:00am Leave your elegant, red-brick **Harbor Court Hotel** (it overlooks the water) to drive or cab up the Charles Street corridor. A former neighborhood of railroad barons, it's now filled with restaurants and boutiques. Stop at the 1806 neoclassical masterpiece, the **Basilica of the Assumption**. Continue past mansion-lined Mount Vernon Square to the **Baltimore Museum of Art**, which holds one of the world's largest Andy Warhol collections.

12:30pm A short drive back to Lexington Market allows you to enjoy the oldest continuously operating market in the United States and the *Preakness Crab Derby.*

1:30pm Head back to the harbor and the American Visionary Art Museum for lunch at **Joy America Cafe**. The food is just what you'd expect—multicultural-Pacific-Rim-fusion-organic with a touch of Southwestern-Italian!

3:00pm The **American Visionary Art Museum**, the newest museum in Baltimore, is the only one in the country restricted to works by self-taught "artists" drawn from various walks of life.

5:00pm Stroll the promenade along Inner Harbor. Stop for oysters on the half shell or steamed shrimp at one of Harborplace's seafood stands.

7:30pm Although the venue changes, the *Triple Crown Ball* is always the highlight of Baltimore's social season. This black-tie traditionbound event has a definite Southern charm. Attractive hostesses clad in jockey satins bring appetizers and drinks while guests review the high-class silent-auction items. At 8:30 p.m., the most entertaining bugler you've ever heard announces dinner with his "Call to Post." The feast is punctuated with blessedly short speeches and hobnobbing. Afterward, a big-name pop band plays and the tony crowd breaks stuffy tradition by packing the dance floor.

Midnight There's still time (till 2 a.m.) for a drink and more dancing—salsa style—at the nearby **Havana Club**.

Day 2. Fri. May 14,1999
(Day 2. Friday   May 19, 2000)

8:00am Have a room-service breakfast while enjoying your room's harbor view and attractive period-reproduction furniture.

9:00am An early start beats long lines at the **National Aquarium**, just steps from your hotel. A self-guided tour takes you past four floors of extraordinary exhibits up to the rooftop rainforest.

11:00am Get a higher perspective on Baltimore from **The Top of the World**, a 27th-floor observatory atop the World Trade Center, the world's tallest pentagonal building. The sights are accompanied by a worthwhile dose of informative exhibits.

Noon At ground level in the Harborplace Amphitheater, watch well-known locals compete in the *Celebrity Crab-Picking Contest*. Then follow the Harborside promenade to **Phillips Harborplace**, a favorite stop for the city's seafood lovers. The famed blue crabs are prepared in a variety of ways—crab cakes, soft-shell crab sandwiches, crab imperial, and steamed crabs. Cap off your meal with some **Thrasher's** fries, flavored with liberal doses of salt and vinegar.

3:00pm Take a two-hour jaunt on **Clipper City**'s replica of an 1854 clipper ship. Major waterfront sites include Fort McHenry, home of the original star-spangled banner that inspired the national anthem.

5:00pm A few blocks from the hotel, Water Street hosts **Bud Light Nights**, a week-long block party with rock bands and copious amounts of anything you want to drink as long as it's Bud. Or head to the **Preakness Pub** (5–8 p.m.) where celebrity jockeys tend bar and tell suprisingly tall tales.

8:30pm Take a short drive to **Charleston**, one of Baltimore's hot new restaurants featuring Southern style and cuisine.

10:00pm Near your hotel, there's live jazz nightly at **Buddies Pub and Jazz Club**. The clientele ranges from bohemian to professional. You can also go to **Pisces** for dancing to Top-40 music, or for a younger, louder scene, the **Baja Beach Club**.

Day 3. Sat. May 15, 1999
(Day 3. Saturday   May 20, 2000)

9:00am Try the new **Donna's** for a complete breakfast that will get you off to a strong start.

11:30am Pimlico Race Course, 20 minutes' drive—with reasonable parking options—offers four ways to enjoy the *Preakness Stakes*, the ninth race of the day. (Gates open at 8:30 a.m., first race is at 11 a.m.) You can join Baltimore's elite in the reserved grandstand (invitation only), sit in the grandstand (ordinary), cruise the infield with the shorts-and-T-shirt crowd (wild), or finesse an invite to sip champagne at the corporate tents clustered around the finish line (fun). Unfortunately, Pimlico's design and large crowds make it difficult to move from one area to another.

4:50pm In the infield, a local radio station's T-shirt give-away—which consists of women giving away their own T-shirts—is over. In the corporate tents, you've consulted psychics to help you pick the winners and downed your final "black-eyed Susan" (a good one has bourbon, Kahlua, triple sec, and orange juice). Joe Kelly sounds the "Call to Post" and prepares you for the singing of "Maryland, My Maryland."

5:00pm Jockey for position to see the big race. In two minutes, the winner will be blanketed with black-

The spirit of Baltimore and the *Preakness* may best be represented by Joe Kelly, the bugler brought in annually from Chicago just for the race. He plays the jazziest "Call to Post" you'll ever hear. "I took a very boring, traditional post call and made it a lot of fun," Joe says. "The audiences love it. They can be losing money, they hear the music, they perk up, they start bopping." Joe's attitude also fittingly represents the spirit of this book. "No matter what your job is or what you're doing," he says, "you can find a way to have fun with it."

eyed Susans (just like the crowd) and paraded into the Winner's Circle. Leave before the 10th race—after collecting your winnings—to get out of the racecourse within a reasonable amount of time.

7:30pm Take a water taxi from the Inner Harbor to the Fell's Point area, where the younger *Preakness* crowd congregates. **Bertha's**, an eccentric and inexpensive restaurant known for its mussels, attracts professionals, locals, and artsy types.

10:00pm A few blocks away, **Bohager's** bar and grill has music and dancing. Spending what's left of your winnings at the **Cat's Eye Pub** (Irish music) or the appropriately named **Horse You Came In On** (soft rock) should be just the thing to get you racing back to Baltimore for next year's *Preakness*.

Alternatives

Two other hotels on the harbor with great views are the **Hyatt Regency Baltimore** and the **Renaissance Harborplace Hotel**.

Time permitting, check out the Mount Vernon area. Its **Walters Art Gallery** houses European paintings and medieval arms and armor. Nearby, the 1826 **Washington Monument**'s winding stairway leads to full-city views, and the **George Peabody Library** has a five-stories-high reading room lined with brass and leather. A good restaurant is **The Brewer's Art**. The elegant **Owl Bar** is a former haunt of F. Scott Fitzgerald and H.L. Mencken.

The Hot Sheet

HOTELS		ADDRESS	PH	FX		PRICE	RMS	BEST ROOMS
Harbor Court Hotel	★	550 Light St.	410-234-0550 800-824-0076	410-659-5925		$$$	203	Harbor vw
Hyatt Regency Baltimore	Alt	300 Light St.	410-528-1234 800-233-1234	410-685-3362		$$$	487	12th fl harbor vw
Renaissance Harborplace Hotel	Alt	202 E. Pratt St.	410-547-1200 800-468-3571	410-539-5780		$$$	622	12th fl harbor vw

RESTAURANTS	DAY	ADDRESS	PH		PRICE	REC	DRESS	FOOD
Bertha's	3	734 S. Broadway	410-327-5795		$$	D/L	Local	Seafood
The Brewer's Art	Alt	1106 N. Charles St.	410-547-6925		$$	D	Kazh	Mediterranean
Charleston	2	1000 Lancaster St.	410-332-7373		$$$	D	Yuppie	Southern
Donna's	3	2 W. Madison St.	410-385-0180		$	B/LD	Kazh	Pastries
Joy America Cafe	1	800 Key Hwy.	410-244-6500		$$	L/D	Kazh, Local	Southwestern, Asian, Italian fusion
Phillips Harborplace	2	301 Light St.	410-685-6600		$$	L/D	Local	Seafood
Thrasher's	2	301 Lake St.	410-837-1325		$	L/D	Local	French fries

NIGHTLIFE	DAY	ADDRESS	PH		COVER	REC*	DRESS	MUSIC
Baja Beach Club	2	55 Market Pl.	410-727-0468		$	P	Local	Rock
Bohager's	3	515 S. Eden St.	410-563-7220		$	M(F)	Local	Jazz, rock
Buddies Pub and Jazz Club	2	313 N. Charles St.	410-332-4200		None	M(F)	Local	Jazz
Cat's Eye Pub	3	1730 Thames St.	410-276-9085		None	M	Local	Jazz, blues, rock, Irish
Havana Club	1	600 Water St.	410-468-0022		None	MP	Yuppie	Salsa
Horse You Came In On	3	1626 Thames St.	410-327-8111		None	M	Kazh	Soft rock, Latin
Owl Bar	Alt	1 E. Chase St.	410-347-0888		None	MP(F)	Local	Swing
Pisces	2	see the Hyatt Regency Baltimore	410-528-1234		None	P(F)	Local	Top 40

SIGHTS & ATTRACTIONS	DAY	ADDRESS	PH		ENTRY FEE
American Visionary Art Museum	1	800 Key Hwy.	410-244-1900		$
Baltimore Museum of Art	1	10 Art Museum Dr.	410-396-7100		$
Basilica of the Assumption	1	408 N. Charles St.	410-727-3564		None
Clipper City	2	301 Light St.	410-539-6277		$$
George Peabody Library	Alt	17 E. Mt. Vernon	410-659-8179		None
National Aquarium	2	510 E. Pratt St.	410-576-3800		$$
The Top of the World	2	401 E. Pratt St.	410-837-8439		$
Walters Art Gallery	Alt	600 N. Charles St.	410-547-9000		$
Washington Monument	Alt	Mt. Vernon Pl.	410-396-0929		$
Baltimore CVB		301 E. Pratt St.	410-659-7300		

Event & Ticket Info

Preakness (Pimlico Race Course, 5201 Park Heights Ave.): Tickets for seats ($45–$70) or standing-only ($12–$20) go on sale the day after Thanksgiving. Seats often sell out by February, but scalped tickets are available on the day of the race. For tickets and information, contact *Pimlico Race Course* (410-542-9400). Hot Tip: Exactly two weeks before the race, returned Horseman's Box seats go on sale ($130–$150), but these great seats sell out within hours.

Triple Crown Ball (Venue to be confirmed): Tickets ($275 CD) should be purchased well in advance from *Preakness Celebration* (410-837-3030).

Bud Lights Nights (Water Street): Get tickets ($3) at the gate.

Celebrity Crab-Picking Contest (Harborplace Ampitheater): Free. For more information, call 410-332-4191.

Preakness Crab Derby (Lexington Market, 400 W. Lexington St.): Free. For more information, call 410-685-6169.

Preakness Pub (Sheraton Inner Harbor Hotel, 300 S. Charles St.): Free. For more information, contact *Preakness Celebration* (410-837-3030).

* M=Live music; P=Dancing (Party); R=Bar only; S=Show; (F)=Food served. For further explanation of codes, see page 14.

 NYC   Baltimore - Washington (BWI) <30 min./$20 No 53°/75° (12°/24°)

  The Fun Also Rises

Memphis in May Barbecue
(Memphis in May World Championship Barbecue Cooking Contest)

| Origin: 1976 | Event ★ ★ ★ ★ ★ ★ City | Attendance: 80,000 |

Memphis is smokin'! One million disciples of blues, beer, and barbecue descend on this city by the Mississippi during the month-long *Memphis in May* festival, highlighted by the world's largest and most prestigious barbecue contest. Although this cookin' of pork grabs the spotlight, the aura of American originals such as Elvis and B.B. King ensure that a trip to the River City means much more than that.

Tom Lee Park, bordering the mighty river, is party central for the *Memphis in May World Championship Barbecue Cooking Contest*. Held the third weekend of the month, more than 240 invited international teams, sporting names like Aporkalypse Now and Swinefeld, compete for pride and prize money. Thirty-three acres of distinctively decorated booths set the stage for wild, noisy, and informal parties, as teams prepare a variety of whole pigs, ribs, shoulders, and both dry and wet spices.

Health codes demand that you be a "guest" of a team in order to sample their barbecue. This simply entails chatting up a team member and getting invited into their area. Don't be shy—arranging "invites" is common and the only way to sample much of what this event offers.

Eating, however, is only part of the action. The Hog Calling, Ms. Piggie, and Showmanship contests will redefine your notion of hams (the human kind). Live music and dancing add fuel to the party fires as afternoon fades into night.

Ever since vaudeville days, when Beale Street was crammed with theaters, musicians have been drawn to Memphis—"I've got a fifth of whiskey and a case of the blues," reads one T-shirt—and it's no accident Elvis turned up here to make famous his blend of blues, gospel, and country sounds. So what if Beale is only four blocks long? The historic stretch of blacktop is packed with clubs and music and can rock until 6 a.m., thanks to its special licensing law.

Tennessee's largest city and home to half a million people, Memphis is easy to get around. The weather, river, Elvis, blues, and barbecue team up for one of the South's spiciest weekends of the year.

Memphis in May Barbecue

Day 1. Thu.   May 20, 1999
(Day 1. Thursday   May 18, 2000)

10:00am Check in at the landmark, perfectly located **Peabody Hotel**, the address of choice in Memphis. Antique luxury and attentive service will make you feel like a Southern aristocrat.

10:30am Across the street from the Peabody, the **Memphis Music Hall of Fame Museum** claims the biggest collection of Elvis mementoes outside of Graceland. Memorabilia-filled display cases trace the history of the blues in Memphis. A few blocks away, continue your musical sojourn with a one-hour tour of **Sun Studio**, where Elvis first recorded.

1:00pm Drive to nearby Overton Square and the **Public Eye** for your first taste of 'cue at this family-oriented restaurant. They serve some of Memphis' best "dry" ribs.

2:30pm The **Memphis Brooks Museum of Art** in Overton Park is a short drive and pleasant afternoon respite. The park and museum building provide an attractive setting for a small but wide-ranging collection.

4:30pm Have a drink at the Peabody's lobby bar, then join visitors who come to see the famous **Peabody Ducks**. At 11 a.m. and 5 p.m. daily, five well-cared-for ducks traverse a red carpet from the elevator to the travertine fountain in the middle of the hotel's elegant lobby. You can follow the ducks home—they live on the roof—for a Thursdays-in-May Sunset Serenade on **The Peabody Rooftop**. If there's a "scene" in Memphis, this is it.

7:00pm (The festival runs 3–11 p.m.) Walk a few blocks to Tom Lee Park for the outrageous *Hog Calling Contest*, followed by a performance of the *Ms. Piggy Contest* winners. Allow time to make the one-mile walk from the festival entrance, past the spectacle of barbecue booths/homes, to the main stage.

9:00pm Take a different path back through the park, exit at Beale Street, and walk to **Elvis Presley's Memphis**. The restaurant serves American cuisine, including many of Elvis' favorites such as meatloaf and grilled peanut-butter-and-banana sandwiches. There's a stage for live '50s-'70s music, a dance floor, and video monitors throughout that supplement live performances with fun-filled Elvis nostalgia.

11:00pm If you're a night owl, drive an hour to gamble in Tunica, Mississippi—which boasts the country's third-largest collection of casinos after Las Vegas and Atlantic City. Or check out Beale Street before the weekend crowds arrive.

Day 2. Fri.   May 21, 1999
(Day 2. Friday   May 19, 2000)

9:00am Drive to **The Arcade** for a traditional Southern breakfast of grits, eggs, and smoked bacon in a 1950s setting. Elvis used to hang out here with friends. His booth is the last one on the left.

10:00am Graceland, a 20-minute drive, is more interesting than most people expect. You'll need at least two hours to take the fascinating tape-guided tour of Elvis Presley's far-from-humble abode and final resting place and to view other exhibits across the street. When you leave Graceland, you'll feel as if you knew the King.

1:00pm Near the Peabody, have lunch at **Cafe Samovar**. Russian food, such as blinis and borscht, makes for a nifty switch from barbecue and Elvis. A nearby alternative is **Ciao Cucina**, a great place for Italian food.

3:00pm Head back to Tom Lee Park for the entertainment highlight—the *Showmanship* competition. Teams lip-sync to popular songs with lyrics irreverently changed to pay homage to pigs and more.

4:00pm Get down to the serious business of barbecue and the high points of the festival. Tension and excitement fill the air as competitors prepare for Saturday's judging. Despite a competitive seriousness, family, friends, and business associates taste, schmooze, and party heavily. Get yourself invited to do the same by becoming a barbecue team's "guest," or buy dinner from the vendors and simply enjoy the sunset and scene.

11:00pm Your nightcap possibilities include Beale Street and the lobby bar at the Peabody.

Day 3. Sat. May 22, 1999
(Day 3. Saturday   May 20, 2000)

9:00am Before walking to the festival, have breakfast in **Cafe Expresso**, the Peabody's pastry-shop-cum-deli.

11:00am Tom Lee Park has undergone a transformation. The music has stopped, trash has disappeared, and barbecue areas have been carefully decorated. Team members don clean aprons or T-shirts with their logos. Tables are sometimes set with crystal, candelabras, flowers, and wine. The judging team arrives (ushered in by a team member who then "guards" the gate), gets a tour and introduction to all team members, and is served the team's cuisine, accompanied by an entertaining verbal description. If the team makes the finals, they will be revisited by different judges a few hours later.

1:00pm Break for lunch at the Peabody's casual **Dux** restaurant. Then drive to the **National Civil Rights Museum**, which has converted the site of Martin Luther King Jr.'s assassination into an emotional exhibit.

6:30pm Find out if your favorite barbecued ribs are, in fact, the world's greatest as the festival culminates with the *awards ceremony*. With a last taste of 'cue and a beer, bid farewell to the friends you've made.

8:30pm If you're hungry, walk to **Automatic Slim's Tonga Club** for a dinner featuring Caribbean, Southwestern, and New York-style cuisine. Admire the zebra skins and modern furnishings of this top rendezvous spot.

10:30pm Nighttime on Beale Street! This lively strip pulsates with jazz, Delta blues, rock, rhythm and blues, and a smattering of gospel. The street will be packed with drinking-age kids, the clubs with adults. A good place to start is **B.B. King's Club & Restaurant**. Down the street is the **Rum Boogie Cafe**, where you can check out guitars that once belonged to the legends who have performed on this grand boulevard of blues.

2:00am After all this living high on the hog, beat the sun back to the Peabody. Then sing the blues about tomorrow's departure before hunkering down to a sleep befitting a king.

Alternatives

Memphis in May's other top weekend is the ***Beale Street Music Festival***, usually held the first weekend in May. This one attracts a younger crowd than the barbecue festival. The usual activity on Beale Street, combined with approximately 80 acts performing on six stages in Tom Lee Park, guarantees a musically fulfilling weekend. ***Elvis Week***, held the beginning of each August, is a kingly series of movies, parties, concerts, and activities.

Memphis' downtown lacks a choice of top-class hotels. For a good location near Beale Street, the **Radisson Hotel Memphis** has a pool, sauna, and exercise room, and the **Holiday Inn Select Downtown** is somewhat better than standard.

Sleep Out Louie's is a popular oyster bar with live music on weekends. The blues clubs on Beale Street are not known for their food (which is mostly 'cue), but a good late-night dive for food and music is **Blues City Cafe**. When you go to the Brooks Museum, a good alternative for lunch is their **Brushmark Restaurant**, which serves an adequate selection of Nouvelle American cuisine. The unusual **Mud Island** includes a scale model of the Mississippi River and a museum devoted to the river, its history, and the people who have lived alongside it.

The Hot Sheet

HOTELS		ADDRESS	PH	FX	PRICE	RMS	BEST ROOMS
Holiday Inn Select Downtown	Alt	160 Union Ave.	901-525-5491 800-465-4329	901-529-8950	$$	192	King Executive
Peabody Hotel	★	149 Union Ave.	901-529-4000 800-732-2639	901-529-3600	$$	520	S. side 10th/11th flrs w/vw of river
Radisson Hotel Memphis	Alt	185 Union Ave.	901-528-1800 800-333-3333	901-526-3226	$$	276	King resort rms face Beale or Union sts

RESTAURANTS	DAY	ADDRESS	PH	PRICE	REC	DRESS	FOOD
The Arcade	2	540 S. Main St.	901-526-5757	$	B/L	Yuppie	Southern
Automatic Slim's Tonga Club	3	83 S. 2nd St.	901-525-7948	$$	D/L	Yuppie	Caribbean fusion
Blues City Cafe	Alt	138 Beale St.	901-526-3637	$	LD	Local	Southern
The Brushmark Restaurant	Alt	1934 Poplar in the Brooks Museum	901-722-3555	$	L	Local	American
Cafe Expresso	3	see the Peabody Hotel	901-529-4000	$	B/LD	Local	Pastries, deli
Cafe Samovar	2	83 Union Ave.	901-529-9607	$	L/D	Yuppie	Russian
Ciao Cucina	2	135 S. Main St.	901-529-0560	$	L/D	Yuppie	Italian
Dux	3	see the Peabody Hotel	901-529-4000	$$	L/BD	Yuppie	Southern
Elvis Presley's Memphis	1	126 Beale St.	901-527-6900	$$	D/L	Local	American
Public Eye	1	17 S. Cooper St.	901-726-4040	$	L/D	Local	Barbecue

NIGHTLIFE	DAY	ADDRESS	PH	COVER	REC*	DRESS	MUSIC
B.B. King's Club & Restaurant	3	143 Beale St.	901-524-5464	$$	MP(F)	Local	Blues, R&B
Blues City Cafe	Alt	see restaurants	901-526-3637	$	M(F)	Local	Blues
Elvis Presley's Memphis	1	see restaurants	901-527-6900	$	MP(F)	Local	Oldies, rockabilly
The Peabody Rooftop	1	see the Peabody Hotel	901-529-4000	$	MP	Local	Rock, blues
Rum Boogie Cafe	3	182 Beale St.	901-528-0150	$	MP	Local	Blues
Sleep Out Louie's	Alt	88 Union Ave.	901-527-5337	None	M	Local	Jazz

SIGHTS & ATTRACTIONS	DAY	ADDRESS	PH	ENTRY FEE
Graceland	2	3764 Elvis Presley Blvd.	901-332-3322	$$
Memphis Brooks Museum of Art	1	1934 Poplar Ave. in Overton Park	901-722-3500	$
Memphis Music Hall of Fame Museum	1	97 S. 2nd St.	901-525-4007	$
Mud Island	Alt	125 N. Front St.	901-576-7241	$
National Civil Rights Museum	3	450 Mulberry St.	901-521-9699	$
The Peabody Ducks	1	see the Peabody Hotel	901-529-4000	None
Sun Studio	1	706 Union Ave.	901-521-0664	$
Memphis CVB		119 N. Riverside Dr.	901-543-5333	

Event & Ticket Info

Memphis in May World Championship Barbecue Cooking Contest (Tom Lee Park): Tickets ($12) are available at the park, or can be purchased in advance through *Memphis in May* or *Ticketmaster* (901-525-1515). For more information, contact *Memphis in May* (901-525-4611 ext. 108).

Alternative Events

Beale Street Music Festival: *Memphis in May*, 901-525-4611 ext. 108

Elvis Week: *Graceland*, 901-322-3322

* M=Live music; P=Dancing (Party); R=Bar only; S=Show; (F)=Food served. For further explanation of codes, see page 14.

 NYC–1   Memphis (MEM) <30 min./$20 Yes/No   61°/81° (16°/27°)

More Barbecue To Chew On

Memphians consider themselves the nation's purveyors of "true" barbecue—they emphasize pork, not beef; pay rigid attention to achieving the right culinary combination of smoke, heat, and time; and specialize in dry-rubbed seasoning (not that gooky stuff most of us call barbecue sauce).

But barbecue is a strong part of American culture everywhere, inspiring nostalgia, patriotism, zeal, and deep divisions in spelling preference. The word *barbecue* was first used around 1666. It derives from French-speaking pirates who called this type of pork feast *de barbe et queue*, which means "from head to tail."

- Seventy-five percent of American households own a barbecue grill; these are used an average of five times per month.

- Forty-two percent of consumers say the most popular form of home entertaining is a barbecue or cook-out party.

- Men do 59 percent of the barbecuing, but women decide to have 57 percent of barbecues.

- The United States is home to about 11,000 barbecue restaurants.

- The most popular occasions for a barbecue and the percentage of the population that participates: Fourth of July (81 percent), Labor Day (70 percent), Memorial Day (66 percent).

There are more than 400 barbecue contests held annually in the United States. The biggest ones are Memphis in May World Championship Barbecue Cooking Contest, the Kansas City American Royal Barbecue Contest, and the World's Championship Bar-B-Que in Houston.

Top Barbecue Competitions

Name	Month	Location	Phone	Attend.	Teams	Prizes
Memphis in May World Championship Barbecue Cooking Contest	May	Memphis, Tenn.	901-525-4611	80,000	240	$40,000
Kansas City American Royal Barbecue Contest	Oct.	Kansas City, Kan.	816-221-9800	45,000	300	$30,000
World's Championship Bar-B-Que	Feb.	Houston, Texas	713-791-9000	175,000	341	trophy
World Pork Expo The Great Pork BarbeQlossal	Jun.	Des Moines, Iowa	515-223-2622	50,000	102	$27,000
Great Lenexa Barbecue Battle	Jun.	Lenexa, Kan.	913-541-8592	25,000	160	$2,500
Blue Ridge Barbecue Festival	Jun.	Tryon, NC	704-859-6236	19,000	66	$17,000
Ribs Burnoff	Jul.	Canton, Ohio	800-533-4302	250,000	56	$4,000
Central California Rib Cookoff	Apr.	Fresno, Calif.	209-432-6766	70,000	80	$2,300

High Times

Observation decks on towers and tall buildings are a feature of most cities in this book. When travelers ascend these universally popular landmarks, they're continuing a tradition thousands of years old. Early humans always surveyed their surroundings from high vantage points—watching for enemies, looking for food, waiting for loved ones to come home. Trees and hills were the first lookouts. Towers built of wood, stones, and bricks followed.

The development of steel and steel-beam construction, however, revolutionized builders' capabilities. Adding high-strength concrete provided compression resistance and minimized vibration. With the addition of elevators, telephones, and electric lights, even the sky no longer seemed the limit.

Built in Chicago in 1885, the first skyscraper was a monument to an insurance company. The Home Insurance Building, at 180 feet tall, employed a totally different concept from traditional towers, with its 11 floors built to be occupied, not just used as lookout posts. It was soon obvious that skyscrapers were a natural in New York City, too, where the best way to maximize scarce and expensive urban land was to build straight up. Surprisingly, several of its tallest skyscrapers were built during the Great Depression, with the Empire State Building taking the "highest" crown in 1931 at 1,250 feet.

The New York/Chicago skyscraper competition heated up a few decades later with the John Hancock Center and Amoco Building in Chicago and the World Trade Center towers in New York. Chicago's Sears Tower took the crown in 1974, at 1,450 feet (not counting twin antennae more than 250 feet tall), and held the "world's tallest" title until the 1997 opening of the Petronas Towers in Kuala Lumpur, Malaysia.

Determining the world's tallest building seems straightforward, but recognized criteria now include four categories. The Sears Tower still qualifies for two "top" honors (height to rooftop and highest occupied floor). New York's World Trade Center One is highest to the top of its antenna. The Petronas Towers are highest in the world to the architectural top. Builders in Tokyo, however, are planning a skyscraper a half-mile high.

CN tower in Toronto at 1,815 feet, though not technically a building, is North America's tallest structure with an observation floor. Visitors to the World Trade Center Two can look out over New York City from the world's highest outdoor viewing platform, 110 floors up, but even cities with more modest skylines boast high points with incredible views, often with restaurants added. Seattle's Space Needle, San Francisco's Embarcadero Skydeck, Houston's Chase Tower Skylobby, St. Louis' Gateway Arch, Boston's Prudential Tower Skywalk, all provide thrills to visitors who come to see the sights.

The Five Tallest Buildings in North America With 100 or More Stories

Building	City	Year Built	Stories	Height Structural Top	Spire/Ant.	Obs. Deck/Rest.(R)
Sears Tower	Chicago	1974	110	1450'	1707'	103
World Trade Center, One	New York	1972	110	1368'	1728'	106R, 107
World Trade Center, Two	New York	1972	110	1362'	1362'	107,110R
Empire State Building	New York	1931	102	1250'	1472'	86
John Hancock Center	Chicago	1969	100	1127'		94, 95R

Indy 500

(The 500 Festival)

Origin: 1911   **Event** ★ ★ ★ ★ ★ **City**   **Attendance:** 400,000

Noise, speed, sun, danger, and courage are the hallmarks of the *Indianapolis 500*, but the days leading up to the big race are filled with the kind of go-for-broke excitement that turns the whole *Indy* package into the "greatest spectacle in racing." Two types of zealot are attracted to *Indy*—racing fans and party fans—and there's more than enough going on to keep everybody's motor running.

The actual race—a few hours around a 2.5-mile oval that circles part of a golf course and accommodates up to 500,000 spectators —is the biggest single sporting event in the world. Cars whiz by at 235 mph, fans debate timeless racing questions, such as the merits of Firestone vs. Goodyear and Bud vs. Miller, and the auto world's latest hero is crowned.

Fans longing for bawdy partying and topless women at the track's infield Snake Pit should be aware that the *Indy 500* has recently become kinder and gentler. Speedway officials have gone out of their way to make the *Indy 500* a more family-oriented event. Organized activities, such as *FanFest*, have replaced Snake Pit debauchery, which is why, unless you're a racing fan, the three days before the race are actually more fun than the race itself.

Most higher-end partying is underwritten by sponsors. With a few strategic phone calls, you could bag a sponsorship connection through a local business back home. You could spend an afternoon at a swanky hospitality suite, at a banquet in the garage of restaurateur/team owner Jonathan Byrd, or at former *500*-driver Stefan Johansson's Karting Center. Even if you don't hook into a private party, your days and nights will be filled.

Indianapolis is the state's capital, with a population of more than 800,000 that spends half a year getting ready for the *Indy 500*, another few months preparing for NASCAR's Brickyard 400, and the rest of the year recuperating. As most locals already know, a few days at *The 500 Festival* are generally enough to teach even the most staunch partyer the value of a pit stop. So, plan for a restful week after leaving this heartland hell raiser.

Day-By-Day Plan For

Indy 500

Day 1. Thu.　May 27, 1999
(Day 1. Thursday　　　　May 25, 2000)

9:00am After a hotel breakfast, drive from your four-star accommodations at **The Westin Hotel Indianapolis** to the City of Speedway. You can't miss the track, it's like approaching Stonehenge—a monument of mythic proportions. Today is *Carburetion Day*, the last chance for *Indy 500* drivers to practice.

10:00am Stop at the **Indianapolis Motor Speedway Hall of Fame Museum**. Worship displays of 30 *Indy 500* winners as well as a variety of classic and antique cars. Drop in on *FanFest* (9 a.m.-6 p.m.), a hands-on entertainment center with race-car simulators.

11:00am Final practice runs start at 11 a.m. Two to three cars at a time take a few turns and crews make last-minute adjustments.

12:30pm Next to the Hall of Fame Museum, grab lunch at the Gasoline Alley Cafe or the Pepsi Pit Stop.

1:30pm Teams compete to fuel and change tires at breakneck speed during the annual *Pit Stop Competition*. Speed here is just as important as on the track. Races have been won and lost in the pits.

3:30pm A *live concert* (until 6 p.m.), entertains the crowds with rock music.

7:30pm Palomino Euro Bistro is a good example of a hip chain of restaurants. The New Italian menu is almost as good as the people-watching scene.

10:00pm Help 5,000 others consume 150 barrels and 200 cases of beer at the *Rally in the Alley* (4 p.m.-midnight), an outdoor dance party sponsored by **Ike and Jonesy's**. The party starts in front of the club, then moves inside after midnight.

Day 2. Fri.　May 28, 1999
(Day 2. Friday　　　　May 26, 2000)

9:00am Stroll to **Acapulco Joe's**, a funky restaurant that serves Mexican food as well as a traditional Hoosier breakfast of biscuits and gravy.

10:00am Make a quick visit to the **Saturday Evening Post Museum**, which houses a collection of *Post* covers from the '50s and '60s.

Noon Head back to the Westin for the *Championship Auto Racing Auxiliary's (CARA)* luncheon fashion show, which started at 11 a.m. Drivers and their wives and children strut in the latest fashions. Or drive to the exquisite **Snow Lion**. One of the few Tibetan restaurants in the United States, it's owned by the Dalai Lama's nephew, Jigme Norbu. If you request your food spicy, the chef will add enough zing to clear any sinus.

2:30pm At downtown's pleasant White River State Park is the **Eiteljorg Museum of American Indians and Western Art**, which has one of the nation's best collections of crafts, sculpture, and painting. Check out the **Canal Walk**, which has paddle boats for rent and a riverside outdoor cafe.

7:00pm Change into formal clothes and head to the Indiana Convention Center for the *Xerox 500 Ball*. Along with dinner and dancing, it features the introduction of the 500 Festival Queen, her court, and the 500 drivers, plus plenty of local VIPs.

Midnight A fun after-party spot—the ball runs until 2 a.m., but gets quiet after midnight—is the **Slippery Noodle Inn**, a historic blues joint that announces to everyone, "dis is it." Apparently that's true. It's been a roadhouse, a way station for the underground railroad, a bordello, a slaughterhouse, and the scene of a murder—with bullet slugs still in the wall to prove it.

Day 3. Sat.   May 29, 1999
(Day 3. Saturday   May 27, 2000)

10:00am After breakfast in your hotel, visit the 🅡 **Indianapolis Museum of Art**. A collection of J.M.W. Turner work is highlighted along with Asian and African art.

Noon *The 500 Festival Parade* marches down Pennsylvania Street, around Monument Circle, and north on Meridian toward 14th Street. About 250,000 spectators show up and many break out the noisemakers, masks, crowns, and red noses that come with each reserved seat.

4:00pm Take a reserved table for high tea at the 🅡 **Canterbury Hotel**. Tea and piano music make for a delightful contrast to the parade hubbub.

5:30pm Hire a **Yellow Rose Carriage** and ride around downtown's hub, Monument Circle. Or take in the 360-degree city view with a drink in the revolving **Eagle's Nest** restaurant atop the Hyatt hotel.

7:00pm Weather permitting, the Indianapolis Symphony Orchestra performs at *The Lilly 500 Family Festival* outdoor concert.

9:00pm Head to Indianapolis' most famous steakhouse, 🅡 the elegant **St. Elmo Steakhouse Restaurant**, which is lauded for its shrimp cocktail as well as its filets and prime rib. Tuxedoed waiters serve you in the Hulman Room, named for the Speedway's patriarch, the late Tony Hulman.

11:30pm You can hang around at 16th Street and Georgetown Road for the infamous *Indy 500*-eve party, but a more lively crowd preps for race day at Broad Ripple Village. Especially after midnight, it's a popular nightspot for young adults and professionals looking for music and bar-hopping in a casual atmosphere. While shopping around for your choice of live-music clubs, stop into **The Vogue**—one of the area's top spots—to put a fast finish on this weekend of classic American partying.

Alternatives

If you stay Sunday for the *Indy 500*, you can show up for the track opening at 5 a.m., even though the gentlemen don't actually start their engines until nearly 11 a.m. There's an early buffet breakfast at the Speedway American Legion.

Getting to the track isn't hard, it's leaving along with hundreds of thousands of others that's a pain. The city's Metro bus is efficient, but still no picnic. If you drive, buy a front-yard parking space from a local, or join veteran fans who park a few miles away and walk in to ensure a faster getaway.

Rent a scanner at the track to hear drivers talking to their crews. Radio frequencies are listed in the newspaper.

Not as stylish as the Westin, **The Hyatt Regency Indianapolis** does offer modern accommodations and a downtown location. Another is the **Omni Severin Hotel**. The best spot in town, the **Canterbury Hotel**, will likely be booked with *Indy* patrons.

Rick's Cafe Boatyard serves great food and has jazz and a quiet elegance. Two casual downtown restaurants are **California Cafe Bar & Grill** and **Buca di Beppo**. From the track, head to **Union Jack Pub**, a favorite local hangout for race-team members and drivers. Knock back beer with traditional American fare, surrounded by great race memorabilia. On Massachusetts Avenue, stop for coffee and dessert at the **Abbey Coffee House**. Broad Ripple Village is a fun daytime stop, with avant-garde restaurants and shops.

Event & Ticket Info (continued from next page)

Carburetion Day (Indianapolis Motor Speedway, 4790 W. 16th St.): Tickets ($10) never sell out and are available at the gate. Admission includes all events inside the Motor Speedway. For more information, contact *Indianapolis Motor Speedway* (317-484-6700).

Championship Auto Racing Auxiliary's Luncheon Fashion Show (Westin Hotel, 50 S. Capitol Ave.): Tickets ($50 CD) can be purchased from *Championship Auto Racing Auxiliary* (317-299-2277).

The Hot Sheet

HOTELS		ADDRESS	PH	FX	PRICE	RMS	BEST ROOMS
Canterbury Hotel	Alt	123 S. Illinois St.	317-634-3000 800-538-8186	317-299-9257	$$	99	City vw
The Hyatt Regency Indianapolis	Alt	1 S. Capitol Ave.	317-632-1234 800-233-1234	317-231-7569	$$	497	City vw
Omni Severin Hotel	Alt	40 W. Jackson St.	317-634-6664 800-843-6664	317-687-3619	$$	424	City vw
The Westin Hotel Indianapolis	★	50 S. Capitol Ave.	317-262-8100 800-937-8461	317-231-3928	$$	573	Dlx rms

RESTAURANTS	DAY	ADDRESS	PH	PRICE	REC	DRESS	FOOD
Abbey Coffee House	Alt	771 Massachusetts Ave.	317-269-8426	$	BLD	Local	Dessert
Acapulco Joe's	2	365 N. Illinois St.	317-637-5160	$	B/LD	Local	Mexican
Buca di Beppo	Alt	35 N. Illinois St.	317-632-2822	$$	D	Local	Italian
California Cafe Bar & Grill	Alt	Circle Center Mall, 3rd level	317-488-8686	$$	LD	Local, Kazh	California
Canterbury Hotel	3	see Canterbury Hotel	317-634-3000	$$	T	Yuppie	Tea, sandwiches
Eagle's Nest	3	see The Hyatt Regency	317-231-7566	$$$$	LD	Yuppie	American
Palomino Euro Bistro	1	49 W. Maryland St.	317-974-0400	$$$	D/L	Yuppie	Mediterranean
Rick's Cafe Boatyard	Alt	4050 Dandy Trail	317-290-9300	$$$	LD	Kazh	American
Snow Lion	2	236 S. Meridian St.	317-955-1680	$	L/D	Kazh	Tibetan
St. Elmo Steakhouse Restaurant	3	127 S. Illinois St.	317-635-0636	$$$$	D	Kazh	Steakhouse
Union Jack Pub	Alt	6225 W. 25th St.	317-243-3300	$$	LD	Local	American

NIGHTLIFE	DAY	ADDRESS	PH	COVER	REC*	DRESS	MUSIC
Ike and Jonesy's	1	12 Jackson Pl.	317-632-4553	$	P(F)	Local	Rock
Slippery Noodle Inn	2	372 S. Meridian St.	317-631-6974	$	MP(F)	Local	Blues
The Vogue	3	6259 N. College Ave.	317-259-7029	$	MP(F)	Kazh	'70s, disco, classic rock

SIGHTS & ATTRACTIONS	DAY	ADDRESS	PH	ENTRY FEE
Canal Walk	2	White River State Park		None
Eiteljorg Museum of American Indians and Western Art	2	500 W. Washington St.	317-636-9378	$
Indianapolis Motor Speedway Hall of Fame Museum	1	4790 W. 16th St.	317-484-6747	$
Indianapolis Museum of Art	3	1200 W. 38th St.	317-923-1331	None
Saturday Evening Post Museum	2	1100 Waterway Blvd.	317-636-8881	None
Yellow Rose Carriage	3	outside The Hyatt Regency	317-634-3400	$$$

Indianapolis CVB		210 S. Capitol Ave.	317-639-4282

Event & Ticket Info

The Indianapolis 500 (Indianapolis Motor Speedway, 4790 W. 16th St.): Tickets ($30 for terrace seats to $140 for penthouse box) generally sell out one year in advance. Requests for reserved seats are accepted only in writing. Order forms are available 13 months prior to the race. Orders are filled after the previous year's race. Contact Indianapolis Motor Speedway (PO Box 24152, Speedway, IN 46224; 317-484-6700).

Since scalping is legal in Indianapolis, you should be able to buy a seat at race time. Additionally, infield access tickets ($20) are available the day of the race.

Xerox 500 Ball (Indiana Convention Center, 100 S. Capitol Ave.): Tickets ($150) are available from The 500 Festival (800-638-4296).

The 500 Festival Parade (Pennsylvania Street, Monument Circle, then north up Meridian to 14th Street): The 45,000 reserved seats ($12–$20) sell out months in advance (this is the largest ticketed parade in North America). Though there's no charge to stand, the crowd makes it difficult to see. For tickets, contact The 500 Festival (800-638-4296).

The Lilly 500 Festival Family Concert (Victory Field, Maryland and West streets): For tickets ($1), which usually sell out by concert time, contact The 500 Festival (800-638-4296).

(continued on previous page)

* M=Live music; P=Dancing (Party); R=Bar only; S=Show; (F)=Food served. For further explanation of codes, see page 14.

 NYC   Indianapolis (IND) <30 min./$25 Yes/No 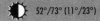 52°/73° (11°/23°)

Start Your Engines

The more than 400,000 spectators whose idea of fun is raw speed, horsepower, and noise make the Indianapolis 500 the largest-attended single-day sporting event on the planet. Auto racing is, in fact, one of the most popular spectator sports in the world, with a long list of car designs and styles of racing to suit every type of fan. To the neophyte, most racing cars might look similar, but track types and sanctioning organizations that govern various races dictate fundamental differences in each design.

Three of the races on our list of the world's most fun places to be—Indy 500, Macau Grand Prix, Monte Carlo Grand Prix—feature similar cars. Each is a midengined, open-wheeled, single-seat racer unsuitable for anything but competition. All are referred to as Formula cars because of certain technical criteria determined by racing's governing bodies. Typically, these criteria restrict the power of the engine in order to limit development costs and top speeds. Also, restrictions make the races more dependent on driver skill, thus avoiding a competition between design technologies.

The Indianapolis 500 is sanctioned by the *IRL* (Indy Racing League), an organization formed in 1996. IRL races are run on oval tracks, with an emphasis on top speed. A competing organization, *CART* (Championship Auto Racing Teams), runs open-wheeled racers, but top speeds may be considerably less, because most CART events are held on curvy road courses that slow down drivers.

Formula One (F1) racing is similar to CART racing, but it's generally concentrated in Europe. F1 racing is sanctioned by the Paris-based FIA (International Automotive Federation). Races are run exclusively on road courses, placing more emphasis on adhesion and traction than on sheer speed. The most famous of the European road races is at Monaco, where drivers blast through the streets of Monte Carlo on a narrow, dangerous course that has remained largely unchanged since the race's inception in 1929. F1 racing is tremendously expensive, but for manu-

facturers, the prestige of a championship is worth the expense, giving rise to a kind of macho snob appeal. When Indy and CART speeds rise, F1 engineers typically up the ante, working feverishly to make sure their cars remain the fastest.

Formula Three (F3) racing is essentially F1's baby brother. The cars are similar in design, only smaller and less powerful. Its main distinction is as a proving ground for racers, so it's common for F3 champions to graduate to F1 status.

The most popular and fastest-growing form of auto racing in the United States is stock-car racing sanctioned by *NASCAR* (National Association of Stock Car Auto Racing). With 32 major races at tracks primarily in the Southeast, NASCAR features American cars and American drivers. The term *stock*, however, is a misnomer. Stock cars may display the names of their showroom counterparts, but the technological similarities end there. Like IRL events, NASCAR races are held primarily on oval tracks, and its cars are designed to reach obscenely high speeds. At the speedway in Daytona, with its long straights and high banks, speeds of more than 220 mph have been recorded.

One of the world's most historically significant races is the 24 Hours of Le Mans *endurance race*. As the oldest race in Europe—run continuously since 1923—the prestige of winning Le Mans is immeasurable. Endurance races involve several classes of automobile, such as world sports cars (single-seat, open-top) and GT-1s (grand-touring cars), which tend to look like street cars, but are far more sophisticated. A lower class is GT-2, which includes heavily modified BMW M3s and Porsche 911s. Most endurance cars are designed for one race and one track only, and are completely rebuilt after each race. An endurance race is a grueling test to prove that a car can handle the punishment and speeds of a racetrack over a long period. If you've ever driven your car on a long road trip, imagine the strain of maintaining that endurance for not only three times as long, but at three or four times the speed.

Also popular in Europe is **rallying**, considered by some to be the most dangerous and exciting form of racing in the world. Rallying involves hurtling heavily modified sedans through all types of terrain, sometimes on dirt roads and through small towns, even at night. Each car contains a driver and a navigator who has carefully plotted the course for maximum speed and must dictate each directional nuance to the driver. The special stages (closed sections of public roads) sometimes use narrow dirt roads that involve great elevation changes, numerous hard turns, and plenty of bumps and ruts. The responsibility for victory weighs heavier on the driver and navigator than on the design of the car.

Amateur **vintage-car racing**, a hobby rather than a professional sport, is gaining popularity. Vintage racing involves driving older, obsolete race cars and road cars around existing road courses. Vintage race cars are all privately owned, races emphasize fun, and no trophies are awarded. In order to ensure safe competition that injures neither drivers nor their extremely valuable toys, cars are grouped in terms of age, type, and engine displacement. It wouldn't be much of a race if a 1920s Morgan was pitted against a mid-'70s Ferrari. Another distinction in vintage racing regards modifications. Some sanctioning groups insist that cars must be raced exactly as they were in their original time period, while others accept some technological upgrades, usually for safety or reliability. HMSA (Historic Motor Sports Association), the sanctioning group running the Monterey Historic Races, is among the most strict, allowing no modification beyond what was available to a car at the time of its manufacture.

A **concours d'elegance** event is based entirely on originality, style, and appearance. A car must have all of its original equipment and it must be operable, but the similarities to racing end there. It's a pure beauty contest, where the paint must shine, the seats must have no cracks, the engine must be spotlessly clean, the body work must be flawless, the wheels and tires must be polished, and the exhaust pipe must be clean of soot or rust. Concours judges check everything meticulously, inspecting carpets for loose threads, examining underbodies for rust, and making sure every part of a car is original and pristine. For a collector, the awarding of a Concours ribbon can immortalize a car, sometimes doubling its value.

"AND THEY'RE OFF ... "

The World's Top Races and Auto Competitions

IRL
- Indianapolis 500, Indianapolis, Ind.; May
- Lone Star 500, Fort Worth, Texas; Jun.
- Vision Air 500, Charlotte, NC; Jul.

NASCAR
- Daytona 500, Daytona Beach, Fla.; Feb.
- Brickyard 400, Indianapolis, Ind.; Aug.
- World 600 at Charlotte Motor Speedway, Charlotte, NC; May

CART
- Toyota Grand Prix of Long Beach, Long Beach, Calif.; Apr.
- Miller Lite 200 at the Milwaukee Mile, Milwaukee, Wis.; May or Jun.
- US 500, Michigan Speedway, Brooklyn, Mich.; Jul.

Formula One
- Monte Carlo Grand Prix, Monte Carlo, Monaco; May
- Belgian Grand Prix, Spa-Francorchamps, Belgium; Aug.
- Italian Grand Prix at Monza, Monza, Italy; Sep.

Rallying
- Royal Auto Club Rally, England; Nov.
- 1000 Lakes of Finland, Finland; Feb.
- New Zealand Rally/Australia Rally; Oct. and Nov.

Endurance Racing
- 24 Hours of Le Mans, Le Mans, France; Jun.
- 24 Hours of Daytona, Daytona Beach, Fla.; Feb.
- 12 Hours of Sebring, Sebring, Fla.; Feb.

Formula Three
- Macau Grand Prix, Taipa Island, Macau; Nov.
- Marlboro Masters of Formula 3, Zandvoort, Holland; Aug.
- British Championship Race, Brands Hatch, England; Sep.

Vintage Racing
- Monterey Historic Races, Monterey, Calif.; Aug.
- Chicago Historic Races, Elkhart Lake, Wis.; Jul.
- Goodwood Festival of Speed, Sussex, England; Jun.

Concours d'Elegance
- Pebble Beach Concours, Pebble Beach, Calif.; Aug.
- Meadow Brook Concours, Rochester, Mich.; Aug.
- Louis Vuitton Classic, New York, NY; Sep.

June 1999

M	T	W	T	F	S	S
	1	2	3	4	5	6
7	8	9	10	11	12	13
14	15	16	17	18	19	20
21	22	23	24	25	26	27
28	29	30				

San Francisco, California, USA

June 2000

M	T	W	T	F	S	S

No event in 2000

Black and White Ball

Origin: 1956	Event ★ ★ ★ ★ ★ ★ ★ City	Attendance: 12,000

Leave the color film at home and prepare yourself for a weekend in monochrome: The *Black and White Ball* turns San Francisco's Civic Center into a set from a glamorous black-and-white film, starring you and 10,000 or so other beautiful people. Too special to happen every year, the biennial ball is the largest one-night arts fund-raiser in the United States—benefiting the San Francisco Symphony—and is probably the world's largest indoor-outdoor black-tie ball.

After a four-year hiatus, 1999 marks the return of the *Black and White Ball* to the Civic Center (many of the buildings were being retrofitted for earthquake safety), meaning that, once again, the party can take advantage of the beautiful City Hall, Opera House, and Symphony Hall. Local professionals and socialites drink, eat, and dance away a night made dreamy by the bay-side fog and twinkling lights of one of the world's most romantic cities. Chinese lanterns hang from trees, balloons float through the air, champagne flows freely, and a laser-and-fireworks show lights up an already-glowing crowd of exquisitely dressed people. Sixteen related venues host more than 50 musical acts.

In keeping with the theme of this first-class event, a weekend itinerary should allow you time to discover the City by the Bay's most elegant diversions. (If you'd like to explore San Francisco's underbelly, see San Francisco Halloween, page 235.) Victorian houses, bay views, parks, and the Golden Gate Bridge are all on the daytime schedule. So is Muir Woods, one of North America's most impressive stands of ancient forest.

Nights begin with fantastic meals—San Francisco is the place where California cuisine originated and the number of outstanding restaurants is extraordinary—then move into the cosmopolitan night-life scenes that have made this city famous (and sometimes, infamous). Choices range from the loud and lusty to the mild and mellow, but all of them exude a familiar feeling—well-known to locals and devoted repeat visitors—that is uniquely San Francisco. You may not leave your heart in San Francisco, but you'll definitely give it a workout.

Black and White Ball

Day 1. Thu.   Jun. 3, 1999

9:00am At the French-inspired **Hotel Monaco**, your small but gorgeous room includes a canopy bed.

9:30am Drive to **Doidge's Cafe**. The breakfasts include fluffy French toast and eggs Benedict with corned-beef hash.

10:30am People-watch and browse along Union Street and nearby Chestnut Street.

Noon Drive to the scenic Pacific Heights and Presidio Heights areas and check out San Francisco's finest homes on your way to **Garibaldi's on Presidio**. This hottest neighborhood restaurant in San Francisco offers upscale Mediterranean lunches.

1:30pm Drive through the Presidio to the Marina. Pass the gorgeous Palace of Fine Arts, circle the entrance to the Golden Gate Bridge, and look for the stately, columned **California Palace of the Legion of Honor**. Views from the art museum and the Rodin sculptures make this a worthwhile detour.

3:30pm Returning from Golden Gate Park, stop for a drink and ocean view at the **Cliff House**.

7:00pm Begin the evening at the city's most comfortable drinking spot, the **Bubble Lounge**. The rest of the evening's venues are within walking distance, so taste various champagnes without worry.

8:00pm Eating at **Vertigo** or **Bix** makes you part of the San Francisco scene. French-accented American cuisine is served in a supper-club atmosphere at Bix—the active bar and live jazz make it a popular meet market. Vertigo, on the ground floor of the Transamerica building, is only a bit more subdued.

10:00pm Have a drink amid the mammarylike light fixtures, rich velvets, and bloated décor of the **Cypress Club** (dinner here is also an option).

11:00pm In the thick of North Beach night life, **Enrico's Sidewalk Cafe** bar has live blues and jazz and a heated sidewalk patio for people-watching. Across the street, **Black Cat** has become another popular spot for jazz.

Day 2. Fri.   Jun. 4, 1999

9:30am Drive to **Il Fornaio** for breakfast on the patio looking out on one of the nation's most attractive urban office parks. The fresh breakfast pastries are a treat.

11:00am Drive past Pier 39, Fisherman's Wharf, and Ghirardelli Square. Across the Golden Gate Bridge, pull off at the vista point at the north end of the bridge.

Noon Drive to **Muir Woods**, 17 miles north of San Francisco. If a noted conservationist says, "This is the best tree-lovers monument that could possibly be found in all the forests of the world," you should name the place after him. The national monument includes 560 acres of redwood forest, with some trees more than 200 feet high and 1,000 years old.

2:00pm On the way back to the city, stop in Sausalito for lunch at **The Spinnaker** restaurant. The main attraction is the view of the water, but the seafood is good.

4:00pm Browse downtown Sausalito's shops or drive into the hills and marvel at houses built on stilts in one of the world's earthquake centers. Wind up the hill (Conzelman Road) for spectacular views of the bridge and city.

5:00pm Back in San Francisco, stay on Lombard Street. The corner of Hyde and Lombard provides one of San Francisco's most magnificent views. It's also the start of the drive down the world's crookedest street.

7:30pm A few blocks from your hotel, have an aperitif

with well-groomed minglers crowding the bar at Wolfgang Puck's **Postrio Restaurant**. Many consider Postrio San Francisco's best restaurant, but ...

8:30pm Nearby, a fun dining experience awaits you at Scala's **Bistro**. A lively crowd fills the restaurant and bar. The menu offers a delicious Mediterranean selection.

10:00pm On the top floor of the Sir Francis Drake hotel, house musicians play big-band or Latin music in the champagne-sipping ambience of **Harry Denton's Starlight Room**. An upscale crowd dances and parties to the backdrop of glowing Union Square-area views.

11:30pm Head to **Harry Denton's Bar and Grill**. This is a longtime favorite of the black-dress, meet-market crowd. The front room has lively jazz. The back restaurant has disco.

Day 3. Sat.   Jun. 5, 1999

9:00am Have breakfast at the **Grand Cafe** in your hotel's art-nouveau restaurant.

10:30am Cab to the **San Francisco Museum of Modern Art** (MOMA). The imposing, modernist structure is the second-largest in America devoted to modern art.

12:30pm Dive into the underwater theme at **Farallon** for outstanding seafood.

2:00pm Browse through San Francisco's premier shopping area, Union Square.

4:00pm On Union Square in the St. Francis Hotel, custom detailing and museum-quality antiques and artifacts deck **The Compass Rose**, which first opened in 1904. Afternoon tea with silver service includes finger sandwiches, scones, cream, berries, and petits fours.

6:00pm You can't dress too elegantly for the ***Black and White Ball***. But while changing, consider the challenge presented by an indoor-outdoor event with five hours of walking and dancing.

7:30pm Jeremiah Tower is one of San Francisco's celebrity chefs, and **Stars**, a California-style brasserie, is his showcase. Another top dinner choice, the nearby **Jardiniere Restaurant** has become a popular new addition to the Civic Center. It serves inventive American cuisine.

9:00pm As soon as you arrive at the ***Black and White Ball***, consult a schedule and map to plan your dancing and music agenda for the evening. Then get giddy on all the complimentary bubbly, live music, finger foods, and mingling. And when you meet some locals, give them some tips on what they should see and do in their great city.

Alternatives

Intimate, luxurious, and always rated among America's best hotels, **Campton Place** is located on Union Square. Rooms are small but elegant. **Inn at the Opera**, in the Civic Center (and near the *Black and White Ball*), has classic European furnishings.

Boulevard is one of the hardest reservations in town to get, but the art-nouveau décor and outstanding American cuisine make it worth a shot. Nearby, **One Market** serves delicious American cuisine in a contemporary setting. In the Italian-flavored, bar-studded North Beach area, **Moose's** has a thriving social scene. For a gourmet dinner, San Francisco's best is **Aqua**, which serves beautifully prepared and presented seafood. Across from Il Fornaio, the famous **Fog City Diner** serves hearty plates of upscale comfort food.

Mercury should be San Francisco's hottest destination by the time you read this. Newly opened in the SOMA area, it has a most unusual and sexy dining room, bar, and nightclub. At the top of Nob Hill, near the landmark Grace Cathedral, the **Top of the Mark**'s 19th-floor views of downtown make it a fine place for a nightcap.

In Golden Gate Park, the **M.H. de Young Memorial Museum** is the counterpart to the Palace of the Legion of Honor, noted for American and African art.

The Hot Sheet

HOTELS		ADDRESS	PH	FX	PRICE	RMS	BEST ROOMS
Campton Place Hotel	Alt	340 Stockton St.	415-781-5555 800-235-4300	415-955-5536	$$$	117	City vw
Hotel Monaco	★	501 Geary St.	415-292-0100	415-292-0111	$$	201	Dntwn vw
Inn at the Opera	Alt	333 Fulton St.	415-863-8400	415-861-0821	$$$	48	

RESTAURANTS	DAY	ADDRESS	PH	PRICE	REC	DRESS	FOOD
Aqua	Alt	252 California St.	415-956-9662	$$$	LD	Dressy	Seafood
Bix	1	56 Gold St.	415-433-6300	$$$	D/L	Yuppie	French, American
Boulevard	Alt	1 Mission St.	415-543-6084	LD	Kazh	New American
The Compass Rose	3	450 Powell St.	415-397-7000	$$	T	Yuppie	High tea
Cypress Club	1	500 Jackson St.	415-296-8555	$$$	D	Yuppie	California, continental
Doidge's Cafe	1	2217 Union St.	415-921-2149	$	B/L	Yuppie	American
Farallon	3	450 Post St.	415-956-6969	$$	L/D	Yuppie	Seafood
Fog City Diner	Alt	1300 Battery St.	415-982-2000	$$	LD	Yuppie	California diner
Garibaldi's on Presidio	1	347 Presidio Ave.	415-563-8841		L/D	Yuppie	California
Grand Cafe	3	see Hotel Monaco	415-292-0101	$	B/LD	Euro, Yuppie	French
Il Fornaio	2	1265 Battery St.	415-986-0100	$$	B/LD	Kazh	Northern Italian
Jardiniere Restaurant	3	300 Grove St.	415-861-5555	$$$	D	Kazh	California, French
Mercury	Alt	540 Howard St.	415-777-1419	$$	D	Kazh	Fusion
Moose's	Alt	1652 Stockton St.	415-989-7800	$$	LD	Euro, Kazh	American
One Market	Alt	1 Market St.	415-777-5577	$$$	LD	Yuppie	Contemporary American
Postrio Restaurant	2	545 Post St.	415-776-7825	$$$	LD	Euro, Yuppie	California
Scala's Bistro	2	432 Powell St.	415-395-8555	$$$	D/L	Euro, Yuppie	Mediterranean
Stars	3	555 Golden Gate Ave.	415-861-7827	$$$	D/L	Kazh	New American
The Spinnaker	2	100 Spinnaker Dr., Sausalito	415-332-1500	$$	L/D	Kazh	Seafood
Vertigo	1	600 Montgomery St.	415-433-7250	$$$	D/L	Euro, Yuppie	California

NIGHTLIFE	DAY	ADDRESS	PH	COVER	REC*	DRESS	MUSIC
Black Cat	1	501 Broadway	415-981-2233	$	M	Kazh	Jazz
Bubble Lounge	1	714 Montgomery St.	415-434-4204	None	R(F)	Kazh	
Cliff House	1	1090 Point Lobos Ave.	415-386-3330	None	R(F)	Local	
Enrico's Sidewalk Cafe	1	504 Broadway	415-982-6223	None	M	Kazh, Euro	Jazz, blues
Harry Denton's Bar and Grill	2	161 Steuart St.	415-882-1333	$$	MP(F)	Euro	Jazz, Top 40
Harry Denton's Starlight Room	2	450 Powell St.	415-395-8595	$	MP	Euro	Jazz, Motown
Top of the Mark	Alt	1 Nob Hill	415-392-3434	$	M	Euro	Jazz

SIGHTS & ATTRACTIONS	DAY	ADDRESS	PH	ENTRY FEE
California Palace of the Legion of Honor	1	Lincoln Park	415-750-3600	$
M.H. de Young Memorial Museum	Alt	75 Tea Garden Dr.	415-750-3600	$
Muir Woods National Monument	2	Muir Woods Rd. off Highway 1	415-388-2596	$
San Francisco Museum of Modern Art	3	151 3rd St.	415-357-4000	$
San Francisco CVB		900 Market St.	415-391-2000	

> ### Event & Ticket Info
> **Black and White Ball** (Civic Center, Van Ness Avenue at Grove Street): Tickets ($165) should be purchased in advance. For tickets and information, contact *San Francisco Symphony Ticket Services* (415-864-6000).

* M=Live music; P=Dancing (Party); R=Bar only; S=Show; (F)=Food served. For further explanation of codes, see page 14.

 NYC –3   San Francisco (SFO) <30 min./$30   Yes   50°/69° (10°/21°)

       *The Fun Also Rises*

June 1999 — Chicago, Illinois, USA — June 2000

Chicago Blues Festival

Origin: 1984 **Event** ★ ★ ★ ★ ★ ★ ★ ★ **City** **Attendance:** 650,000

The blues is a celebration of perseverance in the face of adversity, the will of the human spirit to overcome hardships, and the chance to focus on what's really important: dancing, drinking, and having a good time. A testament to those values, the *Chicago Blues Festival* sets Chicago's buzz meter on high for four days during the first week of June, giving locals and visitors a look at the city at its best—amped, excited, and eager to play.

Although the *Blues Festival* hosts about 60 acts on four stages in Grant Park on the shores of Lake Michigan, chances are you won't recognize many of the names on the play list. No matter. The acts are consistently mind-blowing and the results never fail to do justice to the original American spirit embodied in the blues.

Although the blues was born in the rural, black American South, artists with high hopes for stardom began flocking to Chicago around the turn of the century. Blues rhythms were embraced in Chicago and the tough life that many migrating African-Americans found in the factories and streets of the industrial Midwest provided enough material to give rise to a new, rougher kind of blues—Chicago blues. Legends such as Buddy Guy, Blind Lemon Jefferson,

Muddy Waters, and Howlin' Wolf all spent time in Chicago, and helped make hometown label Chess Records a blues and world leader. Their legacy still courses through the streets of Chicago today.

Like the blues men and women of the past, Chicagoans love a big shebang and the city is as renowned for its musical heritage as for Michael Jordan and bratwurst. The *Blues Festival* also marks the beginning of summer, when the city finally trades its windy winter chill for sunny days in the park. A six-pack of beer, a shakin' tail feather, and a case of the blues are all you need to be a part of the tradition, but in the midst of all the great music, make sure not to miss the cultural and culinary attractions of America's third-largest city.

Chicago Blues Festival

On most days, performances are held on five stages from early afternoon to early evening, with a headliner appearing at the Petrillo Music Shell, 7-9 p.m.

Day 1. Thu.   Jun. 3, 1999
(Day 1. Thursday   June 8, 2000)

9:00am Blow into the Windy City, first breezing through the neoclassical hotel, **The Fairmont**. This is your centrally-located base—mere steps from Michigan Avenue—and regarded as one of the top three hotels in Chicago. The spacious rooms offer views of Grant Park, where the *Blues Fest* takes place.

10:00am Chicago is known for its cutting-edge architecture. A great way to see it while getting to know the city is with a **Chicago Architecture Foundation** walking tour.

Noon Around the corner from the hotel, cross the bridge over the Chicago River to the Tribune Tower. You're at the south end of the Magnificent Mile, a strip of Michigan Avenue loaded with restaurants, art museums, and enough shopping to work your credit card into a sweat.

1:00pm Just off Michigan Avenue, have lunch at the eclectic and upscale **Bistro 110**, well-known for its food and celebrity clientele.

3:00pm It's blues time, baby. Walk or cab to the *Chicago Blues Festival* at Grant Park. The smell of barbecue abounds and the wails of performers with names like "Honeyboy" and "The Root Doctor" hover with the smoke. Grab a cold beverage and wander the festival grounds to get your bearings while taking in as many acts as you can.

9:00pm Chicago has no shortage of sleek restaurants, but the coolest one has to be **56west**. Linger in the European atmosphere after your delicious dinner.

The restaurant crowd eventually files out to be replaced by a collection of on-the-town locals who turn the place into a hip and fun nightclub.

Midnight Nearby is **Narcisse**, another intense bar scene in a very sophisticated setting. A nightspot not to be missed is **The Redhead Piano Bar**. This is an upscale place with a fun and talented pianist who keeps the joint lively.

Day 2. Fri.   Jun. 4, 1999
(Day 2. Friday   June 9, 2000)

9:30am Not far from the hotel is the best breakfast place in town, **Elaine and Ina's Restaurant**. It should be nice enough outside for a patio table.

11:00am Chicago Mercantile Exchange is a half-hour walk away. From the observation level, the trading floor of the "Merc" seems to be a pit of madness—crowded insanity unleashed beneath a board of symbols and numbers. You don't want to miss the trading of pork-bellies futures and options—your lunch may some day depend on the exchanges between the savvy traders below.

Noon Across the street, Chicago's highest point is atop the 110-story **Sears Tower Skydeck** (see page 114). The observation deck is on the 103rd floor. Once the world's tallest building, the Sears Tower has surrendered the title to a skyscraper in Malaysia.

1:30pm Having mastered the art of fun eating, the restaurant group Lettuce Entertain You Restaurants has had a profound influence on Chicago dining. **Scoozi** is one of the group's noted triumphs. Locals and out-of-towners enjoy Italian fare in a lively, colorful setting.

3:00pm Cab to **The Art Institute of Chicago**. Flanked by giant bronze lions, the museum houses more than 300,000 pieces dating from 3000 BC to the present, including many outstanding impressionist and post-impressionist paintings.

7:30pm Before dinner, go to the John Hancock Building and head to the **Signature Lounge** on the 96th floor for panoramic views of Chicago's illuminated skyline.

8:30pm Hudson Club is a swank restaurant with a fresh approach to American cuisine. You should be able to keep an eye on the active bar scene from your table.

10:30pm Cab to **The Second City**, the improvisational-comedy theater that helped catapult the careers of John Belushi, Bill Murray, and Julia Louis-Dreyfus. Arrive 30 minutes early to get good seats.

12:30am In the yuppie-friendly Lincoln Park neighborhood, the high-energy **Kingston Mines** encourages guests to "hear blues, drink booze, talk loud" until 4 a.m.

Day 3. Sat. Jun. 5, 1999
(Day 3. Saturday   June 10, 2000)

9:30am Have breakfast delivered by The Fairmont's attentive room service. Then head to the **Museum of Science and Industry** to experience one of the nation's largest touch-and-feel exhibits, which includes a walk along Yesterday's Main Street and one through a giant heart.

12:30pm Renowned chef Rick Bayless spins his Mexican-influenced spatula at upscale **Topolobampo** and its less formal, adjoining neighbor, **Frontera Grill**.

2:30pm Walk a few blocks to the **Blues Fest**, grab a drink and a patch of grass, and enjoy the show among suburbanites and city-dwellers who have come to stay until the sun sets. Take some time to enjoy the lake view from Buckingham Fountain.

9:30pm When you're ready to leave the blues behind, head back up Michigan Avenue. Have dinner at **Brasserie Jo**, a fine French restaurant with a lively atmosphere that reminds some cosmopolitan diners of La Coupole in Paris.

11:30pm Rush Street is well-known for fun in Chicago. The best place to go is **Jilly's Retro Club**, an upscale disco. To cap off your night they have a piano bar next door playing mostly Sinatra. What better way to end your weekend than with a chorus of "My kinda town, Chicago is ...."

Alternatives

Chicago hosts the world's largest food festival, *Taste of Chicago* (see page 219), spread over 11 days starting at the end of June. Local restaurants set up booths and serve samples of specialties such as pirogis and tomato fritters, while top recording artists from across the charts perform.

It's not as close as The Fairmont to the *Blues Festival*, but **The Drake** is one of Chicago's highest-rated hotels. Completed in 1920, it's set on the northern tip of the Magnificent Mile. The ultrachic **Sutton Place Hotel** is decked out in modern accents of granite, glass, and metal. **The Raphael Hotel** offers Old World character. Although it's located in the center of the city, it's on a quiet, tree-lined street.

Chicago is cooking with Nouveau American cuisine. The best and liveliest options include **Gordon**, which has dancing on weekends; **Harvest on Huron**, with temptations such as macadamia-nut-crusted halibut with papaya-butter sauce; and **Palette's**, which has a jazz pianist and striking décor. For a gourmet meal in a cozy town-house setting, try **Charlie Trotter's**, named for the owner, one of America's top chefs. Another hot spot is **Ben Pao Chinese Restaurant**, with contemporary food and setting. Go to the original **Pizzeria Uno** for Chicago-style pizza.

For more blues, there's **Buddy Guy's Legends** and **Blue Chicago**, both classics, and **House of Blues**, one of the chain of clubs providing somewhat classier food and ambience. For jazz, take a cab to **Green Dolphin Street**. The best performers appear at this large club, which has a bar, dining room, and cool outside porch.

The Hot Sheet

HOTELS		ADDRESS	PH	FX	PRICE	RMS	BEST ROOMS
The Drake	Alt	140 E. Walton St.	312-787-2200 800-553-7253	312-787-4431	$$$	535	Lake Michigan vw
The Fairmont	★	200 N. Columbus Dr.	312-565-8000 800-527-4727	312-856-1032	$$$	764	Grant Park vw
The Raphael Hotel	Alt	201 E. Delaware Pl.	312-943-5000 800-983-7870	312-943-9483	$$	172	Quiet #02 rms
Sutton Place Hotel	Alt	21 E. Bellevue St.	312-266-2100 800-810-6888	312-266-2103	$$$	246	Superior rms

RESTAURANTS	DAY	ADDRESS	PH	PRICE	REC	DRESS	FOOD
56west	1	56 W. Illinois St.	312-527-5600	$$$	D	Yuppie	American, French, Asian
Ben Pao Chinese Restaurant	Alt	52 W. Illinois St.	312-222-1888	$$	LD	Kazh	Chinese
Bistro 110	1	110 E. Pearson St.	312-266-3110	$$	L/D	Local	New American
Brasserie Jo	3	59 W. Hubbard St.	312-595-0800	$$	D/L	Yuppie	French
Charlie Trotter's	Alt	816 W. Armitage Ave.	773-248-6228	$$$	D	Dressy	New American
Elaine and Ina's Restaurant	2	448 E. Ontario St.	312-337-6700	$	B/LD	Yuppie	American breakfast
Gordon	Alt	500 N. Clark St.	312-467-9780	$$$	LD	Dressy, Kazh	New American
Harvest on Huron	Alt	217 W. Huron St.	312-587-9600	$$$	LD	Yuppie	New American
Hudson Club	2	504 N. Wells St.	312-467-1947	$$$	D	Yuppie	Classic American
Palette's	Alt	1030 N. State St.	312-440-5200	$$	D	Yuppie	New American
Pizzeria Uno	Alt	29 E. Ohio St.	312-321-1000	$$	LD	Kazh	Pizza
Scoozi	2	410 W. Huron St.	312-943-5900	$$$	L/D	Kazh	Italian
Topolobampo/Frontera Grill	3	445 N. Clark St.	312-661-1434	$$	L/D	Local	Mexican

NIGHTLIFE	DAY	ADDRESS	PH	COVER	REC*	DRESS	MUSIC
56west	1	see 56west restaurant	312-527-5600	None	R	Yuppie	Contemporary, disco
Blue Chicago	Alt	736 N. Clark St.	312-642-6261	$	MP	Local	Blues
Buddy Guy's Legends	Alt	754 S. Wabash Ave.	312-427-0333	$	M(F)	Local	Blues
Green Dolphin Street	Alt	2200 N. Ashland Ave.	773-395-0066	$	M	Kazh	Jazz
House of Blues	Alt	329 N. Dearborn St.	312-527-2583	$$	MP	Kazh	Blues
Jilly's Retro Club	3	1009 N. Rush St.	312-664-1001	$	P	Kazh	Disco
Kingston Mines	2	2548 Halsted St.	773-477-4646	$$	M(F)	Local	Blues
Narcisse	1	710 N. Clark St.	312-787-2675	None	R(F)	Yuppie	
The Redhead Piano Bar	1	16 W. Ontario St.	312-640-1000	None	M(F)	Yuppie	Jazz
The Second City	2	1616 N. Wells St.	312-337-3992	$$	S	Local	Improv comedy
Signature Lounge	2	875 N. Michigan Ave.	312-787-9596	None	M(F)	Local	Jazz

SIGHTS & ATTRACTIONS	DAY	ADDRESS	PH	ENTRY FEE
The Art Institute of Chicago	2	111 S. Michigan Ave.	312-443-3600	$
Chicago Architecture Foundation	1	224 S. Michigan Ave.	312-922-8687	$
Chicago Mercantile Exchange	2	30 S. Wacker Dr.	312-930-1000	None
Museum of Science and Industry	3	57th St. at Lake Shore Dr.	773-684-1414	$
Sears Tower Skydeck	2	233 S. Wacker Dr.	312-875-9449	$
Chicago CVB		77 E. Randolph St.	312-744-2400	

Event & Ticket Info

Chicago Blues Festival (Grant Park, Columbus Drive): Admission to the *Chicago Blues Festival* is free. For a program listing performers, contact the *Mayor's Office of Special Events*, 312-744-3370.

Alternative Event

Taste of Chicago: *Mayor's Office of Special Events*, 312-744-3370.

* M=Live music; P=Dancing (Party); R=Bar only; S=Show; (F)=Food served. For further explanation of codes, see page 14.

 NYC −1    O'Hare (ORD) <60 min./$35 Midway (MDW) <30 min./$25   No   57°/79° (14°/26°)

June 1999

June 2000

Napa Valley (St. Helena), California, USA

Napa Valley Wine Auction

Origin: 1981   Event ★ ★ ★ ★ ★ ★ City   Attendance: 2,000

The planet's largest charity event focused on food and wine, the ***Napa Valley Wine Auction*** pours a world-famous party into a gourmet extravaganza, creating one spectacular, waistband-expanding three-day gathering. The event raises more than $3 million each year for Napa Valley's health-care institutions, but even if you don't make a single bid, you'll come away with a new appreciation of food, wine, and fun.

The schedule varies from year to year, as do participating wineries. What's consistent is scores of epicurean events that keep crowds happy and full from morning until night. Constant rounds of gourmet meals are prepared by celebrity chefs. Tastings of rare and fine California vintages continue through the weekend. Dozens of events include appearances by celebrity impersonators, boccie ball, art tours, nature walks, and live jazz, zydeco, and rock music.

The social centerpiece is the fancy ***Vintners' Ball***, held at the gorgeous Meadowood Napa Valley resort in St. Helena. Guests are wined and dined with course after course of delicacies prepared by world-renowned chefs. Also held at Meadowood is the ***auction***, a sky's-the-limit nail-biter where some wine lots go for upward of $150,000. Thousands cheer as the bidding paddles go to battle and prices are pushed into the stratosphere.

The wine auction makes June the perfect time to visit famed Napa Valley. This lush and fertile area annually attracts hundreds of thousands of gastronomic pilgrims with its outstanding restaurants and opportunities to

sample vintages from more than 200 wineries—more wineries than in any other region of the world, outside of France. British statesman Benjamin Disraeli might have been disappointed by the ***Napa Valley Wine Auction***—"I rather like bad wine," he said. "One gets so bored with good wine." But a few days in one of the world's premier wine regions is never boring, and it should turn you into a connoisseur of fine wines and great fun.

Napa Valley Wine Auction

Day 1. Thu.   Jun. 3, 1999
(Day 1. Thursday   June 1, 2000)

9:00am With 250 acres of manicured grounds containing pools, fitness and spa facilities, golf courses, and croquet lawns, **Meadowood** is a dream resort. Check into a suite with cathedral-beamed ceilings, plush draperies, and beds luxurious enough to satisfy King Henry VIII.

9:30am Drive to St. Helena for the excellent pastries and cappuccino at **Model Bakery**. Take time to read through your program of auction activities and related events.

11:00am Back at Meadowood, stroll through the nine colorfully decorated tents pitched on velvety lawns. Barrel tasting allows you to sample great wines straight from the fermentation casks. In a preview of Saturday's main auction, bids are taken on selected wine lots and proud vintners present fascinating explanations of how they brought their product from vine to wine. During a silent auction, you get first crack at wines, books, and collectibles created by Napa Valley artists.

1:30pm In various tents, Napa Valley purveyors offer creative gourmet specialties such as herbed grilled prawns, rabbit strudel, and smoked salmon in pastry cones. Choose the perfect wine accompaniment from the wide range of excellent bottled varietals on hand.

3:00pm Drive to **Sterling Vineyards**, 12 miles south of Calistoga on Route 29. Take the aerial sky tram to Sterling's tasting room. The awesome panoramic view of Napa Valley is by far the best at any winery in the state.

6:00pm Choose one of the reliably fun and delicious hospitality events offered at 30 Napa Valley wineries. You can flirt with impersonators of Hollywood stars while enjoying a gourmet dinner and champagne tasting at **Domaine Chandon**. Or go to Far Niente winery to dance to live zydeco music and feast on Southwestern barbecue grilled by a celebrity chef. The **Napa Valley Wine Train** is always a popular selection—wine, dinner, music, and stunning scenery highlight the trip through parts of the 30-mile stretch of flower-covered ground and lush hillsides that make up Napa Valley.

Day 2. Fri.   Jun. 4, 1999
(Day 2. Friday   June 2, 2000)

10:00am Prepare yourself with a room-service breakfast as another 40 vintners open their wineries and homes for feasting, wine tasting, and music. Study your schedule, because you must narrow the options to one. You might choose a vineyard tour, barrel tasting, and lunch at Acacia Winery, overlooking San Francisco Bay. Or go for a game of boccie ball with the Anderson family of Conn Valley Vineyards, followed by a lunch of barbecue and select wines. Other options include a visit to **Clos Pégase** winery. Proprietor, art collector, and winemaker Jan Shrem takes you on a tour of his art collection (it's mildly erotic and loads of fun) then gives a short talk on the history of wine. Afterward, sip a wide range of Clos Pégase wines with brunch on the patio.

2:00pm To get a close-in experience with the natural wonder of Napa, put on your hiking boots and trek to the summit of the mountain behind Pine Ridge Winery (where winemaker Nancy Andrus is an experienced Nepal hiker). Local naturalists and bird-watchers give a wildlife tour along the way to the mountaintop, where you're welcomed with a picnic featuring California cuisine, chilled wines, and live music. You'll go back to your hotel room with a souvenir wicker basket compliments of the winery.

6:30pm At Meadowood, arrive at the ***Vintners' Ball***— the fanciest event of the wine auction—dressed to the nines and sparkling like the vintage champagnes served. This party is the keystone event of the auction.

8:00pm After oysters, shrimp, and other seafood hors d'oeuvres, chefs from all over the country prepare an exquisite four-course meal. Dine inside the giant auction tent, which has been decorated with fantastic sculptures adorning tables and flowers and vines climbing the 20-foot tent poles.

10:00pm In another series of tents, sample a grand array of desserts, from mousses to truffles to ice-cream sundaes. You can dance to live music provided by a big-name talent such as Grammy winner Narada Michael Walden (performing artists change each year).

Day 3. Sat. Jun. 5, 1999
(Day 3. Saturday   June 3, 2000)

9:00am At **Meadowood Grill**, start your day with a fresh and bountiful breakfast that includes bagels with smoked fish, breakfast burritos, hot chocolate, and coffee.

11:00am The first gavel crashes down at 11 a.m. sharp, unleashing the ***Napa Valley Wine Auction*** at Meadowood. In the big tent, nearly 200 barrel lots are on the block. Auctioneers from Christie's exhort bidders to make paddles fly and credit cards jump. Silent auctions continue in nine smaller tents. In another tent, wine and auction-related souvenirs are sold to people who love wine but don't need it in barrel lots. Music, dancing, and other revelry take place throughout the auction, and a festive picnic for all guests accompanies the bidding.

3:00pm Take a break from the auction action to stroll around the grounds, perhaps stopping for a cappuccino and cookies at one of the food booths. Many guests use this time to socialize, network, or sit beneath a shady tree to chat or nap.

6:30pm The last gavel falls and the final banquet begins. Tables are set up in a grassy area under the trees at the base of Meadowood's south hill. A band plays as guests dance between courses that include roasted lamb, fresh and marinated vegetable salads, goat cheese, crusty herb-flecked breads, and homemade fruit pies. This final, perfect evening brings the three days to an earthy, casual, and sensual finish.

Alternatives

High on a hillside, **Auberge du Soleil** in Rutherford is another of Napa Valley's most elegant and romantic hostelries. Spa facilities, a pool, tennis courts, and a romantic restaurant occasionally lure guests out of their suite's immense two-person hot tub (an incredible place to begin a new relationship, or rekindle an old one). **The Inn at Southbridge**, in downtown St. Helena, is the Meadowood's charming little sister. Each of the 21 rooms has homey touches, such as a fireplace, fresh-fruit delivery, and candles. Waterways and fountains gurgle through the lush grounds of the **Vintage Inn** in Yountville. Rooms on the ground floor feature rosebush-bordered patios. Upstairs rooms have cathedrallike beamed ceilings and open verandas—all have fireplaces.

The three days of auction events are so filled with gourmet food you probably won't want to eat anywhere else. But if you stay longer in Napa Valley, try **Mustards Grill**, one of the first major eateries in California to emphasize small side dishes (think *tapas*) in lieu of standard entree meals. **Brix** and **Catahoula** are two more favorite spots. The vine-covered courtyard at **Ristorante Tra Vigne** provides a perfect setting for excellent Italian food.

Napa Valley is not known for its night life, but for the three *B*s: ballooning, bicycling, and bathing (that means mud bathing). There are many choices for each, but Calistoga's **Mountain View Spa** is one of the area's best places for massages, hot tubs, and fresh mud baths.

The Hot Sheet

HOTELS		ADDRESS		PH	FX	PRICE	RMS	BEST ROOMS
Auberge du Soleil	Alt	180 Rutherford Hill Rd.	(R)	707-963-1211 800-348-5406	707-963-1211	$$$$	52	Cottages
Meadowood	★	900 Meadowood Ln.	(S)	707-963-3646 800-458-8080	707-963-3532	$$$$+	84	Cathedral cottage
The Inn at Southbridge	Alt	1020 Main St.	(S)	707-967-9400 800-520-6800	707-963-3532	$$$$	21	Maryville winery vw
Vintage Inn	Alt	6541 Washington St.	(Y)	707-944-1112 800-351-1133	707-944-1616	$$$	200	Mountain vw

RESTAURANTS	DAY	ADDRESS		PH	PRICE	REC	DRESS	FOOD
Brix	Alt	7377 St. Helena Hwy.	(Y)	707-944-2749	$$$	LD	Dressy, Kazh	California Asian
Catahoula	Alt	1457 Lincoln Ave.	(C)	707-942-2275	$$$	LD	Kazh	Southern-inspired American
Domaine Chandon	1	1 California Dr.	(Y)	707-944-2892	$$$$	D/L	Dressy, Yuppie	French-California
Meadowood Grille	3	see Meadowood hotel	(S)	707-963-3646	$$	B/LD	Kazh	American
Model Bakery	1	1357 Main St.	(S)	707-963-8192	$	B/L	Local	Bakery, American
Mustards Grill	Alt	7399 St. Helena Hwy.	(Y)	707-944-2424	$$	LD	Yuppie, Kazh	American grill
Ristorante Tra Vigne	Alt	1050 Charter Oak Ave.	(S)	707-963-4444	$$	LD	Kazh	Northern Italian

SIGHTS & ATTRACTIONS	DAY	ADDRESS		PH	ENTRY FEE
Clos Pégase	2	1060 Dunaweal Ln.	(C)	707-942-4981	None
Mountain View Spa	Alt	1457 Lincoln Ave.	(C)	707-942-5789	$$$$+
Napa Valley Wine Train	1	1275 McKinstry St.	(N)	707-253-2111	$$$$+
Sterling Vineyards	1	1111 Dunaweal Ln.	(C)	707-942-3300	None
Napa Valley CVB		1310 Napa Town Center	(N)	707-226-7459	

Event & Ticket Info

Napa Valley Wine Auction (Meadowood Resort, 900 Meadowood Ln., St. Helena): Only 1,000 tickets ($800 each or $1,500 per couple) that cover all events are sold to the public and must be requested in writing no later than mid-February. If you receive an invitation, reply quickly (overnight mail) as this is first-come first-served. For more information and to request an invitation, contact the *Napa Valley Vintners Association* (800-928-1371 ext. 901).

* C=Calistoga; N=Napa; R=Rutherford; S=St. Helena; Y=Yountville

* M=Live music; P=Dancing (Party); R=Bar only; S=Show; (F)=Food served. For further explanation of codes, see page 14.

 NYC –3   San Francisco (SFO) <120 min./S n/a   Yes   50°/67° (10°/19°)

May/June 1999

May/June 2000

Charleston, South Carolina, USA

Spoleto

(Spoleto Festival USA/Piccolo Spoleto)

Origin: 1977   Event ★ ★ ★ ★ ★ ★ City   Attendance: 72,000

By and large, we don't associate artists with frivolity—tortured souls and unappreciated genius are the shopworn clichés—but Charleston's *Spoleto* festival explodes the notion that fine art can't be fun. The giant performing-arts festival's secret weapon is diversity. Mix poets, painters, dancers, musicians, and actors in one place and everyone's creative energy tends to shine in its most brilliant light.

The result is one of the world's best interdisciplinary arts parties—neither drunken bacchanal nor hoity-toity gathering—a congenial affair where you can take in as much culture as you like against the backdrop of one of the nation's most beautiful cities. Because it's especially dedicated to young artists and contemporary effort, there's always a cutting-edge aura surrounding *Spoleto*. Established artists and critics from around the world show up to catch glimpses of new stars—more than 100 operas, concerts, plays, and other performances are staged during the festival's 17-day run—and hobnob around town with tens of thousands of visitors sampling everything from chardonnay to sushi. Filling in the gaps around the parent gathering, *Piccolo Spoleto*, founded in 1979, is an auxiliary event showcasing the brightest talent of America's Southeast region with more than 400 performing-arts events.

S*poleto*'s party scene takes its cues from the rarefied world of the city's high society, which is largely private and requires skill to penetrate. But the festival itself throws a great street party on its second Saturday and at any rate, the great thing about *Spoleto* is that you can attend a morning chamber concert, have brunch, take a nap, then move on to the next performance and meal.

When you aren't catching a show, you can soak up sunny Charleston's lush gardens, fantastic architecture, distinctive regional cuisine, and irrepressible Southern charm. The city is a walker's paradise, so you're better off ditching the car and strolling through *Spoleto* venues or exploring the area's fabulous beaches. Charleston makes it easy to hop from cafe to cabaret, from performance to pool, from wet swim suit to dry martini, and most important of all, from high art to high fun.

Spoleto

Spoleto performances are generally held mid-afternoon and in the evening. Piccolo Spoleto events are scattered throughout the day. The itinerary assumes you'll be attending performances each afternoon and evening.

Day 1. Thu. Jun. 3, 1999
(Day 1. Thursday June 1, 2000)

9:30am For an unbeatable combination of ambience, location, and comfort, check into the **Planter's Inn**.

10:00am Walk to the Visitor Information Center to catch the video *Forever Charleston*, a great introduction to the city. Narrated by locals, it's accurate, affectionate, lively, and fun.

11:00am Walk 15 minutes to your first *Spoleto* performance. Built in 1736, The Dock Street Theatre— which is actually on Church Street— is where Charles Wadsworth, known as the festival ham, conducts an entertaining chamber-music concert. Take note of performers' names—some years ago, a young singer by the name of Jessye Norman got her stardom-bound start here.

12:30pm On to lunch at **Slightly North of Broad**, a short walk away. The casually elegant restaurant serves contemporary low-country cuisine—examples include shrimp and grits, and grilled tuna topped with fried oysters. Head up Church Street and take note of St. Philip's Episcopal Church. Built in 1847 with its landmark steeple, it was hit hard by Union Army fire. St. Philip's is Charleston's most beautiful church, but on nearby Meeting Street, St. Michael's is the oldest. It was built in 1761.

3:00pm Take your pick of a *Spoleto performance*: music, theater, or dance. All venues are an easy walk from the hotel.

6:30pm Have dinner at **Carolina's**, where the Vietnamese chef mixes Asian and regional ingredients and gets terrific results. Savor excellent seafood in an attractive, shrimp-colored room.

10:30pm After the evening performance, head to **The Clef** for jazz in a comfortable setting. Remember, however, The Clef, like many venues in Charleston, may be hosting official *Piccolo Spoleto* events. It's always a good idea to call ahead in Charleston this time of year.

Midnight Have a nightcap at **Club Habana**. Located above a cigar store, this bordello-style place has an excellent selection of novelty martinis, wines, and after-dinner drinks, including 13 ports, 11 Scotches, and assorted sherries, cognacs, Armagnacs, and Madeiras.

1:00am All those clichés you've heard are true: It's the hour of moonlight, magnolias, and magic. Saunter down Meeting Street to the sepulchral garden of the Circular Congregational Church, across from Hibernian Hall. Established in 1696, the cemetery is the city's oldest, with sequestered nooks and crannies where lovers sneak kisses.

Day 2. Fri. Jun. 4, 1999
(Day 2. Friday June 2, 2000)

8:00am A block from Planter's Inn, order scones, muffins, and coffee at the **Bakers Cafe**.

9:00am Walk 30 minutes to City Marina and take a boat across Charleston Harbor to **Fort Sumter**, where the first shots of the Civil War were fired in 1861. Boats leave at 9:30 a.m. (also noon and 2:30 p.m.) to make the two-hour tour.

12:30pm At **Vickery's Bar & Grill**, indulge in big plates of food, big cocktails, and the sort of low-stress atmosphere that makes GenXers and yuppies all feel at home. Make a note to come back later—the place is lively until its 2 a.m. closing.

3:00pm Again, your afternoon should be taken up by the *Spoleto* performance of your (difficult) choice.

6:30pm One of Charleston's popular spots, known for its lively atmosphere and great food, is **Magnolia's**. It serves New Southern cooking at its best.

10:30pm Have a drink at the **Roof Top at the Vendue Inn**. There's a wonderful view of the waterfront and the city's church spires.

11:30pm Although **Club Tango**'s name is a bit misleading —the music inside actually covers a range of dance genres—this new hot spot tops the list for sophisticated dancing venues in town.

Day 3. Sat.   June 5, 1999
(Day 3. Saturday   June 3, 2000)

8:30am Take advantage of the hotel's room service for a light breakfast.

9:00am Drive or cab 14 miles northwest on Ashley River Road (Highway 61) and spend the morning at the 18th-century **Middleton Place** plantation. The 65 acres of landscaped gardens—punctuated with butterfly lakes and gnarly oaks—are the oldest in America. Take a house tour and watch artisans demonstrating colonial crafts-making.

12:30pm Back in town, have brunch at **Hominy Grill**. The chef's a Southern boy with New York credentials and an Alice Waters philosophy. Try the grilled veggie plate with a cool avocado-and-exotic-rice salad, followed by a comforting slice of buttermilk pie.

3:00pm There's still plenty to choose from at *Spoleto*, but consider taking off the afternoon to rest up for the big evening to come.

6:00pm Dine at **Sonoma Cafe & Wine Bar**, which might as well be called California Comes to Charleston. Fresh ingredients are the stock in trade and the fusion cuisine is beautifully presented in a bustling atmosphere.

8:00pm The first part of tonight's entertainment is a performance that changes from year to year, but it's guaranteed to get you in the mood to party. After the show, the **Saturday Samba** street party continues the theme of the performance. This is the time for you to shed inhibitions, dance, and unleash your artistic side.

11:30pm Sip champagne at the **Bubble Room** or nearby **Club Trio**. Offer a "we shall meet again" toast to *Spoleto*. Like the best performers, Charleston and its top event always leave you wanting a little more.

Alternatives

The *Spoleto Opening Weekend Celebration* includes an elegant black-tie dinner dance, brunch, and a dinner in a historic home. The *Spoleto Festival Finale*, with an orchestra concert and fireworks, is held on the rambling grounds of the Middleton Place plantation.

Charleston Place, a deluxe hotel, shows the city at its finest. **Mills House Hotel** is a beautifully updated historic hotel. **Westin Francis Marion** is a renovated hotel where many *Spoleto* performers stay. All three hotels are conveniently located close to the action.

For contemporary-style cooking in a happening atmosphere, try **Blossom Cafe**. If you prefer refined dining, try the ultraposh **Louis' Restaurant and Bar**. Chef Louis Osteen, a low-country legend, likes to work the crowd. He'll probably drop by and say, "Ah hope you enjoyed your suppah." Another choice is the **Peninsula Grill** at the Planter's Inn. Voted one of the United States' best new restaurants by *Esquire* magazine, it's a fine place for romance, juicy steaks, fresh fish, and an aphrodisiac champagne-and-oyster menu. One of the city's best soul-food restaurants is **Alice's Fine Foods**.

For a night-life alternative, **Zebo Restaurant & Brewery** is a fun microbrewery with surprisingly good food. The **82 Queen** is a lively meeting spot, especially around the bar.

The Hot Sheet

HOTELS		ADDRESS	PH	FX	PRICE	RMS	BEST ROOMS
Charleston Place Orient-Express	Alt	130 Market St.	843-722-4900 800-611-5545	843-722-0728	$$$$	440	Garden and courtyard vw
Mills House Hotel	Alt	115 Meeting St.	843-577-2400 800-874-9600	843-722-0623	$$	214	Downtown vw
Planter's Inn	★	112 N. Market St.	843-722-2345 800-845-7082	843-577-2125	$$	62	Meeting St vw
Westin Francis Marion	Alt	337 King St.	843-722-0600 800-433-3733	843-723-4633	$$	226	Downtown vw

RESTAURANTS	DAY	ADDRESS	PH	PRICE	REC	DRESS	FOOD
Alice's Fine Foods	Alt	468 King St.	843-853-9366	$	LD	Local	Soul food
Baker's Cafe	2	214 King St.	843-577-2694	$	B/L	Local	Pastries
Blossom Cafe	Alt	171 E. Bay St.	843-722-9200	$$$	LD	Yuppie	Mediterranean
Carolina's	1	10 Exchange St.	843-724-3800	$$	D	Kazh	Contemporary, Asian-influenced
Hominy Grill	3	207 Rutledge Ave.	843-937-0930	$	L/BD	Local	Southern
Louis' Restaurant and Bar	Alt	200 Meeting St.	843-853-2550	$$	D	Yuppie	Regional Southern
Magnolia's	2	185 E. Bay St.	843-577-7771	$$$	D/L	Kazh	Southern
Peninsula Grill	Alt	see Planter's Inn	843-723-0700	$$$$	D	Kazh	Southern seafood
Slightly North of Broad	1	192 E. Bay St.	843-723-3424	$$	L/D	Kazh	Regional Southern
Sonoma Cafe & Wine Bar	3	304 King St.	843-853-3222	$$$	D	Kazh	American, Caribbean fusion
Vickery's Bar & Grill	2	15 Beaufain St.	843-577-5300	$	L/D	Local	American, Cuban influence

NIGHTLIFE	DAY	ADDRESS	PH	COVER	REC*	DRESS	MUSIC
82 Queen	Alt	82 Queen St.	843-723-7591	None	R(F)	Kazh	
Bubble Room	3	467 King St.	843-723-5777	$	MP(F)	Local	Rock, funk, pop
The Clef	1	102 N. Market St.	843-722-0732	$	M(F)	Kazh	Jazz
Club Habana	1	177 Meeting St.	843-853-5008	None	R	Local	
Club Tango	2	39 Hutson St.	843-577-2822	$	MP(F)	Kazh	Disco
Club Trio	3	139 Calhoun St.	843-965-5333	None	M(F)	Kazh	Jazz
Roof Top at the Vendue Inn	2	23 Vendue Range	843-577-7970	None	R(F)	Local	
Zebo Restaurant & Brewery	Alt	275 King St.	843-577-7600	$	M(F)	Local	Bluegrass, jazz, pop

SIGHTS & ATTRACTIONS	DAY	ADDRESS	PH	ENTRY FEE
Forever Charleston	1	375 Meeting St.	843-853-8000	$
Fort Sumter	2	171 Lockwood Blvd.	843-722-1691	$
Middleton Place	3	4300 Ashley River Rd.	843-556-6020	$$
Charleston Area CVB		375 Meeting St.	800-868-8118	

Event & Ticket Info

Spoleto Festival USA: To order tickets, call *South Carolina Automated Ticketing/ SCAT* (843-723-0402). For more information, contact *Spoleto Festival USA* (843-722-2764).

Piccolo Spoleto Festival: To order tickets, call *South Carolina Automated Ticketing/SCAT* (843-557-4500). For more information, contact *Piccolo Spoleto Festival* (843-724-7305).

Saturday Samba: Tickets ($75) can be ordered from *Spoleto Festival USA Events Office* (843-724-1192).

Alternate Event

Spoleto Opening Weekend Celebration and **Spoleto Festival Finale**: *Spoleto Festival USA Events*, 843-724-1192

* M=Live music; P=Dancing (Party); R=Bar only; S=Show; (F)=Food served. For further explanation of codes, see page 14.

 NYC   Charleston (CHS) <30 min./$20 No   61°/83° (16°/28°)

June 1999 — Nashville, Tennessee, USA — June 2000

Country Music Fan Fair

(International Country Music Fan Fair)

| Origin: 1972 | Event ★ ★ ★ ★ ★ City | Attendance: 24,000 |

The only thing more sacred than a country star's relationship with God and Momma is his bond with The Fans. Wives come and go, but The Fans stick by, for better or worse—during the arrest for waving a gun on the highway, when he gets caught in the back of a Ford with pants at the ankles, or his failure to get another hit song onto the charts.

For country-music singers and their fans, ***The International Country Music Fan Fair*** is like Christmas, Independence Day, and Woodstock wrapped into one package. Sponsored by the Country Music Association and the Grand Ole Opry, this annual five-day orgy of appreciation pays homage to the ties that bind in country music. Every June, 24,000 die-hard fans from all corners of the United States and the world head south for 35 hours of performances and face time with their beloved stars. And the stars are happy to indulge the fans who pay their bills: One year Garth Brooks signed autographs for 23 straight hours without a break.

For five days, the faithful line up at booths packed into exhibit halls at the Tennessee State Fairgrounds, patiently waiting hour after hour for a photograph with Marty Stuart, Brooks and Dunn, or Patty Loveless. In the grandstand, record labels showcase their best acts and rising stars.

Beyond the fairgrounds, which many fans never leave, is Nashville, which has earned the title of Music City, USA. It's also the state's capital and home to one of the nation's finest universities, Vanderbilt. The past decade has seen Nashville approach its goal of becoming an A-list city. The downtown area, boarded up and depressing in 1990, has been transformed into a thriving tourist destination, while regaining most of its former charm.

Around town there are historic attractions such as the Hermitage (President Andrew Jackson's estate) and the Parthenon, a full-size replica of the original in Athens. With a three-day jaunt to Music City, you can take it all in with a sampling of fan mania, the vaunted Grand Ole Opry, and a crash course in America's music: country. Yahoo!

Country Music Fan Fair

Day 1. Wed. Jun. 16, 1999
Day 1. Wednesday   *June 14, 2000*

9:00am In the heart of Nashville, the **Westin Hermitage Hotel** is the only commercial beaux-arts structure in Tennessee. Built in 1910, the Grecian-and-Tennessee marble in the lobby, and the French doors at the original "ladies entrance," make a grand setting. Have a hearty breakfast at the hotel.

10:00am Drive to the Tennessee State Fairgrounds for the *International Country Music Fan Fair*. Wear comfortable shoes and casual clothes. The daily routine consists of morning, afternoon, and evening shows. Each is a showcase for a different label. The exhibit halls are filled with booths where you can buy memorabilia or sing a voice-over. If you want a star's autograph, hop in line.

1:00pm Your pass entitles you to lunch served with verve by the Oddessa Chuck Wagon Gang. There's also lots of standard fairgrounds junk food.

7:30pm Not far from the hotel is one of Nashville's finer restaurants, **Cafe One Two Three**, which serves eclectic, Southern-accented cuisine.

9:30pm Downtown Nashville should be swinging by now. Start on Second Avenue and Broadway. It's touristy —Hard Rock Cafe, NASCAR Cafe, Planet Hollywood, and Hooters have all moved in—but still a good block for walking, with funky bars, upscale junk shops, cheesy souvenir stands, and the terrific **Wildhorse Saloon**. This high-tech country emporium has free dance lessons, a huge dance floor, and live entertainment.

11:30pm Slide into **Tootsie's Orchid Lounge**, one of the world's greatest dives. Despite its popularity, the joint hasn't had a significant renovation in at least 50 years. During the Grand Ole Opry's heyday, the legendary Hank Williams used to slip out the back door of the Ryman Auditorium to tie one on at Tootsie's. Live performers croon for tips in the front and bands play in the back. Tootsie's looks intimidating from the outside, but walk right in and you'll feel welcome.

Day 2. Thu. Jun. 17, 1999
Day 2. Thursday   *June 15, 2000*

9:00am Drive 15 country miles for breakfast at the **Loveless Restaurant**. Fried chicken, ham, hot biscuits, and hospitality are the specialties.

10:30am Drive a few miles to **The Hermitage**, home of Andrew Jackson. The seventh American president, Old Hickory lived here until his death in 1845. The Greek Revival mansion and 650-acre grounds are splendid.

12:30pm Back in town, lunch at the **Blue Moon Waterfront Cafe**, the one restaurant locals don't want you to know about. Nestled on the Cumberland River, it serves upscale, eclectic seafood.

2:00pm Head back to *Fan Fair* in time for the afternoon show. Finish collecting those autographs.

6:45pm Get an outdoor table at **Sunset Grill** and enjoy New American cuisine at this highly rated restaurant. Try one of more than 60 wines served by the glass.

8:30pm At Riverfront Park, "Dancin' in the District" is in full swing (four bands, 6-10:30 p.m.). These free outdoor concerts are held every Thursday during the summer.

10:30pm Dance to live music in a New York-style dinner club, aptly named **Manhattan's**. Or check into **Gibson's Caffè Milano**, known for performers from Chet Atkins to Yo Yo Ma.

Day 3. Fri.   Jun. 18, 1999
Day 3. Friday   *June 16, 2000*

9:00am Celebrities are often spotted at the **Pancake Pantry**, a local institution. Plow through heaping plates of pancakes, served in every possible style.

10:30am The **Country Music Hall of Fame and Museum** is especially good for people who don't know much about country music or think they don't like it. The museum displays thousands of fascinating items and tributes to country-music legends.

Noon Drive to **Centennial Park** for Nashville's most eccentric attraction, a full-size replica of the Parthenon. The city art museum and the world's tallest indoor sculpture, Athena Parthenos, are inside.

1:30pm Adjacent to the park, Nashville's best barbecue is served at **Hog Heaven**. The pulled-chicken sandwich, with an unusual spicy white sauce, is especially good. Or you could get a burger and malt at **Elliston Place Soda Shop**, a 1939 soda fountain adjacent to the park.

3:00pm Head downtown to the Cumberland River for the two-mile **Nashville City Walk**. The self-guided tour begins at Fort Nashborough in Riverfront Park, where you can ride the whimsical Tennessee Fox Trot Carousel. Follow the green line on the sidewalk to Printer's Alley, the Men's Quarter, Nashville's Historic Black Business District, the State Capitol, and the Tennessee State Museum. Take the tour at the **Ryman Auditorium**, a red-brick 1892 revivalist hall which was home to the Grand Ole Opry from 1943 to 1974.

5:30pm Have an early dinner at **Capitol Grille and Oak Bar**, voted one of the Top 25 New Restaurants in the country by *Esquire*. Choose from a menu of varied, regional American cuisine.

7:00pm Drive to **Opryland Hotel**. A hotel like no other in the world, it has a colossal, nine-acre indoor complex of lush gardens, murals, waterfalls, lakes, rivers, and covered bridges. Walk or shuttle to Opry Plaza. The **Grand Ole Opry Museum** is open late when the Opry's on.

9:00pm Nashville's main attraction since 1925, the **Grand Ole Opry** (the show starts at 7:30 p.m.) is also the longest-running radio show in history. The set is pure corn pone—a red-barn backdrop and a microphone—but the pace is fast and the performances are great. About 20 cast members take the stage, from newcomers to old-timers such as Porter Wagoner. Be sure to pick up some Goo Goo (Grand Ole Opry, according to myth) clusters at the snack bar.

11:00pm You probably have some boot-scootin' left in you, so try **Robert's Western World**, a smoky honky-tonk that old Hank would've loved. Hipsters two-step around the small dance floor. Line dancing is not encouraged, but after a visit here, you'll impress your friends back home with all you've learned in Nashville.

Alternatives

Downtown, **Union Station Hotel** is a beautifully restored Victorian train depot with a breathtaking, 65-foot barrel-vaulted ceiling in the lobby. **Opryland Hotel**, about 15 minutes from downtown, is more of an event hotel, with lots of hubbub. Ask for a room overlooking the gardens, with a private terrace.

If the Grand Ole Opry's not your style, call for the lineup at the **Bluebird Cafe**, where Nashville's finest singer/songwriters practice their craft in an intimate room. It has the best folk, country, and blues in town, even on open-mic nights. The **Bound'ry** serves upscale global cuisine. The **Stockyard Restaurant** in the historic stockyard building is elegant and romantic.

Another Nashville diversion is a stroll at **Cheekwood, Nashville's Home of Art and Gardens**, amid 55 acres of botanical gardens and an art museum.

The Hot Sheet

HOTELS		ADDRESS	PH	FX	PRICE	RMS	BEST ROOMS
Opryland Hotel	Alt	2800 Opryland Dr.	615-889-1000 888-976-1998	615-871-5728	$$$	3,000	Garden and waterway vw
Union Station Hotel	Alt	1001 Broadway	615-726-1001 800-331-2123	615-248-3554	$$	124	Gallery vw
Westin Hermitage Hotel	★	231 6th Ave. N	615-244-3121 800-251-1908	615-254-6909	$$	120	Capitol vw

RESTAURANTS	DAY	ADDRESS	PH	PRICE	REC	DRESS	FOOD
Blue Moon Waterfront Cafe	2	525 Basswood Ave.	615-352-5892	$$	L/D	Local	Seafood
Bound'ry	Alt	911 20th Ave. S	615-321-3043	$$$	D	Yuppie	New Southern, continental
Cafe One Two Three	1	123 12th Ave. N	615-255-2233	$$$	D	Kazh	New Southern, continental
Capitol Grille and Oak Bar	3	see Westin Hermitage Hotel	615-244-3121	$$	D/BL	Kazh	American
Elliston Place Soda Shop	3	2111 Elliston Pl.	615-327-1090	$	L/BD	Local	American
Hog Heaven	3	115 27th Ave. N	615-329-1234	$	L/D	Local	Barbecue
Loveless Restaurant	2	8400 Hwy. 100	615-646-0067	$	B/LD	Local	Southern
Pancake Pantry	3	1796 21st Ave. S	615-383-9333	$	B/L	Local	American
Stockyard Restaurant	Alt	901 2nd Ave. N	615-255-6464	$$$	D	Kazh	American
Sunset Grill	2	2001A Belcourt Ave.	615-386-3663	$$	D/L	Kazh	Nuvo American

NIGHTLIFE	DAY	ADDRESS	PH	COVER	REC*	DRESS	MUSIC
Bluebird Cafe	Alt	4104 Hillsboro Rd.	615-383-1461	$	M(F)	Local	Original country, blues, folk
Gibson's Caffè Milano	2	176 3rd Ave. N	615-255-0253	$$	MP(F)	Kazh	Jazz, country, rock
Grand Ole Opry	3	2802 Opryland Dr.	615-889-6600	$$	S	Kazh	Country
Manhattan's	2	901 2nd Ave.	615-255-2899	None	MP(F)	Yuppie	'30s-'90s
Robert's Western World	3	416 Broadway	615-256-7937	None	MP(F)	Local	Country
Tootsie's Orchid Lounge	1	422 Broadway	615-726-0463	None	MP(F)	Local	Country
Wildhorse Saloon	1	120 2nd Ave. N	615-251-1000	$	MP(F)	Local	Country

SIGHTS & ATTRACTIONS	DAY	ADDRESS	PH	ENTRY FEE
Centennial Park	3	West End and 25th Ave.	615-862-8431	$
Cheekwood, Nashville's Home of Art and Gardens	Alt	1200 Forrest Park Dr.	615-353-2162	$
Country Music Hall of Fame and Museum	3	4 Music Square E	615-256-1639	$
Grand Ole Opry Musuem	3	2804 Opryland Dr.	615-889-7070	None
The Hermitage	2	4580 Rachel's Lane	615-889-2941	$
Nashville City Walk	3	Riverfront Park		None
Opryland Hotel	3	see hotel listing	515-889-1000	None
Ryman Auditorium	3	116 5th Ave. N	615-254-1445	$
Nashville CVB		501 Broadway	615-259-4700	

Event & Ticket Info

Country Music Fan Fair (Tennessee State Fairgrounds, off I-440 between I-65 and I-24): Your ticket (about $90) covers admission all five days, lunches on Wednesday and Thursday, and passes to attractions around town, such as the first-rate Country Music Hall of Fame. Tickets should be purchased by February from *Fan Fair* (615-889-7503).

* M=Live music; P=Dancing (Party); R=Bar only; S=Show; (F)=Food served. For further explanation of codes, see page 14.

 NYC –1   Nashville (BNA) <30 min./$20   Yes   66°/88° (19°/31°)

Summerfest

Origin: 1968   Event ★ ★ ★ ★ City   Attendance: 940,000

Milwaukee, the self-proclaimed City of Fabulous Festivals, hails *Summerfest* as The Big Gig. They might as well call it The Biggest Gig—with 11 stages, more than 2,500 local, regional, and international acts, and about a million spectators, it's arguably the world's largest music festival.

Fans of Hungarian folk opera might be disappointed, but almost no one else will. Each *Summerfest* stage is dedicated to a different musical genre: alternative, rock, jazz, blues, country, folk, big band, zydeco, reggae, and just about anything else you can think of or hum to. All shows are free, with the exception of daily concerts in the 24,000-capacity Marcus Amphitheater that feature some of the biggest names in music.

But *Summerfest* stands for more than music. For 11 days in late June and early July, it jumps with dancing, music, food, fireworks, and Milwaukee's best-known commodity: beer. Opening day is the best day to attend, when the city empties into the lakeside festival grounds to ring in the party with a bang that would make Milwaukeans' Bavarian forebearers proud. *Summerfest* ranks with Munich's legendary Oktoberfest as one of the world's premier beer blowouts.

Milwaukee has been making beer since about 1822, when founder Solomon Juneau started brewing a frontier pilsner here.

Business thrived as the area filled with waves of thirsty immigrants—mostly Germans. Beer quickly became a central factor in Milwaukee's economy and culture, and before long, the city was a prosperous, industrial giant. It attracted immigrants from around the globe, making Milwaukee a surprisingly cosmopolitan, land-locked island of cultures. Pabst, Blatz, Stroh's, Schlitz, and of course, the monolithic Miller were all born and raised in Milwaukee, a k a Brew City.

Milwaukee's beer-loving, northern European heritage remains conspicuous in its night life, which is synonymous with its pub life. Milwaukee's cuisine sways toward steak, cheese, potatoes, and heavy Teutonic platters relished by the city's founders. There are also enough attractions in this city of more than 600,000 to keep you hopping when you're not enjoying one of the biggest and best music festivals in the world.

Summerfest

Day 1. Thu. Jun. 24, 1999
(Day 1. Thursday   June 29, 2000)

10:00am Rich with Old World charm and elegance, the **Pfister Hotel** is a 20-minute walk from *Summerfest*. It's even closer to the night life of the historic Third Ward and Milwaukee's East Side. Musicians playing the festival tend to stay here, so check the lobby for familiar faces.

10:30am Wander around the neighborhood, then head to Lake Michigan and the **Milwaukee Art Museum** for its noon opening. The 20,000-piece collection is strong in 19th-century German art and American sculpture, photography, and painting, including two of Andy Warhol's soup cans.

1:45pm Not far away, *Summerfest* is already crawling with party-goers. Before entering the Henry W. Maier Festival Grounds, walk through the parking lots closest to the entrance. Milwaukee's own Harley-Davidson company commandeers them for the arrival of thousands of Harleys in an unofficial, thundering opening-day parade of leather and chrome.

2:00pm The booths of more than 45 restaurants sell foods that include bratwurst, pizza, braised-beef medallions, and *focaccia* sandwiches. *Summerfest* stages and dancing areas are surrounded and separated by crafts peddlers, games of chance, and carnival rides. There are also corporate-sponsored activities, including in-line skating exhibitions, volleyball games, and tents where you can spend cash on CDs and other music stuff.

6:30pm Cab to the popular **Coerper's Five O'Clock Club**, a diamond-in-the-rough dinner spot with dim lighting, dark accents, and vinyl booths. You can choose from one entree: steak (it's the best in Milwaukee). A well-balanced meal here means a brandy old-fashioned before and after the main course.

8:30pm Catch one more show—and, of course, one more beer—at the *Fest*. Everywhere you look, a banner, decorated tent, or a three-stories-high inflated can reminds you of Milwaukee's drink of choice. But there's no sign of the so-called King of Beers in this town. This is Brew City, where local flavors rule. Wrap your hands around a cold one and join the dancing and people-watching. Or sit by the lake and enjoy the melodies from the many stages blending together into a symphony.

10:35pm Day One finishes with a fireworks extravaganza—the ***Big Bang*** at the Big Gig. You can see the show from anywhere on the grounds, but people start gathering at 9:30 p.m. for spectacular lakeside views.

11:30pm When *Summerfest* closes, follow the crowd and walk five minutes to the historic Third Ward. On Water Street, stop into the **Milwaukee Ale House**, *the* place to continue the *Summerfest* celebration. Patrons quaff house-brewed beer, dance, and sing on a two-level deck over the Milwaukee River.

Day 2. Fri. Jun. 25, 1999
(Day 2. Friday   June 30, 2000)

10:00am Bear Brew Coffee, around the corner from the Pfister, serves some of the best breakfast pastries in town.

10:30am Walk along the Milwaukee Riverwalk toward a cluster of interesting shops on Old World Third Street. Sample some of Wisconsin's homemade cheeses, honeys, and mustards at the Wisconsin Cheese Mart. Stop into Milwaukee landmark Usinger's Famous Sausage. They've been making "America's finest sausage" since 1880. Between shops, duck into **Buck Bradley's Saloon & Eatery** to pull up one of 40 stools to the gorgeous cherrywood and rose-granite bar—it's the longest one east of the Mississippi River.

Noon Cross the street to **Mader's Restaurant**, which has kept its German cuisine and atmosphere authentic since 1902. Feast like a Bavarian prince on specialties such as sauerbraten, Wiener schnitzel, or liver-dumpling soup, surrounded by an impressive collection of medieval armor and art. Mader's adjacent **Knight's Bar** serves lighter fare and more than 200 beers. Dark wood, stained glass, and furniture from Baron von Richtofen's castle emanate Old World ambience.

2:00pm The **Milwaukee Public Museum** is the star of a three-museum complex that includes the Humphrey IMAX Dome Theater and Discovery World-The James Lovell Museum of Science, Economics and Technology. It's a wonderful natural-history museum with walk-through exhibits including the "Streets of Old Milwaukee."

6:30pm From the hotel, walk around the corner to dinner at **Louise's Trattoria** for a California-comes-to-Milwaukee dinner. **Taylor's** has a nice bar. Or head to **Eagan's on Water** to order your favorite cocktail, concocted from among the more than 400 liquors displayed behind the bar.

10:00pm Close the day back on Old World Third Street at two of Milwaukee's better clubs—the retro-chic **Velvet Room** and the **Emerald City** dance club.

Day 3. Sat.   Jun. 26, 1999
(Day 3. Saturday   July 1, 2000)

9:30am Take a short walk to the contemporary **Cafe Knickerbocker**. On the outdoor patio, soak up the sun while you eat light and tasty pancakes, waffles, or omelets.

10:30am It's a worthwhile cab ride to **America's Black Holocaust Museum**, which provides a history of racial injustice in a thought-provoking exhibit.

Noon Two blocks from the hotel is **Elsa's on the Park**. There are spectacular views of St. John's Cathedral and to-die-for burgers at this swank but inviting lunch spot.

1:30pm Back to *Summerfest* to catch anything you may have missed Thursday—such as, maybe, the human cannonball or the water-ski show. You can try winning a car in the Hole-In-One golfing contest in between musical performances. Or shop around for more music.

7:30pm After dressing up a bit, stop into Pfister's elegant **Lobby Lounge** for an aperitif among *Summerfest* musicians.

8:30pm Cab to Brady Street, the eclectic epicenter of Milwaukee's East Side neighborhood. Among Milwaukee's upper echelon of eateries, **Sanford Restaurant** is a cozy hot spot offering impeccable contemporary American cuisine created by an award-winning chef. A good alternative for Italian food is **Mimma's Cafe**.

10:30pm Up & Under Pub has been popular since long before the East Side's current renaissance, attracting renowned blues acts from across the country. The new **Hi Hat Lounge** has a jazzier feel. If you still haven't had enough music, you could always stay another day—along with summer, *Summerfest* is still just getting started.

Alternatives

The **Wyndham Milwaukee Center Hotel**, located in the heart of downtown's Theater District, is an attractive old building, with rooms decorated in what it calls Flemish-Renaissance style. The newly developed art-deco, all-suite **Hotel Metro** is another good downtown choice.

If you can't get a table at Coerper's, **Butch's Old Casino Steak House** is great for steak, as well as beautiful pork chops and succulent lamb shanks. One of the city's only true late-night restaurants is **Pizza Man,** home to the largest collection of wines in the city—all available by the glass—and a menu that surpasses pizza, with such treats as wild-boar ravioli and *escargot* in a white-wine sauce. For an excellent German restaurant, look no further than **Karl Ratzsch's**.

The Hot Sheet

HOTELS		ADDRESS	PH	FX		PRICE	RMS	BEST ROOMS
Hotel Metro	Alt	411 E. Mason St.	414-272-1937	414-223-1158		$$	65	Spa suite
Pfister Hotel	★	424 E. Wisconsin Ave.	414-273-8222 800-558-8232	414-273-0747		$$$	300	Lake vw
Wyndham Milwaukee Center Hotel	Alt	139 E. Kilbourn Ave.	414-276-8686 800-996-3426	414-276-8007		$$$	221	Grand king city vw

RESTAURANTS	DAY	ADDRESS	PH	PRICE	REC	DRESS	FOOD
Bear Brew Coffee	2	708 N. Milwaukee St.	414-224-8877	$	B/LD	Local	American
Butch's Old Casino Steak House	Alt	555 N. 7th St.	414-271-8111	$$	D	Kazh	American
Cafe Knickerbocker	3	1028 E. Juneau Ave.	414-272-0011	$	B/LD	Local	Continental
Coerper's Five O'Clock Club	1	2416 W. State St.	414-342-3553	$$	D	Kazh	American
Elsa's on the Park	3	833 Jefferson St.	414-765-0615	$	L/D	Local	American
Karl Ratzsch's	Alt	320 E. Mason St.	414-276-2720	$$$	D	Kazh	German
Knight's Bar	2	see Mader's Restaurant	414-271-3377	$	L/D	Local	German
Louise's Trattoria	2	801 N. Jefferson St.	414-273-4224	$$	D/L	Kazh	Italian
Mader's Restaurant	2	1037 N. Old World 3rd St.	414-271-3377	$$	L/D	Local	German
Mimma's Cafe	3	1307 E. Brady St.	414-271-7337	$$$	D	Kazh	Italian
Pizza Man	Alt	1800 E. North Ave.	414-272-1745	$$	LD	Local	Italian
Sanford Restaurant	3	1547 Jackson St.	414-276-9608	$$$	D	Kazh	Contemporary American

NIGHTLIFE	DAY	ADDRESS	PH	COVER	REC*	DRESS	MUSIC
Buck Bradley's Saloon & Eatery	2	1019 N. Old World 3rd St.	414-224-8500	None	R(F)	Local	
Eagan's on Water	2	1030 N. Water St.	414-271-6900	$$	R(F)	Kazh	
Emerald City	2	1101 N. Old World 3rd St.	414-226-2489	None	P	Local	Jazz, blues
Hi Hat Lounge	3	1701 N. Arlington St.	414 225-9330	None	M(F)	Local	Jazz
Lobby Lounge	3	see Pfister Hotel	414-273-8222	None	M(F)	Kazh	Piano
Milwaukee Ale House	1	233 N. Water St.	414-226-2337	$	MP(F)	Local	Swing, rock, blues, folk
Taylor's	2	795 N. Jefferson St.	414-271-2856	None	R	Local	
Up & Under Pub	3	1216 E. Brady St.	414-276-2677	$	M(F)	Local	Blues
Velvet Room	2	730 N. Old World 3rd St.	414-319-1190	None	MP(F)	Local	Jazz, swing

SIGHTS & ATTRACTIONS	DAY	ADDRESS	PH	ENTRY FEE
America's Black Holocaust Museum	3	2233 N. 4th St.	414-264-2500	$
Milwaukee Art Museum	1	750 N. Lincoln Memorial Dr.	414-224-3200	$
Milwaukee Public Museum	2	800 W. Wells St.	414-278-2700	$
Greater Milwaukee CVB		510 W. Kilbourn Ave.	800-554-1448	

Event & Ticket Info

Summerfest (Henry W. Maier Festival Park): Tickets ($9 Fri./Sat., $8 other days) are available at the gate. For more information, contact *Milwaukee World Festival Inc.* (800-273-3378 or 414-273-2680)

For headliner shows at the Marcus Amphitheater, an additional ticket ($10-$25) should be ordered in advance (starting in April) through *Ticketmaster* (414-276-4545 or 800-359-2525).

* M=Live music; P=Dancing (Party); R=Bar only; S=Show; (F)=Food served. For further explanation of codes, see page 14.

 NYC −1 General Mitchell (MKE) <30 min./S<20 Yes/No 59°/80° (15°/27°)

Magic in the Air

Ka-boom! Showers of red, blue, and amber burst like flowers in the sky, with tendrils trailing slowly down. White flashes zig-zag up and explode into sparkles. Lights streak across the sky with long fiery tails, stars erupt into sprays, and waterfalls of sparks appear to thundering reverberations.

Nearly every event in this book accentuates the excitement with fireworks. While the loud noise produced by igniting saltpeter, sulfur, and charcoal packed into bamboo tubes 2,000 years ago in China was used to drive away evil spirits, now the booms, hisses, and spectacular colors are intended to summon the spirits of fun and awe.

There are thousands of Fourth of July fireworks celebrations all over the United States. But fireworks also light up the sky at state and local fairs, festivals, amusement parks, parades, and many other events. Some celebrations even bring fireworks indoors. Louisville, Ky., claims the largest fireworks show in the country on opening day of the Kentucky Derby Festival, when nearly 34,000 shells splash spectacular designs high in the sky over the Ohio River, building up to the grand finale of a 6,000-foot "wall of fireworks" re-creating a fiery Niagara Falls.

How can you judge a fireworks show? Money doesn't necessarily buy the best shows—costs can reach $2,500 a minute for choreographed productions, but a well-planned state-fair show can bliss out a crowd for less than $10,000. Several competitions claim to evaluate the best, including contests in Spain, Stockholm, Cannes, and Monte Carlo. Many US contenders consider a gold Jupiter from Montréal's Benson & Hedges International competition to be the most prestigious. Between May and July, more than 1.5 million people in Montréal thrill to nine nights of magnificent pyromusical displays, the largest fireworks-and-music spectacle in the world. While fireworks normally serve as background to festivals and events, these nights hail pyrotechnicians as true artists.

Montréal's jury ignores decibels, looking instead for subtleties and richness of composition. The brilliance of the colors, quality and originality of the fireworks, and precision synchronization between the sound effects and fireworks are crucial. Entrants choreograph shows to all kinds of music, including classical, dance, electronic, rock, and movie themes. Some use lasers, giant water screens, narration, and other effects. But the most critical aspect of each show is how well its presentation inspires emotion and imagination.

Ongoing research and development make fireworks shows more exciting and popular all the time. For years, white and amber were the only colors available. But as pyrotechnicians experiment with new mixes of chemicals and salts, the skies can be lit with yellow, red, green, blue, and, most recently, pastels as well as a wide range of other colors, such as aqua and fuscia. Shells can now reach more than a thousand feet into the sky and be seen for miles.

All fireworks shows used to be dangerously hand-fired with torches set to the fuses of each shell. Most still are. But increasingly, shows are choreographed on computers and either electrically-fired by flipping switches to ignite prewired shells or computer-fired with the touch of button.

Different countries have signature designs that are mixed into fireworks celebrations. Asian fireworks tend to be large yet quiet and colorful, displaying elegant flowers. Europe builds great rockets and candles, with the French especially known for glitzy, silvery, and glamorous designs. England favors screaming hummers and streaking serpents. South American fireworks are flamboyant, while Italians like noisy celebrations with loud finales.

European fireworks productions, less constricted by liability concerns, often differ from those in North America, working the whole sky with great wide tableau, rockets, and other fireworks not seen in the United States. European laser shows might scan the audience or shoot moving beams into its midst, creating spectacular effects American laws don't allow.

Multimedia productions sometimes add lasers to create pencil-thin beams. When a beam is projected onto a screen—whether a building, a mountainside, or smoke from fireworks—it produces a small dot of bright light. But rapid motion causes the human eye to perceive that dot as a line, much the way that swishing sparklers can "write" in the air. Laser light can be shot through an oscillating crystal and then recombined into 40 million colors. While some fireworks purists disdain lasers, laser artists claim their creations add dramatic impact and extend audience attention.

Typical fireworks shows surprisingly run just 18 to 23 minutes (though multimedia productions tend to last longer). Some of the most famous displays, such as the nightly fireworks choreographed to music at Disney theme parks, may run only five to 15 minutes. Even in such short bursts, fireworks still provide a thrill that is as unique as it is timeless.

Here are some terms you might want to use to impress your friends while watching those incredible displays of sound and light:

Effects

Aerials: fireworks that explode high in the sky

Battle in the clouds: a number of salutes timed to explode in succession, sounding like a fusillade of musketry

Chrysanthemum: shells that break into trails of fine lines, like flowers bursting forth

Comet: a shell that streaks across the sky, displaying a long, fiery tail that drops sparkles along its trail

Diadems: ejected cardboardlike strips or disks that flicker brightly as they fall in a cluster

Fountain: a tall spray of sparks

Fuse: a string of woven threads containing gunpowder that ignites the charges at the base of the shell

Hummer: an aerial spinning device that makes a screaming or humming sound

Pattern: a configuration of stars that explodes to create desired shapes, such as five-pointed stars and hearts

Peonies: stars that burst from a central core without trails

Potato: a basic aerial shell that breaks into a shower of color

Roman candle: a tube containing alternating layers of compacted black powder and single stars that rise one at a time into the sky

Salute: a loud, concussive report and flash of light to punctuate a display

Serpent: a small tube that shoots in erratic colorful streaks across the sky

Set piece: an illumination placed on a frame set into the ground that outlines a picture or words in colored fire

Strobes: a cluster of flashing silvery lights that float down slowly in the sky

Weeping willow: a star that burns so slowly as it falls through the sky that it suggests elegant, drooping willow branches

Whistle shell: a noisemaker that shrieks as it streaks across the sky after a shell burst

Hardware

Mortar: a launching tube made of heavy cardboard or metal sunk into the ground or mounted in racks

Parachute: used to suspend various effects, including flares, colored chains, or illuminated flags

Shell: the hard paper container, weighing between one and 160 pounds and shot from a launcher that carries fireworks into the sky

Stars: hundreds of chemical pellets in different sizes packaged together to ignite at the height of a shell's climb, bursting into planned patterns

Philadelphia, Pennsylvania, USA

Fourth of July

(Sunoco Welcome America)

Origin: 1993   Event ★ ★ ★ ★ ★ ★ ★ ★ City   Attendance: 1,000,000

Ever since the Founding Fathers converged on Philadelphia in 1776 to put their John Hancocks on the Declaration of Independence, Philadelphians have made certain their *July 4* soiree is the best in the country. Celebrating America's birthday in America's birthplace, more than two million revelers flock to Philly's green lawns and riverside parks for a series of food fests, parades, outdoor concerts, and fireworks shows that paint the city's summer nights in red, white, and blue.

Philly's well-preserved historic setting makes it the perfect place for celebrating the nation's birth. About 40 free events are scheduled between the end of June and the *Fourth of July*. Top names in popular music give free outdoor concerts and, on July 3, fireworks light the sky over Penn's Landing on the Delaware River. Not bad for opening acts, but the main event comes on *Independence Day*, when the Benjamin Franklin Parkway is invaded by an army of all-American floats. Another outdoor concert warms up the crowd for the grand fireworks display above the Philadelphia Museum of Art and Schuylkill River. The spectacular pyrotechnics are accompanied by patriotic songs performed by the Philly Pops.

America's fifth-largest city is best-known for cheese steaks and hoagies, but there's much more to the city than unforgettable sandwiches. In 1994, Philadelphia was voted by readers of *Condé Naste Traveler* as America's best restaurant city. The Philadelphia Orchestra enjoys a reputation that places it among the best in the world. The vast Philadelphia Museum of Art houses 2,000 years' worth of art. And when the sun goes down, hedonists can partake of the chic new nightclub scene along the banks of the Delaware River. The City of Brotherly Love has been dubbed "America's Friendliest City." Helpful natives and a treasure-trove of historic sites make Philadelphia an easy city for first-timers to explore.

Sure, taxation without representation was good spin, but America has always been about the pursuit of happiness and the right to peaceable assembly. Find out what really fueled the American Revolution during the week when all of Philly transforms into one big historic block party.

Fourth of July

Day 1. Fri.   Jul. 2, 1999
(Day 3. Wednesday   *July 5, 2000)*

9:00am Your perfectly appointed **Omni Hotel** is located in the center of the Independence National Historical Park. Have breakfast in its **Azalea Room** as you look out onto the Second Bank of the United States, a beautiful Greek Revival building.

10:30am A walk through Philadelphia's city center will take you to **Reading Terminal Market**, housed in the old Reading Railroad (do not pass go, do not collect $200) station. Restaurants and food stalls serve everything from Chinese to soul food to Pennsylvania Dutch specialties.

Noon Have **Rick's Philly Steaks** grill you a cheese steak. Before leaving the market try one of the city's famous soft pretzels.

1:00pm Walk to the **Rodin Museum**, which houses the largest collection of the master's sculptures outside France. The nearby **Philadelphia Museum of Art** follows with one of America's largest art collections. European masters are featured alongside a Hindu temple, 12th-century French cloister, and Japanese teahouse.

7:30pm You've had time to rest up for a night on the town. Start with a drink at the 40-foot mahogany bar inside **Circa**—located in an impressive 100-year-old building—then enjoy creative versions of classic American cuisine. After dinner hours, Circa turns into a dance club frequented by attractive young professionals.

10:00pm If you'd prefer live music, cab to **Warmdaddy's for Blues**, a New Orleans-style blues club that draws a prosperous clientele for big-name performers.

12:30am On bar-hopping South Street, **The Monte Carlo Living Room** encourages you to put your dancing shoes on for Top-40 music before calling it a night.

Day 2. Sat.   Jul. 3, 1999
(Day 1. Monday   *July 3, 2000)*

10:00am After breakfast at the **Down Home Diner** in the Reading Terminal Market, walk to the **Franklin Institute Science Museum**. It's crammed with interactive science exhibits, highlighted by the famed Franklin Institute heart. Wander into blood vessels large enough to accommodate a tall man and hear the deafening thud of a beating heart.

Noon Try the Belgian crab cakes at nearby **Bridgid's**, a sophisticated eatery specializing in Belgian cuisine. Or order to-go at **Ben's**, the institute's cafeteria, and picnic on the lawns of nearby Fairmount Park.

1:30pm Stroll through the Philadelphia Museum's azalea gardens to picturesque **Boat House Row**, a series of Victorian mansions along the Schuylkill River. Then walk through **Fairmount Park**, the world's largest landscaped city park, measuring some 8,900 acres. Begin at Lemon Hill, an elegant mansion noted for its oval-shaped rooms.

4:30pm Fortify yourself (it will be a while before dinner) amidst Old World elegance at the **Rittenhouse Hotel**. This charming establishment is Philly's premier spot for high tea.

7:30pm From your hotel, walk five minutes to **Penn's Landing** for the free, outdoor pop *concert*. You can probably snag an open spot along the retaining wall to the left of the stage, which beats showing up at 5 p.m. to ensure a seat. The concert is followed by fantastic *fireworks* over the Delaware River.

10:15pm When the pyrotechnics are over, head to the trendy **Rock Lobster**. This lively outdoor riverside restaurant serves steak and shellfish dishes amid a festive but casual atmosphere.

Midnight Nearby, **Katmandu**, Philly's best summertime outdoor nightclub, is already jammed with partyers dancing to live and recorded music. If you prefer an indoor club, try **Egypt** or **The Eighth Floor**, or squeeze in all three on your way to bed.

Day 3. Sun.   Jul. 4, 1999
(Day 2. Tuesday   July 4, 2000)

9:30am After a room-service breakfast, stroll outside along with performers in 18th-century costumes who set the stage for a memorable birthday. In front of Independence Hall, the ***Liberty Medal*** ceremony includes stirring speeches by award recipients. Past winners have included Nelson Mandela, Yitzak Rabin, and Ted Turner.

11:00am If you don't choose to rub elbows with Philadelphia's political and business elite at the ***Philadelphia Liberty Medal Luncheon***, stick around for "Ben Franklin's Greatest Hits," a musical-comedy skit that recounts the major events in Franklin's life. The show is followed by a mass exodus to the **Liberty Bell**, where descendants of signers of the Declaration of Independence get to ring the revered artifact.

12:30pm Nearby, **City Tavern**, an 18th-century eatery with restored Revolutionary charms, has a quaint dining room decorated with period furniture. The costumed staff serves delicious American culinary classics and unusual ales while a quartet plays period music in the salon.

2:00pm Explore the historic district and Society Hill from a horse-drawn carriage—while a local at the reins gives his salty take on Revolutionary history. Don't miss **Independence Hall**, where the Declaration of Independence was signed; Christ Church, where many of the Founding Fathers prayed for liberty; the elegant First Bank of the United States, America's first major building in the Greek Revival style; and Carpenters' Hall, where the First Continental Congress convened in 1774. Another interesting stop is Franklin Court, an open-air, skeletal version of Ben's home that leads to an unusual post office and museum.

6:00pm An evening of red-white-and-blue festivities begins with a ***parade*** that turns onto Ben Franklin Parkway at 16th Street. The parade proceeds to the Philadelphia Museum of Art, which serves as the backdrop for a ***concert*** by pop superstars, along with patriotic music by the Philly Pops. Food stands are plentiful and make the most sense for dinner.

10:00pm A spectacular ***fireworks*** show above the museum caps the evening. As crowds disperse, vie for space at the **Swan Lounge** in the nearby Four Seasons hotel. According to historian Benson Bobrick, most of the secret planning for the revolution took place in taverns and inns, so before taking your leave, hoist a final grog for patriotism's sake and toast every Tom, George, and Benjamin in the bar.

Alternatives

The **Park Hyatt Philadelphia** makes an excellent second choice for a hotel. Like the Omni, it's located on Independence Park. Although its location is less appropriate for this occasion, the **Four Seasons Philadelphia** is generally recognized as the city's top hotel.

Brasserie Perrier is the more hip and lively sister of the famous **Le Bec-Fin**, which is often ranked as Philadelphia's, if not the nation's, best restaurant. **Striped Bass**, a beautiful all-seafood restaurant, is a strong challenger to the title. **Zanzibar Blue** is another popular late-night hangout, featuring recorded dance music and live jazz.

The Hot Sheet

HOTELS		ADDRESS	PH	FX	PRICE	RMS	BEST ROOMS
Four Seasons Philadelphia	Alt	1 Logan Sq.	215-963-1500 800-332-3442	215-963-9562	$$$$	365	Logan Circle vw
Omni Hotel	★	401 Chestnut St.	215-925-0000 800-843-6664	215-925-1263	$$$	150	Vw of Independence Park
Park Hyatt Philadelphia	Alt	1415 Chancellor Ct.	215-893-1776 800-233-1234	215-732-8518	$$$	170	Stratford rms have bdrm and lr w/city vw

RESTAURANTS	DAY	ADDRESS	PH	PRICE	REC	DRESS	FOOD
Azalea Room	1	see Omni Hotel	215-925-0000	$	B/LD	Local	New American
Ben's	2	20th St. and Ben Franklin, see the Franklin Institute	215-448-1200	$	L	Local	Salad, pasta, cheese steaks
Brasserie Perrier	Alt	1619 Walnut St.	215-568-3000	$$	LD	Kazh	Italian, French w/Asian influence
Bridgid's	2	726 N. 24th St.	215-232-3232	$	L/D	Local	Belgian
Circa	1	1518 Walnut St.	215-545-6800	$$	D	Yuppie	New American
City Tavern	3	212 Walnut St.	215-413-1443	$$	L/D	Local	Traditional fayre
Down Home Diner	2	12th and Arch sts., inside Reading Terminal Mkt.	215-627-1955	$	B/LD	Local	American, Southern
Le Bec-Fin	Alt	1523 Walnut St.	215-567-1000	$$$$	D	Dressy	Haute French
Rick's Philly Steaks	1	12th and Arch sts., inside Reading Terminal Mkt.	215-925-4320	$	L	Local	Cheese steaks
Rittenhouse Hotel	2	210 W. Rittenhouse Sq.	215-546-9000	$$	T	Kazh	High tea
Rock Lobster	2	Pier 13-15, near Columbus Blvd.	215-627-7625	$$	D/L	Local	Steak and shellfish
Striped Bass	Alt	1500 Walnut St.	215-732-4444	$$$$	LD	Dressy, Kazh	Seafood

NIGHTLIFE	DAY	ADDRESS	PH	COVER	REC*	DRESS	MUSIC
Egypt	2	520 N. Delaware Ave.	215-922-6500	$	P	Local	Top 40
The Eighth Floor	2	800 N. Delaware Ave.	215-922-1000	$	P	Local, Kazh	'70s, progressive
Katmandu	2	417 N. Columbus Blvd. at Pier 25	215-629-7400	$	MP(F)	Local	Reggae, Top 40
The Monte Carlo Living Room	1	150 South St.	215-925-2220	$	P(F)	Yuppie, Kazh	Top 40
Swan Lounge	3	see Four Seasons hotel	215-963-1500	None	R	Dressy, Kazh	
Warmdaddy's for Blues	1	4 S. Front St.	215-627-2500	$	M(F)	Local	Blues
Zanzibar Blue	Alt	2000 S. Broad St.	215-732-4500	$$	M	Local	Jazz

SIGHTS & ATTRACTIONS	DAY	ADDRESS	PH	ENTRY FEE
Boat House Row	2	on Schuylkill River		None
Fairmount Park	2	River Dr., Belmont Ave., or Kelly Dr.	215-685-0000	None
Franklin Institute Science Museum	2	2222 N. 20th St.	215-448-1200	$
Independence Hall	3	5th and Chestnut st.	215-597-8974	None
Liberty Bell	3	Market St. betw. 5th and 6th sts.	215-597-8974	None
Penn's Landing	2	Delaware River, Lombard to Market St.	215-922-2386	None
Philadelphia Museum of Art	1	26th St. and Ben Franklin Pkwy.	215-763-8100	$
Reading Terminal Market	1	12th and Arch sts.	215-922-2317	None
Rodin Museum	1	22nd St. and Ben Franklin Pkwy.	215-763-8100	$
Philadelphia CVB		16th and John F. Kennedy Blvd.	800-321-9563	

Event & Ticket Info

Fourth of July: Most activities, including the recommended concerts, are free. For more information, call *Philadelphia Visitors Center* (800-777-5883).

Philadelphia Liberty Medal Luncheon (Philadelphia Marriott, 1201 Market St.): For tickets ($150 CD) and information, contact *Greater Philadelphia First* (215-575-2200).

* M=Live music; P=Dancing (Party); R=Bar only; S=Show; (F)=Food served. For further explanation of codes, see page 14.

 NYC Philadelphia (PHL) <30 min./$20   No 67°/87° (19°/31°)

June/July 1999

Boston, Massachusetts, USA

June/July 2000

Boston Harborfest

Origin: 1982 Event ★ ★ ★ ★ ★ ★ ★ City Attendance: 2,500,000

Big-time partying in America began in Boston on December 16, 1773. That's the date some 7,000 citizens came to the Old South Meeting House, spilled into the streets protesting imperial oppression, and just maybe exceeded modern DMV standards for legal blood-alcohol content.

Close to midnight on that fateful day when British officials refused for the final time to take their tea back home, almost a hundred men disguised as Mohawk Indians suddenly appeared outside Old South's doors, and the cry "To the wharves!" rang out. When the night was over, nearly 60 tons of tea leaves were floating in the harbor and America had enjoyed its first raging party, the Boston Tea Party.

These days, the town's big shindig, **Harborfest**, gives thanks to Samuel Adams, Paul Revere, John Hancock, and all the other colonists who gave us the freedom to hear the Boston Pops perform Tchaikovsky's *1812 Overture* while watching an awesome fireworks display overhead. The week-long festival features more than 170 events that not only celebrate Boston's role in the American Revolution, but its rich maritime history. More than two million visitors come to **Harborfest** to view the USS *Constitution*, go on whale-watching cruises, see free jazz and rock concerts, and watch the Independence Day Parade. The highlight of the weekend is the Boston Pops concert on the Esplanade. The Pops play patriotic favorites while three tons of pyrotechnic showers burst overhead in a deafening crescendo.

Even with all the **Harborfest** happenings, try to visit as many of Boston's other top attractions as you can. The Museum of Fine Arts, Boston has an excellent collection of early-American paintings. The Freedom Trail brings you historic sites of the American Revolution, including one of the country's oldest pubs, the Green Dragon Tavern. During the Revolutionary period, Sam Adams held many meetings in the bar's secret back room. Venture inside, give a toast to this incendiary speaker, and do your duty as an American (or sympathetic ally) by downing a beer with his name on it.

Boston Harborfest

Day 1. Fri. Jul. 2, 1999
(Day 1. Sunday *July 2, 2000)*

8:30am Arrive at **The Ritz-Carlton Boston**, directly across from the Boston Public Garden and within walking distance of all *Harborfest* events. Built in 1927, its exquisite rooms have hosted Winston Churchill, Bette Davis, and Jackie O.

9:30am Say hello to the swans in the Public Garden as you walk to Beacon Hill for breakfast at **Panificio**. The waffles with fresh fruit are sublime.

10:30am Head back to Beacon Street and start along the Freedom Trail. Toss away your map and follow the red line that takes you past 16 monumental sites and into the city's cherished neighborhoods—Beacon Hill, with century-old brick brownstones; the North End, with winding streets and a lively Italian community; and Charlestown, home to the Battle of Bunker Hill and now the resting spot for America's most celebrated ship, the USS *Constitution*. Stop at the graves of Paul Revere, Samuel Adams, and John Hancock; the Old South Meeting House; and Boston's number-one attraction, Quincy Market, a renovated historic district now filled with shops and restaurants.

1:00pm Lunch at **Ye Olde Union Oyster House**, the oldest restaurant in continuous service in America. Opened in 1826, this is where Daniel Webster had his daily breakfast of three dozen oysters with several tumblers of brandy, and where John F. Kennedy often dined on lobster stew.

2:30pm Part Two of the Freedom Trail brings you to Boston's oldest building, the home of Paul Revere, then across the Charlestown Bridge to reach Old Ironsides and Bunker Hill. Return via the $1 ferry ride from the Charleston Navy Yard and cab back to The Ritz.

7:00pm Head to the 62nd-floor **John Hancock Observatory** in the John Hancock Building. A terrific light display traces the history of Boston.

8:30pm Dine at one of Boston's newest and hottest restaurants, **Clio**, in the swank Eliot Suite Hotel. Chef Ken Oringer gets rave reviews for his continental fare, served at intimate tables.

10:30pm Cab to **Aria** and plop down on an overstuffed sofa for an after-dinner drink. Afterward, salsa and tango the night away at **Europa**'s Latin night.

12:30am If you have energy for more, try **Trattoria Il Panino**—the restaurant and dance floors are split among five levels.

Day 2. Sat. Jul. 3, 1999
(Day 2. Monday *July 3, 2000)*

9:30am **Charlie's Sandwich Shoppe** is an old-time urban diner with famous banana and blueberry pancakes. This is strictly a local joint so be prepared to talk about the Red Sox and the Celtics.

10:30am Cab to the **Museum of Fine Arts, Boston** to view the excellent permanent collection. Gilbert Stuart's well-known portrait of George Washington is here along with works by Winslow Homer, Fitz Hugh Lane, and French impressionists.

12:30pm Stroll to the **Isabella Stewart Gardner Museum** where the cafe serves lobster bisque and a wide selection of salads and sandwiches. The courtyard is filled year-round with flowers.

3:00pm Cab to the corner of Newbury and Fairfield streets. Walk down Newbury Street, Boston's low-key version of New York's Fifth Avenue, back toward The Ritz. Here, you'll find the finest boutiques in Beantown. Stop for a drink at an outdoor place such as **Armani Cafe** or the very hip **Sonsie**.

6:00pm Walk 20 minutes to City Hall Plaza to see a popular band perform at the *Party on the Plaza*.

8:30pm Eat at **La Bettola**, where chef Rene Michelena has won honors from *Esquire*, *Bon Appétit*, and *Food and Wine* magazines.

10:30pm On your way back to the hotel you can try **The Big Easy Bar**, a large but comfortable dance hall. **Mercury Bar**, a bit more mellow, is another good choice for an upscale scene and great snack food.

Day 3. Sun. Jul. 4, 1999
(Day 3. Tuesday   July 4, 2000)

8:30am Breakfast at The Ritz cafe on the first floor of the hotel.

9:30am Stroll to Boston City Hall for a *flag-raising ceremony* and *parade*. If you want good seats for the evening's Boston Pops performance, you'll have to head to the Esplanade immediately after the parade and plant yourself for the remainder of the day.

1:30pm Cab to Cambridge for lunch in Harvard Yard at **Up Stairs at the Pudding**. The restaurant is situated above the Hasty Pudding Playhouse, home to Harvard's famous theatrical group. Ask for a table in the garden.

2:30pm Tour America's most celebrated campus, then head to Harvard Square to people-watch. Ecuadorian musicians, mimes, heavy-metal guitarists, beggars, and jugglers all entertain the bespectacled Harvard intellectuals.

5:00pm Cab to downtown Boston before the crowds get too thick. Head to The Four Seasons' **Bristol Lounge**. Year after year, their martini is voted the best in town by *Boston Magazine*.

8:00pm The Main Event. You can try to squeeze into the Esplanade or you can walk across Longfellow Bridge to Cambridge and see the fireworks with far fewer people. You won't be able to see the Pops from there, but you can certainly hear them.

10:30pm There's no better late-night dining scene than **Mistral**. Owned by famed nightclub impresario Seth Greenberg, Mistral is known for excellent French food in a stylish Provençal setting.

12:30pm Insomniacs head to **Wally's Cafe** for late-night jazz and blues. It's the kind of place where you can get some help bringing your Fourth to an end with a fifth.

Alternatives

A *Harborfest* highlight is *Chowderfest*, a chowder-cooking contest where the public is invited to sample.

L ocated on the edge of the Boston Public Garden, **The Four Seasons Boston** has the same views as The Ritz. One of the city's finest boutique hotels, **The Eliot Suite Hotel** has undergone an elegant renovation.

H amersley's Bistro has been awarded four stars (the highest ranking) by the *Boston Globe*. At hip **Biba**, tables overlook the Boston Public Garden. **Grill 23 & Bar** is one of the city's best steakhouses. **Legal Sea Foods** is a chain, but worth a visit. **Les Zygamotes** (French for "the muscles that make us smile"), is a buzzing bistro. The trendy **Restaurant Zinc** has great food, a beautiful zinc bar, lots of noise, and late hours. Terrific outdoor tables at **29 Newbury** allow you to enjoy New American cuisine while people-watching.

R egattabar in the Charles Hotel features high-caliber jazz acts such as Sonny Rollins and Herbie Hancock. **Lizard Lounge** is known for its eclectic mix of acid-jazz and rock. One of few remaining 17th-century taverns is the **Green Dragon Tavern**, which has live music on weekends.

T he **John F. Kennedy Library and Museum** will bring back memories of the president and his era. **Boston Harbor Whale Watch** cruise, which lasts about five hours, will also reward you with the best views of Boston's skyline.

The Hot Sheet

HOTELS		ADDRESS	PH	FX	PRICE	RMS	BEST ROOMS
The Eliot Suite Hotel	Alt	370 Commonwealth Ave.	617-267-1607 800-443-5468	617-536-9114	$$$	95	
The Four Seasons Boston	Alt	200 Boylston St.	617-338-4400 800-332-3442	627-423-0154	$$$$	400	Garden vw
The Ritz-Carlton Boston	★	15 Arlington St.	617-536-5700 800-241-3333	617-536-1335	$$$$	275	Newbury vw

RESTAURANTS	DAY	ADDRESS	PH	PRICE	REC	DRESS	FOOD
29 Newbury	Alt	29 Newbury St.	617-536-0290	$$	LD	Local, Yuppie	American eclectic
Armani Cafe	2	214 Newbury St.	617-437-0909	$$$	T/LD	Yuppie	Italian
Biba	Alt	272 Boylston St.	617-426-7878	$$$$	LD	Kazh	American eclectic
Charlie's Sandwich Shoppe	2	429 Columbus Ave.	617-536-7669	$	B/L	Local	American
Clio	1	see The Eliot Suite Hotel	617-536-7200	$$$	D	Kazh	American
Grill 23 & Bar	Alt	161 Berkeley St.	617-542-2255	$$$	D	Dressy	Grill house
Hamersley's Bistro	Alt	553 Tremont St.	617-423-2700	$$$	D	Yuppie, Local	Country French
La Bettola	2	480A Columbus Ave.	617-236-5252	$$$	D	Kazh	Italian, Asian
Legal Sea Foods	Alt	35 Columbus Ave.	617-426-4444	$$	LD	Yuppie, Local	Seafood
Les Zygamotes	Alt	129 South St.	617-542-5108	$$$	LD	Kazh	French
Mistral	3	223 Columbus Ave.	617-867-9300	$$$	D/L	Dressy, Kazh	French, Mediterranean
Panificio	1	144 Charles St.	617-227-4340	$	B	Local	American
Restaurant Zinc	Alt	35 Stanhope St.	617-262-2323	$$$	D	Kazh, Local	French, fish
Sonsie	2	327 Newberry St.	617-351-2500	$	T/LD	Kazh	New American
Up Stairs at the Pudding	3	10 Holyoke St., Cambridge	617-864-1933	$$$	L/D	Kazh	Italian, French
Ye Olde Union Oyster House	1	41 Union St.	617-227-2750	$$$	L/D	Kazh	Seafood

NIGHTLIFE	DAY	ADDRESS	PH	COVER	REC*	DRESS	MUSIC
Aria	1	246 Tremont St.	617-330-7080	$	P	Kazh	Techno, Top 40
The Big Easy Bar	2	1 Boylston Pl.	617-351-7000	$	M	Kazh	Top 40, funk, '70s/'80s
Bristol Lounge	3	see The Four Seasons hotel	617-338-4400	None	M	Kazh	Jazz
Europa	1	51 Stuart St.	617-482-3939	$	P	Kazh	Latin, disco
Green Dragon Tavern	Alt	11 Marshall St.	617-367-0055	$	M	Local	Rock
Lizard Lounge	Alt	1667 Massachusetts Ave.	617-547-1228	$	R	Local	Jazz, hip-hop, alternative
Mercury Bar	2	116 Boylston St.	617-482-7799	$	P(F)	Local	Top 40
Regattabar	Alt	1 Bennett St., Cambridge	617-864-1200	$$	M	Local	Jazz
Trattoria Il Panino	1	295 Franklin St.	617-742-8240	None	MP(F)	Kazh	Top 40, '70s, '80s
Wally's Cafe	3	427 Massachusetts Ave.	617-424-1408	None	M	Local	Blues, jazz, Latin jazz

SIGHTS & ATTRACTIONS	DAY	ADDRESS	PH	ENTRY FEE
Boston Harbor Whale Watch	Alt	60 Rowes Wharf	617-345-9866	$$
Isabella Stewart Gardner Museum	2	280 Defend Way	617-566-1401	$
John F. Kennedy Library and Museum	Alt	O. William T. Morrissey Blvd., Dorchester	617-929-4523	$
John Hancock Observatory	1	200 Clarendon St.	617-572-6429	$
Museum of Fine Arts, Boston	2	465 Huntington Ave.	617-267-9300	$
Boston CVB		147 Tremont St.	617-536-4100	

Event & Ticket Info

Boston Harborfest: Most events are free. For more information, contact *Boston Harborfest* (617-227-1528).

Party on the Plaza (City Hall Plaza on Cambridge Street): Free

Chowderfest (City Hall Plaza on Cambridge Street): Tickets ($5) can be purchased at the event.

* M=Live music; P=Dancing (Party); R=Bar only; S=Show; (F)=Food served. For further explanation of codes, see page 14.

 NYC   Logan (BOS) <30min./$20 No 65°/81° (18°/28°)

  The Fun Also Rises

Montréal Jazz Festival
(Festival International de Jazz de Montréal)

Origin: 1979   Event ★ ★ ★ ★ ★ ★ ★ City   **Attendance:** 1,500,000

In a city calling itself the City of Festivals, the ***Montréal Jazz Festival*** is the biggest and most joyful fete of the year. Often called the best jazz festival in the world—2,000 musicians from 25 countries get crowds moving at 400 shows—this event rates as one of Canada's best annual shindigs.

The ***Jazz Fest*** really ought to be called the Montréal Music Festival and Street Party. From noon until the early-morning hours, 1.5 million music lovers and social animals pack six square blocks, all of them closed to vehicular traffic. Musicians play free concerts on eight outdoor stages, turning the area into a party that reverberates with the sounds of jazz, blues, world beat, African, zydeco, rhythm and blues, and most other party-music genres. Every night, concerts and galas crank up eight indoor venues, which range from elegant theaters in Place des Arts, to some downright weird and very alternative nightclubs. Bands aren't the only acts in town—jugglers, unicyclists, illusionists, mimes, and performance artists help fill the festival site with sights. Throughout the area, jazz bars and food kiosks keep energy levels high.

So much happens at the festival that it's tempting to linger at party central. But by breaking away from the festival scene, you'll be able to enjoy cosmopolitan Montréal's beauty and vitality. Whether in Old Montréal, the Latin Quarter, or amid striking downtown architecture,

Montréal is a great walking city. Old Montréal, with its narrow cobbled streets, is an especially worthwhile side trip. Don't forget to take part in the most popular local sport—people-watching from the city's sidewalk cafes.

Montréal is actually two cities, one above ground, one below. During summer you may never see the 18 miles of subterranean pedestrian malls, but you will enjoy plenty of restaurants and bars with 3 a.m. closing times. Nearly three-quarters of metropolitan Montréal's 3.5 million citizens are French, making it the largest French population outside Paris. And as in Paris, although English is spoken, the language you'll understand best here is the local *joie de vivre*.

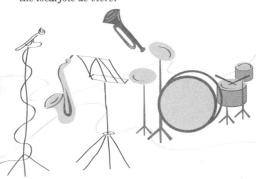

Montréal Jazz Festival

Day 1. Tue.   Jul. 6, 1999
(Day 1. Tuesday   July 4, 2000)

9:30am The attractive **L'Hôtel de la Montagne** has a posh lobby, intricately detailed marble and artwork, and rooms that offer nice views of the beautiful Mont-Royal Park.

10:30am Explore the Old Port. Then hire a *calèche* (a type of horse-drawn carriage), for a tour of Old Montréal's quaint cobbled streets. More than any other place in North America, Old Montréal really feels like Europe.

12:30pm Cab to lunch at the very French **L'Express**, marked only by its name painted on the sidewalk. Mingle at the bar with Montréalers drenched in style—from their attitudes to their designer ensembles—before having delicious bistro fare.

2:00pm Do some window-shopping on Rue St-Denis, then sit, have coffee, and people-watch from one of the streetfront terraces. The sidewalk traffic— Montréalers are very fashion conscious—is excellent for those who appreciate contemplating the better half of the human condition.

4:00pm The **Musée d'Art Contemporain** is one of Montréal's most worthwhile attractions. Enter from Place des Arts and browse through shows featuring artists working on the latest edge of modern art, many of whom tend to come from Québec.

6:00pm Leaving the museum, you'll be in the thick of *festival activity*. Grab some festival food and find a place to watch the concert. Festival themes change each year, but the outdoor extravaganza practically guarantees good time for the more than 100,000 people who show up.

11:00pm Walk to **Shed Café** for excellent late-night food and drink. Afterward, if there's a crowd outside, follow it to one of the many clubs in the area.

You'll be excused for not playing on, however, since tomorrow promises to be an even-busier day.

Day 2. Wed.   July 7, 1999
(Day 2. Wednesday   July 5, 2000)

9:00am Montréal is famous for its bagels. Find out why by ordering a bagel with cream cheese and lox at **Eggspectation**, a short walk from the hotel.

10:30am Cab to one of the city's top attractions, the **Montréal Biodôme**, an environmental museum that allows you to enter the Amazon rainforest, the Arctic, or two other climate areas filled with so much flora that you'll believe you're really there.

12:30pm It's a short ride to **Schwartz's Montréal Hebrew Delicatessen** to enjoy Montréal's famous smoked meat—which is similar to corned beef— and an old-fashioned cherry Coke. It's a long way from posh, but it's a visitor's don't-miss and Montréalers flock there, too.

2:00pm Today's *free concerts* have started. Pick up a copy of *The Gazette* for the complete performance schedule and the paper's picks for the day. You can watch outdoor concerts from stageside tables until around 6:30 p.m., when crowds become larger and denser. Scope out the area to familiarize yourself with all eight stages before the crowds show up.

6:00pm On your way back to your hotel, stop up, way up, at one of the best terrace bars in Montréal, **737**. You'll get a great view from its 45th-floor perch.

8:00pm Allow enough time to find the theater showing your choice of ***headliner concerts***, which is probably at Place des Arts. If you choose one of the Les Événements concerts at Salle Wilfrid-Pelletier, book a seat near the front for the best view or—for optimal acoustics—in the middle of the first row under the balcony overhang. In Théâtre

Maisonneuve, home of Les Grand Concerts, all seats offer good views, but sit toward the rear of the first section for the best acoustics.

10:15pm Cab to dinner at **Ferreira Café Trattoria** for an unusual Portuguese-inspired meal with an attractive crowd and setting.

12:15am Funkytown is the hot club downstairs from the Restaurant Alexandre. Afterward, walk to **Thursdays** (it's now Thursday, after all), where you can have a nightcap in the bar upstairs or dance until 3 a.m. in the club below.

Day 3. Thu.　Jul. 8, 1999
(Day 3. Thursday　　　　July 6, 2000)

9:30am Walk to **Chez Cora**. Along with basic breakfasts such as bacon and eggs and fruit, you can try *cretons*, a Québecois dish made from ground pork.

10:30am The **Montréal Museum of Fine Arts** has one of the best permanent collections in North America. Its great range of works spans centuries and disciplines.

12:30pm Have lunch at **Globe**, where the casually attractive atmosphere perfectly suits the healthy lunch menu.

2:00pm It should be an afternoon of great jazz at the *festival*, capped with a drink at **Jello Bar**. Have one or two of the many martini concoctions and bask in the '50s-style sophistication of its lounge.

7:30pm Dinner is at **Mediterraneo**, where you'll find Montréal's hip crowd eating California-Italian cuisine.

9:30pm If you crave a cigar or that type of atmosphere, try **Wax**, above the restaurant Primadonna. Or try **Diva Bar and Lounge**, as notable for its décor as for the smartly dressed group of regulars who drink there.

11:00pm Still in the neighborhood, you can exercise your dance muscles at **Club Di Salvio**. When you're ready, catch a cab back to the hotel, where, until as late as 3 a.m., you can dance to a live orchestra amid starry skies near the rooftop swimming pool at **Terrasse Magnétic**.

Alternatives

Coming on the heels of the *Jazz Festival* is the extraordinary ***Just for Laughs Comedy Festival***, which draws more than a million people to laugh with established stars and up-and-coming comedians.

If you're coming to Montréal primarily for jazz, consider **Hotel Wyndham Montréal**. This is the hotel where the festival's jazz musicians traditionally stay, and where some of them meet to jam from midnight to 4 a.m. in the hotel lounge. All you have to do is walk out the door to be in the middle of the free-concert area. Another option is the recently redecorated **Le Westin Mont-Royal** hotel. Its spacious rooms—only 12 to a floor—include living rooms.

Hip dinner alternatives are **Restaurante Primadonna** and **Buena Notte**. Another popular restaurant is **Weinstein's and Gavino's.** Many people consider **Toque!** to be Montréal's finest restaurant, where the clientele is surprisingly animated amid expensive surroundings.

The **Casino de Montréal** provides a complete evening of entertainment—dinner, nightclub show, gaming—in elegant surroundings. Just in case you can't get enough, Montréal's best-known jazz club is **Biddle's Jazz & Ribs Inc.**, where you can have chicken and ribs while listening to the music of veteran bassist Charlie Biddle and his illustrious sidemen.

Mont-Royal, with its lighted cross atop the peak, dominates the island city's skyline. Its natural park is a favorite with locals as a place to exercise, picnic, or just sit and enjoy nature. A taxi can take you partway up the mountain to enjoy wonderful views, day or night. The **Montréal Botanical Garden,** next to the Biodôme, has the largest Chinese Garden outside of Asia, and a creepy but cool collection of bugs and other small, scary things at its renowned Insectorium.

The Hot Sheet

HOTELS		ADDRESS	PH	FX	PRICE	RMS	BEST ROOMS
L'Hôtel de la Montagne	★	1430 rue de la Montagne	514-288-5656 800-361-6262	514-288-9658	$$	135	Mont-Royal, "04"
Hôtel Wyndham Montréal	Alt	1255 Jeanne-Mance	514-285-1450 800-361-8234	514-285-1243	$$	600	Mtn vw
Le Westin Mont-Royal	Alt	1050 rue Sherbrooke Ouest	514-284-1110 800-228-3000	514-845-3025	$$$	300	Above 8th fl, mtn or city vw

RESTAURANTS	DAY	ADDRESS	PH	PRICE	REC	DRESS	FOOD
Buena Notte	Alt	3518 blvd. St-Laurent	514-848-0644	$$	LD	Kazh	Italian
Chez Cora	3	1425 Stanley	514-286-6171	$	B	Local	Québecois breakfast
Eggspectation	2	198 av. Laurier	514-278-6411	$	B/LD	Kazh	Breakfast
L'Express	1	3927 rue St-Denis	514-845-5333	$$	L/BD	Kazh	French
Ferreira Café Trattoria	2	1446 rue Peel	514-848-0988	$$	D/L	Kazh	Mediterranean, Portuguese
Globe	3	3455 blvd. St-Laurent	514-284-3823	$$	L/D	Kazh	California fusion
Mediterraneo	3	3500 blvd. St-Laurent	514-844-0027	$$	D	Kazh	Mediterranean
Restaurante Primadonna	Alt	3479 blvd. St-Laurent	514-282-6644	$$$	LD	Kazh	Italian, sushi
Schwartz's Montréal Hebrew Delicatessen	2	3895 blvd. St-Laurent	514-842-4813	$	L/BD	Local	Deli
Shed Café	1	3515 blvd. St-Laurent	514-842-0220	$	T/BLD	Kazh	Continental
Toque!	Alt	3842 rue St-Denis	514-499-2084	$$	D	Kazh	French
Weinstein's and Gavino's	Alt	1434 rue Crescent	514-288-2231	$	LD	Kazh	Italian

NIGHTLIFE	DAY	ADDRESS	PH	COVER	REC*	DRESS	MUSIC
737	2	Place Ville Marie, Penthouse 3	514-397-0737	None	R(F)	Kazh	
Biddle's Jazz & Ribs Inc.	Alt	2060 rue Aylmer	514-842-8656	None	M(F)	Kazh	Jazz
Casino de Montréal	Alt	1 av. de Casino	514-392-2746	None	MS(F)	Kazh	Cabaret
Club Di Salvio	3	3519 blvd. St-Laurent	514-845-4337	$	P	Yuppie	Disco
Diva Bar and Lounge	3	3481 blvd. St-Laurent	514-282-6644	$	MP	Kazh	R&B
Funkytown	2	1454 rue Peel	514-282-8387	None	P	Kazh	Disco
Jello Bar	3	151 rue Ontario Ouest	514-285-2621	None	MP	Kazh	Jazz, swing
Terrasse Magnétic	3	see L'Hôtel de la Montagne	514-288-5656	None	MP	Kazh	Dance
Thursdays	2	see L'Hôtel de la Montagne	514-288-5656	None	P	Yuppie	Pop, R&B
Wax	3	3481 blvd. St-Laurent	514-282-0919	$	MP	Kazh	Soul, R&B

SIGHTS & ATTRACTIONS	DAY	ADDRESS	PH	ENTRY FEE
Mont-Royal Park	Alt	Av. du Royal and Av. du Parc	514-844-4928	None
Montréal Biodôme	2	4777 Pierre de Coubertin	514-868-3000	$
Montréal Botanical Garden	Alt	4101 rue Sherbrooke E	514-872-1400	$
Montréal Museum of Fine Arts	3	1379-1380 rue Sherbrooke Ouest	514-285-2000	$
Musée d'Art Contemporain	1	185 rue Ste-Catherine Ouest	514-847-6226	$
Greater Montréal CTB		1001 Square Dorchester	514-844-5400	

Event & Ticket Info

Montréal International Jazz Festival (Rue Ste-Catherine between Jeanne-Mance and Boulevard St-Laurent): Of 400 performances, almost 300 are free. Tickets for selected shows ($10-$50) can be ordered from *Admission Ticket Network* (800-361-4595). For more information, contact *Montréal International Jazz Festival* (888-515-0515).

Alternative Event

Just for Laughs Comedy Festival: Just For Laughs, 514-790-4242

* M=Live music; P=Dancing (Party); R=Bar only; S=Show; (F)=Food served. For further explanation of codes, see page 14.

 NYC   Dorval (YUL) <30 min./$20 No 61°/80° (16°/27°) 1.51 Canadian Dollars

July 1999

July 2000

Minneapolis, Minnesota, USA

Aquatennial

(Minneapolis Aquatennial Festival)

| Origin: 1940 | Event ★★★ City | Attendance: 800,000 |

Put away the ice-fishing poles—when the Land of 10,000 Lakes thaws out, the only cold thing you want to get your hands on is a frosty beverage. With winters as hellish as they often are in Minneapolis, the natives have a well-earned right to step outside and take advantage of the relief summer brings.

That happens in earnest the third full week of July—the warmest and driest time of year—when 800,000 warm-weather lovers come to *Minneapolis Aquatennial* to play outdoors during The 10 Best Days of Summer (as the festival bills itself). Minnesota ranks near the top of US cities for number of boats per capita, but that doesn't include those entered in the famed Milk Carton Boat Races. *Aquatennial* is a celebration of the importance of the area's rivers and lakes and these races are one of the signature events. Creations have included a six-foot soda-pop machine, a living room (complete with couch and TV), and a carnival with a working Ferris wheel—all made from milk cartons. The largest vessel to sail was in 1993—in honor of Desert Storm veterans, a replica of an aircraft carrier was constructed from 25,000 milk cartons and carried 150 people.

Offbeat entertainment is the hallmark of the 59-year-old festival. What other gala can boast the record for the world's largest root-beer float, made in a swimming pool? Or an event in which people slide into 1,000 pounds of aqua-colored gelatin?

Large crowds line Hennepin Avenue for the Grande Day and torchlight parades showcasing the best Minnesota high-school bands, floats, and celebrities. Not to be missed are the Aqua Jesters, the *Aquatennial*'s award-winning clown brigade known for zany routines.

Aquatennial is no Mardi Gras—Minnesotans may share the same river as people from New Orleans, but they don't have nearly as many warm days to practice dancing without clothes on—but with a Twin Cities population of roughly 2.5 million shedding a collective case of cabin fever, this is often a party of epic proportions.

Aquatennial

Day 1. Fri.   Jul. 16, 1999
(Day 1. Friday   July 14, 2000)

9:00am The **Nicollet Island Inn** is your home for the weekend. Built from limestone in 1893, the hotel is one of the few remaining buildings associated with the early development of Nicollet Island, directly across the Mississippi River from downtown Minneapolis. Rooms are decorated with period furniture and the service is tops.

10:00am After breakfast in the hotel dining room overlooking the Mississippi River, stroll around Nicollet Island and check out its 19th-century houses. Take in the picturesque sights of the Mississippi Mile. For a guided tour, stop at the **Minnesota Historical Society** office.

12:30pm Have *tapas* at **Bobino Cafe and Wine Bar**. Then head to St. Anthony Main for a **Minneapolis RiverCity Trolley** ride across the Stone Arch Bridge through downtown Minneapolis.

2:00pm Visit **The Walker Art Center** and **Minneapolis Sculpture Garden**. Check out one of the nation's finest and most visited collections of 20th-century art. Stroll the grid of alleys and courtyards, dotted with more than 40 contemporary sculptures.

5:00pm Have an espresso at the **Loring Cafe & Bar**, a gathering place for latter-day bohemians.

6:00pm *Aquatennial* kicks off with the *Hennepin Avenue Block Party*. Whoop it up with 50,000 or more of those friendly and attractive Minnesotans you've heard about. (Travelers partial to classic Scandinavian good looks are often pleasantly surprised to find themselves surrounded by Minnesota's stunning progeny of largely Nordic ancestors.) Local bands—sometimes national acts such as the Smashing Pumpkins, who performed in 1998—play free concerts.

8:00pm Scores of vendors hawk all kinds of carnival-type food and drinks until late into the evening, but break for a dinner of great chili at **The Loon Cafe**. Then head back to the party.

11:00pm Continue the party at either **The Gay 90s**, a formerly all-gay club becoming more and more mixed, or **South Beach**, a dance club trying to appeal to a slightly upscale crowd.

Day 2. Sat.   Jul. 17, 1999
(Day 2. Saturday   July 15, 2000)

9:00am Have an espresso, croissant, and artsy conversation at **The New French Café and Bar**. With the feel of a Parisian bistro, it's a favorite hangout for Twin Cities' culture vultures and worth the wait to get in. Then walk to Hennepin Avenue for the *Aquatennial Grande Day Parade*. Bands, floats, and celebrities will do the elbow-elbow, wrist-wrist thing.

1:00pm Lunch at the hip **Palomino Euro-Bistro**. Standout design and reliably good food have made this chain a hit in many cities.

2:30pm Cab to the **Minneapolis Institute of Arts**. It boasts an extensive collection of African and Asian art, with artifacts from 500 BC to the present.

4:00pm OK, it doesn't register on the hip-meter, but you should see it, nonetheless. The Twin Cities' largest attraction—in more ways than one—is the **Mall of America**, the largest shopping mall in the world. Drive or cab to the shopping, dining, and entertainment mecca, 12 miles south of downtown. Referred to by locals as the megamall, it features 350 retail shops, an 18-hole miniature-golf course, live-music venues, sports bars, and a seven-acre amusement park.

8:00pm Dine at **Goodfellow's**, a five-star restaurant known for its award-winning wine collection and gourmet dishes. The art-deco interior is almost as classy as the food.

10:00pm For after-dinner coffee, make it Irish. **Kieran's Irish Pub** is a little out of the way, but the walk and the music will do you good.

11:30pm Take your earplugs to **First Avenue**, the home-town nightclub most associated with Prince's rise to world superstardom. The club provided the setting for his movie, *Purple Rain*, and remains atop the city's list of after-dark spots. It's a dark cavern with a giant dance floor, tables overlooking the club from a balcony, and disco-dancer cages flanking the stage.

Day 3. Sun.   Jul. 18, 1999
(Day 3. Sunday   July 16, 2000)

10:00am Have coffee in your hotel before taking a 10-minute cab ride to Lake Nokomis for the *Milk Carton Boat Races*. Marvel at the things people can make with idle time on their hands.

Noon Cab to the **Fine Line Music Cafe** for brunch. Incredible live gospel ensembles serenade you while you eat.

2:00pm More than two million people have boarded the **Jonathan Padelford** riverboats for narrated Mississippi River cruises. You'll see landmarks such as St. Anthony Falls and get spectacular views of the downtown skyline.

3:30pm Drive to the **Frederick R. Weisman Art Museum** at the University of Minnesota. Frank O. Gehry's building is stunning and the 20th-century American art is fascinating.

7:30pm Have an unforgettable dinner at **D'Amico Cucina**. One of Minnesota's top restaurants, it's known for impeccable service and Italian dishes you don't see at most Italian restaurants.

10:00pm Although they attract younger crowds, two popular dance clubs are **Tropix** and **Quest Club**, both downtown. By the time you get back to the

hotel, three days of *Aquatennial* partying should have you convinced there really is something different in the water here.

Alternatives

St. Paul hosts **Winter Carnival**, which draws an even larger crowd to carve ice, build snowpeople, and do the winter thing. If you enjoy watching parades in freezing weather, you may want to check it out.

The **Hyatt Whitney Hotel** provides comfortable rooms with great views of the Mississippi River. The **Minneapolis Marriott City Center** is a contemporary hotel near the downtown shopping district and close to many attractions and restaurants.

Try the **Pickled Parrot** for award-winning barbecue ribs. Enjoy a relaxing meal at the semiformal **Murray's**. You may be hungry enough to try the infamous 28-ounce Silver Butterknife Steak, but there are less ambitious menu items. **Cafe Brenda** offers lots of good choices for vegans. If the idea of Caribbean fare in Minnesota appeals to your sense of the surreal, the kitschy **Chez Bananas** is fun.

Mary Tyler Moore Alert: Don't be shy about throwing your hat into the air—thousands of tourists do it—for a snapshot at the corner of Eighth Street and Nicollet Mall. That's where television's Mary Richards did it.

Minnehaha Falls is one of the country's most famous and romantic urban sites. Immortalized in poet Henry Wadsworth Longfellow's 1855 poem *The Song of Hiawatha*, the park also includes the Stevens House, home of Minneapolis' first Euro-American settler from 1850 to 1855.

Two good reasons for crossing over to St. Paul are Summit Avenue and **The Dakota Bar and Grill**. The former has the nation's longest stretch of intact residential Victorian architecture, including some homes open to tour. The latter has the best jazz in town and a restaurant that serves Minnesota's other aqua specialty, baked walleye.

The Hot Sheet

HOTELS		ADDRESS	PH	FX	PRICE	RMS	BEST ROOMS
Hyatt Whitney Hotel	Alt	150 Portland Ave.	612-339-9300 800-233-1234	612-339-1333	$$	96	Bi-level river vw
Minneapolis Marriott City Center	Alt	30 7th St. S	612-349-4000 800-638-8108	612-332-7165	$	583	City vw
Nicollet Island Inn	★	95 Merriam St.	612-331-1800 800-331-1800	612-331-6528	$$	24	Corner rm river vw

RESTAURANTS	DAY	ADDRESS	PH	PRICE	REC	DRESS	FOOD
Bobino Cafe and Wine Bar	1	222 Hennepin Ave.	612-623-3301	$$	L/D	Local	American, continental
Cafe Brenda	Alt	300 1st Ave. N	612-342-9230	$$	LD	Local	Vegetarian
Chez Bananas	Alt	129 N. 4th St.	612-340-0032	$$	LD	Local	Caribbean
D'Amico Cucina	3	100 N. 6th St.	612-338-2401	$$$	D	Kazh	Italian
The Dakota Bar and Grill	Alt	1201 E. Bandana Blvd.	612-642-1442	$$$	D	Kazh	Regional American
Fine Line Music Cafe	3	318 1st Ave.	612-338-8100	$$	B/LD	Local	American
Goodfellows	2	40 S. 7th St.	612-332-4800	$$$	D	Kazh, Dressy	Regional American
The Loon Cafe	1	500 1st Ave. N	612-332-8342	$	D/L	Local	American
Loring Cafe & Bar	1	1624 Harmon Pl.	612-332-1617	$	T/LD	Local	Espresso
Murray's	Alt	24 S. 6th St.	612-339-0909	$$	LD	Kazh	Steakhouse
The New French Café and Bar	2	128 N. 4th St.	612-338-3790	$	B/LD	Kazh, Local	French
Palomino Euro-Bistro	2	825 Hennepin Ave.	612-339-3800	$$	L/D	Yuppie	Mediterranean
Pickled Parrot	Alt	26 N. 5th St.	612-332-0673	$$	LD	Kazh	Caribbean, Southwestern

NIGHTLIFE	DAY	ADDRESS	PH	COVER	REC*	DRESS	MUSIC
The Dakota Bar and Grill	Alt	1021 E. Bandana Blvd.	612-642-1442	$$	M(F)	Kazh, Dressy	Jazz
Fine Line Music Cafe	Alt	see Fine Line restaurant	612-338-8100	$	MP(F)	Local	Jazz, reggae, blues, rap, rock, gospel
First Avenue	2	29 N. 7th St.	612-338-8388	$	MP(F)	Local	Alternative rock
The Gay 90s	1	408 Hennepin Ave.	612-333-7755	$	P(F)	Local	Disco, R&B, country
Kieran's Irish Pub	2	330 2nd Ave. S	612-339-4499	None	M(F)	Local	Irish
Quest Club	3	110 N. 5th St.	612-338-3383	$	MP	Kazh	Reggae, rock
South Beach	1	325 1st. Ave.	612-204-0790	$	MP(F)	Local	Hip-hop, R&B, '70s, '80s
Tropix	3	400 3rd Ave. N	612-333-1006	$	MP	Local	Rock

SIGHTS & ATTRACTIONS	DAY	ADDRESS	PH	ENTRY FEE
Frederick R. Weisman Art Museum	3	333 E. River Rd.	612-625-9494	None
Mall of America	2	Hwy. 494 and Cedar Ave.	612-883-8800	None
Minneapolis Institute of Arts	2	2400 3rd Ave. S	612-870-3131	None
Minneapolis Sculpture Garden	1	Vineland Pl. and Lyndale Ave.	612-375-7622	None
Minnehaha Falls	Alt	Minnehaha Pkwy. in Minnehaha Park		None
The Walker Art Center	1	725 Vineland Pl.	612-375-7636	$

OTHER SIGHTS, SHOPS & SERVICES

	DAY	ADDRESS	PH	
Minneapolis RiverCity Trolley	1	S.E. Main St.	612-204-0000	$
Minnesota Historical Society	1	125 S.E. Main St.	612-627-5433	$
Padelford Packet Boat Co.	3	Boom Island Park	651-227-1100	$
Greater Minneapolis CVA		40 S. 7th St.	612-348-7000	

Event & Ticket Info

Minneapolis Aquatennial Festival: All events are free. For information, contact *Minneapolis Aquatennial* (612-331-8371).

Grande Day Parade (Hennepin at Block E): A limited number of grandstand seats are available for the parade. Tickets ($6) are available from *Minneapolis Aquatennial* (612-331-8371).

Milk Carton Boat Races (Lake Nokomis): Bleacher seating ($2) is sold on site.

Alternative Event

St. Paul Winter Carnival: St. Paul Festivals and Heritage Foundation, 651-223-4700

* M=Live music; P=Dancing (Party); R=Bar only; S=Show; (F)=Food served. For further explanation of codes, see page 14.

 NYC –1   Minneapolis-St. Paul (MSP) <30 min./S<20   Yes/No   61°/82° (16°/28°)

Calgary Stampede

Calgary, Alberta, Canada

| Origin: 1912 | Event ★ ★ ★ ★ ★ ★ ★ City | Attendance: 1,100,000 |

If you've ever wanted to watch a full-size chuck wagon bite the dust in a blaze of glory, or hear a defeated cowboy swear a blue streak at a two-ton piece of twisting livestock, the *Calgary Stampede* is the place to be. At this annual Western bash, visitors get so close to the action —in the grounds and on the city streets—that there really are no spectators here, just participants.

For 10 days every July, Calgary becomes the world's biggest and best party town. The celebration of Old West spirit is highlighted by a world-class rodeo, but public gatherings for pancake feasts, square-dancing, two-stepping, beer-guzzling, and all-night partying are the real purpose (and fun).

Each day, the afternoon *rodeo* and evening *Rangeland Derby* showcase the dangerous world of the professional cowboy. The rodeo equivalent of an auto-race crash is a cowpoke getting booted in the head by a bronc or bull. Only lunatics really want to see that sort of thing, but the possibility of calamity will keep you nervously clutching your seat bottom.

Away from the *Stampede* grounds, the Western spirit rages. Day and night, country bands belt out tunes all over town. Two-steppers and line dancers congregate at outdoor hoedowns. Those too shy to dance gather nerve by joining local saloons and clubs that spill over with 10-gallon hats and the cowboy's drink of choice— a shot of whiskey with a beer chaser.

During *Stampede*, denim rules this otherwise-cosmopolitan city of 800,000. Cowboy-clad customs and immigration officers work the airport. Hotels put up Western-themed façades. Local business types get to ditch their suits for jeans in the office, proving that cowboy couture can be *très* chic.

An hour outside Calgary, Banff National Park is the country's best place to view the majestic beauty of the Canadian Rockies. Lake Louise, possibly the most beautiful lake in the world, is the centerpiece of this stunning park, making the scenic drive a perfect topper to a weekend at one of the world's great events.

Calgary Stampede

Day 1. Fri. Jul. 16, 1999
(Day 1. Friday July 14, 2000)

8:45am Upon entering **The Palliser**, you'll get a "Howdy ma'am, sir," from the doorman. The lobby of the traditional and elegant hotel is done up like a regal barn, with pine planks framing the check-in counter and bales of hay scattered about. Built in 1914, The Palliser is *Stampede* central and your west-facing room provides a breathtaking view of the mountains.

9:00am For a genuine **Western Breakfast**, grab some free flapjacks from a chuck wagon on Stephen Avenue Walk, along the Eighth Avenue Mall, one block from the hotel. This is your first chance to get an idea of what *The New York Times* meant when it said the *Stampede*'s two million visitors create "a raucous party that turns the entire city into a Western theme park."

10:30am Stroll down the mall to **Lammle's Western Wear** and ditch your city-slicker ensemble for dude duds. This upscale store carries boots, Western shirts and vests, denim, cowboy hats, bolo ties, skirts, dresses, and beaded shirts.

Noon In Eau Claire Market, lunch in the Big Skye Dining Room or on the outdoor deck at **OutWest**, an eatery with the ambience of a Western-movie set. Try a bowl of buffalo chili, ribs grilled with blackstrap barbecue sauce, or aged Alberta steak or prime rib. For the less easily satisfied, ostrich is also on the menu.

1:00pm Cab to the hotel, drop off your purchases, and grab a light jacket on the way back out.

1:30pm Walk the few blocks to the *Stampede* grounds and take your seat for the *Rodeo*. This is the tension-building warm-up for the finals.

4:30pm Check out the Daily Events Schedule. It lists all free exhibits, shows, entertainers, and activities. Make your way down the incredibly clean midway, with its neon cacophony, barkers, and games of chance. Pig races and livestock competitions are the draw here. Or take your chances on the Ejection Seat (an amazing bungee contraption).

7:00pm Have a cold beer and chow down on a barbecue steak, beef-on-a-bun, or all-you-can-eat Western buffet.

8:00pm With thundering hooves and flying dust, the *Rangeland Derby* pits four chuck wagons and 16 outriders in a race down the Half Mile of Hell. The *Grandstand Show* follows with energetic song, dance, and comedy routines.

11:30pm Don't miss the *fireworks show*, an awe-inspiring pyrotechnic light-and-laser spectacle.

11:45pm Still on the fairgrounds, party to live country music at Nashville North, or Top-40 music at the outdoor Coca-Cola stage. Close out the night with a swing through the casino.

Day 2. Sat. Jul. 17, 1999
(Day 2. Saturday July 15, 2000)

9:00am Walk to Olympic Plaza for entertainment in *Rope Square*. Grab a coffee and only enough pancake-chuck grub to stave off your appetite until brunch.

10:30am Drive 90 minutes to Banff National Park. Mountain weather can change quickly, so take extra clothing and, of course, extra film.

12:15pm At your reserved table in the Banff Springs Hotel's **Alberta Dining Room**, take in views of staggering mountains while enjoying an excellent buffet brunch.

2:00pm Ride the **Sulphur Mountain Gondola** to the "top of the world." Walk off your brunch along the Vista Trail walkway to Sanson's Peak. Then soak in the natural mineral waters of the **Banff Upper Hot Springs**.

6:30pm Try the **Grizzly House**, which features fondue specialties and wild game, including rattlesnake. Or return to Calgary for dinner at **Teatro**, which features Italian-inspired regional cuisine in a historic bank building.

10:00pm Check out **Cowboys Dance Hall**, which you'll have heard about by this time. A favorite nightspot, its vast arenalike structure may be packed, but there's also an outside keg party. Slipping $20 to the doorman should get you past the line. A great alternative is **Dusty's Saloon,** just a couple of blocks from the *Stampede* grounds. Morning, noon, and night, there's a party at Dusty's.

Day 3. Sun.   Jul. 18, 1999
(Day 3. Sunday   July 16, 2000)

10:30am Stroll to breakfast at the **1886 Buffalo Cafe**. Established long before the surrounding trendy Eau Claire Market, this tiny restaurant is known for omelets with a choice of 19 fillings. If there's a line, hang tough—it's worth the wait.

12:30pm Grab a cab and head for the *Stampede* grounds. The 1:30 p.m. *rodeo finals* are filled with thrills and spills, as cowboys and cowgirls compete for $300,000 in prize money. Choose from a variety of carnival-style food and beverages on sale throughout the grounds.

7:00pm Change into your new Western wear at the hotel. Since the *Stampede* is on, you'll be appropriately dressed, even for an evening in tonight's tony establishments.

8:00pm If you're hooked on chuck-wagon races, stay for the finals. Otherwise, cab to Eau Claire and unwind as you dine on the patio of the **River Cafe** in Prince's Island Park, along the Bow River. This chic cafe features Canadian, wood-fired cuisine and an extensive selection of Northwestern wines.

11:00pm Wrap up the evening at **The Palace Nightclub** on Stephen Avenue Walk. The popular Palace retains its classy flair, while exchanging its usual Egyptian theme for *Stampede* style and country bands.

Alternatives

The **Calgary Marriott Hotel**, just a block from The Palliser, is probably the best modern hotel in town and within easy walking distance of the *Stampede* grounds. Opened in late 1998, the **Sheraton Suites Calgary Eau Clair** is close to the action in Eau Claire. This all-suite hotel delivers terrific service and amenities. If you stay in Banff, the **Banff Springs Hotel** is the grande dame of the area.

La Caille on the Bow is a terrific place for dinner with a river view, an outdoor patio, and both casual and elegant dining rooms. Another great choice is **Mescalero**, a cozy, local favorite specializing in Southwestern wood-grilled entrees presented with artistic flair. If you can't get enough cowboy fare, pay a visit to **Buzzards Cowboy Cuisine**. Surrounded by Western memorabilia, you can hitch up your blue jeans and try son-of-a-bitch stew, buffalo steak, or prairie oysters (calves' testicles sautéed in herbs, lemon juice, and white wine). A breakfast alternative is **Break The Fast Cafe**, with a funky, fun atmosphere.

Convenient and hopping, The Palliser's **Paralyzer Room** is a cabaret-style saloon featuring live bands and a Western buffet. Keep in mind that The Palliser offers a wonderful weekend brunch. The Western club that attracts the cowboys is **Ranchman's Restaurant**.

If you have enough time, take a trip to the observation terrace of the **Calgary Tower**, just a block from The Palliser. One of the city's tallest buildings, it gives a great panoramic view of Calgary and the Rockies on a clear day.

The Hot Sheet

Hotels		Address	Ph	Fx	Price	Rms	Best Rooms
Banff Springs Hotel (Canadian Pacific Hotels)	Alt	Banff Springs	403-762-2211 800-441-1414	403-762-5755	$$$$	777	Mtn vw
Calgary Marriott Hotel	Alt	110 9th Ave. SE	403-266-7331 800-266-7331	403-262-8442	$$	383	Downtown vw
The Palliser (Canadian Pacific Hotels)	★	133 9th Ave. SW	403-262-1234 800-441-1414	403-260-4260	$$$	405	Mtn vw
Sheraton Suites Calgary Eau Clair	Alt	255 Barclay Parade SW	403-266-7200 888-784-8370	403-266-1300	$$	325	River valley vw

Restaurants	Day	Address	Ph	Price	Rec	Dress	Food
1886 Buffalo Cafe	3	187 Barclay Parade SW	403-269-9255	$	B	Local	Breakfast
Alberta Dining Room	2	see Banff Springs Hotel	403-762-6860	$$$	B/LD	Yuppie	Buffet brunch
Break The Fast Cafe	Alt	516 9th Ave. SW	403-265-5071	$	BL	Local	Ukrainian
Buzzards Cowboy Cuisine	Alt	140 10th Ave. SW	403-264-6959	$$	LD	Local	Steakhouse
Grizzly House	2	207 Banff Ave.	403-762-4055	$$	D/L	Local	Fondue
La Caille on the Bow	Alt	805 1st Ave. SW	403-262-5554	$$	LD	Dressy, Kazh	Contemporary, continental
Mescalero	Alt	1315 1st St. SW	403-266-3339	$$	LD	Kazh	Contemporary Southwestern
OutWest	1	151 Eau Claire Market	403-262-9378	$$	L/D	Local	Regional American
The Palliser	Alt	see The Palliser hotel	403-262-1234	$$$	BL	Kazh	Brunch
River Cafe	3	in Prince's Island Park	403-261-7670	$$	D/L	Yuppie	Organic game
Teatro	2	200 8th Ave. SE	403-290-1012	$$	D/L	Kazh	Italian

Nightlife	Day	Address	Ph	Cover	Rec*	Dress	Music
Cowboys Dance Hall	2	826 5th St. SW	403-265-0699	$$$	MP(F)	Kazh	Country, pop
Dusty's Saloon	2	1088 Olympic Way SE	403-263-5343	$	MP(F)	Local	Country
The Palace Nightclub	3	219 8th Ave. SW	403-263-9980	$	MP	Local	Country
Paralyzer Room	Alt	see The Palliser hotel	403-262-1234	$	MP(F)	Local	Country
Ranchman's Restaurant	Alt	9615 Macleod Trail	403-253-1100	$	MP(F)	Local	Country

Sights & Attractions	Day	Address	Ph	Entry Fee
Calgary Tower	Alt	101 9th Ave. SW	403-266-7171	$
Sulphur Mountain Gondola	2	End of the Mountain	403-762-2523	$$
Banff Upper Hot Springs	2	101 Mountain Ave.	403-762-1515	$
Lammle's Western Wear	1	211 Stephen Ave. SW	403-266-5226	None
Calgary CVB		131 9th Ave. SE	800-661-1678	

Event & Ticket Info

Calgary Stampede Rodeo (Stampede Park, Olympic Way and 14th Avenue SE): Tickets ($18-$40) should be ordered close to one year in advance for good seats. A limited number of "rush seat" tickets ($9) go on sale each day 90 minutes prior to show time. Infield seats, close to the action by the chutes, sell out within hours. Infield seats for 1999 are sold out. For 2000, call early on August 16, 1999. Contact *Calgary Stampede* (800-661-1767).

Rangeland Derby and Grandstand Show: Tickets ($21-$45) for the grandstand are best for the chuck-wagon races. Contact *Calgary Stampede* (800-661-1767).

Stampede Park has a separate admission charge for those not already holding tickets for the Rodeo or the Rangeland Derby.

* M=Live music; P=Dancing (Party); R=Bar only; S=Show; (F)=Food served. For further explanation of codes, see page 14.

 NYC −2 Calgary (YYC) <30 min./$20   Yes 47°/76° (8°/24°) 1.51 Canadian Dollars

Caribana

Toronto, Ontario, Canada

Origin: 1967	Event ★ ★ ★ ★ ★ City	Attendance: 1,500,000

Like snow in June, like peanut butter and chocolate, the great joy of Toronto's *Caribana* is the mind-boggling combination of two seemingly disparate elements. When hard-core Caribbean partying plows head first into hard-core Anglo culture, the result is one of the most exciting blends of opposites since Dylan discovered electricity.

One of North America's largest and most exuberant street parties, *Caribana* takes place in Toronto, a city with a history of straight-laced refinement. Over the past few decades, however, immigration from every corner of the globe has dramatically changed the face of the Ontario capital. To celebrate the heritage of the largely Caribbean and Latin influx, *Caribana* gathers more than a million happy people to grind to traditional calypso, steel-drum music, and soca, a calypso offshoot originally called soul calypso that pumps up the energy and volume.

The carnival traditions of the Carib and Latin worlds are well-known, and *Caribana* evokes them all. Musical competitors vie for the Calypso Monarch crown and the trophy for best steel band. Others opt for jump-ups, sunset cruises, or the mas (short for "masquerade") drama of the king-and-queen competition. Excitement peaks at the *Caribana Parade*. Flatbed trucks jammed with brightly costumed dancers and bands follow a two-mile lakeside route, cheered on by half a million drinking, dancing spectators. On the water side of Lakeshore Boulevard, crowds gather around food stands to sample traditional island fare such as *roti* and patties. Liberal use of the beer tents is a favorite way to beat the afternoon heat.

Since most *Caribana*-weekend activities are held close to Lake Ontario, it's easy to slip away to find out what else makes Toronto tick. The city's world-renowned restaurants, ethnic neighborhoods, museums, galleries, and live theater have been touted by *National Geographic*, *Fortune*, and the *Utne Reader*. Just beyond the city limits lies one of the world's most awe-inspiring natural sights: Niagara Falls. The city is clean, the locals are friendly, and for this weekend at least, dancing in the streets is the top priority. Who says Canada and the Caribbean have nothing in common?

Caribana

Day 1. Thu. July 29, 1999
(Day 1. Thursday   August 3, 2000)

9:30am The **Westin Harbour Castle**'s twin, modern high-rises have a prime location, central to the festivities and convenient to downtown. Make sure to ask for a room with a view of the lake or city.

10:30am Take a tour of **Casa Loma**, a mock-medieval castle built in 1914 with an intriguing mix of furnished suites, secret passages, underground tunnels, and magnificent gardens.

12:30pm Lunch at **Prego della Piazza**, an oasis of calm in midtown surrounded by boutiques, towering office blocks, and old churches. Exquisitely prepared meals earn consistently high ratings.

2:30pm Walk to the **Royal Ontario Museum**, commonly known as ROM. Famous for its East Asian collection, new additions include a wing dedicated to European decorative arts and a working paleontology lab.

6:00pm Join the financial-district crowd for a drink at a popular after-work spot, **Jump Cafe & Bar**.

8:00pm Walk to the **Mercer Street Grill**, a funky-from-the-outside eatery that's popular with hotshots from the nearby financial district. It's acclaimed for Asian-accented fish and meat dishes and an extensive wine list.

10:00pm For dancing, you have two fun options: Latin style at **Cha Cha Cha** or the jazzy **Easy & The Fifth**.

Day 2. Fri. July 30, 1999
(Day 2. Friday   August 4, 2000)

8:00am Have breakfast at the **Studio Cafe** in the Four Seasons hotel. Designed to evoke the atmosphere of an artist's loft, the dining room is adorned with pieces from notable Canadian artists.

9:00am Set off to **Niagara Falls**, a 90-minute drive. Park on the Niagara Parkway. Walk or take the People Mover to Table Rock House for great views of Horseshoe Falls and the smaller American Falls. Ride on *Maid of the Mist*, an open boat that carries you into the maelstrom at the base of Horseshoe Falls. (You'll be issued waterproof gear.) The Table Rock Scenic Tunnels are a drier but equally dramatic alternative, opening onto viewing portals right under Horseshoe Falls.

1:00pm Take Winston Churchill's advice and follow the prettiest afternoon drive in the world to historic Niagara-on-the-Lake. Along the way, a good lunch stop is the **Queenston Heights Restaurant**. It has a varied menu—seafood, chicken, beef, etc.—but the restaurant sits high on the Niagara Escarpment and the real draw is its spectacular view of the Niagara River.

2:00pm In Niagara-on-the-Lake, Fort George is a fascinating reconstruction of the original (which was destroyed in 1812) and there are plenty of stores, cafes, and restaurants along Queen Street.

6:00pm Return to Toronto to join the crowd at the ferry terminal beside your hotel for the ***Sunset Cruise***. Remember, Toronto is on island time for ***Caribana***, so go with the flow and be prepared for a late start. Most of your fellow passengers will have Caribbean roots and will definitely know how to have a party. Once on board, live bands—local and from the West Indies—drive up the tempo. Rum drinks and beer are plentiful and there's a tasty Caribbean spread.

11:30pm A number of Caribbean dance parties dot the city, most of them put on in association with ***Caribana***. Check the local newspaper. Or hit the entertainment district and check out **Limelight** or **Whiskey Saigon**.

2:00am Late-night hunger pangs can be assuaged at **Pearl Court**, where Cantonese and Szechwan dishes are served until 4 a.m., or at **Fran's**, a long-established, 24-hour hamburger joint.

Day 3. Sat. July 31, 1999
(Day 3. Saturday   August 5, 2000)

9:00am Take the hotel shuttle to Union Station and walk to the **CN Tower**, the world's tallest tower at 1,815 feet. At the observation level, you can step on to the glass floor and see the ground beneath your feet—a frightening 1,122 feet below. Half the fun is seeing the traumatizing effect this has on folks of all ages. The Space Deck, at 1,464 feet, has the world's highest observation gallery.

10:30am Head for **Masquerade Caffè Bar**. Steaming bowls of latte, flaky croissants, fresh fruit, and yogurt are standard breakfast fare.

11:30am Armed with sunscreen, a hat, and comfortable shoes, get to Lakeshore Boulevard West and the *Caribana Parade* route. Crowds don't build until several hours later, but the earlier you arrive, the better the chance you'll have of finding a spot in the shade. By late afternoon, you'll thank yourself.

Noon Wander through the marketplace and lunch on whatever suits your mood—fresh coconut, hamburgers, sweet corn, *roti*, jerk chicken, and pilau are all available. Exotic bevies include *mauby*, ginger beer, and sorrel. Around you, people will not be shy about whooping it up, greeting long-lost friends and acquaintants, exchanging shouts and hugs, waving to Moko Jumbies (traditional African characters who walk on stilts), and singing and dancing to the live calypso, soca, steel-drum, reggae, and samba bands. By 6 p.m., the parade is usually finished and all of the day's winners will have been announced.

7:30pm Have a great meal on your last night in Toronto at **Zoom Caffè & Bar**. The décor, presentation, and clientele are all top-notch.

9:30pm Get back in the Caribbean mood at **The Bamboo**, a hip nightclub with live bands—tonight will be reggae—and people-watching upstairs at its Treetop Lounge.

11:30pm If you want to slow down a bit, head to the **Top o' the Senator** for a nightcap and some of the best jazz around. Have a final drink and reflect on a city that can be as energetic, stimulating, or relaxed as suits its mood. If you haven't yet discovered Toronto's charm and sophistication, a *Caribana* weekend is the most fun way to get to know this fascinating and diverse city.

Alternatives

Sheraton Centre Toronto and the **Royal York** are conveniently located downtown for easy access to most *Caribana* activities. Both hotels are also popular with weekend-getaway travelers. In midtown's trendy Yorkville, it's difficult to beat **The Four Seasons Toronto** for luxurious rooms and always-dependable service.

The **Art Gallery of Toronto** has the world's largest public collection of Henry Moore sculptures and a fabulous accumulation of Inuit and contemporary Canadian art. It also often hosts large touring exhibits. For somewhat quirkier edification, the **Bata Shoe Museum** has the world's most comprehensive collection of shoes, spanning some 4,500 years. It includes everything from 18th-century, French chestnut-crushing clogs to space boots.

A hip alternative lunch or dinner spot is **Splendido**. **Canoe** restaurant is 54 floors up and has food equal to its exquisite views. The Annex, one of Toronto's trendiest residential neighborhoods, boasts some of the city's best ethnic shopping and dining. In a cozy Markham Street house you'll find **Southern Accent**, where Cajun and Creole dishes are excellent. **Mildred Pierce** is a groovy restaurant renowned for its Sunday brunch and over-the-top décor. An icon on the Toronto bar scene, the **Roof Lounge** at the Grand Bay Hotel Toronto is a longtime haunt of literary types. John Irving and the late Robertson Davies are two great writers who have called Toronto their home.

The Hot Sheet

HOTELS		ADDRESS	PH	FX	PRICE	RMS	BEST ROOMS
The Four Seasons Toronto	Alt	21 Avenue Rd.	416-964-0411 800-268-6283	416-964-2301	$$$	380	Lake vw
Royal York	Alt	100 Front St. W	416-368-2511 800-828-7447	416-368-9040	$$	1,537	Lake vw
Sheraton Centre Toronto	Alt	123 Queen St. W	416-361-1000 800-325-3535	416-947-4874	$$$	1377	City Hall vw
Westin Harbour Castle	★	1 Harbour Sq.	416-869-1600 800-228-3000	416-869-1420	$$$	985	South Tower harbour vw

RESTAURANTS	DAY	ADDRESS	PH	PRICE	REC	DRESS	FOOD
Canoe	Alt	66 Wellington St. W	416-364-0054	$$$	LD	Dressy	New Canadian
Fran's	2	55 St. Clair W	416-925-6337	$	T/BLD	Local	Hamburgers
Masquerade Caffè Bar	3	181 Bay St.	416-363-8971	$	B/LD	Local	Pastries
Mercer Street Grill	1	36 Mercer St.	416-599-3399	$$$	D	Yuppie	Fusion
Mildred Pierce	Alt	99 Sudbury St.	416-588-5695	$$	B/LD	Kazh	American
Pearl Court	2	633 Gerrard St.	416-463-8778	$$	T/BLD	Kazh	Chinese
Prego della Piazza	1	150 Bloor St. W	416-920-9900	$$	L/D	Euro	Italian
Queenston Heights Restaurant	2	14184 Niagara Parkway	905-262-4274	$$	L/D	Local	American
Southern Accent	Alt	595 Markham St.	416-536-3211	$$	D	Kazh	Cajun, Creole
Splendido	Alt	88 Harboard St.	416-929-7788	$$$	LD	Yuppie	Continental
Studio Cafe	2	see The Four Seasons Toronto hotel	416-928-7330	$$	B/LD	Kazh	Continental
Zoom Caffè & Bar	3	18 King St. E	416-861-9872	$$	D/L	Kazh	New Latin

NIGHTLIFE	DAY	ADDRESS	PH	COVER	REC*	DRESS	MUSIC
The Bamboo	3	312 Queen St. W	416-593-5771	$	MP(F)	Local	Reggae
Cha Cha Cha	1	11 Duncan St.	416-598-3538	None	P	Kazh	Latin, disco
Easy & The Fifth	1	225 Richmond St. W	416-979-3000	$	P	Kazh	Top 40, Latin, jazz, blues
Jump Cafe & Bar	1	Commerce Court E, Yonge and Wellington sts.	416-363-3400	None	R(F)	Kazh	
Limelight	2	250 Adelaide St. W	416-593-6126	$	P	Kazh	Top 40, '70s, '80s
Roof Lounge	Alt	4 Avenue Rd.	416-924-5471	None	R	Kazh	
Top o' the Senator	3	253 Victoria St.	416-364-7517	$$	M(F)	Kazh	Jazz
Whiskey Saigon	2	250 Richmond St. W	416-593-4646	$	P	Local	Rock, '80s retro

SIGHTS & ATTRACTIONS	DAY	ADDRESS	PH	ENTRY FEE
Art Gallery of Toronto	Alt	317 Dundas St. W	416-979-6648	None
Bata Shoe Museum	Alt	327 Bloor St. W	416-979-7799	$
Casa Loma	1	1 Austin Terrace	416-923-1171	$
CN Tower	3	301 Front St. W	416-360-8500	$$
Niagara Falls	2	80 mi. south of Toronto	905-356-6061	None
Royal Ontario Museum	1	100 Queen's Park	416-586-8000	$$
Metropolitan Toronto CVB		255 Front St. W	800-363-1990	

Event & Ticket Info

Caribana: Most of the events are free. For more information, contact *Caribbean Cultural Committee/Caribana* (416-465-4884).

Caribana Sunset Boat Cruise (Ferry Dock, at foot of Bay Street): Tickets ($40) should be ordered in advance. Contact *Caribbean Cultural Committee/ Caribana* (416-465-4884).

* M=Live music; P=Dancing (Party); R=Bar only; S=Show; (F)=Food served. For further explanation of codes, see page 14.

 NYC Lester B. Pearson (YYY) <30 min./$20 Yes/No 59°/79° (15°/26°) 1.51 Canadian Dollars

July 1999

July 2000

Cheyenne, Wyoming, USA

Cheyenne Frontier Days

Origin: 1897 Event ★ ★ ★ ★ City Attendance: 400,000

Cowboys have figured out a lot of cool things to do with cattle—wrangle 'em, rope 'em, ride 'em, rustle 'em, eat 'em—but *Cheyenne Frontier Days* has to be the best thing they've come up with so far. Justly known as "the daddy of 'em all," *Frontier Days* is a century-old rawhide rodeo, Wild West show, and summertime hoedown rolled into one rowdy spectacle that's unlike any other American gathering. Real cowboys and cowgirls still exist and it seems like every last one of 'em rides into town for this annual buckskin bacchanal.

With $500,000 in prize money at stake, the competition and personal rivalries grow fierce as more than 1,000 top-ranked cowboys compete in the world's largest outdoor rodeo arena. Tension builds through roping events, bull riding, barrel racing, steer wrestling, bulldogging, bronco riding, and the absolutely bizarre chuck-wagon races. Crowds roar as teams load wagons with a stove and grub, race on a figure-eight course, and pound down the track to the finish line—often on two wheels. This is the only rodeo in the United States to which Canadian teams bring their unique, home-grown racing tradition. Then comes the *Frontier Days Wild Horse Race* climax. Mayhem prevails as 12 three-man teams try to saddle and race horses judged too wild for the arena events.

Sleepy Cheyenne's tourist attractions are mostly found in the nearby Rocky Mountains. But during *Frontier Days*, Cheyenne's modest head count of 55,000 more than doubles, so there's plenty more to chew on when the broncs aren't bucking. The *Frontier Days Parade* is a cavalcade of history that rolls from the state capitol to the Union Pacific tracks, where Cheyenne began as a prairie outpost. Along the midway, neon lights illuminate the careening rides, side shows, and games of chance that surround a giant merchandise mart where everything Western is bartered. Country-music stars and rodeo-circuit favorites mount stages around town nightly to make cowpokes and visitors feel at home with laughin', hollerin', and dancin'.

Day-By-Day Plan For

Cheyenne Frontier Days

Day 1. Thu.   Jul. 29, 1999
(Day 1. Thursday   *July 27, 2000)*

9:00am Make **Little America Hotel** your temporary home on the range. The rooms are standard-issue Americana, but it's comfortable and just ten blocks from downtown Cheyenne.

11:00am Yoked shirts and cowboy boots are *de rigueur* this weekend. **The Wrangler** or **Just Dandy** are top spots to shop for dude gear hip enough to wear after the *Frontier Days* weekend.

12:30pm At the fairgrounds, rodeo tickets and hearty grub are found at **The Cowboy Cafeteria**, where cowboys and families feast on 'cue, beans, buns, and corn on the cob.

1:15pm The **Grand Entry Parade** passes the grandstands signaling the start of a full day of **rodeo** events, where cowboys demonstrate the skills and courage that helped tame the West and introduced words such as *broncobusting* and *lassoing* to the English language.

5:00pm While postrodeo traffic thins, visit the **Frontier Park Indian Village**, where the Wind River Dance Group lives and performs Native American dances daily.

7:30pm Drive to **Los Amigos** Mexican restaurant, where Carroll Leger smothers just about every item on the menu with his specialty—green chile and pork.

9:00pm A mile north at **The Horn's Cowboy Bar**, winners of the Wild Horse Races keep tradition alive by literally drinking from their victory boots. Hundreds pack this combination Bavarian beer hall/*Animal House*/Old West saloon to two-step to regional bands. Go ahead and close down the joint, since—as Waylon sings it—"the girls all get prettier at closing time." (And the guys get louder, if nothing else.)

Day 2. Fri.   Jul. 30, 1999
(Day 2. Friday   *July 28, 2000)*

7:00am Hit the free pancake breakfast (7–9 a.m.) in downtown's city center parking lot. No after-church Sunday social, this is where 10,000 locals and visitors sit on hay bales enjoying hotcakes and ham fresh from the griddle. Entertainment is provided by The Chugwater Philharmonic String Quartet—a fast-moving country-music-and-comedy show that's an annual crowd favorite.

9:00am If you're willing to forgo the rodeo, make the 70-mile drive on I-80 to the **Snowy Range of the Rocky Mountains**. After crossing an 8,640-foot pass, take Highway 130 west to Centennial (population 100) for a look at the boxcar museum and a public library consisting of a rack of paperback novels.

Noon Have lunch at **The Old Corral** in the town's newest building (which is still old enough to have housed The Old Corral for 70 years). The steak and chicken dinners are excellent, but there's also a cowpoke surprise: the state's best salads. Continue on scenic Highway 130, passing wildflowers, the sapphire waters of Lake Marie, and good spots for midsummer snowball fights.

5:00pm Back in Cheyenne, proceed to **Lexie's** for an early dinner of American favorites.

7:00pm *The Cheyenne Frontier Days Night Show* begins when the wild-and-woolly chuck-wagon races kick up dust and inspire spectators to hoot and holler. Between heats, womens barrel racing ratchets up the excitement. Western-music concerts in front of the grandstands get boots stompin' and hands clappin'. It can get cool and breezy at night, so consider bringing a coat or blanket.

10:30pm Get your boots to the dance floor at the **Hitching Post Inn** or **The Cowboy Bar**.

Day 3. Sat.   Jul. 31,1999
(Day 3. Saturday   July 29, 2000)

9:30am A cannon blast signals the long and strong **Frontier Days Parade**. Find a place a block south of the capitol building where you can sit in the shade on the grass. Thousands of spectators enjoy more than 1,000 horses, marching bands, historic vehicles, and antique autos. Ladies costumed in turn-of-the-century finery ride in the world's largest collection of horse-drawn vehicles. Floats carry folks dressed in the traditional wear of Native Americans, cowboys, cowgirls, gamblers, and gunslingers.

Noon Walk down Capitol Avenue to **The Albany**, a local favorite and Cheyenne's oldest cafe. The prime-rib roast-beef sandwich is among the more popular lunch orders.

1:15pm Head back to the stands for the **rodeo semi-finals** or take the two-hour **Cheyenne Street Railway Trolley** tour. Retired teachers dish up details of Cheyenne's history as you cruise past famous and infamous sights, buildings, homes, and museums, including the **Cheyenne Frontier Days Old West Museum** at Frontier Park.

3:00pm Cross the road from the Frontier Park complex to **Lions Park**, where you can take a dip in Sloan's Lake, Cheyenne's original swimmin' hole with beach and paddle-boat rentals. Don't leave without visiting **Cheyenne Botanic Gardens and Solar Conservatory**. The lush oasis retreat seems far away from the heat and dust of the rodeo arena.

7:30pm About 10 minutes south of town on I-80, the Terry Bison Ranch serves delicious buffalo steaks and lamb chops in its **Senator's Steak House**.

9:30pm Don't miss the *Frontier Days*' party finale (and highlight) starring Ricky and the Red Streaks at **The Coach Room**. Ricky's bawdy humor and cookin' band has made this hilarious act the *Frontier Days* favorite since the 1970s. Rodeo royalty and the cattle corporate crowd drink Black Velvet and rest their $1,000 boots on the bar's brass rail. Mix with direc-

tors of other Western shows, *Frontier Days* committeemen, and various Western celebs before saying "happy trails" and riding off into the sunset.

Alternatives

If you can manage to stay until Sunday, be sure to catch the **rodeo finals**. The events are basically the same, but the excitement level tends to be higher when most of the prize money is on the line.

Little America Hotel's charm and views make it the prime place to stay on the frontier, but the newly built and conveniently located **Holiday Inn** is a good option. Also suited to the *Frontier Days* experience is the **Hitching Post Inn**, which combines Old West style with luxury amenities. The inn also houses two good beef restaurants, the **Carriage Court Restaurant** and the **Cheyenne Cattle Company**. Both have earned awards from the Wyoming Beef Council.

Cheyenne folks know meat, and local restaurants tend to focus on it—**The Little Bear Inn** is yet another solid option— but for a change from Western meals, **The Twin Dragons** restaurant has a lunch buffet featuring Mandarin, Peking, Hunan, and Szechwan specialties.

Cheyenne's night life is mostly downtown. If you've already become a regular at the Hitching Post or The Cowboy Bar, check out the **Cheyenne Club** for kit-shickin' live music. The **Mayflower Tavern** is another *Frontier Days* favorite with cowboys—and sometimes their horses. Even during the day, the **Wigwam** is a popular watering hole and meeting place.

An hour's drive northwest of Cheyenne, the **Diamond Guest Ranch** offers horseback riding, hay rides, trout fishing, a dance hall, steakhouse, bar, and cabin rentals. At the **Wyoming Hereford Ranch,** you're welcome to inspect the facilities of a cattle-breeding operation that has produced world-renowned stock since 1883.

The Hot Sheet

HOTELS		ADDRESS	PH	FX	PRICE	RMS	BEST ROOMS
Hitching Post Inn Resort and Conference Center Best Western	Alt	1700 W. Lincolnway	307-638-3301 800-221-0125	307-778-7194	$$	157	New section, Bldg 4 or 5
Holiday Inn	Alt	204 Fox Farm Rd.	307-638-4466 800-465-4329	307-638-3677	$$	245	Laramie Range vw
Little America Hotel	★	2800 W. Lincolnway	307-775-8400 800-445-6945	307-775-8425	$$	188	Facing golf course

RESTAURANTS	DAY	ADDRESS	PH	PRICE	REC	DRESS	FOOD
The Albany	3	1506 Capitol Ave.	307-638-3507	$	L/D	Local	Beef
Carriage Court Restaurant	Alt	see the Hitching Post Inn	307-638-3301	$$	LD	Local	Beef
Cheyenne Cattle Company	Alt	see the Hitching Post Inn	307-638-3301	$$	LD	Local	Beef
The Cowboy Cafeteria	1	Frontier Park	307-778-7222	$	L/D	Local	Burgers, hot dogs
Lexie's	2	216 E. 17th St.	307-638-8712	$$	D/BL	Local	American
The Little Bear Inn	Alt	Little Bear Road N, I-25N, Exit 16	307-634-3684	$$	D	Local	Steak
Los Amigos	1	620 Central Ave.	307-638-8591	$	D/L	Local	Mexican
The Old Corral	2	2750 W. Hwy 130, Centennial	307-745-5918	$	L/BD	Local	Chicken, steak, salads
Senator's Steak House	3	I-25, 51 Service Rd. E	307-634-4994	$$	D	Local	Chuck-wagon dinner
The Twin Dragons	Alt	1809 Carey Ave.	307-637-6622	$	D	Local	Chinese

NIGHTLIFE	DAY	ADDRESS	PH	COVER	REC*	DRESS	MUSIC
Cheyenne Club	Alt	1617 Capitol Ave.	307-635-7777	$	MP	Local	Country
The Coach Room	3	see the Hitching Post Inn	307-638-3301	$$	MP	Local	Country, oldies
The Horn's Cowboy Bar	1	312 S. Greeley Hwy.	307-637-3800	None	MP	Local	Country
Mayflower Tavern	Alt	112 W. 17th St.	307-632-7999	None	R	Local	
Wigwam	Alt	1600 Central Ave.	307-635-9096	None	MP	Local	Country

SIGHTS & ATTRACTIONS	DAY	ADDRESS	PH	ENTRY FEE
Cheyenne Botanic Gardens and Solar Conservatory	3	710 S. Lions Park Dr.	307-637-6458	$
Cheyenne Street Railway Trolley	3	309 W. Lincolnway	800-426-5009	$
Diamond Guest Ranch	Alt	40 miles north of Cheyenne, Chugwater (I-25)	800-932-4222	None
Cheyenne Frontier Days Old West Museum	3	4610 N. Carey Ave.	800-778-7290	$
Lions Park	3	520 W. 8th St.	307-637-6429	None
Snowy Range of Rocky Mts.	2	130 miles west of Cheyenne		
Wyoming Hereford Ranch	Alt	1600 Hereford Ranch Rd., east of Cheyenne	307-634-1905	None

OTHER SIGHTS, SHOPS & SERVICES

	DAY	ADDRESS	PH	ENTRY FEE
Just Dandy	1	1607 Capitol Ave.	307-635-2565	None
The Wrangler	1	1518 Capitol Ave.	307-634-3048	None
The Cheyenne Area CVB		309 W. Lincolnway	800-426-5009	

Event & Ticket Info

Cheyenne Frontier Days (Frontier Park, Carey Ave. and 8th Ave.): There is no charge for admission to the park, the **parades**, **Frontier Park Indian Village**, or the **Pancake Breakfast** (Lincoln Way and Carey Ave.). Tickets for reserved seating for the **rodeo** ($10-20) and **The Cheyenne Frontier Days Night Show** ($18) go on sale in January. The best seats for the **rodeo** which are over or close to the chutes, sell out months in advance. Some **Night Shows** sell out in advance. For tickets or information, contact *Frontier Days* (800-227-6336).

* M=Live music; P=Dancing (Party); R=Bar only; S=Show; (F)=Food served. For further explanation of codes, see page 14.

 NYC – 2   Cheyenne (CYS) <30 min./$5 Denver (DEN) <120 min./NA   Yes   50°/85° (10°/29°)

The Fun Also Rises

August 1999

Carmel/Monterey (Pebble Beach), California, USA

August 2000

Concours d'Elegance

(Pebble Beach Concours d'Elegance)

| Origin: 1950 | Event ★ ★ ★ ★ ★ City | Attendance: 12,000 |

Be careful not to spill your champagne—the interior of that '29 Benz you're looking at costs about the same as your annual mortgage payments. Better, anyway, to use the free-flowing bubbly here to lubricate a conversation with one of the engaging well-to-dos or car buffs with encyclopedic knowledge who are drawn to this event each year like royalty to caviar.

Renowned as the Super Bowl of auto shows, Sunday's posh *Concours d'Elegance* vintage-car show sparkles with stars, chrome, and champagne flutes while a backdrop of Pacific Ocean breakers, jazz, and classical music provides auxiliary atmosphere. The prestigious Pebble Beach Golf Course turns into a time machine as many of the 9,000 attendees don fashions that were *haute couture* when some of the show's oldest vehicles first chugged past horse-drawn carriages. Some take a little of the *Concours* home by successfully bidding on rare and classic cars shown by Christie's and the Blackhawk Collection. Most, however, are content simply sipping champagne and watching while the smart set cruises for top-drawer trophies to display in their passenger seats.

The *Concours Italiano* begins a weekend of official events. The show highlights Italian design in more than 450 new and vintage motor vehicles and in a fashion show, while 10,000 guests examine vehicles and fashion models, shop, and use car tales to broach conversation. Car-club parades and multimillion-dollar auto auctions provide further distractions. From Friday until Sunday at Laguna Seca, the *Monterey Historic Automobile Races* send 360 sporty vintage cars buzzing and backfiring around the racetrack while visitors explore tents displaying auto-related expos and demos.

Amid the Monterey Peninsula's dramatic coastline and lush valleys are four of California's most scenic towns. Carmel-by-the-Sea (Carmel for short) is an upscale, ocean-side resort village. Inland, Carmel Valley attracts bikers, golfers, hikers, and wine tasters. The exclusive gated community of Pebble Beach includes rugged coast and ultraluxury resorts. Monterey is the only real city on the peninsula, with shopping, dining, and entertainment options catering to a wide range of visitors.

Concours d'Elegance

Day 1. Fri.   Aug. 27, 1999
(Day 1. Friday   August 18, 2000)

8:30am Get settled at the gorgeous **La Playa Hotel**. Overlooking the Pacific, the hotel forms a horseshoe around meticulously landscaped gardens and a heated pool.

10:00am Have breakfast at the award-winning **From Scratch Restaurant**. At an outdoor table, enjoy cheese blintzes or a custom-made omelet.

11:30am The ***Concours Italiano*** began at 8:30 a.m., so you've missed some of the drive-by presentations of Italian cars. No problem. Once off the runway, vehicles are positioned throughout the green where you can take a closer look. A love of Italian vehicles brings together an interesting mix of country-club types, middle-class families, Italians, and car guys. At noon, you can check out the preview of Italian fall fashions, complete with a catwalk and models.

1:00pm Local Italian restaurants vend fresh foods in the main dining tent. Line up before the fashion show finishes at 1 p.m.

3:00pm Beat the end-of-show rush and drive through one of the most beautiful areas on earth, the **Big Sur Coast**. Stop less than one-third of the way along the 90-mile scenic drive at **Nepenthe** (about an hour's drive) for a drink, a bite to eat, and a great view of the coast. Then return home.

7:30pm The Santa Fe-themed **Rio Grill** consistently wins awards for its wine list and food. Spend social time at the bar with a friendly wine-and-cheese crowd, then order an entree hot off the oak-wood smoker.

9:30pm Carmel is a place for romantic evening strolls and window-shopping. Ocean Avenue is the main strip for both.

10:30pm Cap your night at a local pub. **Sade's** may fit only 35 customers, but it's a good place to meet actual Carmelites. Across Ocean Avenue, **Red Lion Tavern** re-creates ye olde English drinking place and serves fish 'n' chips and bangers 'n' mash. **Hog's Breath Inn** has four fireplaces and a nice patio. Nearby **Jack London's** ends the Carmel pub crawl at 2 a.m.

Day 2. Sat.   Aug. 28, 1999
(Day 2. Saturday   August 19, 2000)

9:00am For today's races, wear casual, comfortable clothes and prepare for hot sunshine. If you really want to fit in, wear jeans and a T-shirt featuring a car-company logo.

10:00am The laid-back **Old Monterey Cafe** won a "Best on the Monterey Peninsula" award and is worth the 30-minute drive. It features 100 omelet toppings and six different Benedicts.

11:00am A 20-minute drive away, warm-ups for the ***Monterey Historic Automobile Races*** are underway. The auto parade and races start at noon. Spend the day on the paddock, where you can check out displays and vendors and get good views of the race. Shady tents showcase concept cars and promotional displays.

1:30pm Near Laguna Seca, **Tarpy's Roadhouse Cafe** occupies an old vine-covered stone villa. The chefs transform American staples into *haute cuisine*. Sample wine at the **Ventana Vineyards** tasting room before leaving.

3:30pm Consistently rated as the finest in the United States, Monterey's **Monterey Bay Aquarium** displays more than 300,000 marine animals and plants. A major recent addition is the Outer Bay exhibit, which is viewed through the largest window on earth.

6:00pm The Cannery Row area is worth a stroll, although the tourist commercialism must make the sardines turn over in their cans. Count the number of times you spot John Steinbeck's name.

7:30pm Have dinner at **Montrio**, where international ® influences flavor the dishes. The restaurant is housed in a 1910 firehouse.

9:00pm Two blocks from Montrio, the Italian restaurant **Cibo** draws an animated crowd to its bar for live jazz. Across from Cibo, bids are taken until midnight on exotic and rare cars at the *Monterey Sports and Classic Car Auction*.

10:30pm Stroll along Alvarado Street. Live music at **Viva Monterey** is usually good. At **McGarrett's**, you can choose from three dance floors with completely different vibes.

Day 3. Sun. Aug. 29, 1999
(Day 3. Sunday   August 20, 2000)

8:30am Dressing in elegant or vintage attire for the *Concours d'Elegance* will maximize your mingling power. Don't forget comfortable shoes and something warm for when the fog rolls in.

9:30am At **Patisserie Boissière**'s, order from the extensive coffee list. There's also an in-house bakery with pastries and tea breads.

10:30am The main event. At the *Concours d'Elegance*, car fanatics spend hours beholding vintage vehicles situated around the 18th hole of the Pebble Beach golf course. Be on the lookout for celebrity regulars such as Clint Eastwood and Jay Leno. Sip cocktails and listen to jazz while mixing with a set as polished as the autos. Cars compete for awards, but most guests are too enraptured with each other to devote sustained attention to competitions. Be sure to stop into The Lodge at Pebble Beach courtyard to see new and extraordinary concept cars.

1:00pm Near The Lodge, the **Pebble Beach Market** ® fixes burgers and fresh deli foods. Order and join other ocean-side picnickers on the grass back at the *Concours*.

4:00pm Before leaving, trek to the Peter Hay Golf Course where the *Blackhawk Collection Exposition of Classic Cars* silently auctions collectible cars.

7:30pm Locals and visitors come to **Il Fornaio** for ® California-fresh Italian dishes, house-baked breads, and a thriving social scene. Choose a table on the ocean-view terrace.

9:30pm Carmel closes down early, so bid farewell to the Age of Elegance by taking a moonlit walk along the beach by your hotel as stars twinkle like ancient headlights on the Milky Way.

Alternatives

The best places to stay any time—and especially during the collector-car weekend—are **Inn at Spanish Bay** and **The Lodge at Pebble Beach**. However, both hotels limit that weekend's guests to participants in the *Concours d'Elegance*, event sponsors, and others directly involved in the *Concours*. Other options include the **Highlands Inn**, a stone lodge set on a rugged hillside above a dramatic drop to the ocean. The **Monterey Plaza Hotel** is stylish and centrally located on Monterey Bay and comes with the usual load of luxury amenities.

An alternative plan for your first afternoon is to drive into Carmel Valley and exchange your car for a horse at **Holman Ranch**. Ride or hike in **Garland Ranch Regional Park**'s 4,462-acres. Or taste tannins at **Galante Vineyards**, **Bernardus Winery**, or **Château Julien**. You can also visit **Carmel Mission** (the Basilica of Mission San Carlos Borromeo del Rio Carmelo), a well-restored and excellent example of the Franciscan missions in California.

Concours d'Elegance (18th Fairway at The Lodge at Pebble Beach): Purchase tickets ($50 CD) at least a month in advance through *United Way* (831-372-8026). For more information, contact *Concours d'Elegance* (831-659-0663). (continued on next page)

The Hot Sheet

HOTELS		ADDRESS	PH	FX	PRICE	RMS	BEST ROOMS
Highlands Inn	Alt	Hwy. 1, 4 miles south of Carmel	831-624-3801 (CS) 800-682-4811	831-626-1574	$$$$	142	Ocean vw
Inn at Spanish Bay	Alt	2700 17 Mile Dr.	(M) 831-647-7500 800-654-9300	831-644-7960	$$$$	269	Ocean vw
La Playa Hotel	★	Camino Real at 8th Ave.	(CS) 831-624-6476 800-582-8900	831-624-7966	$$	80	Pool deck or ocean vw
The Lodge at Pebble Beach	Alt	17 Mile Dr.	(M) 831-624-3811 800-654-9300	831-644-7960	$$$$	161	Ocean vw
Monterey Plaza Hotel	Alt	400 Cannery Row	(M) 831-646-1700 800-631-1339	831-646-0285	$$$	285	Ocean vw

RESTAURANTS	DAY	ADDRESS	PH	PRICE	REC	DRESS	FOOD
From Scratch Restaurant	1	3626 The Barnyard	(CS) 831-625-2448	$$	B/LD	Local	American
Il Fornaio	3	Ocean Ave. at Monte Verde	(CS) 831-622-5100	$$$	D/BL	Kazh	Italian
Montrio	2	414 Calle Principal	(M) 831-648-8880	$$$	D/L	Local	American, continental
Nepenthe	1	Hwy. 1, Big Sur	831-667-2345	$$$	T/LD	Local	American
The Old Monterey Cafe	2	489 Alvarado St.	(M) 831-646-1021	$	B/L	Local	Omelets
Patisserie Boissière	3	Mission St.	(CS) 831-624-5008	$	B/LD	Local	American
Pebble Beach Market	3	17 Mile Dr. (across from The Lodge)	(M) 831-625-8528	$	L/BD	Local	Deli
Rio Grill	1	101 Crossroads Blvd. at Hwy. 1 and Rio Rd.	(CV) 831-625-5436	$$	D/L	Kazh	Southwestern
Tarpy's Roadhouse Cafe	2	Monterey-Salinas Hwy. 68, 1 mi. east of airport	(M) 831-647-1444	$	L/D	Local	American

NIGHTLIFE	DAY	ADDRESS	PH	COVER	REC*	DRESS	MUSIC
Cibo	2	301 Alvarado St.	(M) 831-649-8151	None	M(F)	Kazh	Jazz
Hog's Breath Inn	1	San Carlos St.	(CS) 831-625-1044	None	R	Local	
Jack London's	1	San Carlos St. (betw. 5th and 6th sts.)	(CS) 831-624-2336	None	R(F)	Local	
McGarrett's	2	321 Alvarado St.	(M) 831-646-9244	$	P	Local	Top 40
Red Lion Tavern	1	Su Vecino Ct.	(CS) 831-625-6765	None	R(F)	Local	
Sade's	1	Lincoln St. and Ocean Ave.	(CS) 831-624-0787	None	R(F)	Local	
Viva Monterey	2	414 Alvarado St.	(M) 831-646-1415	None	M(F)	Local	Contemporary

SIGHTS & ATTRACTIONS	DAY	ADDRESS	PH	ENTRY FEE
Bernardus Winery	Alt	5 W. Carmel Valley Rd.	(CV) 800-223-2533	None
Big Sur Coast	1	Hwy. 1	(M)	None
Carmel Mission	Alt	Rio Rd. off of Hwy. 1	(CS) 831-624-9848	None
Château Julien	Alt	8940 Carmel Valley Rd.	(CV) 831-624-2600	None
Galante Vineyards	Alt	18181 Cachagua Rd.	(CV) 800-425-2683	None
Garland Ranch Regional Park	Alt	9 miles inland on Hwy. 1	(CV) 831-659-6063	None
Monterey Bay Aquarium	2	886 Cannery Row	(M) 831-648-4888	$$
Ventana Vineyards	2	Hwy. 68 and Hwy. 218	(M) 831-372-7415	None
Holman Ranch	Alt	Holman Rd.	(CV) 831-659-6054	$$$
Monterey Peninsula CVB		380 Alvarado St.	(M) 831-648-5350	

Event & Ticket Info

(continued from previous page)

Blackhawk Collection Exposition of Classic Cars (Peter Hay Golf Course, the Lodge at Pebble Beach): Free. For more information, call 510-736-3444.
Concours Italiano (Quail Lodge Resort, 8205 Valley Greens Dr., Carmel): Purchase tickets ($40) up to three weeks before the event from *Concours Italiano* (425-688-1903) or at the gate.
Monterey Historic Automobile Races (Laguna Seca Raceway, Hwy. 68, Salinas): For tickets ($35), call 800-327-7322.
Monterey Sports and Classic Car Auction (Monterey Conference Center, Doubletree Hotel, 2 Portola Plaza): For tickets ($25 at the door) and information, call 800-211-4371.

* CV=Carmel Valley; CS=Carmel-by-the-Sea; M=Monterey
* M=Live music; P=Dancing (Party); R=Bar only; S=Show; (F)=Food served. For further explanation of codes, see page 14.

 NYC –3   Monterey (MRY) <30 min./$20 San Jose (SJC) <90 min./$n/a   Yes   52°/68° (11°/20°)

 The Fun Also Rises

September 1999 · Seattle, Washington, USA · September 2000

Bumbershoot

(Bumbershoot, The Seattle Arts Festival)

Origin: 1971   Event ★★★★★ City   Attendance: 250,000

There's a buzz in Seattle and it isn't from the coffee. It comes from **Bumbershoot** (slang for "umbrella"), an annual Labor Day weekend celebration that's become one of the largest arts festivals in the United States. Set against the stunning backdrop of Puget Sound and the Olympic Mountains, this food, culture, and music explosion runs 12 hours a day for four days, attracting top local and international bands as part of an awesome program.

Nestled among dark-green pine trees, embraced by fresh ocean breezes, shadowed by the 605-foot Space Needle, and loaded with as many as 28 indoor and outdoor stages, **Bumbershoot** attracts a fun-loving and usually mellow crowd. More than 2,500 artists, authors, filmmakers, poets, and musicians give praise to the human spirit in the 74-acre Seattle Center—a legacy of the 1962 Seattle World's Fair and now the festival's home. Barbecued salmon, Northwest art, experimental films, ballet, and opera provide the subtext, but the real draw here is music. Crowds as large as 20,000 often gather to watch music-world legends bring familiar and cutting-edge sounds to music-crazy Seattle. While listening, fans work on tans during the day and watch the stars at night. Forty food and beverage booths appease the hungry.

When **Bumbershoot** festivities end at 11 p.m. each night, party-goers walk a few blocks to hip Belltown, or farther, to the music scene in historic Pioneer Square. During the days, visitors can hop ferries for 10-minute rides to West Seattle or two-hour trips to Victoria, British Columbia. Hikers can visit the nearby Olympic and Cascade mountains and wander among old-growth forests. City attractions include the Seattle Art Museum and Pike Place Market, the oldest farmers market in the United States.

Twenty years ago, Seattle was a sleepy city known for timber and salmon. These days, music, food, coffee, and computer-culture booms continue to make this Northwest gem—with an area population of 2.3 million—one of the country's most visited cities. **Bumbershoot** collects the best of Seattle into one glorious weekend.

Bumbershoot

Day 1. Fri.   Sept. 3, 1999
(Day 1. Friday   September 1, 2000)

10:00am *Snazzy* characterizes the **Hotel Monaco**. Enjoy the lobby mural and Mediterranean-eclectic interior design. Opened in 1997, the Monaco has fast become the happening hotel for travelers.

10:30am Dressed in comfortable clothing, walking shoes, and a lightweight jacket (you now blend with the locals), stop into one of Seattle's famed coffeehouses and order an energy-boosting latte, Seattle's drink of choice.

11:30am Walk to Westlake Shopping Center and the Monorail at the top of the mall. After a two-minute elevated-train ride, you'll be at Seattle Center, site of **Bumbershoot**. Your ticket admits you to all performances and exhibitions on a first-come-first-served basis.

12:30pm Select from a multitude of regional food and drink specialties for lunch and grab a seat on the grass. Study the festival program. More than 2,000 acts, performances, and spectacles take time to sort out.

3:00pm Stroll the grounds and get your bearings at the gigantic international fountain. With sprays of cooling water, it serves as a central meeting place. Meander around the art market, taking mental note of which piece of Northwest art to buy later. Locate the Opera House, Budweiser Mainstage, Literary Stage, rock arena, and playhouse, where continuous screenings of independent short films are held.

6:30pm Exit at the Space Needle gate and hop into the elevator bound for the **Space Needle Restaurant**. At 520 feet, the observation deck offers a 360-degree view of Puget Sound, bays, lakes, rivers, and snow-capped Mount Rainier. Have dinner at a window table in the revolving restaurant while watching a spectacular sunset unfold.

8:30pm Catch the last show at the festival. If the performer is well-known, be prepared to wait in line for 30 minutes or more.

11:00pm Exit at the Broad Street gate and walk ten minutes to Belltown, where there's no shortage of night-life options. **Queen City Grill** is known for its Friday singles scene. And **2218** puts on a lively weekend salsa party. **The Crocodile Cafe** is a hot spot for the sounds Seattle made famous—grunge and alt rock.

Day 2. Sat.   Sept. 4, 1999
(Day 2. Saturday   September 2, 2000)

9:00am Stroll 10 blocks to **Le Panier Very French Bakery** at **Pike Place Market**. If you're lucky, you'll be able to snag a window table, watch the crowd, and enjoy a homemade pastry with a steaming bowl of French-style coffee.

10:00am Join the Pike Place crowd browsing past fresh produce, flowers, restaurants, and gift shops. Be prepared to duck the flying fish heads being thrown as you walk past the Pure Food Fish Market.

11:00am Walk six blocks to gracefully restored Pioneer Square, where loggers built the original Skid Road to slide logs downhill to the waterfront. (As Seattle's economic center migrated north, Skid Row was abandoned to the homeless and indigent.) Meet at Doc Maynard's public house for the humorous **Underground Tour**, a walk through subterranean Seattle.

1:30pm A local favorite since 1938, **Ivar's Acres of Clams** has fresh seafood and stunning views of Elliott Bay.

3:00pm Walk along the water and up the 16,000-square-foot staircase-turned-park called the Harbor Steps. At the top you'll find the spectacular Robert Venturi-designed **Seattle Art Museum**. Enjoy outstanding collections of African, Pacific Northwest, and contemporary American art.

5:30pm Walk back to the Hotel Monaco in time to relax at an hour-long wine tasting in the lobby next to the fireplace. Free only to guests, the featured wines are chosen from the highly rated vineyards of Washington and Oregon.

7:00pm Head back to **Bumbershoot** for the Saturday-night headliner. Food concessions dot the stadium, so you won't go hungry.

11:00pm Stop at **Dmitriou's Jazz Alley** to catch the last nationally renowned jazz act of the evening. **The Ballard Firehouse Food & Beverage Company** has live rock or blues.

1:00am If you're not ready for the party to end, cab to **13 Coins** for a late-night snack. It's been a Seattle institution for more than 30 years.

Day 3. Sun. Sept. 5, 1999
(Day 3. Sunday   September 3, 2000)

10:00am Walk to the Four Seasons Olympic hotel for its famous Sunday brunch among the palms at **The Garden Court**.

11:30am Instead of more **Bumbershoot**, board a ferry at piers 55 and 56 to **Tillicum Village** for a four-hour visit to Blake Island. Your trip will include a buffet featuring Pacific salmon, baked Northwest Coast Native American-style on cedar stakes over alder fires.

4:30pm Have a final cup of Seattle coffee at the original **Starbucks** at Pike Place Market.

7:00pm Watch the sun set behind the Olympic Mountains while sampling from one of Seattle's most honored wine lists at **Ray's Boat House**, a local favorite for leisurely boaters and high-powered business types.

While **Bumbershoot** captures the spirit of the city's reputation for wet weather, according to the Seattle-King County News Bureau, Seattleites buy more sunglasses per capita than residents of any other city in the United States.

9:00pm Dress smartly for dinner at **El Gaucho**, Seattle's trendiest elegant restaurant. It's known for flaming steaks. After dinner, be part of Seattle's casual social scene at its big bar or in one of two cigar lounges.

Alternatives

The **Four Seasons Olympic**, three blocks from Westlake Center, has been fully restored to its original 1920s Renaissance Revival splendor— it may be Seattle's most elegant hotel. Another older hotel, the **Mayflower Park Hotel**, adjacent to the Westlake Shopping Center, could not be more convenient to **Bumbershoot**.

You'll probably eat lots of stall food at *Bumbershoot*, but you can also try the acclaimed **Sazerac** restaurant in the Hotel Monaco, where dishes are accompanied by sparkling city views. **McCormick and Schmick's Seafood Restaurant** is a regional favorite. The largest outdoor deck in Seattle, overlooking Elliott Bay, is at **Anthony's Bell Street Diner**. Order from a wide range of food that includes Northwest seafood delicacies such as charcoal-grilled salmon with sun-dried tomato butter.

The aircraft industry's presence can be enjoyed at the **Museum of Flight** where you'll see more than 50 full-size aircraft. The **Washington Park Arboretum** is a huge park with a unique collection of plants from around the world, along with a gorgeous **Japanese Garden**.

With an extra day, go to Victoria, BC, via *The Victoria Clipper*, a turbo-jetted ferry. Victoria harbor is pretty, but the fountains and flowers at **The Butchart Gardens Ltd.** are the island's highlight and well worth the short bus ride. End your visit with high tea (starting at 3:30 p.m.) at the luxurious **Empress Hotel**.

The Hot Sheet

HOTELS		ADDRESS	PH	FX	PRICE	RMS	BEST ROOMS
Four Seasons Olympic (Regent Hotels)	Alt	411 University St.	206-621-1700 800-223-8772	206-682-9633	$$$$	450	Dlx corner rms w/ prt wtr vw
Hotel Monaco (Kimpton Hotels)	★	1101 4th Ave.	206-621-1770 800-945-2240	206-621-7779	$$$	189	Corner rm w/city vw
Mayflower Park Hotel in Westlake Center	Alt	405 Olive Way	206-382-6990 800-426-5100	206-382-6996	$$	172	Corner rm w/city vw

RESTAURANTS	DAY	ADDRESS	PH	PRICE	REC	DRESS	FOOD
13 Coins	2	125 Boren Ave. N	206-682-2513	$$	BLD	Local	Varied
Anthony's Bell Street Diner	Alt	2201 Alaskan Way	206-448-6688	$$	LD	Local	Seafood
The Garden Court	3	see Four Seasons Olympic hotel	206-621-1700	$$$	BLD	Kazh	Continental
El Gaucho	3	2505 1st Ave.	206-728-1337	$$$	D	Kazh, Dressy	American, steaks
Ivar's Acres of Clams	2	Pier 54	206-624-6852	$$	L/D	Local	Seafood
McCormick and Schmick's Seafood Restaurant	Alt	1103 1st Ave.	206-623-5500	$$	LD	Kazh	Seafood
Le Panier Very French Bakery	2	1902 Pike Pl.	206-441-3669	$	B	Local	Continental
Sazerac	Alt	1101 4th Ave.	206-624-7755	$$	D/BL	Local, Kazh	Southern American
Space Needle Restaurant	1	219 4th St. N	206-443-2100	$$$$	D/BL	Dressy, Kazh	American
Starbucks	3	1912 Pike Pl.	206-448-8762	$	T	Local	Coffee, pastries

NIGHTLIFE	DAY	ADDRESS	PH	COVER	REC*	DRESS	MUSIC
2218	1	2218 1st Ave.	206-443-0707	$	P(F)	Kazh	Jazz, disco
The Ballard Firehouse Food & Beverage Company	2	5429 Russell Ave. NW	206-784-3516	$	M(F)	Local	Blues, rock
The Crocodile Cafe	1	2200 2nd Ave.	206-448-2114	$	M(F)	Local	Alternative, rock, grunge
Dmitriou's Jazz Alley	2	2033 6th Ave.	206-441-9729	$$	M(F)	Kazh	Jazz
Queen City Grill	1	2201 1st Ave.	206-443-0975	None	R(F)	Local	
Ray's Boat House	3	6049 Seaview Ave. NW	206-789-3770	$$	R(F)	Local, Kazh	

SIGHTS & ATTRACTIONS	DAY	ADDRESS	PH	ENTRY FEE
The Butchart Gardens Ltd.	Alt	800 Benvenuto Ave.	250-652-4422	$$
The Empress Hotel	Alt	721 Government St.	250-384-8111	$$$
Japanese Garden	Alt	1501 Lake Washington Blvd.	206-684-4725	$
Museum of Flight	Alt	9404 E. Marginal Way S	206-764-5720	$
Pike Place Market	2	1st Ave.	206-682-7453	None
Seattle Art Museum	2	100 University St.	206-654-3100	$
Tillicum Village, Blake Island	3	2200 6th Ave., Ste. A04	206-443-1244	$$$$+
Underground Tour	2	Pioneer Square	1-888-608-6337	$
Washington Park Arboretum	Alt	2300 Arboretum Dr. E	206-543-8800	None

OTHER SIGHTS, SHOPS & SERVICES

The Victoria Clipper	Alt	Pier 69 in Seattle	800-888-2535	$$$$+

Event & Ticket Info

Bumbershoot, The Seattle Arts Festival (Seattle Center): Daily adult tickets ($14) are available at the *Seattle Center* during the festival. For advance tickets, call *Ticketmaster* (206-628-0888) beginning in August. For more information, call *One Reel Special Events Hotline* (206-281-8111).

Seattle-King County Visitor Information	Convention Center, 8th Ave. and Pike	206-461-5840

Victoria—Area Code 250

* M=Live music; P=Dancing (Party); R=Bar only; S=Show; (F)=Food served. For further explanation of codes, see page 14.

 NYC −3   Seattle/Tacoma (SEA) <60 min./$35   No   52°/69° (11°/21°)

August/September 1999

August/September 2000

Reno (Black Rock City), Nevada, USA

Burning Man

Origin: 1986   Event ★ ★ ★ ★ ★ ★ ★ ★ City   Attendance: 10,000

It's the fourth-largest metropolitan area in Nevada, but don't bother looking for it on the map. It appears for a single week each year, then sinks without a trace into the miles-deep dust of an ancient lake bed. It's Black Rock City, home to the ***Burning Man*** festival, an eclectic mix of offbeat art, impromptu performance, and cultural experimentation that draws 10,000 or so free spirits to the middle of nowhere each Labor Day weekend.

Tall as a five-story building, trimmed with neon and stuffed with fireworks, the Man is an impressive piece of work, but the real story is in the culture that has sprung up around it. ***Burning Man*** has become a magnet for many strange and unexpected offerings. Surrealist sculptors and solar-powered multimedia auteurs share the stage with musicians, painters, dancers, poets, and gearheads. People labor all year to construct elaborate theme camps ranging from potluck barter bars to full-tilt circus sideshows. Costumes abound, including the ever-popular birthday suit. There are two daily newspapers in operation along with a dozen or so pirate radio stations. There's even an opera.

Burning Man's motto—"No spectators"—means no matter how hard you try, you can't avoid becoming part of the show. It's an intensely participatory event, with no proscenium to separate the players from the crowd. Be prepared to interact with people.

There's no on-site vending and little for sale in nearby towns, so you'll need to bring all your own gear and supplies. Likewise, you'll need to take everything with you when you leave. ***Burning Man*** provides sanitation and basic safety services, but no dumpsters. One of the few rules is that the desert has to be restored to its natural state of pristine emptiness when this counterculture Eden disappears for another year.

It's hot, it's dusty, and it's a lot of work to get there. But once you've made it to Black Rock City, you'll understand why so many people call it home, if only for a few days each year.

Burning Man

Day 1. Fri.   Sept. 3, 1999
(Day 1. Friday   September 1, 2000)

10:00am From the Reno airport, skip the slot machines and make a beeline for your rental RV. Try to reserve one with a roll-out side-awning, and see if you can get a few folding chairs thrown in along with the standard "housekeeping package" of linens and kitchenware—you'll appreciate having a shady place to relax, have a drink, and people-watch during the day. Remember, there are no RV hookups in Black Rock City. You'll need to be self-contained or carry generator fuel.

11:30am Reno is your last chance to really shop, so make the most of it: ice chest, cold drinks, sun block, trash bags, earplugs, food, lip balm, ice, and more cold drinks. You won't be that hungry—the desert is a natural appetite suppressant—but you will be thirsty. Make sure you have at least a gallon of water per person per day in addition to all the beer, wine, juice, and soft drinks you can carry. Hats and sunglasses are survival essentials in the desert. Shopping for *Burning Man* is an art and a science—it's a good idea to check the festival's Web site (www.burningman.com) for suggestions on what to pack.

1:00pm Drive the 120 miles north from Reno to the *Burning Man* site. The solitude and beauty of this terrain makes the desert a paradise for many people.

3:00pm If nowhere does in fact have a middle, you can hear it talking to itself in Gerlach, Nevada, population 300. One gas station, no stores, five bars, and the *Burning Man* ticket office, located in what was once a jailhouse. If you're hungry, stop by Bruno's Country Club for a plate of Bruno's famous ravioli. Be sure to stop in the bar and check out Bruno's fine collection of memorabilia from land speed-record teams, including Richard Noble's Thrust SSC, the first vehicle to break the sound barrier on land.

5:00pm Roll into Black Rock City and set up camp. If you've got questions, stop one of the khaki-clad Danger Rangers, the festival's well-trained volunteer force. Have a drink and introduce yourself to your neighbors. Like any town, Black Rock City has different neighborhoods with different flavors. Get to know yours—its citizenry and major landmarks—before it gets dark. Interacting with folks is the essence of *Burning Man*.

8:30pm Raise a glass to the spectacular desert sunset, slip into (or out of) your hottest outfit, then set out for an evening of surreal entertainment. A full schedule of Saturday-night performances culminates in the opera, an allegorical fantasy with spectacular costumes, original music, and (no kidding) a burning stage. Kind of like the Met, but with a looser dress code and bigger explosions.

Midnight Put a little distance between yourself and the bright lights by relaxing under a gorgeous desert sky and spending quality time with billions of burning stars. Afterward, you can dance or head back to the RV for late-night socializing with a set of neighbors straight out of *The Twilight Zone*.

Day 2. Sat.   Sept. 4, 1999
(Day 2. Saturday   September 2, 2000)

Dawn If you're a morning person, head out to the *Burning Man* at sunrise and look for Java Cow, a bizarre creature known to dispense coffee to the early-rising faithful.

10:00am Better yet, sleep in, then shuffle over to center camp when you're good and ready and order a latte at the coffee bar, *Burning Man*'s sole concession to commerce and its de facto social hub. Sit in the shade of many parachutes and read the *Black Rock Gazette*, the town's leading daily. Along with several pirate radio stations, it's part of *Burning Man*'s always-entertaining media.

11:00am If you feel energetic, take a stroll around camp before it gets too hot. Soak up the ambience of the theme camps and try your hand at some of the arts workshops, such as casting molten aluminum at Recycling Camp or assembling your own burnable offering from scrap lumber.

Midday Take a tip from the desert wildlife and lay low during the hottest part of the day. Drink water *constantly*. Don't resist the urge to nap—it's your body's way of telling you there's a huge party tonight. There's a lot to see, but don't worry, it'll all still be there when you wake up.

Late afternoon In the spectacular golden light of the late-day desert, check out some of the theme camps you've missed or pay return visits to the ones where you've made friends. Don't forget to get your *Burning Man* passport stamped at all your theme-camp stops —it'll make a great souvenir when you get home.

Dusk Showtime! Put on your finest regalia and head to center camp for the Cacophonists' Cocktail Party, a *Burning Man* tradition started by the San Francisco Cacophony Society, the loose network of pranksters and urban adventurers who nurtured this event through its formative years. Formal attire is always appropriate, but if you have an idea for a crazy costume, you should please the crowd by wearing it. After a few rounds (BYOB, of course), follow the sound of drums to the burning of the Man, the festival's climactic spectacle. Skyrockets scream from its upraised arms, tracing bright arcs across the sky, until at last it collapses into the biggest bonfire you've ever seen.

Night Shake all night at the big community dance. Remember those earplugs you bought back in Reno? This is where they'll come in handy. Share all your remaining beverages and treats with your new friends. At some point, you'll probably be treated to a speech or appearance by Larry Harvey, the event's originator, who is known by the trademark Stetson he's almost never seen without. (He wears the hat as a tribute to his late father.) Harvey is an eccentric idealist who began this event in San Francisco in 1985 by burning an eight-foot structure on the beach as a reaction to a severe romantic breakup. Now, his community of friends has grown, graduate thesis papers have been written about him and his event, and he's been invited to speak at Harvard University about this idyllic community that comes together in the desert each year. Because of the way he speaks in fits and stutters, many of his friends believe Harvey is possessed—by friendly spirits.

Day 3. Sun. Sept. 5, 1999
(Day 3. Sunday   September 3, 2000)

Morning Donate at least an hour to the group clean-up effort, more if you can spare it. *Burning Man* has a strong environmental aesthetic and the citizens of Black Rock City take great pride in "leaving no trace" when they pack up and leave. Don't be surprised if you make some friends in the process. Now that you're a veteran, inquire about becoming a Danger Ranger volunteer at next year's gathering.

Noon Head back to Reno—coming from *Burning Man*, prepare for massive culture shock as you approach the neon-lit gambling oasis—with an empty ice chest and a chapped smile on your face. Start making your list of things to bring next year.

Event & Ticket Info

Burning Man (Nowhere Somewhere, Nevada): Tickets ($100 on site, $80 before August 15) can be purchased at the event, but it's best to get them ahead of time from *The Burning Man Project* (415-863-5263) so that you can receive the official Survival Guide and other helpful planning tools.

 NYC –3   Reno/Tahoe Cannon (RNO) <30 min./S15   Yes   39°/82° (4°/28°)

Living Fantasies

"**L**ife," as John Lennon said, "is what happens when you're making other plans." Despite how great things may have worked out, there comes a time when you find yourself wondering, What if … ?

What if you'd kept playing baseball? Kept practicing music and taken that club gig? Run away and become a cowboy? Whatever it is, what if you'd followed that dream? Now, how can you tell without abandoning the life you've worked so hard to build?

Fantasy camps started in the 1980s with baseball camps for people who wanted to play as hard as they worked. Now, many other sports and interests have camps. Some, such as golf, tennis, and gourmet-chef fantasy camps, may be only onetime deals. But many return each year, running from a few days to a week or more.

Whether you save the day with a home run, winning basket, or miraculous touchdown, there's a camp that lets you join some of the top athletes in the game in daily practices and "championship" games. You can also be an umpire, coach, scorekeeper, or announcer. Sports camps not your passion? Then live the life of a jazz great, fighter pilot, astronaut, or brewmeister.

Baseball Camps

Imagine you're up with the bases loaded, playing for your favorite pro team. The crowd's chants turn to a roar as you send a dinger into the cheap seats, bringing home three of the game's greatest heroes and winning the game. Your home-run trot is a thing of beauty. Your all-star teammates mob you at the plate.

Most baseball teams hold fantasy camps, although not always every year. Camps usually are held in Florida or Arizona and include several team members and legends of the game. Call your favorite baseball team's headquarters for more information.

The Doubleday Country Inn and Farm near Harrisburg, Pa. (717-789-2456), re-creates "the olden days" when one could ride horses on the wooded hillsides and play baseball on converted cornfields. At the camp, former major leaguers join you in twilight games.

Other baseball fantasy camps include:

Carl Yaztrzemski Baseball Camp	888-333-1881
Cooperstown Baseball Camp	800-726-7314
Field of Dreams Fantasy Camp	800-443-8981
Heroes In Pinstripes Fantasy Camp	606-474-2514
Tony Oliva's Baseball Fantasy Camp	888-333-1881
Ultimate Week Adult Baseball Fantasy Camp	800-525-6387
World Series of Fantasy Baseball	888-333-1881

Other Camps

Maybe you'd rather be standing at the free-throw line, score tied, no time left on the clock. Your pro-basketball teammates, legends all, watch anxiously as you take your shot—then burst into wild cheers as, no sweat, you drain the winning charity toss. If you're a hoops junkie, try Angela Beck's **Lasers Women's Fantasy Basketball Camp** (San Jose, Calif.; 408-271-1500), **Sports Legends Fantasy Camp** (Dallas, Texas; 800-937-5107), or the **Washington Wizards-Wes Unseld Fantasy Camp** (Washington, DC; 202-661-5000).

You can also score touchdowns at the **Green Bay Experience Fantasy Football Camp** (800-945-7102) or put your opponent in the dreaded camel clutch at the **Pro Wrestling Fantasy Camp** (510-785-8396).

Not all fantasies center on sports. You can jam with jazz greats at **Jazz Fantasy Camp** (Rhinelander, Wis.; 715-369-1500) or Moravian College's **Summer Jazz Fantasy Camp** (Bethlehem, Pa.; 610-861-1650). Pump adrenalin as a military fighter pilot at **Aviation Challenge Camp** (Huntsville, Ala.; 800-637-7223) or aim for the stars at the **Space Academy's Fantasy Astronaut Camp** (Huntsville, Ala.; 800-637-7223).

Taste the grit and relive the battles at **Civil War Adventures Camp** (800-624-4421). Drive those doggies home on an **American Wilderness Experience Cattle Drive** (800-444-0099). Or kick back and savor some classic suds at the **Homebrewers Fantasy Camp** (800-636-1331).

September 1999

September 2000

Big Muddy
(Big Muddy Blues & Roots Music Festival)

Origin: 1992 Event ★★★★ City Attendance: 50,000

As a young man, W.C. Handy slept on the St. Louis levee and soaked up sounds of the Mississippi River, which he later wove into his world-famous "St. Louis Blues." On Labor Day weekend, you can hear great musicians play the blues in the very place the music got its start.

Like Handy, you'll "hate to see the evenin' sun go down" after a day at St. Louis' *Big Muddy Blues & Roots Music Festival*, an annual event held north of downtown in historic Laclede's Landing. Each year, some 50,000 fun seekers flood the landing's quaint cobblestone streets, now lined with trendy shops, offices, restaurants, and nightclubs. Local and internationally famous blues greats—plus a few jazz and gospel artists— perform Saturday and Sunday on a series of outdoor stages while appreciative throngs eat, drink, and get anything but blue.

St. Louis sits at the northern end of a musical corridor that connects the city to two other river towns, Memphis and New Orleans. But the St. Louis version of the blues has a different flavor—a quirky mixture of soul and rhythm and blues that locals proudly call their own.

Part Southern, part Eastern, and part Midwestern, St. Louis was founded in 1764— when it could still rightfully be called the Gateway to the West—but has diversified while becoming the eighteenth most populous city in the United States. Among its assets are lovely historic neighborhoods, private places lined with breathtaking mansions, and a surprisingly vibrant night life. It also has another renowned festival, the delightful Japanese Festival—that takes place every year at the same time as *Big Muddy*—in the country's largest traditional Japanese garden.

The Western frontier is farther away these days—closer to Japan than to St. Louis, if you want to get technical —but St. Louis' trademark Gateway Arch is still a beacon to travelers coming from all directions in search of a piece of pure America. With its mix of music, food, and river scenery, *Big Muddy* isn't a festival that could take place only in America—it's a festival that could take place only in St. Louis.

Big Muddy

Day 1. Fri. — Sep. 3, 1999
(Day 1. Friday — September 1, 2000)

9:00am There'll be lots of activity in the gorgeous lobby of your hotel, the **Hyatt Regency St. Louis**, an integral part of the Union Station redevelopment. The six-story vaulted ceiling is one of the features of this commercial complex.

9:45am Drive to University City—15 minutes from downtown—for breakfast at the best of several **St. Louis Bread Company** outlets. This casual bakery/cafe is known for its freshly baked breads, pastries, and bagels.

10:30am Stroll down Delmar Boulevard. The eclectic shops in University City's "loop" make it one of the funkiest areas in town. Sidewalks embedded with bronze stars make up the **St. Louis Walk of Fame**.

Noon Eat at pop-culture paradise **Blueberry Hill**. Order a terrific hamburger, see the world's greatest juke-box, and check out memorabilia from Elvis, Chuck Berry, and 1950s TV shows. Or watch root beer rattle off the line while having lunch at **Fitz's**, a restaurant-cum-bottling-plant.

1:30pm Drive to Forest Park, site of the 1904 World's Fair and one of the nation's largest urban parks. Along its winding streets are the History Museum, St. Louis Science Center, St. Louis Zoo, and your stop, the **Saint Louis Art Museum**. The art and sculpture collections are particularly good. Just east of the park is the Central West End—gawk at the mansions on its luxurious private streets, especially Washington Terrace, then drive past the boutiques, pubs, and cafes of the business district. Stop at the inspiring **Cathedral of Saint Louis**, which has the world's largest collection of mosaic art—41.5 million pieces in all.

4:00pm On Route 66, 10 minutes away, is a south-side institution. **Ted Drewes Frozen Custard** is known for its delicious frozen custard and "the concrete," a milkshake so thick it will not spill (they say), even when turned upside down.

5:00pm Return to your hotel at **St. Louis Union Station**, a renovated station that contains more than 100 shops and restaurants. Enjoy a drink in the Grand Hall, which has been restored to its 1894 glory.

8:30pm **Harry's** is a favorite with locals and visitors in part because of the celebrity clientele, and in part because of the very good smokehouse dishes. Book ahead.

10:00pm Hang out at **Harry's**—it's a scene on Friday nights—and enjoy the band playing on the patio. Afterward, try nearby **Club Utopia,** a dimly lit disco with the smoky, dry-ice effect of a big-time show.

Day 2. Sat. — Sep. 4, 1999
(Day 2. Saturday — September 2, 2000)

9:00am Breakfast in the Hyatt's dining room, then go via Metro Link or car to the **Gateway Arch**, architect Eero Saarinen's gleaming tribute to the opening of the West. The tallest man-made monument in the United States, it's an impressive sight from a distance, extraordinary close-up. Tram to the top, 630 feet up, for a spectacular view. The short film on the building of the arch is worthwhile. Do a quick tour of the Museum of Westward Expansion at the same location.

12:30pm Explore the arch grounds, getting a look at the Mississippi River, historic Eads Bridge, and riverboats moored at the levee.

1:15pm Lunch at **Joseph's Italian Cafe**, a casually elegant restaurant that serves light entrees.

2:30pm Laclede's Landing, which makes use of restored 19th-century warehouses, cast-iron street lamps, and cobblestone streets, is the site of *Big Muddy*. Spend the afternoon listening to live performances by blues greats such as Otis Rush and Booker T. Jones on one of four stages. More music emanates from some of the half-dozen clubs in the area.

6:30pm Drive to the suburb of Clayton, a bustling business district that changes into a center of fine eating by night. **Crazy Fish Fresh Grill** is one of the town's hottest spots, with a great clientele and cross-cultural cuisine. Another fun choice is **Cardwell's**, which has California-style food.

8:30pm Drive to *Big Muddy* to catch late-evening performers and glistening lights on the river.

10:00pm Nearby, try the **Broadway Oyster Bar**, with its jazz- or blues-filled patio, and its neighbor, **BB's Jazz, Blues & Soups**. BB's is open later than many clubs, so musicians who finish gigs elsewhere often stop by to jam.

Midnight Reminisce about Ol' Blue Eyes with a nightcap at **The Summit**, or dance at **AJ's**, off the lobby of the Adam's Mark Hotel. The dark ambience at the hip **Living Room** is softened by sofas and chairs tucked into nooks.

Day 3. Sun. Sep. 5, 1999
(Day 3. Sunday   September 3, 2000)

10:00am Drive to the quaint Soulard neighborhood for brunch at **Patty Long's 9th Street Abbey**, which serves eclectic American food in a renovated 19th-century church.

11:30am Drive past nearby sights, such as the Anheuser-Busch Brewery, with its elegant Clydesdale stables. See Lafayette Square—with its restored Victorian painted-lady-style houses—and the Compton Heights neighborhood. Its opulent mansions were built by early beer barons. Tower Grove Park is an 1868 Victorian treasure with gazebos and lily ponds.

1:00pm Next to Tower Grove is the **Missouri Botanical Gardens**, home of the *Japanese Festival*. Wear comfortable shoes and tour the grounds, especially the scented garden, a re-created rainforest in the geodesic-domed Climatron. As part of the *Japanese Festival*, you'll see dancers, drummers, *ikebana*, bonsai, and martial-arts exhibitions.

4:00pm Head to *Big Muddy* and have an early meal in one of the many restaurants in Laclede's Landing while people-watching and listening to more great blues. Try **Hannegan's Restaurant & Pub**. It serves good, basic American dishes.

9:30pm As the festival winds down, drive to Soulard to sample the night life at local clubs such as **John D. McGurk's Irish Pub and Restaurant** (Irish music) or **1860s Hard Shell Cafe and Bar** (live blues and rock). Or return to the loop for more blues at **Blueberry Hill** or **Riddle's Penultimate Wine Bar**. Having now sampled the best of St. Louis, you won't have to go crying the blues for at least another year.

Alternatives

In Clayton, **The Ritz-Carlton St. Louis** is a fine representative of the chain, and **Seven Gables Inn** has romantic suites, each differently furnished with antiques. The grande dame of downtown St. Louis hotels is **The Mayfair Wyndham Grand Heritage Hotel**. This 1920s-era hotel started the industry-wide custom of placing chocolates on pillows when actor Cary Grant was a guest.

St. Louis' best restaurant is the elegant **Tony's**. The style may feel formal, but the Italian dishes are first-rate.

City Museum is one offbeat museum that may warrant squeezing into your schedule. It's described as a whimsical "warehouse of adventure," with a working glass studio, giant fish tank, and walk-through whale.

The Hot Sheet

HOTELS		ADDRESS	PH	FX	PRICE	RMS	BEST ROOMS
Hyatt Regency St. Louis	★	1 St. Louis Union Station	314-231-1234 800-233-1234		$$	538	Union Station vw
The Mayfair Wyndham Grand Heritage Hotel	Alt	806 St. Charles St.	314-421-2500 800-757-8483	314-421-0770	$$	182	City vw
The Ritz-Carlton St. Louis	Alt	100 Carondelet Plaza	314-863-6300 800-241-3333	314-863-7486	$$	301	City vw
Seven Gables Inn	Alt	26 N. Meramec St.	314-863-8400 800-433-6590	314-863-8846	$$	32	Garden court vw

RESTAURANTS	DAY	ADDRESS	PH	PRICE	REC	DRESS	FOOD
Blueberry Hill	1	6504 Delmar Blvd.	314-727-0880	$	L/D	Local	American
Cardwell's	2	8100 Maryland Ave.	314-726-5055	$$$	D/L	Dressy, Kazh	California
Crazy Fish Fresh Grill	2	15 N. Meramec St.	314-726-2111	$$	D/L	Kazh	Seafood
Fitz's	1	6605 Delmar Blvd.	314-726-9555	$	L/D	Local	American
Hannegan's Restaurant & Pub	3	719 N. 2nd St.	314-241-8877	$$	D/L	Kazh	American
Harry's	1	2144 Market St.	314-421-6969	$$	D/L	Local	American
Joseph's Italian Cafe	2	705 N. Broadway	314-421-6366	$$	L/D	Kazh	Italian
Patty Long's 9th Street Abbey	3	1808 S. 9th St.	314-621-9598	$$$	B/LD	Kazh	American
St. Louis Bread Company	1	6309 Delmar Blvd.	314-726-6644	$	B/LD	Local	American
Ted Drewes Frozen Custard	1	6726 Chippewa (Old Route 66)	314-481-2652	None	T	Local	
Tony's	Alt	410 Market St.	314-231-7007	$$$$	D	Dressy	Italian

NIGHTLIFE	DAY	ADDRESS	PH	COVER	REC*	DRESS	MUSIC
1860s Hard Shell Cafe and Bar	3	1860 S. 9th St.	314-231-1860	$	MP(F)	Kazh, Local	Blues, R&B
AJ's	2	4th and Chestnut sts., Adam's Mark Hotel	314-241-7400	$	MP(F)	Kazh, Local	'70s-'90s
BB's Jazz, Blues & Soups	2	700 S. Broadway	314-436-5222	$	MP(F)	Kazh, Local	Blues
Blueberry Hill	3	see Blueberry Hill restaurant	314-727-0880	$$	MP(F)	Kazh	Blues, R&B
Broadway Oyster Bar	2	736 S. Broadway	314-621-8811	$	M(F)	Local	Blues, jazz
Club Utopia	1	326 S. 21st St.	314-588-7332	$	MP	Kazh, Local	Hip-hop, Top 40
Harry's	1	see Harry's restaurant	314-421-6969	None	MP(F)	Local	Rock
John D. McGurk's Irish Pub and Restaurant	3	1200 Russell Blvd.	314-776-8309	None	M	Local	Irish
The Living Room	2	1014 Locust St.	314-436-9928	$	MP	Kazh	Rock, house DJ
Riddle's Penultimate Wine Bar	3	6307 Delmar Blvd.	314-725-6985	None	M(F)	Kazh, Local	Blues, jazz
The Summit	2	200 N. Broadway	314-436-2770	None	MP(F)	Kazh	Sinatra

SIGHTS & ATTRACTIONS	DAY	ADDRESS	PH	ENTRY FEE
Cathedral of Saint Louis	1	4431 Lindell Blvd.	314-533-2824	None
City Museum	Alt	701 N. 15th St.	314-231-2489	$
Gateway Arch	2	Jefferson National Expansion Memorial Park	314-425-4465	$
Missouri Botanical Gardens	3	4344 Shaw St.	314-577-9400	$
Saint Louis Art Museum	1	Forest Park, 1 Fine Arts Dr.	314-721-0072	None
St. Louis Union Station	1	Market St. betw. 18th and 20th sts.	314-421-6655	None
St. Louis Walk of Fame	1	6504 Delmar Blvd.	314-727-7827	None
St. Louis CVB		1 Metropolitan Sq., Ste. 1100	800-916-0040	

* M=Live music; P=Dancing (Party); R=Bar only; S=Show; (F)=Food served. For further explanation of codes, see page 14.

 NYC −1   Lambert St. Louis (STL) <30 min./$20   Yes/No   59°/80° (16°/27°)

  The Fun Also Rises

September 1999

September 2000

Cincinnati, Ohio, USA

Riverfest

Origin: 1977   Event ★ ★ ★ ★ City   Attendance: 500,000

No doubt about it, summertime is the season for fiestas, festivals, and fetes of every stripe. But one city saves its party power for the very end, proudly hosting America's biggest farewell-to-summer extravaganza and holding one of the nation's best fireworks displays to usher in the cooling breezes of autumn.

Held on the Sunday of Labor Day weekend, Cincinnati's *Riverfest* attracts swarms of people to the banks of the Ohio River for games, music, food, and, of course, lots of sun. The biggest attraction, however, is an explosive fireworks show that lights up the sky, the river, the city, and the faces of about 500,000 spectators. Once launched over the Ohio River from a single barge, the 30-minute extravaganza now utilizes two bridges and three barges—one dedicated entirely to the grand finale—to create a lavish pyrotechnic show. Partyers pack surrounding high-rises, hillsides, parks, and streets, tune their radios to the WEBN-FM simulcast, turn up the volume, then rip off the knobs. Rozzi's Famous Fireworks does the show every year that never fails to leave audiences roaring with approval.

Cincinnati has had plenty of reasons to celebrate since being founded in 1788.

A national and regional leader since early times, it's been home to three US presidents (Howard Taft, Benjamin Harrison, and Ulysses S. Grant). With its scenic Ohio River border, it's a pretty city, providing the area's nearly two million residents with inspiring architecture, outdoor sculpture, a gorgeous skyline (especially at night), and a full complement of visual and performing arts.

Cincinnati is often unfairly regarded as a hub city. If you're from the East Coast or West Coast or have a *New Yorker*/Steinberg view of the United States, you may be surprised when you fly to Cincinnati—and land in Kentucky. The Ohio city shares plenty with its southern neighbor, including an airport. It's a conservative city that, paradoxically, is filled with people who like to let their hair down. Throughout the year, Cincinnatians find excuses to throw parties, but *Riverfest*—when the seasons change with a huge bang—is their favorite event.

Day 1. Fri.   Sep. 3, 1999
(Day 1. Friday   September 1, 2000)

8:30am The Cincinnatian Hotel is the lodging of choice for visiting dignitaries, celebrities, and presidents. Luxurious amenities give this landmark regal splendor—from the French second-empire exterior to the eight-story atrium rising above a magnificent walnut-and-marble staircase.

9:00am Walk five minutes to **The Cincinnati Coffee Company** for freshly baked pastries with the "world's finest coffees, espressos, and cold drinks."

10:00am Around the corner from the hotel stands the Tyler-Davidson Fountain. Its splendor and starring role in the opening credits of *WKRP in Cincinnati* have made it one of the most photographed spots in the city. Take a few steps and grab an elevator 48 floors to the observation deck of **Carew Tower**, downtown's tallest building. You'll get panoramic views of the Ohio River and surrounding valleys in Ohio, Indiana, and Kentucky.

11:15am Head around the corner to The Atrium Building, take the Skywalk over the highway, past Cinergy Field, and down to the cobbled wharf at Public Landing—about a 15-minute walk. There's a great view of the Roebling Suspension Bridge, built more than a century ago. If it appears oddly familiar, that's not *déjà vu*: The bridge served as a prototype for its world-famous descendant in Brooklyn. Follow the Riverwalk east, along the Serpentine Wall, and into Bicentennial Commons at Sawyer Point, where stages and tents are already set up for *Riverfest*. People-watch or just gaze over the river as fireworks barges get ready for Sunday night and massive industrial barges mingle with pleasure boats.

1:00pm At the end of the park, the **Montgomery Inn Boathouse** overlooks the river. Roll up your sleeves and dig into some of the best ribs in the world (according to experts such as Bob Hope and Johnny Bench).

3:00pm A scenic plan for Friday afternoon is a trip to Eden Park. It's filled with lakes, fountains, walkways, and gardens, and is home to the renowned **Cincinnati Art Museum**, which displays masterpieces and art objects spanning thousands of years.

6:00pm Close by is the so-called Greenwich Village of Cincinnati, Mount Adams. Stop by the Immaculata Church for a terrific view of the Ohio River, before having dinner at a view table at the first-class **Celestial Restaurant**.

9:00pm Take in some jazz at the restaurant's **Incline Lounge** or settle into the outdoor patio at **Mount Adams Pavilion** for river views and local bands.

Day 2. Sat.   Sep. 4, 1999
(Day 2. Saturday   September 2, 2000)

9:00am One of the best kitchens in town is in your hotel, so take advantage of exceptional service and cuisine in the Victorian ambience of **The Palace**.

10:00am Tour the old German neighborhood, Over-the-Rhine. It's said to have the country's largest collection of 19th-century Italianate buildings. They're now filled with antique and art galleries, coffeehouses, and clubs.

Noon Drive to the **Taft Museum** for a look at its fantastic collection of European and American art. It's housed in a mansion originally built for descendants of Cincinnati native William Howard Taft.

1:30pm At **Skyline Chili**, try a Cincinnati favorite, a three-way. No, it has nothing to do with massage oils and velvet robes: It's spaghetti topped with chili and cheese.

2:00pm Head to **Graeter's Confectionery**, the oldest surviving ice-cream manufacturer in America. Try to divine the "secret, old-world creaming methods" that make their scoops so rich and smooth.

3:30pm All the charm of a 19th-century German village is alive and well at MainStrasse Village in Covington, Kentucky. Start at the **Cathedral Basilica of the Assumption**, an example of Gothic design, with trappings that include the world's largest stained-glass window. Once you've had your fill of flying buttresses, explore the area's streets, which buzz with art and entertainment for the weekend.

7:00pm Catch a **BB Riverboat** cruise on an authentic Mark Twain-era stern-wheeler. Enjoy dinner as the big paddle wheel turns and the sun sets.

9:30pm Back on shore, drive to Covington's **Dee Felice Cafe** for old-fashioned New Orleans décor and Dixieland jazz that carries on late into the night.

11:30pm End up—or maybe spend your whole evening—at The Waterfront, the hippest upscale restaurant-and-nightclub complex in the area. Have steak or lobster at **South Beach Grill at the Waterfront**, a hot spot for sports stars and other celebrities. Have drinks at **Las Brisas** or dance at **Fusion**.

Day 3. Sun.   Sep. 5, 1999
(Day 3. Sunday   September 3, 2000)

11:00am Have Sunday brunch in the Westin Hotel's gorgeous **Albee**, overlooking Fountain Square. Walking there, you'll encounter ambitious *Riverfest* attendees heading for the river with blankets under their arms, hoping to get squatter's rights to good viewing spots for the evening's fireworks.

1:30pm Stroll to the riverfront, which should already be hopping with activity. Boats fill the docks and celebrants hang out on picnic blankets, people-watch, toss Frisbees, and nosh on snacks from the tents of more than 20 restaurants. There's a sand-volleyball tournament, a rubber-duck regatta, and a wide range of live music on three stages. One thing that's missing, however, is booze, since it's prohibited on the festival grounds.

9:00pm The ***Toyota/WEBN Fireworks*** show begins at 9:05 p.m. and continues for more than 30 minutes, so make sure you're comfortable wherever you end up watching them. Bring a radio, because the fireworks are choreographed.

10:00pm After the smoke clears, the nearby Mount Adams bars and restaurants are popular for celebrating. Listen to live jazz and blues in the courtyard of **Blind Lemon** or **City View Tavern**. The **Mount Adams Bar & Grill** accommodates your farewell nightcap until 2:30 a.m.

Alternatives

Cincinnati's other big party is **Oktoberfest-Zinzinnati**, which started in 1976 and now draws 500,000 revellers to the nation's largest Oktoberfest celebration. Whether it's the world's largest kazoo band (20,000 people) or world's largest chicken dance (48,000 people), beer and the festival spirit will have you doing crazy things.

A hotel option is the **Omni Netherland Plaza**, an art-deco masterpiece with pierced nickel-silver wall sconces and a spectacular sea-horse fountain. **The Westin Hotel** is centrally located and offers deluxe rooms overlooking Fountain Square.

Cincinnati prides itself on its dining options, the *crème de la crème* being **Maisonette**, the only restaurant in America to retain a top-star rating for more than 30 years. Trendy downtown restaurants include **Ciao Cucina**, **Plaza 600**, and **Redfish Looziana Roadhouse and Seafood Kitchen**. If you want to sneak a real meal in during *Riverfest*, Plaza 600 serves Sunday brunch and Redfish serves Sunday dinner. For after-dinner drinks and live music each weekend night, there's **Havana Martini Club**. There are dueling pianos at **Howl at the Moon Saloon** on the Kentucky side of the river.

The Hot Sheet

HOTELS		ADDRESS	PH	FX	PRICE	RMS	BEST ROOMS
The Cincinnatian Hotel	★	601 Vine St.	513-381-3000 800-942-9000	513-651-0256	$$	148	Atrium vw
Omni Netherland Plaza	Alt	35 W. 5th St.	513-421-9100 800-843-6664	513-421-4291	$$	619	Carew Tower vw
The Westin Hotel	Alt	21 E. 5th St.	513-621-7700 800-973-8461	513-852-5670	$$	448	Fountain Sq vw

RESTAURANTS	DAY	ADDRESS	PH	PRICE	REC	DRESS	FOOD
The Albee	3	see the Westin Hotel	513-852-2740	$$	B/LD	Kazh	American
BB Riverboats	2	1 Madison Ave.	606-261-8500	$$$	D	Local	American
Celestial Restaurant	1	1071 Celestial St.	513-241-4455	$$$	D/L	Yuppie	French, continental
Ciao Cucina	Alt	700 Walnut St.	513-929-0700	$$	LD	Kazh	Italian
The Cincinnati Coffee Company	1	39 E. 7th. St.	513-361-0300	$	B/L	Local	Pastries, sandwiches
Graeter's Confectionery	2	41 E. 4th St.	513-381-0653	$	T/BL	Local	Ice cream
Maisonette	Alt	114 E. 6th St.	513-721-2260	$$$	LD	Dressy	French
Montgomery Inn Boathouse	1	925 Eastern Ave.	513-721-7427	$$$	L/D	Kazh	Ribs
The Palace	2	see The Cincinnatian Hotel	513-381-3000	$$	B/LD	Dressy	American
Plaza 600	Alt	600 Walnut St.	513-721-8600	$$	LD	Kazh	American
Redfish Looziana Roadhouse and Seafood Kitchen	Alt	700 Race St.	513-929-4700	$$	LD	Kazh	Cajun, creole
Skyline Chili	2	254 E. 4th St.	513-241-4848	$	L/D	Local	Chili
South Beach Grill at the Waterfront	2	14 Pete Rose Pier	606-581-1414	$$$	D	Kazh, Yuppie	American

NIGHTLIFE	DAY	ADDRESS	PH	COVER	REC*	DRESS	MUSIC
Blind Lemon	3	936 Hatch St.	513-241-3885	None	M(F)	Local	Acoustic folk, jazz
City View Tavern	3	403 Oregon St.	513-241-8439	None	R(F)	Local	
Dee Felice Cafe	2	529 Main St.	606-261-2365	None	M(F)	Local	Jazz, Dixieland
Fusion	2	14 Pete Rose Pier	606-581-1414	$	P	Kazh	Rock, hip-hop
Havana Martini Club	Alt	580 Walnut St.	513-651-2800	$	M	Yuppie	Jazz, blues
Howl at the Moon Saloon	Alt	101 Riverboat Row	606-581-2800	$	M	Local	Dueling pianos
Incline Lounge	1	1071 Celestial St.	513-241-4455	None	MP	Kazh	Jazz, swing
Las Brisas	2	14 Pete Rose Pier	606-581-1414	$	MP	Local	Top 40
Mount Adams Bar & Grill	3	938 Hatch St.	513-621-3666	None	R(F)	Kazh	
Mount Adams Pavilion	1	949 Pavilion St.	513-744-9200	$	MP(F)	Kazh	Rock, alternative

SIGHTS & ATTRACTIONS	DAY	ADDRESS	PH	ENTRY FEE
Carew Tower	1	441 Vine St.	513-241-3888	$
Cathedral Basilica of the Assumption	2	1140 Madison Ave.	606-431-2060	None
Cincinnati Art Museum	1	953 Eden Park Dr.	513-721-5204	$
Taft Museum	2	316 Pike St.	513-241-0343	$
Greater Cincinnati CVB		300 W. 6th St.	513-621-2142	

Event & Ticket Info

Riverfest: The day's events are free. For more information and schedule of events, contact *Cincinnati Recreation Commission* (513-352-4000).

Toyota/WEBN Fireworks: For information, call *WEBN-FM* (513-749-3764).

Alternative Event

Oktoberfest-Zinzinnati: The Downtown Council, 513-579-3191

Cincinnati—Area Code 513 Covington—Area Code 606

* M=Live music; P=Dancing (Party); R=Bar only; S=Show; (F)=Food served. For further explanation of codes, see page 14.

 NYC   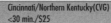 Cincinnati/Northern Kentucky(CVG) <30 min./$25   Yes   57°/80° (14°/27°)

Street Scene

Origin: 1984	Event ★ ★ ★ ★ ★ ★ City	Attendance: 85,000

There are a lot of people out there who think San Diego is California's best-kept secret—and they haven't even been to *Street Scene* yet! It's scary to imagine how many out-of-towners might pack up and move out to this mainland paradise once they get a three-day Street Scene peek at all the music, food, culture, and natural beauty that makes San Diego unique.

Street Scene is unusual for being a raging, over-21-crowd party on Friday and Saturday that turns into a mellow family event on Sunday. But no matter what day it is, the festival's combination of food, music, and cultural celebrations keeps happy crowds buzzing around San Diego's turn-of-the-century Gaslamp Quarter. There's a mix of mini-festivals that includes the Wine & Garlic Festival, Via Caliente (a jalapeño heaven or hell, depending on your tolerance), Taste of San Diego (samples from the city's finest restaurants), and the Microbrewery Festival. Jazz, R&B, rock, swing, reggae, zydeco, and even gospel music propel revelers through reliably beautiful Southern California nights.

Just south of Los Angeles and just north of the Mexican border, San Diego has a look and feel all its own. The ubiquitous Spanish and Mexican architecture is a point of civic pride. Balboa Park is one of the most beautiful city parks in the world. Old Town and the Gaslamp Quarter preserve the city's history. The San Diego Zoo is internationally recognized as the best in the world.

The mighty Pacific Ocean plays a big part in the everyday lives of San Diegans. Coastal weather patterns bring sunny, warm days all year. Gorgeous white-sand beaches along the city's coast are perfect for swimming. Surfing, diving, and ocean fishing are also popular. San Diego's harbor, one of California's largest, is home to fishing boats, yachts, clippers, and the US Navy's primary Pacific Coast fleet.

Tequila shots, tacos, tank tops, and tans, however, are the primary lure in September. At *Street Scene*, you won't find a shortage of any of the local specialties.

Street Scene

Day 1. Thu. Sep. 9, 1999
(Day 1. Thursday *September 7, 2000)*

9:30am Admire San Diego Bay from your room at the **Hyatt Regency San Diego**, where all rooms have bay views. You're also close to the *Street Scene* here.

10:30am Head for San Diego's jewel, Balboa Park. Its lush gardens and Spanish architecture house fascinating museums of all kinds. The largest museum in the city, the **San Diego Museum of Art**, includes an impressive collection of European, Asian, American, Indian, and contemporary California art. Visit the **Timken Museum of Art** next door for a sampling of Russian icons.

12:30pm Lunch at the Museum of Art's **Sculpture Garden Restaurant**. Good American dishes are served with nouvelle touches.

1:30pm Wander Balboa Park's exquisite gardens and visit some of its many other museums. The **Museum of Man** exhibits Mexican history and Indian culture of the Americas. The **Aerospace Museum** spans the history of flight from gliders to the Wright Brothers to space.

4:30pm The view from your room is good, but it's better with a cocktail at the **Top of the Hyatt** lounge.

6:30pm The trendy Gaslamp Quarter started out as the 1867 vision of Alonzo Horton, who offered lots to people who promised to build houses. Renovated in the 1970s, it's now a thriving district for music and food, sometimes referred to as "the New Orleans of the West Coast." Though *Street Scene* doesn't begin until tomorrow, get your bearings by wandering its streets and alleys and popping into a pub for a drink.

7:30pm Fio's Cucina Italiana has earned more than 50 dining awards. Executive chef Robert Gaffney's innovative Italian dishes add California, French, and Pacific Rim influences to entrées such as lobster ravioli with saffron sauce and chive oil.

9:30pm Jim Croce and wife Ingrid used to serve grand dinners to their friends Jimmy Buffet, James Taylor, Arlo Guthrie, Bonnie Raitt, and The Manhattan Transfer before retiring to all-night jam sessions. Croce hit the big time with songs such as "Time in a Bottle" and "Bad, Bad Leroy Brown," but died shortly thereafter in a plane crash. Ingrid, who moved with Jim to San Diego just a month before he died, opened Croce's as a tribute to her husband. **Croce's Jazz Bar** features live jazz every night. Its **Top Hat Bar & Grille** is the place to be for live rhythm and blues.

Midnight Ole Madrid may be the hottest club in San Diego, judging from the fashion-plate lines outside. You can beat the lines by having dinner there. The food isn't Spanish or all that great, but the views from the balcony tables are a treat.

Day 2. Fri. Sep. 10, 1999
(Day 2. Friday *September 8, 2000)*

8:30am Try one of the hearty breakfasts at the Horton Grand Hotel's **Ida Bailey's** restaurant, named for the Gaslamp Quarter's most notorious madam at the turn of the century.

10:00am Morning is feeding time, so get to the **San Diego Zoo** early to see the animals at their liveliest. An aerial tramway and narrated bus tour give good overviews of one of the world's largest collections of animals exhibited in natural landscapes.

2:30pm Back at the Gaslamp Quarter, have a late lunch at **Osteria Panevino**. Tuscan ambience and brick-oven pizzas have made this a popular restaurant for lunch and dinner.

5:00pm Dive into *Street Scene*. It doesn't really matter where you start. Pick your favorite type of music and head for a stage, then dance your way past festival and food booths into the night.

8:00pm Walk to one of the trendiest spots in the Gaslamp Quarter. The **Dakota Grill & Spirits** offers mesquite-grilled and wood-fired meats and pizzas, along with microbrewed beers. Afterward, return to *Street Scene* and catch the final acts.

12:15am Head for the city's best underground (literally) dancing at the **Blue Tattoo**. The location for television's *Silk Stalkings*, it requires "proper dress," but is worth the effort.

Day 3. Sat. Sep. 11, 1999
(Day 3. Saturday   September 9, 2000)

9:00am Mexican food fanatics praise the **Old Town Mexican Cafe**'s *pozole* soup for breakfast. If pork and hominy don't stimulate your appetite, you're sure to find a breakfast dish that will at San Diego's favorite Mexican restaurant.

10:00am Visit **Old Town San Diego State Historic Park**, which commemorates the first permanent settlement in California. Plaza Vieja was the center of town and the scene of bullfights. Casa de Machado depicts everyday life in early, Mexican San Diego.

Noon Relax in Southern California style. Head to La Jolla (pronounced *La Hoy-ah*) for a Mediterranean lunch at **Trattoria Acqua**. Choose between pastas and sandwiches on fresh *focaccia*.

1:30pm La Jolla's white crescent beaches, warm ocean, and great surfing are irresistible. Swimmers head for the southern end of La Jolla Shores Beach, while surfers take over the northern end. La Jolla Cove is a natural tide-pool area where starfish, hermit crabs, sea cucumbers, and other sea life abound at low tide.

5:30pm Plenty relaxed, head back to *Street Scene* for a few late-afternoon beers and maybe some chips, salsa, and mariachi music.

8:00pm If you haven't filled up on festival food, try **Blue Point Coastal Cuisine** for seafood and a hopping bar scene. Return to the festival for closing acts and rub shoulders with a large and lively crowd.

12:15am Wind up the night dancing to Top-40 and disco music at the **E Street Alley**.

Alternatives

The **Horton Grand Hotel**, an elegant Victorian hotel complete with a ghost and horse-drawn carriages, also offers modern amenities. Its Gaslamp District location makes it either noisy or convenient, depending on your perspective. The beachfront **Hotel del Coronado**, an imposing Victorian National Historic Landmark, recalls turn-of-the-century, high-society summer holidays. The **Sheraton San Diego Hotel & Marina** offers luxury in a resort setting on Harbor Island.

Taka has been voted one of San Diego's best Japanese restaurants by both diners and restaurant critics. **Rainwater's**, an intimate downtown restaurant known for its prime steaks, is a good dinner alternative. Greek food is excellent at the **Athens Market Taverna**, where the owner fusses over her customers. If you skipped the festival Friday or Saturday night, you can listen to a mariachi band and then dance to salsa and merengue bands at **Casa Guadalajara** in Old Town. **Cafe Sevilla** offers a Flamenco show with dinner and a Euro-Latin disco afterward. In La Jolla, **George's Ocean Terrace** provides a wonderful ocean vantage point. The restaurant downstairs is more casual and popular with locals.

If you loved the San Diego Zoo but need more animals, go to the **San Diego Wild Animal Park** in nearby Escondido. **Mission Basilica San Diego de Alcala** was the first mission in American California and it makes for an interesting visit. Another mission you may want to visit is Mission Beach, a wide, sandy ocean beach. Black's Beach is decorously referred to as Clothing Optional.

The Hot Sheet

HOTELS		ADDRESS	PH	FX	PRICE	RMS	BEST ROOMS
Horton Grand Hotel	Alt	311 Island Ave.	619-544-1886 800-542-1886	619-239-3823	$$	132	Courtyard vw
Hotel Del Coronado	Alt	1500 Orange Ave.	619-435-6611 800-468-3533	619-522-8262	$$$$	692	Ocean front vw
Hyatt Regency San Diego	★	1 Market Pl.	619-232-1234 800-233-1234	619-233-6464	$$$$	875	Bay vw
Sheraton San Diego Hotel & Marina	Alt	1380 Harbor Island Dr.	619-291-2900 800-325-3535	619-692-2337	$$$	1,044	Ocean front vw

RESTAURANTS	DAY	ADDRESS	PH	PRICE	REC	DRESS	FOOD
Athens Market Taverna	Alt	109 West F St.	619-234-1955	$$	LD	Kazh	Greek
Blue Point Coastal Cuisine	3	565 5th Ave.	619-233-6623	$$$	D	Kazh	Seafood, American
Cafe Sevilla	Alt	555 4th Ave.	619-233-5979	$$	D	Yuppie	Spanish
Dakota Grill & Spirits	2	901 5th Ave.	619-234-5554	$$	D/L	Yuppie	American, Southwestern grill
Fio's Cucina Italiana	1	801 5th Ave.	619-234-3467	$$	D	Kazh	Northern Italian
George's Ocean Terrace	Alt	1250 Prospect St.	619-454-4244	$$	LD	Kazh, Local	American
Ida Bailey's	2	see Horton Grand Hotel	619-544-1886	$$	B/D	Yuppie	American
Old Town Mexican Cafe	3	2489 San Diego Ave.	619-297-4330	$	B/LD	Local	Mexican
Osteria Panevino	2	722 5th Ave.	619-595-7959	$$	L/D	Kazh	Italian
Rainwater's	Alt	1202 Kettner Blvd.	619-233-5757	$$$	LD	Euro	Chop house
Sculpture Garden Restaurant	1	1450 El Prado Way	619-696-1990	$$	L/D	Local	American
Taka	Alt	555 5th Ave.	619-338-0555	$$	D	Kazh	Japanese
Trattoria Acqua	3	1298 Prospect St.	619-454-0709	$	L/D	Yuppie	Northern Italian

NIGHTLIFE	DAY	ADDRESS	PH	COVER	REC*	DRESS	MUSIC
Blue Tattoo	2	835 5th Ave.	619-238-7191	$	P	Kazh, Dressy	Dance
Casa Guadalajara	Alt	4105 Taylor St.	619-295-5111	$	P(F)	Kazh	Salsa
Croce's Jazz Bar	1	802 5th Ave.	619-233-4355	$	M(F)	Kazh	Jazz
E Street Alley	3	E Street Alley btwn. 4th and 5th aves.	619-231-9200	$	P(F)	Kazh	Top 40, funk, '70s, '80s
Ole Madrid	1	755 5th Ave.	619-557-0146	$	P(F)	Euro	House, Latin
Top Hat Bar & Grille	1	802 5th Ave.	619-233-4355	$	M(F)	Kazh	R&B
Top of the Hyatt	1	see Hyatt hotel	619-232-1234	None	R(F)	Kazh	

SIGHTS & ATTRACTIONS	DAY	ADDRESS	PH	ENTRY FEE
Aerospace Museum	1	2001 Pan American Pl.	619-234-8291	$
Mission Basilica San Diego de Alcala	Alt	10818 San Diego Mission Rd.	619-281-8449	$
Museum of Man	1	1350 El Prado Way	619-239-2001	$
Old Town San Diego State Historic Park	3	Twiggs and Congress sts.	619-220-5422	None
San Diego Museum of Art	1	1450 El Prado Way	619-232-7931	$
San Diego Wild Animal Park	Alt	15500 San Pasqual Valley Rd.	760-747-8702	$$
San Diego Zoo	2	2920 Zoo Dr.	619-234-3153	$$
Timken Museum of Art	1	1500 El Prado Way	619-239-5548	None
San Diego CVB		11 Horton Plz.	619-232-3101	

Event & Ticket Info

San Diego Street Scene
(5th Avenue at Market Street):
Tickets ($30) are available at the gate for Friday or Saturday. A combined ticket ($50) for Friday and Saturday is sold in advance through *Ticketmaster* (800-488-5252). Sunday tickets ($20) should be purchased at the gate. For more information, contact *Street Scene* (619-557-0505).

* M=Live music; P=Dancing (Party); R=Bar only; S=Show; (F)=Food served. For further explanation of codes, see page 14.

 NYC −3   San Diego (SAN) <30 min./$10   Yes/No   62°/76° (17°/24°)

September 1999 · Honolulu, Hawaii, USA · September 2000

Aloha Festival

| Origin: 1947 | Event ★ ★ ★ ★ ★ City | Attendance: 300,000 |

Hula girls and sunsets. Mai tais on a catamaran at dusk. Plumeria-scented trade winds that cool sun-kissed skin. If these are clichés, bring on a Hawaiian paradise full of them. Any time's fine to ease into the aloha spirit, but Hawaii's *Aloha Festivals*, held each autumn, provide a great excuse to visit one of earth's perfect places.

The festivals encompass more than 300 events on all six major Hawaiian Islands, including the most visited island of Oahu, site of the state's capital, Honolulu. Oahu's *Aloha Festival* is anchored by two ho'olaule'a celebrations—with lei and food booths, music from metal to rap to Hawaiian, and entertainment including traditional hula—that draw residents and visitors by the thousands.

Aloha Week was created in 1947 as a cultural celebration of Hawaii's music, dance, and history. After the tragic toll World War II took on the islands, quickly it became a welcome peacetime ritual. *Aloha Festivals*, as the events were renamed in 1991, were scheduled in the fall for two reasons: to honor the makahiki, the ancient Hawaiian season of music, dance, and feasting, when war was not a permissible activity; and to attract visitors to the islands after the summer season. Today, the festivals revolve around a series of free street parties and are still centered mostly on music and food. The Oahu festival opens in front of the Iolani Palace with a presentation of the annual Royal Court, young people who have gone through a year-long process of selection and training. Once the playground of King Kamehameha, Honolulu boasts having the only royal palace in the United States.

Upon arrival at Honolulu International Airport, you'll definitely want to lose yourself for a few days, get out your SPF-15, "rubba slippas" (beach sandals, also known as flip-flops), and just hang loose. Sure, for great resorts, seasoned travelers probably think of the outer islands when they think of Hawaii. But Oahu, especially during the *Aloha Festivals*, is the place to be for both natural beauty and three days of exciting restaurants, night life, and attractions.

The Fun Also Rises

Aloha Festival

Day 1. Fri. Sep. 10, 1999
(Day 1. Friday   September 15, 2000)

10:00am You could probably spend the whole day hanging at your hotel, **Halekulani**, the "House without a Key," which offers 456 elegant rooms built around an 80-year-old beach house in the middle of Waikiki. Instead, start by hiking 45 minutes into **Manoa Falls**. You'll pass through a soothing, green rainforest before arriving at the cool freshwater pool at the top of the trail.

12:15pm Drive downtown and do a tour of **Iolani Palace**. Make reservations in advance. In the Blue Room, Queen Liliuokalani was dethroned, marking the beginning of United States annexation maneuvers.

1:30pm Take a long walk down King Street to the Chinatown Historic District at the end of town farthest from Diamond Head. If you're hungry, stop for dim sum at **Legend Seafood Restaurant**. Or near the Chinatown Cultural Plaza, snack on manapua (meat- and curry-filled buns) at the **Royal Kitchen**.

5:30pm A small crowd gathers for the festival's opening ceremony, including music and a hula performance, which takes place in a gorgeous setting in front of the palace.

6:30pm Follow the Royal Court in procession to the **Ho'olaule'a** fun. You won't have trouble locating food booths and music stages. Alcohol isn't served on the streets, so most party-goers pop in and out of downtown's many pubs between mingling, eating, dancing, and people-watching sessions on the crowded closed-off streets.

10:00pm After the festivities end, head to Aloha Tower Marketplace on the harbor. At the **Gordon Biersch Brewery**, kick back with local music and microbrews.

11:30pm It's a short drive to **Mystique,** one of the best club venues in town, with an intimate jazz area separated by glass from the disco. Watching people dance to disco while you're listening to jazz is a kick.

Day 2. Sat. Sep. 11, 1999
(Day 2. Saturday   September 16, 2000)

8:30am Start early on just another day in paradise. Beginning at the entrance to the crater on Diamond Head Road, hike up hills and stairs for a spectacular view of the Waikiki sprawl from **Diamond Head**.

10:00am You've earned a treat—breakfast at the **Hau Tree Lanai** in the New Otani Kaimana Beach Hotel. The fried rice and eggs is a local favorite and you can watch Kaimana Beach begin to hum with local and tourist activity.

11:00am Third in attendance for rose parades, behind the Rose Bowl Parade and the Portland Rose Festival's parade, the **Aloha Festivals' Floral Parade** draws thousands to the streets and millions via television. Each island sends its own pa'u princess and escorts, decorated with their island's special flowers. These ladies and their costumes are beautiful sights to see. The beginning of the parade will just be reaching the end of the parade route at the corner of Kalakaua and Kapahulu avenues in Waikiki. It lasts two hours, but you can walk the route in reverse (45 minutes).

1:00pm "Eh, bruddah, try one chicken katsu plate lunch from **Grace's**. Two scoops rice with shoyu on top. Broke da mouth." Translation: The chicken plate at Grace's, a true local legend, will knock your socks off. So will the rest of Hawaii's "local food," a calorie-laden melting pot of cultural influences that include teriyaki from Japan, fried rice and dim sum from China, sweet bread from Portugal, and lau laus and poi from the South Pacific.

2:00pm Nearby, the **Honolulu Academy of Arts**, housed in beautiful 70-year-old building, has one of the world's finest collections of Asian and Pacific art, along with American and European works. OK, afterward you can go to the beach.

6:30pm Relax at the Halekulani's **House without a Key** with a drink, a sunset, and possibly a slack-key guitar.

8:30pm Drive downtown to the Harbor Court Building and its dramatic entrance to **Palomino**. The crowd, having drinks and contemporary Italian fare at tables or the white-marble bar, is as chic as the décor.

10:30pm Atop of Ala Moana hotel, the sedate and jazzy longtime favorite **Nicholas Nickolas** has late-night dining and live music. Off the lobby, **Rumours** has disco into the early hours with high-tech lighting and two dance cages for customer use. This place is loaded with tourists cutting loose.

Day 3. Sun. Sep. 12, 1999
(Day 3. Sunday   September 17, 2000)

8:30am The buffet breakfast at the **Rainbow Lanai** at the Hilton Hawaiian Village hotel is worth a detour. It offers the island's greatest variety of foods in bright, pleasant surroundings.

9:30am Drive the Pali Highway to Kailua. About halfway (20 minutes), stop for a magnificent view of the island at the **Pali Lookout**.

10:30am Kailua Beach is windsurfing heaven (the Kailua end of the beach is used primarily by singles and couples). For spectacular views, hike the nearby **Kaiwa Ridge Trail**.

1:30pm On your way back to town, stop for lunch at the **Chart House**. Check out the view of the sprawling gardens below in Haiku Plantation while enjoying coconut-encrusted shrimp.

4:00pm **Duke's Canoe Club** gets hopping Sunday afternoons. Great music and a fun mix of locals and tourists ensure lots of mai tais and people-watching, both in the bar and on the beach.

7:00pm Drive to **Roy's** in Hawaii-Kai for a fine meal, complete with interesting interior and exterior views. Chef Roy Yamaguchi put Hawaii's version of Pacific Rim cuisine on the culinary map.

10:00pm Make a final circuit of dance spots, including the **Esprit Lounge** in the Sheraton Waikiki for a live show band that keeps a tanned and happy crowd dancing all night. If you can manage, stay late enough to "accidentally" miss tomorrow's flight back to earth.

Alternatives

The second weekend of the ***Aloha Festivals*** moves the ***Ho'olaule'a*** to Waikiki—turning a street party into a beach party.

The size of the **Hilton Hawaiian Village** may put off some people, but you can get one of the best view rooms on Oahu at a reasonable price, along with an outstanding beachfront. Or you could stay at the more secluded **Kahala Mandarin Oriental** hotel.

Dine at romantic **La Mer** (reservations required). The cuisine is Asian-inspired French—it could be argued that this is dining at a spiritual level. Ask for a table with a Diamond Head view. The **Captain's Table Restaurant and Lounge** has live Hawaiian music 6–9 p.m. Brunch at the Kahala Mandarin's **Plumeria Beach Cafe**. The Japanese dishes, in particular, are outstanding. Before or after eating, check out the dolphin feedings at 11 a.m.

If you want to explore more of the island, drive to the North Shore. Stop at the **Polynesian Cultural Center** and sample its many eating options (including an evening luau) amid seven model villages representing Hawaii, Samoa, Tonga, Fiji, New Zealand, Tahiti, and the Marquesas.

The Hot Sheet

HOTELS		ADDRESS	PH	FX	PRICE	RMS	BEST ROOMS
Halekulani	★	2199 Kalia Rd.	808-923-2311 800-367-2343	808-926-8004	$$$$+	456	Diamond Head vw
Hilton Hawaiian Village	Alt	2005 Kalia Rd.	808-949-4321 800-445-8667	808-951-5458	$$$	2,545	"01" rms w/2 balc
Kahala Mandarin Oriental	Alt	5000 Kahala Ave.	808-739-8888 800-367-2525	808-739-8800	$$$$	371	Beachfront vw

RESTAURANTS	DAY	ADDRESS	PH	PRICE	REC	DRESS	FOOD
Chart House	3	46336 Haiku Rd.	808-247-6671	$$$	L/D	Kazh, Local	American
Grace's	2	1296 Beretania St.	808-593-2202	$	L/BD	Local	Local cuisine
Hau Tree Lanai	2	2863 Kalakaua Ave.	808-921-7066	$$	B/LD	Kazh, Local	American, Japanese
La Mer	Alt	see Halekulani hotel	808-923-2311	$$$$+	D	Dressy	French, Asian influences
Legend Seafood Restaurant	1	100 N. Beretania St.	808-532-1868	$$	L/BD	Kazh	Chinese
Palomino	2	66 Queen St.	808-528-2400	$$$	D/L	Yuppie	Continental
Plumeria Beach Cafe	Alt	see the Kahala Mandarin Oriental hotel	808-739-8888	$$$	BLD	Kazh	Local cuisine
Rainbow Lanai	3	2005 Kalia Rd.	808- 949-4321	$$	B/LD	Kazh	Continental
Roy's	3	6600 Kalanianaole Hwy.	808-396-7697	$$$	D	Kazh	Pacific Rim
Royal Kitchen	1	Kukui and River sts.	808-524-4461	$	L/B	Local	Chinese

NIGHTLIFE	DAY	ADDRESS	PH	COVER	REC*	DRESS	MUSIC
Captain's Table Restaurant and Lounge	Alt	2570 Kalakaua Ave.	808-922-2511	None	M(F)	Kazh	Hawaiian
Duke's Canoe Club	3	2335 Kalakaua Ave.	808-922-2268	None	M(F)	Local	Hawaiian
Esprit Lounge	3	2255 Kalakaua Ave. at the Sheraton Waikiki	808-922-4422	None	MP(F)	Local	Contemporary
Gordon Biersch Brewery	1	1 Aloha Tower Dr.	808-599-4877	None	MP(F)	Kazh, Local	Contemporary Hawaiian, rock
House without a Key	2	see Halekulani hotel	808-923-2311	None	M(F)	Kazh	Hawaiian
Mystique	1	500 Alamoana Blvd.	808-533-0061	$	P(F)	Kazh	Jazz
Nicholas Nickolas	2	410 Atkinson Dr. at the Ala Moana hotel	808-955-4466	None	MP(F)	Kazh	Top 40
Rumours	2	410 Atkinson Dr. at the Ala Moana hotel	808-955-4811	$	MP(F)	Kazh	Top 40, '60s, '70s

SIGHTS & ATTRACTIONS	DAY	ADDRESS	PH	ENTRY FEE
Diamond Head	2	Monsarrat Ave. at 18th St.	808-971-2525	None
Honolulu Academy of Arts	2	900 S. Beretania St.	808-532-8701	$
Iolani Palace	1	King and Richards sts.	808-522-0832	$
Kaiwa Ridge Trail	3	Kaelepulu St. and Aalapapa Dr.		None
Manoa Falls	1	north end of Manoa Rd.		None
Pali Lookout	3	Pali Hwy. to Kailua		None
Polynesian Cultural Center	Alt	55370 Kamehame Hwy.	808-293-3333	$$$
Hawaii CVB		2270 Kalakaua Ave.	808-924-0266	

Event & Ticket Info

Aloha Festivals: Many events are free, including the **Floral Parade** and **Ho'olaule'a**, but some performances and activities require admission fees. For a brochure with a schedule of activities and admission information, call *Aloha Festivals* (800-852-7690 or 808-545-1771).

* M=Live music; P=Dancing (Party); R=Bar only; S=Show; (F)=Food served. For further explanation of codes, see page 14.

 NYC −5   Honolulu (HNL) <30 min./$25   Yes   73°/87° (23°/31°)

  The Fun Also Rises

September 1999
Santa Fe,
New Mexico,
USA
September 2000

Fiesta de Santa Fe

| Origin: 1712 | Event ★ ★ ★ ★ City | Attendance: 75,000 |

Santa Fe's wild side ignites during the riotous *Fiesta de Santa Fe*, a series of fiery (literally) parties that makes September the best time of year to visit one of the most scenic capital cities in the United States. Held on the weekend after Labor Day, the event begins Friday night when Zozobra, a 40-foot-tall puppet, is torched near the central plaza as 50,000 spectators cheer. Accompanied by dancers, fireworks, and heart-rending groans representing the bizarre puppet's death cries, it's all done in a joyous effort to banish gloom from the lives of the onlookers.

Once Zozobra has disappeared in a dark cloud of flames and smoke, a party rages until midnight in Santa Fe's historic Plaza with the *Baile de la Gente* street dance. The rest of the weekend is a combination of 300 years of tradition and Santa Fe-style fun. The *Gran Baile de la Fiesta* (Fiesta Ball), the *Historical, Hysterical Parade*, and the *Desfile de los Niños* (Children's Pet Parade) are all part of the entertainment.

Santa Fe's reputation for world-class art, opera, and cuisine is really nothing new. Founded by order of the Spanish Crown in 1609—13 years before the Pilgrims landed at Plymouth Rock—the city was a center of art, culture, and religion from the start. Its population is only 65,000, but Santa Fe's rich mix of museums and more than 150 art galleries makes it the third-largest art market in the country. With more than 200 restaurants, Santa Fe is also considered the gastronomic center of the Southwest.

St. Francis Cathedral, built by papal decree in 1851 to tame the "unruly and godless" local inhabitants, presides over Santa Fe. Getting around town on foot is easy, allowing you to enjoy the Santa Fe-style architecture which, like the food, reflects a combination of Anglo, Native American, and Spanish cultures. You may want a car for day trips into the high desert of northern New Mexico, the mythic source of the pure air and magical atmosphere that inspire the *Fiesta de Santa Fe*.

Fiesta de Santa Fe

Day 1. Fri.　Sep. 10, 1999
(Day 1. Friday　　September 8, 2000)

9:00am The **Inn of the Anasazi** is a gem in the heart of Santa Fe. It's attractive, environmentally sensitive, and comfortable, and it provides a contemporary Santa Fe feel.

10:00am Stroll a few blocks to **Santa Fe Baking Co.** and stake out an outdoor table. Enjoy gourmet coffee and home-baked pastries. Reading material includes international newspapers and a good selection of magazines.

11:00am Explore the compact heart of Santa Fe. The new **Georgia O'Keeffe Museum**, located just west of the Plaza, houses the most extensive collection of O'Keeffe paintings in the world. Two blocks east of the Plaza, the **Institute of American Indian Arts Museum** features a mix of 7,000 works by Native American artists, the widest range of contemporary Native American art in the United States. In between museum visits, stop at one of the many food booths set up in the Plaza for *Fiesta*. Sample roast mutton on fried bread, fajitas, and ice-cold watermelon juice.

Noon At the Plaza bandstand, you'll see the *Fiesta*'s Opening Ceremonies, followed by entertainment all afternoon. Don't miss the ***Entrada de Don Diego de Vargas*** in the Plaza. It's an interesting reenactment—complete with costumes—of the conqueror's entrance into the city.

3:00pm Continue your exploration with a tour of the **Palace of the Governors** that includes a history museum. Built in 1610, it's the oldest public building in continuous use in the United States. Outside, Native American craftspeople sell exquisite silver, turquoise jewelry, and pottery in one of the oldest open-air markets in the country.

5:00pm Cab to Fort Marcy Park, where you'll be part of the singing, dancing, and giddy atmosphere surrounding the dusk burning of **Zozobra**. Created from chicken wire, muslin, and shredded paper, the giant puppet requires 600 hours of work to complete. Constructed at a secret location by volunteers of the local Kiwanis Club, the giant image has a different look every year.

8:30pm Have dinner at one of Santa Fe's hottest restaurants, **Geronimo**, on gallery-lined Canyon Road. Guests are welcomed with a glowing fire and sophisticated yet relaxed Southwestern décor. A menu standout is crispy, red-corn chiles rellenos stuffed with roast duck.

10:30pm The Plaza is alive with the traditional music and dancing of the ***Baile de la Gente*** (9 p.m.–midnight). Put on your most outgoing persona and get invited to one of the many private *Fiesta* parties in town.

Day 2. Sat.　Sep. 11, 1999
(Day 2. Saturday　　September 9, 2000)

10:00am After a relaxed breakfast at the hotel, it's time for the ***Desfile de los Niños*** (Children's Pet Parade). Kids and their pets produce laughs and smiles as they wind from Cathedral Park down Paseo de Peralta, Palace Avenue, Sandoval Street, and San Francisco Street back to the park. The *Fiesta* is now in full swing. Food, traditional entertainment, and an arts-and-crafts market filled with authentic Southwestern creations are the major attractions until midnight.

12:30pm Go to Canyon Road for a casual lunch at **El Farol**. Have *tapas* on the front patio. After lunch, take a walk along Canyon Road. It's filled with arts-and-crafts galleries.

5:30pm For great margaritas, head to the **Belltower** bar in the lobby of the La Honda Hotel.

7:30pm Walk to Water Street and the **Coyote Cafe**. Known to food lovers all over the world, this star of the Sante Fe culinary scene has a modern ambience, but the food is pure Southwest. The New Mexican Black Angus rib chop is a must.

9:00pm For more than 100 years, the *Gran Baile de la Fiesta* has been one of the most eagerly awaited annual events in Santa Fe. A public homage to Don Diego de Vargas and La Reina, it's noteworthy for magnificent costumes. The splendidly dressed De Vargas and La Reina, with entourage in tow, sweep through the ballroom accompanied by mariachis and a big band playing traditional Spanish tunes. If you don't know the *ranchera*, *cumbria*, or *valtes*, don't worry, there's contemporary dance music as well.

11:30pm For a lively scene and more dancing, you could go back to **El Farol**. Or for a complete change of style, try the chic new **A Bar** martini and jazz club.

Day 3. Sun. Sep. 12, 1999
(Day 3. Sunday   September 10, 2000)

10:30am Definitely worth the wait in line, **Cafe Pasqual's** is always packed with diners in search of great Southwestern breakfasts. Then while away the morning back at the *Fiesta* in the Plaza.

2:00pm Be sure to attend the wacky *Historical, Hysterical Parade*.

3:00pm Although the *Fiesta* continues in the Plaza until 5 p.m., take a detour to the **Museum of International Folk Art**. It houses a truly amazing collection—probably the largest of its kind—that's both fun and enriching.

7:30pm Tonight's dinner is at your hotel. The **Anasazi** serves food that combines New Mexican and Native American influences in an elegant Southwestern setting.

9:30pm At **Vanessie of Santa Fe**, pianist Doug Montgomery is a local favorite. This nightspot is also a great place to reflect on the mix of dancing in the street, history, and natural beauty that makes *Fiesta de Santa Fe* so spectacular.

Alternatives

For a taste of Old Santa Fe with modern amenities, **La Fonda Hotel** is the place to hang your hat. Located on the Plaza, this classic hostelry features adobe architecture, hand-carved furniture, fireplaces, and balconies. With its award-winning Pueblo architecture and wonderful views, the **Inn at Loretto** is another excellent choice. The **Inn of the Governors** is a small and intimate hotel with kiva fireplaces in the garden patio.

Another restaurant high on everyone's list is **Santacafe**, where fusion cuisine is served in a romantic setting. **Pranzo Italian Grill** features northern Italian dishes in an elegant, contemporary setting. Ask for a table on the open-air roof garden.

For an amazing day trip, wander through the ancient cliff dwellings and kivas at **Bandelier National Monument** on the Jemez Mountain Trail. You can climb ladders into these nearly thousand-year-old Anasazi pueblos and get an insider's view of life in this ancient civilization.

In striking contrast is the nearby Los Alamos National Laboratory, the home of the Manhattan Project, where the atomic bomb was developed. Today, you can visit its **Bradbury Science Museum** for exhibits describing the history of the laboratory, as well as demonstrations of its research activities.

Farther north, past Abiquiu on Highway 84, you can get a close-up look at the majestic, otherworldly natural beauty of northern New Mexico. Take a 45-minute hike from Ghost Ranch, where Georgia O'Keeffe spent much of her painting life, to the top of Chimney Rock.

The Hot Sheet

HOTELS		ADDRESS	PH	FX	PRICE	RMS	BEST ROOMS
Inn at Loretto	Alt	211 Old Santa Fe Trail	505-988-5531 800-727-5531	505-984-7988	$$$	141	Mountain, river vw
Inn of the Anasazi	★	113 Washington Ave.	505-988-3030 800-688-8100		$$$	59	Deluxe
Inn of the Governors	Alt	234 Don Gaspar St.	505-982-4333 800-234-4534	505-989-9149	$$$	100	City vw
La Fonda Hotel	Alt	100 E. San Francisco	505-982-5511 800-523-5002	505-988-2952	$$	153	Loretto Chapel vw

RESTAURANTS	DAY	ADDRESS	PH	PRICE	REC	DRESS	FOOD
Anasazi	3	see Inn of the Anasazi	505-988-3030	$$$	D/BL	Kazh	Asian-influenced Southwestern
Cafe Pasqual's	3	121 Don Gaspar St.	505-983-9340	$$	B/LD	Local	Southwestern
Coyote Cafe	2	132 W. Water St.	505-983-1615	$$$$	D	Kazh	Modern Southwestern
El Farol	2	808 Canyon Rd.	505-983-9912	$	L/D	Local	Spanish, Southwestern
Geronimo	1	724 Canyon Rd.	505-982-1500	$$	D/L	Kazh	New American
Pranzo Italian Grill	Alt	540 Montezuma St.	505-984-2645	$$	LD	Kazh	Italian
Santa Fe Baking Co.	1	201 Galisteo St.	505-995-0751	$	B/L	Local	American
Santacafe	Alt	231 Washington St.	505-984-1788	$$$	LD	Kazh	New American

NIGHTLIFE	DAY	ADDRESS	PH	COVER	REC*	DRESS	MUSIC
A Bar	2	331 Sandoval St.	505-982-8999	$	MP	Kazh	Jazz, rock, swing
Belltower	2	see La Fonda Hotel	505-982-5511	None	R	Local	
El Farol	2	see El Farol restaurant	505-983-9912	$	MP(F)	Kazh	Salsa, flamenco, R&B, rock
Vanessie of Santa Fe	3	434 W. San Francisco St.	505-982-9966	None	M(F)	Local	Jazz, pop, classical

SIGHTS & ATTRACTIONS	DAY	ADDRESS	PH	ENTRY FEE
Bandelier National Monument	Alt	Hwy. 4, 8 miles west of White Ranch	505-672-0343	$
Bradbury Science Museum	1	Central and 15th sts.	505-667-4444	None
Georgia O'Keeffe Museum	1	217 Johnson St.	505-995-0785	$
Institute of American Indian Arts Museum	1	108 Cathedral Pl.	505-988-6211	$
Museum of International Folk Art	3	706 Camino Lejo St.	505-827-6350	$
Palace of the Governors	1	100 W. Palace St.	505-827-6483	$
Santa Fe CVB		201 W. Marcy St.	800-777-2489	

Event & Ticket Info

Fiesta de Santa Fe: Most activities are free. For information, contact the *Santa Fe CVB* (800-777-2489). **Grand Baile de Fiesta** (Sweeney Convention Center, 201 W. Marcy St.): Order tickets ($15) well in advance from the *Santa Fe Fiesta Council* (505-988-7575).

* M=Live music; P=Dancing (Party); R=Bar only; S=Show; (F)=Food served. For further explanation of codes, see page 14.

 NYC −2 Santa Fe (SAF) <30min./$20 Albuquerque (ABQ) <60 min./$30 Yes 50°/81° (10°/27°)

Balloon Fiesta

(Kodak Albuquerque International Balloon Fiesta)

Origin: 1972	Event ★★★★★★ City	Attendance: 1,500,000

With nearly 1,000 multicolored balloons ascending at dawn into the clear Southwestern sky, nearly all of them framed by the dusky Sandia mountains, it's no wonder Albuquerque's **Balloon Fiesta** is the most photographed event in the world. Official sources claim 25 million pictures are snapped during the event's nine days, which are highlighted by mass ascensions, target and precision competitions, and as much color as a roll of film can handle.

Albuquerque's unique "box" geography—mountain formations hold in mostly glorious weather patterns—makes for perfect ballooning conditions. But it's not just the professionals who get high here. Visitors can take rides along the majestic Sandia Mountains or make graceful circuits over the Rio Grande.

While most events in this book pulsate into the early hours, in Albuquerque you get up in the dark hours for spectacular daybreak events. Dusk is the other time to be outside, as hundreds of brilliantly lit, tethered balloons sway against sunset skies, creating a surreal skyscape of colors.

The **Balloon Fiesta** takes over and transforms Albuquerque, but the city still offers lively night life along with award-winning restaurants. Though its population is about 500,000, Albuquerque has a small-town feel consistent with its history as a frontier crossroads and trading center. Old Town,

the four-block "village" at the heart of the city since 1706, is a charming adobe area lined with galleries, cafes, and winding brick walkways.

Within an hour's drive of Albuquerque are awe-inspiring natural areas such as Petroglyph National Monument, with 17,000 ancient Indian writings carved into black rock from five extinct volcanoes. Native Americans carry on the centuries-old traditions of their ancestors with ceremonial dances and skillful artisanship. The big skies and muted-color desert vistas that seem to go on forever continue to inspire great art, much of which is showcased in museums and art galleries throughout the city. In October, visitors come to Albuquerque for the brilliant balloons, but most leave equally colored with a new appreciation of the artistry and grace of New Mexico's ancient and modern cultures.

Balloon Fiesta

Day 1. Thu.   Oct. 7, 1999
(Day 1. Thursday   October 12, 2000)

9:00am Accented with antique frescoes, beamed ceilings, and Spanish-tile floors in the lobby, **La Posada de Albuquerque** is native son Conrad Hilton's first hotel.

10:00am Start your day with a visit to the **Albuquerque Museum of Art and History**. It combines an interesting sculpture garden with Native American art and historical displays.

11:00am Explore Old Town's sheltered walkways, winding brick paths, and quaint patios on the museum's walking tour.

12:30pm Across the street from the museum is a wonderful spot for a light lunch. **Seasons Rotisserie & Grill** serves pastas, sandwiches, and American cuisine in an upscale, casual setting.

2:30pm Visit the **National Atomic Museum**. It features models of the first atomic bombs, aircraft, rockets, missiles, and nuclear weapons.

5:30pm Leave radioactivity for a more benign kind of glow. Head for Balloon Fiesta Park and the *Special Shapes Rodeo Glow*. Sailing ships, cows, tennis shoes, and pink dragons are lit up with a host of other character balloons to create a fascinating menagerie against the sky. Balloons start inflating—and parking lots fill up—at 5:30 p.m. Pilots set off "burns" synchronized to music at dusk, about 7 p.m.

8:00pm Stay for the *fireworks show*, which, against the brilliant stars of the desert sky, is one of the most beautiful in the world.

9:00pm Get pampered in a turn-of-the-century brick building at the **Artichoke Cafe**, an Italian-French-American bistro with exquisite dinners.

11:00pm Relax at the seductive **Martini Grille**, the perfect finish to a perfect day. The nearby **Club Rhythm and Blues** has good music.

Day 2. Fri.   Oct. 8, 1999
(Day 2. Friday   October 13, 2000)

5:30am Don't worry, your 4 a.m. wake-up call will be worth the pain. Hurry to Balloon Fiesta Park for the *Dawn Patrol*, a haunting ceremony that sends one luminous, solitary balloon into the dawn sky to greet the sun as it climbs over the Sandias.

7:00am Remember all those crazy-shaped balloons you saw glowing in last night's sky? Now watch them all rise together in the dramatic *Special Shapes Ascension*.

11:00am Not long ago, Route 66 ran through three time zones and eight states, from Chicago to Los Angeles. Today it has all but vanished, but the **66 Diner** still serves a mean brunch while paying homage to this special part of American history.

12:30pm Head east out of Albuquerque on I-40, then north on New Mexico Highway 14, and pick up the road to the Sandia Crest and the Turquoise Trail. Wind through the Cibola National Forest for breathtaking views at 10,000 feet and above. Continue through old mining towns (gold, silver, turquoise, and coal), stopping at artists' shops between the views. Or ...

12:30pm Visit one of the many Native American pueblos within an hour's drive of Albuquerque. Fall is the perfect time to catch harvest ceremonies, which are heralded by hypnotic drumming and gorgeously feathered and beaded dancers. Try the Indian fry bread, hot and honey-drizzled, straight from the pan.

6:15pm Take in an incredible sunset on the **Sandia Peak Tramway**, the world's longest aerial tramway. You'll be lifted from the desert floor, above canyons and lush forests, to the top of Sandia Peak, where panoramic views take in more than 11,000 square miles

7:00pm *High-class* takes on new meaning at the **High Finance** restaurant atop Sandia Peak. The steaks, seafood, and pastas are superb (if you can tear yourself away from the awesome panoramic views long enough to order). Or ...

7:00pm If you're craving downtime, head back to the hotel and **Conrad's Downtown**, La Posada's excellent restaurant. Featuring award-winning recipes from Jane Butel, a celebrated cookbook author synonymous with Southwestern cuisine (her Southwestern Cooking School is just off the lobby), Conrad's is great for feasting and people-watching. Try one of three versions of traditional Spanish paella while flamenco-guitar music plays in the background.

9:00pm Stop by **The Lobby Bar** at La Posada for blues and jazz in one of the city's popular meeting spots.

11:00pm Dance at the Crowne Plaza's **Pyramid Club**, where there's plenty of high-energy music from the '70s, '80s, and '90s.

Day 3. Sat.   Oct. 9, 1999
(Day 3. Saturday   October 14, 2000)

5:00am If you missed the Dawn Patrol yesterday, go today, but don't miss the *Mass Ascension* at 7 a.m. Nearly a thousand balloons take off together for an unforgettable dawn. You could be in one of them by splurging on a *World Balloon* ride.

9:00am Head back to La Posada de Albuquerque for a leisurely breakfast at **Conrad's Downtown**.

10:30am New Mexico boasts the art, history, and culture of 19 Native American tribes. Learn how climate and geography made each one unique at the **Indian Pueblo Cultural Center**, where traditional dance performances and art demonstrations are held on weekends.

12:30pm Savor culinary history with lunch at **La Placita Restaurant**, Albuquerque's oldest restored

hacienda. It serves New Mexican and American cuisine in a Spanish atmosphere.

2:30pm See Native American art at **Petroglyph National Monument** on the city's west side. Several walking trails, ranging from easy to moderately difficult, wind around 17,000 petroglyphs carved into volcanic rock.

5:30pm The *Night Magic Glow* is one of the most anticipated events of the week. Balloons are slowly inflated until the sky is filled with the fantastic sight of hundreds of luminous balloons pulsating with light.

8:30pm Stay for the *fireworks*, a spectacular end to a fiesta day.

9:30pm The **Metropolitan Grill** has the rare combination of exquisitely prepared food and great prices. Its New American cuisine combines Asian, Mexican, Italian, French, and Southwestern influences into a collection of small plates that change with the seasons. Sample several for a filling dinner for the same price as an entree.

11:30pm Two-step to country music at the **Midnight Rodeo** or settle in next door at its Gotham Room and shake your booty to dance music.

Alternatives

At the **Sheraton Old Town**, you can wake up each morning to 300 years of history and culture. The **Crowne Plaza Pyramid** hotel has the dramatic, 10-story Aztec Pyramid Atrium. The **Hyatt Regency Albuquerque** has an attractive lobby and standard Hyatt rooms.

Stephens restaurant was named one of America's 50 best restaurants by *Condé Nast Traveler* magazine. **McGrath's Bar & Grill** is a good eating choice, serving well-prepared American fare in an attractive room. **Terra, an American Bistro** is a good stop for dishes made with familiar ingredients. Two small unusual museums are the **American International Rattlesnake Museum** and the **Turquoise Museum**.

The Hot Sheet

HOTELS		ADDRESS	PH	FX	PRICE	RMS	BEST ROOMS
Crowne Plaza Pyramid	Alt	5151 San Francisco Rd. NE	505-821-3333 800-227-6963	505-828-0230	$$	311	Mtn vw
Hyatt Regency Albuquerque	Alt	330 Tijeras NW	505-842-1234 800-233-1234	505-766-6749	$$	395	Mtn vw
La Posada de Albuquerque	★	125 2nd St. NW	505-242-9090 800-777-5732	505-242-8664	$$	113	Mtn vw
Sheraton Old Town	Alt	800 Rio Grande NW	505-843-6300 800-237-2133	505-842-8426	$$	188	City vw

RESTAURANTS	DAY	ADDRESS	PH	PRICE	REC	DRESS	FOOD
66 Diner	2	1405 Central Ave. NE	505-247-1421	$	B/LD	Local	American
Artichoke Cafe	1	424 Central SE	505-243-0200	$$	D	Kazh	French, American
Conrad's Downtown	2	see La Posada hotel	505-242-9090	$$	D/BL	Kazh	Southwestern
High Finance	2	45 Tramway NE	505-243-9742	$$$	D/L	Kazh	American
La Placita Restaurant	3	208 San Felipe	505-247-2204	$$	L/D	Local	New Mexican
McGrath's Bar & Grill	Alt	see Hyatt Regency Albuquerque hotel	505-766-6700	$$	BLD	Kazh	American, continental
Metropolitan Grill	3	519 Central NW	505-224-9040	$$	D/L	Kazh	New American
Seasons Rotisserie & Grill	1	2031 Mountain Rd. NW	505-766-5100	$$	L/D	Kazh	American
Stephens	Alt	1311 Tijeras NW	505-842-1773	$$	D	Dressy	American
Terra, an American Bistro	Alt	1119 Alameda NW	505-792-1700	$$	LD	Local	American

NIGHTLIFE	DAY	ADDRESS	PH	COVER	REC*	DRESS	MUSIC
Club Rhythm and Blues	1	3523 Central Ave. NE	505-256-0849	$	M	Kazh	Jazz, blues
The Lobby Bar	2	see La Posada hotel	505-242-9090	$	M(F)	Kazh	Flamenco, jazz
The Martini Grille	1	4200 Central SE	505-255-4111	None	M(F)	Kazh	Piano bar
Midnight Rodeo	3	4901 McLeod NE	505-888-0100	$	P(F)	Local	Country, rock
Pyramid Club	2	see Crowne Plaza Pyramid	505-821-3333	$	P(F)	Kazh	Disco, retro

SIGHTS & ATTRACTIONS	DAY	ADDRESS	PH	ENTRY FEE
Albuquerque Museum of Art and History	1	2000 Mountain Rd. NW	505-242-4600	None
American International Rattlesnake Museum	Alt	202 San Felipe NW	505-242-6569	$
Indian Pueblo Cultural Center	3	2401 12th St. NW	505-843-7270	$
National Atomic Museum	1	Wyoming Blvd. SE	505-284-3243	$
Petroglyph National Monument	3	4735 Unser NE	505-899-0205	None
Sandia Peak Tramway	2	Tramway Rd. at Tramway Blvd.	505-856-7325	$$
Turquoise Museum	Alt	2107 Central NW	505-247-8650	$
Albuquerque CVB		20 1st Plaza Bldg. NW	800-733-9918	

Event & Ticket Info

Albuquerque International Balloon Fiesta (Balloon Fiesta State Park, Interstate 25 at Tramway): Daily tickets ($4) are purchased at the gate. Five-day tickets ($15), which eliminate the need to wait in lines, can be ordered from *Albuquerque International Balloon Fiesta* (888-422-7277).

World Balloon, the official ride concession for *Balloon Fiesta*, arranges rides ($225 per person). For more information, contact *World Balloon* (505-293-6800).

---

* M=Live music; P=Dancing (Party); R=Bar only; S=Show; (F)=Food served. For further explanation of codes, see page 14.

 NYC −2   Albuquerque (ABQ) <30 min./$15   Yes   44°/71° (7°/22°)

  The Fun Also Rises

Great American Beer Festival

Origin: 1982   **Event** ★ ★ ★ ★ ★ **City**   **Attendance:** 35,000

Had Danny and the Juniors been writing songs in the '90s instead of the '50s, they might have ended up singing, "Let's go to the hops." The opportunity to taste 1,700 different one-ounce samples of creative brews from more than 400 breweries worldwide now makes this event the must-do pilgrimage for malt worshipers and seekers of good times. It also makes October the best time to visit Denver.

Denver's first permanent structure was a saloon, so it's no surprise that the city was ground zero for the microbrewery craze in the United States. In the downtown area, 15 microbreweries are within stumbling distance of each other and the tightly knit community of local brewers enthusiastically welcomes the Great American Beer Festival every fall. The Napa Valley of beer, Denver brews more beer than any other American city and it has the country's highest number of home-brewers (though Portland, Ore., argues with both claims).

Denver has a thriving downtown, with a diverse mix of people, theaters, shops, and restaurants. Old West charm has been restored in the lower downtown area (LoDo to locals), where Victorian buildings house art galleries, pubs, coffeehouses, and chic boutiques. Horse-drawn carriages and people-powered bicycle buggies comfortably commingle with downtown traffic.

The city is a walker's dream. Everywhere you want to be downtown is within a short hike, with the help of free shuttles that run every few minutes. Locate the mountains—visible from everywhere—and you know which way is west. It's a safe city, where urban revitalization has lured wealthy young professionals to fill LoDo lofts, and so unpretentious you'll swear you belong here shortly after arriving.

With more than two million people in the metropolitan area, there's much beyond the beer culture to explore in this town-turned-city. There are fine museums and restaurants and, of course, the Rocky Mountains in the backyard. But frothy brew is reason enough to make a Denver excursion. Just don't forget to bring your bottle of aspirin, because it's a helluva hopping weekend when Denver becomes one giant beer tent.

Great American Beer Festival

Day 1. Thu.   Oct. 7, 1999
(Day 1. Thursday   October 5, 2000)

10:00am Check into the **Adam's Mark Hotel Denver**. This is the festival's headquarters hotel, where high ceilings and open spaces help the most stressed-out traveler relax.

10:30am Walk to Civic Center Park, one of more than 200 city parks. Next to its statues and gardens is the **Colorado State Capitol**. Stand on the fifteenth step and you're exactly 5,280 feet above sea level, a living testament to Denver's handle, the Mile High City. Walk to the top of the dome for great city views.

11:30am The **Colorado History Museum** showcases frontier history with exhibits featuring cowboys, Indians, explorers, fur trappers, and miners.

1:30pm Wander to the 16th Street Mall, a tree-lined city street that provides the downtown pulse—free shuttle buses run its mile length every few minutes. Hit **Tommy Tsunami** for lunch. The décor highlights all kinds of funky, Asian pop culture. Pacific Rim cuisine and a sushi bar offer a nice lunch selection.

3:00pm On Wynkoop Street, the **Tattered Cover Book Store** is America's largest independent bookstore and arguably its best. Oversize chairs and cappuccinos are its signature. This is not just any bookstore—you'll be amazed.

4:00pm The nearby **Wynkoop Brewing Company** is Colorado's first brew pub. Check out the impressive pool room, with its tin ceilings and heavy oak beams.

8:00pm It's a short drive to one of the best and hippest Denver restaurants, **Barolo Grill**. The bar scene is worth a stop.

10:00pm You'll be arriving before the crowds, but cab to **The Church**, a converted house of worship now dancing to a different tune (rock, alternative). Candles, stained glass, and old pews add a creepy-cool effect. Afterward, head to the **Supreme Court Cafe and Nightclub** in your hotel. The beer-fest crowd makes this a better-than-normal scene.

Day 2. Fri.   Oct. 8, 1999
(Day 2. Friday   October 6, 2000)

9:30am You only live once, so it's **Ellyngton's** in the Brown Palace Hotel for breakfast. This beautiful hotel—a tourist attraction itself—has entertained every president since Calvin Coolidge.

11:00am Where did you get the money to pay for that breakfast? Walk to the **US Mint** and find out on a short tour.

11:45am Walk to the **Denver Art Museum** and enjoy one of the nation's finest collections of Native American art and artifacts, part of its vast collection.

1:30pm The **Falling Rock Tap House** has the best pub food in town. Brothers Chris and Steve Black avoided creating another brew pub, and, instead, started a tap house that serves 69 draft beers (a number everyone remembers). This is where Denver's beer aficionados hang out.

3:00pm A short walk will settle your stomach for the twists and turns at **Elitch Gardens Amusement Park**, adjacent to downtown. A 100-foot-high Ferris wheel and a 350-foot-high observation tower offer spectacular 360-degree views. Plenty of scary rides mix with flower gardens, lakes, and lagoons.

5:30pm Walk four blocks to the ***Great American Beer Festival*** in the Colorado Convention Center. Taste 1,700 different beers? No way! Alums and local brewers have a suggestion: Pick a strategy each time you attend a tasting. Select your favorite style—lager, stout, ale, etc.—and taste only within that category. Or pick a region of the country and taste beers only from that area. Upstairs, you'll find education-made-easy by interactive computer play, *Singled Out*-style game shows, and the history of beer and brewing on display.

9:30pm Cab to **The Denver Chophouse & Brewery**, an outstanding eatery where the power players of Denver dine. Try the fontina cheese and sage-stuffed Iowa pork chops. Under the restaurant is **Sing Sing**, a dueling-pianos bar with a sunken stage and wraparound bar. Nicknamed DrunkDrunk, the edge-loving crowd sings along, often only inches from out-of-control.

12:30am Nearby is the **Purple Martini**, where an amazing selection of martini concoctions is fashioned by show-off bartenders.

Day 3. Sat.   Oct. 9, 1999
(Day 3. Saturday   Oct. 7, 2000)

9:30am Dixon's Downtown Grill attracts the cell-phone crowd, which comes for abundant breakfasts of anything eggs. Big booths along a wall of windows give great views of the 16th Street people parade.

11:00am Catch the Light Rail to the **Black American West Museum & Heritage Center**, a small but fascinating collection of memorabilia celebrating the contribution of African-Americans to the region's development.

12:30pm Return to Larimer Square for a light Italian lunch at **Josephina's Ristorante**.

2:00pm Back to the Brewhaha for another shot at one-ounce samplers, more beer culture, and a new strategy. Freebies abound, from key chains to coasters emblazoned with creative logos from well-known to obscure breweries, so don't forget to pocket souvenirs.

4:30pm The special afternoon session ends in time for you to take a hotel break or just hang out.

6:30pm Head to Larimer Square for dinner at **Cadillac**

Ranch. Everything cowboy and Cadillac adorns this must-visit steak establishment, famous for its outstanding service and signature smoked prime rib.

8:00pm Larimer Square, Denver's oldest street, is full of shops, bars, cafes, and Victorian charm. Take a left at 16th Street, walk one block and turn right on Market Street to **Brendan's Market Street Pub**, the best place in town to hear live blues. This basement club has cramped quarters and tables circling the tiny dance floor—lots of dirty dancing done here—but it draws top talent.

10:30pm Walk to **El Chapultepec** for the best live jazz in town. National talent frequently drops in for a set after playing a concert, making this tiny, smoky legend well worth its cramped quarters.

Midnight Last call is **The Cruise Room**, a popular place for nightcaps in the 100-year-old Oxford Hotel. With its vintage jukebox and art-deco allure, it's all Denver attitude and atmosphere, playful and plenty laid-back. Not a bad finish to put on a weekend at the hops.

Alternatives

The grande dame of Denver hotels is the **Brown Palace**. Everything about it is elegant. The historic **Oxford Hotel** has antique-filled rooms. The **Hyatt Regency Denver** is a reliable downtown option.

Jax Fish House is relaxed, but upscale. It serves seafood in a charming atmosphere. **Palomino Euro Bistro**, part of the chain, is another scene/seen restaurant. The **Buckhorn Exchange** is a Denver institution with wild game decorating the walls and your plate.

If you brought your boots, you might want to try some boot-scootin' at the **Grizzly Rose**.

Popular day trips go to Central City and Black Hawk. These mining-towns-turned-gambling-meccas are restored in an Old West style, with almost 40 casinos.

The Hot Sheet

HOTELS		ADDRESS	PH	FX	PRICE	RMS	BEST ROOMS
Adam's Mark Hotel Denver	★	1550 Court Pl.	303-893-3333 800-444-2326	303-626-2544	$$	1,225	Mtn vw
Brown Palace	Alt	321 17th St.	303-297-3111	303-312-5900	$$$	230	City vw
Hyatt Regency Denver	Alt	1750 Welton St.	303-295-1234 800-233-1234	303-293-2565	$$	511	City vw
Oxford Hotel	Alt	1600 17th St.	303-628-5400 800-228-5838	303-628-5553	$$	80	Corner rms

RESTAURANTS	DAY	ADDRESS	PH	PRICE	REC	DRESS	FOOD
Barolo Grill	1	3030 E. 6th Ave.	303-393-1040	$$	D	Kazh	Northern Italian
Buckhorn Exchange	Alt	1000 Osage St.	303-534-9505	$$$	LD	Kazh	American Western
Cadillac Ranch	3	1400 Larimer Sq.	303-820-2288	$$$	D/L	Local	Steakhouse
The Denver Chophouse & Brewery	2	1735 19th St.	303-296-0800	$$$	D/L	Kazh	Seafood
Dixon's Downtown Grill	3	1610 16th St.	303-573-6100	$	B/LD	Kazh	American breakfast
Ellyngton's	2	321 17th St.	303-297-3111	$$$	B/L	Dressy	Brunch buffet
Falling Rock Tap House	2	1919 Blake St.	303-293-8338	$	L/D	Local	Pub food
Jax Fish House	Alt	1539 17th St.	303-292-5767	$$$	D	Kazh	Seafood
Josephina's Ristorante	3	1433 Larimer Sq.	303-623-0166	$$	L/D	Kazh	Italian
Palomino Euro Bistro	Alt	1515 Arapahoe St.	303-534-7800	$$	LD	Kazh	Mediterranean
Tommy Tsunami	1	1432 Market St.	303-534-5050	$$	L/D	Kazh	Pacific Rim

NIGHTLIFE	DAY	ADDRESS	PH	COVER	REC*	DRESS	MUSIC
Brendan's Market Street Pub	3	1625 Market St.	303-595-0609	$	MP(F)	Local, Kazh	Blues
El Chapultepec	3	1962 Market St.	303-295-9126	None	M(F)	Local	Jazz
The Church	1	1160 Lincoln St.	303-832-3528	$	MP(F)	Euro	Retro, techno, progressive, disco, industrial
The Cruise Room	3	see the Oxford Hotel	303-628-5400	None	R(F)	Yuppie	
Grizzly Rose	Alt	5450 N. Valley Hwy.	303-295-1330	$$	M	Local	Country
Purple Martini	2	1336 15th St.	303-820-0575	None	R(F)	Kazh	
Sing Sing	2	1735 19th St.	303-291-0880	$	M(F)	Local	Rock, dueling pianos
Supreme Court Cafe and Nightclub	1	see Adam's Mark Hotel	303-893-3333		MP(F)	Kazh	R&B, Motown
Wynkoop Brewing Company	1	1634 18th St.	303-297-2700	None	R(F)	Kazh	

SIGHTS & ATTRACTIONS	DAY	ADDRESS	PH	ENTRY FEE
Black American West Museum & Heritage Center	3	3091 California St.	303-292-2566	$
Colorado History Museum	1	1300 Broadway	303-866-3682	$
Colorado State Capitol	1	200 E. Colfax Ave.	303-866-2604	None
Denver Art Museum	2	100 W. 14th Ave.	303-640-4433	$
Elitch Gardens Amusement Park	2	2000 Elitch Circle	303-595-4386	$$$
US Mint	2	320 Colfax Ave.	303-844-3582	None
Tattered Cover Book Store	1	1628 16th St.	303-436-1070	None
Denver Metro CVB		1668 Larimer St.	303-892-1112	

Event & Ticket Info

Great American Beer Festival (Currigan Exhibition Hall, 14th and Champa streets): Tickets ($30) are available at the door. The event sometimes sells out each day in later hours. Advance tickets ($25) go on sale in August. For more information, contact *Association of Brewers/ Great American Beer Festival* (303-447-0126).

* M=Live music; P=Dancing (Party); R=Bar only; S=Show; (F)=Food served. For further explanation of codes, see page 14.

 NYC −2   **Denver (DEN)** <60 min./$30   Yes   37°/67° (3°/19°)

October 1999   Washington, DC, USA   October 2000

Taste of DC

| Origin: 1990 | Event ★★★★ City | Attendance: 1,200,000 |

Talk about a perfect day: It's Indian summer and you're in the nation's capital, walking along storied Pennsylvania Avenue during the *Taste of DC*, which claims to be the largest annual outdoor festival on the East Coast. The White House is your backdrop and Capitol Hill lies directly ahead. Pennsylvania Avenue is closed off and electric with excitement generated by tens of thousands of people, music booming from three stages, and a symphony of alluring smells from cuisine prepared by Washington eateries. There are dozens of reasons to visit Washington, DC, any time of year, but the fall weather and *Taste of DC* celebration makes the when-to-go decision a no-brainer.

Taste of DC, a quintessential "Taste of ..." event that lures about 1.2 million visitors, was created to showcase the astonishing variety that makes DC one of the great world capitals. It's an event made for wandering and stopping and eating and drinking and wandering some more. Let yourself be swept up by the currents of people surging along five blocks of Pennsylvania Avenue. People-watching, beer-tasting, and free concerts also will pull you in different directions. With variety as its mantra, the DC Committee to Promote Washington selects nationally known music groups and 40 local restaurants to fuel the event. Add to this an international crafts bazaar, and your plate is full—even without leaving Pennsylvania Avenue.

The absence of an annual let-your-hair-down festival in Washington must have something to do with the fact that there are too many politicians in town. Or perhaps its population of 600,000 can handle only one gigantic bash every four years (Inauguration Day may be America's best party). But along with the *Taste*, attractions outside the festival could keep you busy for weeks—the Smithsonian Institution alone requires several trips to completely explore. With its atmosphere of diplomacy, bevy of historical landmarks and museums, ethnic diversity, and refined night life, DC is a town both righties and lefties can endorse.

Taste of DC

Day 1. Fri.   Oct. 8, 1999
(Day 1. Friday   *October 6, 2000)*

8:00am Stay at the historic and elegant beaux-arts **Willard Inter-Continental Hotel**, where Nathaniel Hawthorne stayed and Martin Luther King Jr. composed his "I Have a Dream" speech while a guest. Begin your stay with a tour of the nearby **White House**. Your congressman can arrange a VIP tour ticket for you—otherwise, line up on East Executive Avenue, next to the Treasury Building.

Noon Try the very fresh fish and atmosphere at **Kinkead's**, a short walk away. Downstairs is quick and casual; upstairs serves full lunches.

1:30pm The **Smithsonian Institution** is an incredible collection of 14 separate, world-class museums. These include art museums, such as the Freer Gallery of Art and the Hirshhorn Museum and Sculpture Garden, as well as the National Museum of American History and the National Museum of Natural History. There's too much to see in one day, so plan your visit at the **Smithsonian Information Center**.

4:30pm Have a coffee or predinner drink in the Willard's acclaimed bar, **Round Robin**. The collection of wall portraits depicts famous hotel guests from Walt Whitman to Charles Dickens.

7:00pm Head to Washington's eclectic Adams-Morgan district for dinner at **Cities,** where the menu varies according to the featured city and the food is always well-prepared. Dinner or your concierge will get you into the swank **Prive**, a membership-only disco located upstairs. You may not want to leave until its 3 a.m. closing, but …

9:00pm Nearby **Felix Restaurant & Lounge** will be a scene tonight, with dancing in the lounge. On your way back to the hotel, stop in at **Ozio's** or **Rumors,** two of downtown's best meeting places.

Day 2. Sat.   Oct. 9, 1999
(Day 2. Saturday   *October 7, 2000)*

9:30am From the hotel, stroll a couple of blocks north to **Reeve's** for a full breakfast. Then enjoy the varied collection of European and American art at the **National Gallery of Art**.

Noon Walk to Union Station, the beautifully restored train station, for lunch at **B. Smith's.** The stylish ambience well suits the New American cuisine.

2:00pm Take a quick, guided tour of the **US Capitol**, where US senators and representatives are supposed to earn their livings.

4:00pm The massive *Taste of DC* is in full swing. Start by selecting from the concerts that begin on the hour from stages on Ninth and 12th streets.

7:30pm Drive to Georgetown to catch **The Capitol Steps**' political-satire revue. Taking aim at similar targets, **The Gross National Product** is often just as funny.

9:30pm Dine at **Cafe Milano**, where foreign diplomats often sit next to supermodels or basketball stars. Milano's phenomenal success comes from its jet-set atmosphere, as well as its light pastas and pizzas.

11:30pm You'll find a fun crowd and good beer at **Nathan's**, **Clyde's**, or a host of other Georgetown hangouts. A few blocks away, **Sequoia**'s patio-bar scene makes it a consistent local favorite.

1:30am Good food after midnight? **Bistro Français** serves nightcaps until late, along with its famed chicken and *pommes frites.*

Day 3. Sun. Oct. 10, 1999
(Day 3. Sunday   October 8, 2000)

10:00am Breakfast in the hotel and then brace yourself for the sobering **US Holocaust Memorial Museum**. Artifacts, photos, films, and interactive exhibits tell the story of Jewish persecution by the Nazis in one of the world's finest museums.

1:00pm From Creole to Ethiopian, forty local restaurants at **Taste** represent the city's culinary variety, so you're sure to find something for lunch. Stand in line for food on Ninth Street, so that while you wait you can clearly view the stage and hear the music. Enjoy more bands, global cuisine, and the crafts bazaar, which sells everything from Mexican silver to Moroccan sandals. Don't miss the street performers, who often create quite a buzz.

7:00pm Head to **Cafe Atlantico**'s three-tiered dining room for a dinner of pan-Latin cuisine. Loosen up with a *caipirinha,* a boisterous Brazilian cocktail involving Brazilian moonshine, sugar, and lime. Try a medley of Argentinean grilled meats, the quail *tamal fingido* with corn and chile, or the snapper Veracruz.

9:30pm Cab to **Blues Alley**, the oldest jazz supper club in the United States. It's schedule often looks like a Who's Who of the jazz and blues world—all the legends have played the stage here at one time or another. Close out the weekend driving past the Reflecting Pool, which is flanked by the **Lincoln Memorial** and the **Washington Monument** (you can take an elevator to the top of the latter). The monuments, breathtakingly lit and mirrored on the water, will remind you of much of the drama and history that has placed Washington at the center of the modern world.

Alternatives

Washington's biggest annual event is the **Fourth of July Celebration**. If you can't be in Philadelphia or Boston, DC is a spectacular place to spend the holiday, complete with a parade, the Smithsonian Festival of American Folklife, concerts, and fireworks.

Between Georgetown and Foggy Bottom, the **Four Seasons Hotel** is noted for its contemporary elegance. The dignified **Hay-Adams Hotel** is the capital's most prestigious temporary address, barring its neighbor, the White House.

> As someone once observed, "Washington is considered the world's most important city, just not in the United States."

Washington's wide range of neat restaurants includes **Red Sage**, a Southwestern import that is a Congressional-staffer hangout; **Les Halles**, whose satisfying French-American cuisine has made it a DC institution; **Bombay Club**, the city's best Indian restaurant, with an exuberant décor and exquisite tandooris and *thalis* that lure luminaries, from Jodie Foster to the First Family; the **Old Ebbitt Grill**, an institution serving politicos since 1856 in its wood-and-brass saloon; **Jaleo**, a chic spot to satisfy your *tapas* craving; and **Cashion's Eat Place**, an Adams-Morgan spot where you'll be charmed by the atmosphere and the food. Smartly dressed guests, mesmerized by go-go dancers at **Club Zei**, dance to a state-of-the-art sound system.

Washington's landmarks and other museums are too numerous to list here, but if you have extra time, try to visit **The Phillips Collection**, America's first modern-art museum. It's located in the gallery-filled DuPont Circle neighborhood and includes Renoir's masterpiece, *Luncheon of the Boating Party*. The **National Air and Space Museum** is the most visited museum in the world. Its attractions range from the Wright brothers' 1903 *Flyer* to an exhibit that allows you to walk on a re-created moon surface. The **Vietnam Veterans Memorial** is one of the more moving memorials in the nation. **Ford's Theatre**, the site of Lincoln's assassination, has a small museum.

The Hot Sheet

HOTELS		ADDRESS	PH	FX	PRICE	RMS	BEST ROOMS
Four Seasons Hotel	Ålt	2800 Pennsylvania Ave.	202-342-0444 800-332-3442	202-342-3442	$$$$+	257	Georgetown, garden vw
Hay-Adams Hotel	Alt	1 Lafayette Sq.	202-638-6600 800-424-5054	202-638-2716	$$$$	143	White House or St. John's Church vw
Willard Inter-Continental Hotel ★		1401 Pennsylvania Ave. NW	202-628-9100 800-327-0200	202-637-7307	$$$$	341	Capitol and Washington Monument vw

RESTAURANTS	DAY	ADDRESS	PH	PRICE	REC	DRESS	FOOD
B. Smith's	2	50 Massachusetts Ave. NE	202-289-6188	$$	L/BD	Kazh	Southern
Bistro Français	2	3128 M St. NW	202-338-3830	$$	D/L	Local	French
Bombay Club	Alt	815 Connecticut Ave. NW	202-659-3727	$$	LD	Formal	Indian
Cafe Atlantico	3	405 8th St. NW	202-393-0812	$$	D/L	Local	Brazilian
Cafe Milano	2	3251 Prospect St. NW	202-333-6183	$$	D/L	Local	Italian
Cashion's Eat Place	Alt	1819 Columbia Rd. NW	202-797-1819	$$	D	Kazh	American
Cities	1	2424 18th St. NW	202-328-2100	$$	D	Kazh	Varies
Jaleo	Alt	480 7th St. NW	202-628-7949	$$	LD	Kazh	Spanish
Kinkead's	1	2000 Pennsylvania Ave. NW	202-296-7700	$$	L/D	Local	Seafood
Les Halles	Alt	1201 Pennsylvania Ave. NW	202-347-6848	$$	LD	Local	French, American
Old Ebbitt Grill	Alt	675 15th St. NW	202-347-4801	$$	BLD	Local	American
Red Sage	Alt	605 14th St. NW	202-638-4444	$$$	LD	Yuppie, Kazh	American Southwestern
Reeve's	2	1306 G St. NW	202-628-6350	$	B/L	Local	American breakfast

NIGHTLIFE	DAY	ADDRESS	PH	COVER	REC*	DRESS	MUSIC
Blues Alley	3	1073 Wisconsin Ave. NW	202-337-4141	$$	M(F)	Local	Jazz
The Capitol Steps	2	1055 Jefferson St. NW	202-298-8222	$$$	S	Kazh	
Club Zei	Alt	1415 Zei Alley NW	202-842-2445	$	MP	Local	International
Clyde's	2	3236 M St. NW	202-333-9180	None	R(F)	Local	
Felix Restaurant & Lounge	1	2406 18th St. NW	202-483-3549	$	MP	Kazh	Funk
Nathan's	2	3150 M St. NW	202-338-2000	None	R(F)	Local	
Ozio's	1	1835 K St. NW	202-822-6000	$	MP	Kazh	International
Prive	1	2424 18th St. NW	202-328-2100	None	P(F)	Kazh	Dance
Round Robin	1	see the Willard hotel	202-628-9100	None	R	Yuppie, Kazh	
Rumors	1	1900 M St. NW	202-466-7378	$	P(F)	Kazh	Top 40
Sequoia	2	3000 K St. NW	202-944-4200	None	R(F)	Local	
The Gross National Product	2	3135 K St. NW	202-783-7212	$$	S	Kazh	

SIGHTS & ATTRACTIONS	DAY	ADDRESS	PH	ENTRY FEE
Ford's Theatre	Alt	511 10th St. NW	202-638-2367	None
Lincoln Memorial	3	23rd St. NW	202-426-6841	None
National Air and Space Museum	Alt	6th St. and Independence Ave. SW	202-357-1400	None
National Gallery of Art	2	4th St. & Constitution Ave. NW	202-737-4215	None
The Phillips Collection	Alt	1600 21st St. NW	202-387-2151	$
Smithsonian Institution	1	1000 Jefferson Dr. SW	202-357-2700	None
US Capitol	2	Capitol Hill NW	202-225-6827	None
US Holocaust Memorial Museum	3	100 Raoul Wallenberg Pl. SW	202-488-0400	None
Vietnam Veterans Memorial	Alt	Constitution and Bacon aves.	202-634-1568	None
Washington Monument	3	15th St. NW	202-426-6841	None
White House	1	1600 Pennsylvania Ave. NW	202-456-2200	None
Smithsonian Information Ctr.	1	1000 Jefferson Dr. SW	202-357-2700	None
Washington Visitor's Center		1212 New York Ave. NW, 6th fl.	202-789-7000	

Event & Ticket Info

Taste of DC: All events are free. For more information, contact the DC Committee to Promote Washington (202-724-5430).

Alternative Event
Fourth of July Celebration:
National Park Service, 202-619-7222

* M=Live music; P=Dancing (Party); R=Bar only; S=Show; (F)=Food served. For further explanation of codes, see page 14.

 NYC 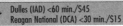 Dulles (IAD) <60 min./$45 Reagan National (DCA) <30 min./$15 No 44°/68° (7°/14°)

If It's Tuesday, It Must Be Alligator Lasagna ...

Eating well gives joy to life and food festivals in America leave no aspect of that joy unexplored. From a few hundred invitation-only attendees to millions gorging together, from regional cuisine to the truly exotic, from fast food to gourmet—food festivals cover the gastronomic gamut. Festivals may honor one type of food with a smorgasbord of endless variations.

They may showcase an ethnic cuisine. They may feature amateur cook-off competitions or samples from high-class restaurants. Some, such as the Taste of Chicago, America's biggest food and music festival, may feature top entertainment, rides, and exhibits, in addition to dozens of food vendors and gourmet restaurants. Whatever your preference, dozens of delicious events await you throughout the year.

You could build a complete meal traveling to food festivals, awakening to the World's Largest Pancake Breakfast in Springfield, Mass., with syrup from either Vermont's or New York's maple festivals. Add South Carolina's World Grits Festival before a spicy Creole lunch at Louisiana's gumbo or jambalaya festivals. For dinner, start with appetizers at the Great Wisconsin Cheese Festival and Alabama's National Peanut Festival, where the streets are paved with peanuts for the Goober Parade. Make chili your next course at the Republic of Texas Chilympiad, as nearly 600 contestants dazzle festival-goers in the State Men's Championship Chili Cook-Off. Grab your main course from the World's Largest Skillet at Kentucky's World Chicken Festival, garnished with garlic from the Gilroy (Calif.) Garlic Festival ("the smelliest party on the continent") or honey from the Ohio Honey Festival, where possibly deranged volunteers sport living-bee beards.

For vegetables, try artichokes from the Castroville (Calif.) Artichoke Festival, potatoes from North Dakota's Potato Bowl, or Vidalia onions from Georgia's festival. Choose fruit from Michigan and South Carolina peach festivals. At the latter, you can also exercise away calories in the Tour de Peche bicycle race. Prefer strawberries? The succulent fruit inspires festivals all over the country—from Tennessee to Texas to California—drawing enormous crowds. The Florida Strawberry Festival is one of the best, where nearly a million visitors savor strawberries along with the finest country-music entertainers in the business.

If you're more of an old salt than a landlubber, you won't want to miss Maryland's St. Mary's County Oyster Festival. If you're terminally devoted to oysters, get tickets (only 2,250 are available) to Virginia's Chincoteague Oyster Festival. Other festivals across the country celebrate scallops, clams, lobsters, crawfish, catfish, mullet, and more. Adventurous gourmands can travel light years beyond calimari at The Great Monterey Squid Festival in California.

Dessert addicts, don't despair. Wisconsin's Chocolate City Festival or the chocolate-chile ice cream at Arizona's La Fiesta de los Chiles may convince you to skip dinner altogether.

This all too tame for you? Then you're ripe for the Sweetwater (Texas) Rattlesnake

Roundup, where you can eat western diamondback rattlesnakes that can grow to eight feet. Or head to Kansas, where women in the Pit Hissers roundup crew welcome men's help in gathering dinner at the Rattlesnake Roundup and Prairie Folk Festival. You may prefer Anahuac, Texas, where a three-to-one alligators-to-people ratio doesn't stop townspeople from chowing down on their amphibian friends at their Gatorfest.

Gastronomically speaking, it's possible to travel the world without leaving the States. One of the biggest international cuisine festival's is Bronx African-American & Caribbean Heritage Festival, with millions eating curried goat, conch, and other delicacies. Ohio's Oktoberfest-Zinzinnati is one of the largest German festivals in the world. Kutztown's German festival, in the heart of Pennsylvania Dutch country, strives for authenticity in every detail. Sophia Loren once said, "Everything you see I owe to spaghetti," so if you want a figure like hers, go to Buffalo, NY, for its Italian Heritage & Food Festival. Of course, as somebody else once pointed out, "The trouble with eating Italian food is that five or six days later you're hungry again." Solve that at Arizona's Matsuri Festival of Japan, where spaghetti turns into *yaki soba* (pan-fried noodles). Stay for the prestigious Heard Museum Guild Indian Fair & Market, where you can sample Native American fry bread, Hopi stew, or *piki*, a thin Hopi bread made with blue cornmeal and rabbit brush plant.

If you still can't decide, there are plenty of multiethnic food festivals. You may want to spend the summer in Milwaukee, where the United Festivals run from June to September, celebrating first Asian foods, then Polish, and on through Italian, German, African, Irish, Mexican, and Native American.

There are also some decidedly weird food festivals. Nearly a 100,000 visitors delight in slimy okra-eating contests at the Okra Strut in South Carolina. You can catch the Product Costume Style Show at the Texas Citrus Festival, where clothes are made with seed buttons, onionskin collars, pulverized tangerine rinds, and other local agricultural products.

Or dine on emu kebabs at the Texas Watermelon Thump and dandelion wedding soup at the Dandelion Mayfest.

Then there are the organic Viagras: Horseradish, chiles, artichokes, tomatoes, yams, and Georgia's rampant kudzu vine (it grows a foot a day) have all been regarded at one time or another as aphrodisiacs. Stockton (Calif.) Asparagus Festival and any of a number of oyster fests claim libidinous side effects. But don't confuse erotic seafood with Montana's Rocky Mountain Oyster Feed, where brave souls, delirious from nonstop country music, feast on calf testicles, just like those at Oklahoma's Calf Fry Festival.

After all this, you may swear off down-home events for more refined festivals, where gourmet restaurants treat visitors to their most exquisite fare. Cities all over the United States hold "Taste" festivals that showcase top area restaurants. Santa Fe's Wine & Chile Fiesta features cooking demonstrations by nationally-recognized chefs, horseback rides to mesa-top campfire breakfasts, and delicacies from more than 60 of the town's renowned restaurants. In the Northwest, 300,000 know a good thing when they taste it at the Bite of Seattle, which showcases dozens of local restaurants. In California, the La Jolla Festival of the Arts and Food Faire combines showings by more than 175 award-winning US artists with a variety of cuisines from more than 20 international gourmet restaurants. Nearby, the Taste of San Diego is part of the state's largest annual food-and-music festival.

What's missing from US festivals, though, is the kind of action you may not have seen since college-cafeteria days. Fair-goers to Brussels' *Gilles de Binche* end up in a huge orange-throwing melee. And tomatoes may lose their aphrodisiac potential if you spend much time in Buñol, Spain at *La Tomatina*, the greatest food fight in the world, where you'll be bathed in half a million (120 tons) smashed tomatoes.

Whether you eat the food, wear it, parade in it, throw it, or bathe in it, there are enough culinary events out there to satisfy the appetite of even the hungriest festival-goer.

Menu

Event Name	City	State	Phone	Month	#Days	Att. (000)	
Central New York Maple Festival	Marathon	NY	607-849-3278	Apr.	3	60	BREAKFAST
World Grits Festival	St. George	SC	803-563-3255	Apr.	3	45	
Vermont Maple Festival	St. Albans	VT	802-524-2444	Apr.	3	40	
Gumbo Festival	Bridge City	LA	504-436-4712	Aug.	3	100	LUNCH
Jambalaya Festival	Sorrento	LA	504-622-2331	Apr.	3	25	
Republic of Texas Chilympiad	San Marcos	TX	512-396-5400	Sep.	N/A	N/A	
National Peanut Festival	Dothan	AL	334-793-4323	Nov.	9	136	
Heard Museum Guild Indian Fair & Market	Phoenix	AZ	602-252-8840	Mar.	2	20	
Kudzu Takeover Day and Crafts Fair	Lumpkin	GA	912-838-6262	Aug.	1	14	
Rattlesnake Roundup & Prairie Folk Festival	Sharon Springs	KS	913-852-4473	May	3	2	AFTERNOON SNACK
Rocky Mountain Oyster Feed	Clinton	MT	406-825-4968	Sep.	5	13	
Dandelion Mayfest	Dover	OH	216-932-2145	May	2	10	
Calf Fry Festival	Vinita	OK	918-256-7133	Sep.	2	10	
Gatorfest	Anahuac	TX	409-267-4190	Sep.	3	25	
Sweetwater Rattlesnake Roundup	Sweetwater	TX	915-235-5466	Mar.	3	30	
Fiery Food Festival	Pasco	WA	509-545-0738	Sep.	2	50	
Great Wisconsin Cheese Festival	Little Chute	WI	414-788-7390	Jun.	3	15	
Matsuri Festival of Japan	Phoenix	AZ	602-262-5071	Feb.	2	40	
The Great Monterey Squid Festival	Monterey	CA	408-649-6544	May	2	30	
Boggy Bayou Mullet Festival	Niceville	FL	850-678-1615	Oct.	3	175	
World Chicken Festival	London	KY	606-878-6900	Sep.	4	20	
Mudbug Madness	Shreveport	LA	800-551-8682	May	3	120	
St. Mary's County Oyster Festival	Leonardtown	MD	301-863-5015	Oct.	2	25	
Maine Lobster Festival	Rockland	ME	800-562-2529	Aug.	5	10	DINNER
Yarmouth Clam Festival	Yarmouth	ME	207-846-3984	Jul.	3	150	
Bourne Scallop Festival	Bourne	MS	508-759-6000	Sep.	3	50	
World Catfish Festival	Belzoni	MS	800-408-4838	Apr.	1	20	
Bronx African-American and Caribbean Heritage Festival	Bronx	NY	718-367-1754	Sep.	1	15	
Italian Heritage & Food Festival	Buffalo	NY	716-874-6133	Jul.	5	100	
Oktoberfest-Zinzinnati	Cincinnati	OH	800-246-2987	Sep.	2	N/A	
Chincoteague Oyster Festival	Chincoteague	VA	804-336-6161	Oct.	N/A	N/A	
Gilroy Garlic Festival	Gilroy	CA	408-842-1625	Jul.	3	123	GARNISHES
International Horseradish Festival	Collinsville	IL	618-344-2884	Jun.	2	10	
Phelps Sauerkraut Festival	Phelps	NY	315-548-5691	Aug.	4	10	
Ohio Honey Festival	Oxford	OH	513-868-5891	Sep.	3	20	
Castroville Artichoke Festival	Castroville	CA	408-633-2465	Sep.	2	N/A	
Stockton Asparagus Festival	Stockton	CA	209-467-8001	Apr.	3	80	
Vidalia Onion Festival	Vidalia	GA	912-538-8687	Apr.	4	60	SIDE DISHES
Potato Bowl	Grand Forks	ND	800-866-4566	Sep.	7	N/A	
Okra Strut	Irmo	SC	803-781-9878	Sep.	2	60	
East Texas Yamboree	Gilmer	TX	903-843-2413	Oct.	3	100	
Tomato Festival	Jacksonville	TX	903-586-2217	Jun.	1	10	
Florida Strawberry Festival	Plant City	FL	813-752-9194	Mar.	11	850	
Peach Festival	Romeo	MI	810-752-4436	Sep.	4	N/A	FRUITS
South Carolina Peach Festival	Gaffney	SC	864-489-5721	Jul.	2	25	
Texas Citrus Festival	Mission	TX	956-585-9724	Feb.	4	800	
Texas Watermelon Thump	Luling	TX	830-875-2082	Jun.	3	35	
La Fiesta de los Chiles	Tucson	AZ	520-326-9686	Oct.	2	12	
Boston Scooper Bowl	Boston	MA	617-632-3300	Jun.	6	25	DESSERTS
Kutztown Pennsylvania German Festival	Kutztown	PA	800-963-8824	Jun.	9	50	
Chocolate City Festival	Burlington	WI	414-763-6044	May	3	100	
La Jolla Festival of the Arts and Food Faire	La Jolla	CA	619-456-1268	Jun.	N/A	N/A	
Taste of San Diego	San Diego	CA	619-236-1212	Sep.	3	85	ADDITIONAL
Taste of Chicago	Chicago	IL	312-744-3315	Jun.	11	3,650	
Santa Fe Wine & Chile Festival	Santa Fe	NM	505-438-8060	Sep.	5	2	
Bite of Seattle	Seattle	WA	206-232-2982	Jun.	11	N/A	
United Festivals	Milwaukee	WI	414-273-3950	Jun.	N/A	N/A	

G-Wiz, You Call This Fun?

The modern age of the amusement park began in 1884 when the world's first roller coaster was built at New York's Coney Island. By today's standards, the first coaster was about as exciting as a Congressional filibuster. Coney's Switchback Railway ride stood 15 feet tall and ran a heart-stopping four mph. Well, you gotta start somewhere.

In the old days, people looking for amusement were likely to take stately rides to the country or, if they really wanted a wild time, organize picnics. Today's fun-lover is looking for more: sensory intensity, excitement, and an adrenalin rush that puts one's concentration squarely on the moment at hand. After all, it's hard to let your mind wander when you're hurtling downhill on a pair of skinny tracks at nearly 90 mph.

Newer and faster rides began to evolve at the early amusement parks, which were called trolley parks because they were operated and serviced by trolley companies. By the 1950s, though, automobiles had put most trolley companies out of business. Only the best, most well-run amusement parks struggled on and even they appeared to be on their last legs.

Then the amusement gods sent a savior to Earth. Walt Disney took old ideas of fun and dressed them up in modern 1955 concepts, combining rides, shows, restaurants, and, most important, a theme. Disneyland became an immediate smash. Other companies soon expanded on Disney's idea. Now, enormous theme parks such as Six Flags and Great America set the definition for amusement parks. (Walt Disney World in Florida has become a category unto itself, see page 223.) The latest twist, water parks, sends nearly 10 million people a year laughing and screaming down water-filled tubes and slides.

The 250 million people who visit amusement parks each year don't need the word *fun* in the park's name—although it's used more than any other adjective—to know that the sights, smells, sounds, and action promise a good time. Some go for the entertainment. Most get pleasure from just being out with lots of people. But for those not

lucky enough to be astronauts or fighter pilots, there may be no better source for an instant adrenalin rush than a roller coaster. Speed, force, and velocity are natural allies for destruction, making roller coasters the maximum thrill you can get in a safe environment.

Today's coasters often take off with riders standing or hanging from the bottoms of the rails. They make loops and corkscrews and heart-stopping drops. They provide lots of heart-in-the-mouth "air time" that lifts riders off their seats. Veteran riders know that front seats give smoother rides, but more extreme G-forces. Third seats on nonlooping coasters are best for negative Gs (weightless "hang time"). Back seats offer the most severe force of the drops. Sitting over the wheels gives rougher jolts.

Many parks also use propellers, bungee cords, swings, and other devices to create the G-forces and sudden drops thrill-seekers crave. But no matter what the method, for most of us, amusement parks still provide the mental and physical challenge thrill-seekers call the ultimate fun.

Top Ten Best-Attended US Theme Parks (annual attend.)

Disneyland, Anaheim, Calif.—15,000,000
The Magic Kingdom, Walt Disney World,
  Lake Buena Vista, Fla.—13,803,000
Epcot, Walt Disney World, Lake Buena Vista, Fla.—11,235,000
Disney-MGM Studios, Walt Disney World,
  Lake Buena Vista, Fla.—9,975,000
Universal Studios Florida, Orlando, Fla.—8,400,000
Universal Studios Hollywood, Universal City, Calif.—5,400,000
Sea World of Florida, Orlando, Fla.—5,100,000
Busch Gardens, Tampa, Fla.—4,170,000
Six Flags Great Adventure, Jackson, NJ—4,000,000
Sea World of California, San Diego, Calif.—3,890,000

October 1999

M	T	W	T	F	S	S
				1	2	3
4	5	6	7	8	9	10
11	12	13	14	15	16	17
18	19	20	21	22	23	24
25	26	27	28	29	30	31

Orlando (Lake Buena Vista), Florida, USA

October 2000

M	T	W	T	F	S	S
						1
2	3	4	5	6	7	8
9	10	11	12	13	14	15
16	17	18	19	20	21	22
23	24	25	26	27	28	29
30	31					

Disney World

(Walt Disney World)

A FunGuide 100 Destination

Admit it. There's a kid in you that just loves the idea of wallowing in *Disney World*. Rides, attractions, and even large, fuzzy cartoon characters never completely lose their appeal, but the park's often-overlooked emphasis on entertainment for grown-ups is a bigger draw than many fun-seekers realize.

The Orlando offspring of the California original that invented the concept "theme park," *Disney World* has grown into a recreation district unrivaled perhaps anywhere on the globe. It covers 47 square miles—that's about twice the size of Manhattan Island—and in addition to the Magic Kingdom (more-or-less a facsimile of California's Disneyland) there's: Epcot Center, a world's-fair-cum-shopping-mall specializing in global iconography and corporate sponsorship; the Disney-MGM Studios, an ersatz production facility spiked with rides and shows; Disney's new 500-acre Animal Kingdom, an ostensibly cage-free salute to our relationship with animals; and two after-dusk entertainment zones, including a gated-admission nightclub island.

For much of the year, neophytes will find Walt's huge, shrewd machine defies concise touring plans. Tables for good restaurants are tied up weeks ahead, scampering moppets clog every artery, and lines for the best attractions can top two hours (summer and holidays are the worst). Industry estimates point to *Disney World*'s theme parks posting an average of more than 100,000 admissions a day in 1997. So the perfect time to visit is when you'll encounter the shortest lines and the fewest families: early and mid-November, early December, and mid-January are all quiet. Mid-October is the best time to find sublime weather and breathing room between the tourists.

What follows is a mere greatest-hits itinerary, rather than a top-to-bottom expedition strategy. You need a solid week to fully navigate it all, because *Disney World* also includes three lavishly themed water parks, five-and-a-half immaculately groomed golf courses, a *Fantasia*-inspired miniature golf course, and more. Today's *Disney World* adds up to a unique, 25,000-room resort/playground for everyone who refuses to stop being a kid, at least once in a while.

Disney World

Day 1. Thu. Oct. 14, 1999
(Day 1. Thursday October 19, 2000)

8:00am Check in at Disney's **Grand Floridian Resort and Spa**, Mickey's premium digs, themed after turn-of-the-century Florida resorts. Then drive or monorail to Epcot Center to be inside the gates before the "official" 9 a.m. opening. Ride Spaceship Earth, a fast-aging attraction about communication, inside the 180-foot-high silver golf ball. Make a beeline for the brand-new Test Track, the ambitious speed ride simulating vehicle-performance testing. Skip the GM car showroom and head for *Honey, I Shrunk the Audience*, an 18-minute, 3-D cinematic crowd-pleaser with surprising tactile effects. These three are Epcot's big kahunas—you'll want to knock them off first thing.

10:15am Ride Journey into Imagination, an archetypal Disney *magnum opus* about creativity, then head to Living with the Land, a boat ride through dioramas and greenhouses that show how man can dominate Mother Nature through technology. Also tour The Living Seas.

11:45am Leave Future World and enter World Showcase. Take a quick spin through the Mexico pavilion, but pass on the seductive-looking boat ride—it's a sorry infomercial for south-of-the-border tourism. Head to Norway and experience the cheery Maelstrom, the only real ride in World Showcase. The oft-missed Stave Church Gallery is a sanctuary from the throng.

12:30pm Tender a hearty *koldtbord* at Norway's **Restaurant Akershus** (make reservations), one of Epcot's more successful eateries. Continue your tour of the World Showcase arena with China, Western Europe, Japan, Morocco, the United Kingdom, and Canada. Of several promotional movies, *Impressions de France* is the best; the patriotic *American Adventure* is a large-scale, 29-minute production.

4:00pm Return to Future World and Body Wars, a ride about a miniaturized voyage through the human body. Walk through Innoventions, a huge area exhibiting consumer products. If you stay late, have a snack and catch the incredible fireworks around the lake at 9 p.m.

9:30pm Bus to Downtown Disney and **Bongo's Cuban Cafe** (no reservations; a wait is likely after 8 p.m.), a camp tribute to Ricky Ricardo's Havana, complete with Cuba libres and music. After dinner, stop at *Planet Hollywood*, more a tourist attraction than a place to eat. Take in the music and scene at the **House of Blues**—it's modeled after an old-time Mississippi juke joint and showcases folk art from the Mississippi Delta (a Gospel brunch burns down the house on Sundays).

Day 2. Fri. Oct. 15, 1999
(Day 2. Friday October 20, 2000)

8:30am Enter the Magic Kingdom and head down Main Street to the Central Plaza in front of Cinderella Castle to get into position for the rope drop. At 9 a.m., bolt for Space Mountain and ride. Then quickly cross the park to Frontierland and experience Splash Mountain and Big Thunder Mountain Railroad. The three mountains are the park's biggest attractions and will grow long lines as the day wears on.

10:30am Ride the Jungle Cruise, Pirates of the Caribbean, and Haunted Mansion, a triumvirate of Disney classics. Head back to Tomorrowland—grab a snack at **Cosmic Ray's Starlight Cafe** (the veggie burgers are decent) before tackling the technoterror of Alien Encounter. Rinse that nasty aftertaste with the new Buzz Lightyear's Space Ranger Spin and the frisky Timekeeper. Wrap up your magical day with Fantasyland's It's a Small World, a saccharine rejoinder to your day at Epcot.

3:30pm Monorail to the Grand Floridian for afternoon tea at the **Garden View Lounge**. Relax poolside or on the lakefront beach, or check out the Grand Floridian's spa.

6:30pm Take the bus to Disney's BoardWalk Resort. Dinner at the **Flying Fish Cafe** (make reservations two weeks ahead) is a seafood treat amid a frolicking carny/sealife ambience.

8:30pm After dinner, explore Disney's wood-decked BoardWalk entertainment area, themed with an East Coast seaside leitmotif. **Jellyrolls Dueling Pianos** is pure fun. Try the **Atlantic Dance Hall** for martinis and occasional big-band dancing, or chill out in **The Belle Vue Room**, a 1930s sitting room adorned with antique radios playing nostalgic shows.

Day 3. Sat.   Oct. 16, 1999
(Day 3. Saturday   October 21, 2000)

8:00am Be at the front entrance to Animal Kingdom in time for opening. Head straight for Countdown to Extinction, a rollicking thrill ride into the Cretaceous era. Do the Kilimanjaro Safaris, a 20-minute adventure through the main wildlife enclosure (animals are most visible in the early morning). Walk the Gorilla Falls trail—note the detail of Harambe village.

10:00am Travel to the ruins of Asia and ride Tiger Rapids Run, a raft ride through a burning forest; walk the Maharajah Jungle Trek to see the Bengal tigers. Finish at the Tree of Life, a fabulous cement icon with more than 300 animals carved into its trunk. At its base is a theater where you'll find *It's Tough To Be a Bug*, a hilarious 3-D movie.

11:15am Board a bus for the Disney-MGM Studios. Ride Star Tours, a motion simulator based on the *Star Wars* franchise, and see *Muppet Vision*, another 3-D movie, starring the Muppets' cornball antics.

12:30pm Lunch at the **Hollywood Brown Derby** (make reservations), where drawings of legendary characters ornament the walls.

1:30pm Note the start time for the afternoon parade (usually 1:30 or 3:00 p.m.) and time your visit to the Tower of Terror to coincide with it. The studios' biggest hit, the Tower is a prodigious, special-effects-enhanced free fall that rates among Disney's best. Also see the Indiana Jones Adventure, the Great Movie Ride's history of Hollywood, and the Magic of Disney Animation (where *Mulan* was made). The Backlot Tour provides little filmmaking insight, but lots of crowd-pleasing explosions. Of several musical shows, the *Hunchback of Notre Dame* is the snazziest.

6:00pm Finish at the studios with the first performance of *Fantasmic*, a fireworks-and-laser spectacular held after dusk.

8:00pm Monorail to dinner at the **California Grill**. A tribute to Wolfgang Puck-style cuisine, it's Disney's best restaurant. Located on the 15th floor of the Contemporary Resort, it has a great view of the Kingdom fireworks show (make reservations at least two weeks ahead).

10:00pm Head downtown to **Pleasure Island**, a theme park for nightclubbing—country, jazz, rock, and disco are housed in first-class venues. The quirky Adventurer's Club is an improvisational all-night sketch set in a 1930s social club for world explorers. The nightly New Year's Eve street party starts at 11 p.m, providing a perfect way to close out one fun three-day chapter and ring in another.

Alternatives

The Michael Graves-designed **Walt Disney World Swan** and **Dolphin**, where over-the-top Floridian colors and themes meet postmodern whimsy, are two good alternative hotels. The Dolphin, particularly, epitomizes fun. It also has a nightclub, the **Cocabanana Club**.

Disney's three water parks are a blast. The most thrilling is Blizzard Beach, a mock ski resort where the world's highest water slide (fashioned after a ski jump) towers over the Florida landscape.

The Hot Sheet

HOTELS		ADDRESS	PH	FX		PRICE	RMS	BEST ROOMS
Grand Floridian Resort and Spa	★	4401 Grand Floridian Way	407-934-7639	407-824-3186		$$$$+	900	Lodge tower or vw of Seven Seas Lagoon
Walt Disney World Swan (Westin) and Dolphin (Sheraton)	Alt	1200-1500 Epcot Resorts Blvd.	407-934-3000 800-248-7926	407-934-4710		$$$$+	2267	Club rm w/ balc and resort vw

RESTAURANTS	DAY	ADDRESS	PH	PRICE	REC	DRESS	FOOD
Bongo's Cuban Cafe	1	Downtown Disney, West Side	407-828-0999	$$	D/L	Kazh, Local	Cuban
The California Grill	3	4600 N. World Dr., Contemporary Resort, 15th flr.	407-939-3463	$$$	D	Kazh	American, seafood
Cosmic Ray's Starlight Cafe	2	at the Magic Kingdom	407-939-3463	$	L	Kazh, Local	American
Flying Fish Cafe	2	on the BoardWalk	407-939-5100	$$$	D	Kazh	American, seafood
Garden View Lounge	2	at the Grand Floridian Resort and Spa	407-824-3000	$$	T	Kazh	Afternoon tea
Hollywood Brown Derby	3	at Disney-MGM Studios	407-934-7639	$$	L/D	Kazh	American, seafood
Restaurant Akershus	1	at Epcot Center	407-939-3463	$$	L/D	Kazh, Local	Norwegian, seafood

NIGHTLIFE	DAY	ADDRESS	PH	COVER	REC*	DRESS	MUSIC
Atlantic Dance Hall	2	on the BoardWalk	407-939-5100	$	P	Kazh	'60s, '70s & '80s
The Belle Vue Room	2	lobby of the BoardWalk Inn	407-939-5100	None	R	Kazh	
Cocabanana	Alt	see Swan and Dolphin hotels	407-934-3000	None	M	Kazh	Disco
House of Blues	1	Downtown Disney West Side	407-934-2583	$ – $$$$+	M	Kazh	Varies
Jellyrolls Dueling Pianos	2	on the BoardWalk	407-939-5100	$	M	Kazh, Local	Varies
Pleasure Island	3	Downtown Disney	407-934-7781	$$	MP	Kazh, Local	Wide variety

Hot Tip: Disney Resort guests (including Swan and Dolphin) may take advantage of an early-admission program called Surprise Mornings. Each of the main theme parks is opened 60 to 90 minutes early two or three days each week—the result is minimal lines for the big attractions at first, but higher-than-usual attendance by late morning. Either take advantage of the early-admission policy by arriving at 7:30 a.m., or skip the assigned Surprise Morning park for that day (the itinerary provided does not incorporate the early-admission days).

Event & Ticket Info

Walt Disney World offers a variety of ticket options. Most convenient is the length of stay pass which provides unlimited admission to all attractions (including Pleasure Island and water parks) from the morning of your arrival through the night of your departure. Prices vary based on the number of nights. Purchase tickets in advance through the *Walt Disney Travel Company* (800-828-0228).

* M=Live music; P=Dancing (Party); R=Bar only; S=Show; (F)=Food served. For further explanation of codes, see page 14.

 NYC Orlando (ORL) <30 min./$25 Yes/No 66°/83° (19°/28°)

October 1999 — Key West, Florida, USA — October 2000

Fantasy Fest

Origin: 1979   Event ★ ★ ★ ★ ★ ★ ★ City   Attendance: 100,000

if your fantasies have ever included watching a gorgeous sunset on a sandy beach with daiquiri in hand, then dancing in the streets until morning with the world's friendliest and most imaginative extroverts, *Fantasy Fest* may be your dream come true. An international cast of revelers explore and exhibit their own fantasies during this 10-day festival that's one of the country's wildest and most colorful. If party god Bacchus were to star in a Looney Tunes cartoon, the result might look like *Fantasy Fest*.

The festival's grand finale is a lunatic twilight parade down Duval Street, the city's main drag, that draws as many as 70,000 people—twice the population of the island. The giddy crowd mills around, gawking at one outrageous costume after another. Local saloons throw rambunctious parties that don't wind down until 4 a.m.

Key West's always been famous for its *laissez-faire* attitude, but during *Fantasy Fest*, the city's casual "no dress code" rule is, well, modified. Spirited revelers roam the streets in costumes that range from amazing to absurd—the recent 20-foot, spaghetti-spouting spaceship qualified as both. Annual themes—"BC," "Call of the Wild," "Lost in the '60s"—inspire costume ideas. And though nudity is not allowed, body paint usually squeaks by as a costume.

Fantasy Fest began in 1979 when local merchants threw a Halloween party hoping to entice a few out-of-towners to the town's empty off-season hotels and restaurants. Hundreds came in costume to watch a ragtag parade that included a Rolls-Royce whose famous naked-lady hood ornament was replaced by a real naked lady, painted gold. Wire-service photos intrigued revelers and got the festival rolling.

Now, the fantasy takes over this picturesque and friendly island. Most of Key West's many excellent restaurants and 150-plus bars encourage the craziness. There's something perversely fun about dining at a four-star restaurant when the table to your left is occupied by a family of coneheads and the one to your right includes a group of burly men in petticoats.

Fantasy Fest

Day 1. Thu. Oct. 28, 1999
(Day 1. Thursday *October 26, 2000)*

10:30am Check into the **Ocean Key House Resort and Marina**. With Jacuzzi suites at the edge of the harbor, it puts you in the center of the action.

11:00am Walk four blocks along the historic waterfront to **Pepe's Cafe** and select from omelet and pancake specials. Established in 1909, it's Key West's oldest restaurant.

Noon Across the street at funky **B.O.'s Fish Wagon**, grab eats for your afternoon sailing trip. Proprietor Buddy Owen is a Conch (or Key West native, it's pronounced *konk*) who'll box you up famous Square Grouper fish sandwiches—named after the bales of marijuana that used to wash ashore during Key West's smuggling days.

1:00pm Don't miss Key West's greatest attraction: North America's only living coral reef. The **Sebago Catamaran** will sail you comfortably to the reef for a three-and-a-half-hour snorkeling adventure with beer and wine on the trip back.

6:00pm A block from your hotel is the world-famous, nightly **Mallory Square Sunset Celebration**. Jugglers, acrobats, and musicians perform, as oglers await the glorious, sometimes-applauded sunsets over the Gulf of Mexico.

7:30pm Dine at the Pier House Resort's popular **Harbor View Cafe** where, tonight, your highly coveted table on the waterfront patio becomes a theater box seat for ...

9:00pm ... the annual **Pretenders in Paradise International Costume Contest**. The biggest contest of the festival, it's set on a huge stage on the beach. Professional costume builders come from around the world to entertain the standing-room-only crowd. Amateur-division entries are often hysterical.

11:00pm Head up Whitehead Street to the **Green Parrot Bar**, the oldest bar in Florida. This working-class rock-and-roll club holds a raucous costume contest open to all.

Day 2. Fri. Oct. 29, 1999
(Day 2. Friday *October 27, 2000)*

9:00am Wait in line at **Camille's** on Duval for a satisfying breakfast. Try the French toast made with homemade bread.

10:30am Stroll down Duval, the Historic District's main thoroughfare, to the **Shipwreck Historium**. It celebrates Key West's nautical history and the "wrecking" business that once made Key West the wealthiest city in America. Cross the street to **The Mel Fisher Maritime Museum** to see examples of $200 million in gold, silver, and emeralds salvaged from the richest Spanish shipwreck ever.

Noon Stop into the European-style sidewalk cafe, **Mangoes**, for a gourmet pizza and views of the Duval bustle.

2:00pm The **Street Fair** on Duval gets rolling with arts, crafts, food, beer, beer, and more beer. Shop for costumes and accessories for tomorrow's big parade. Visit **Fast Buck Freddie's** to watch master mask-maker Michael Stark create fantastic masks and headdresses.

3:00pm Stop at **Flamingo Crossing**, a homemade-ice-cream shop with unusual flavors, such as sour sop and key lime.

4:00pm Wander all the way up Duval Street to the clothing-optional **Atlantic Shores Resort Pool Bar** for a cold drink. No matter what you wear, you'll be overdressed.

5:00pm Walk to the Key West Cemetery, famous for headstones with epitaphs such as "I told you I was sick" and "At least I know where he's sleeping tonight." It's the staging area for the *Masquerade March*, a wacky procession of grown-ups that trick-or-treats its way through bars and guest houses en route to The Ocean Key House's Sunset Pier.

7:00pm A block from the pier, **Bagatelle** serves exquisite Caribbean cuisine. A table on the wraparound veranda is perfect for watching the growing chaos in the streets.

9:00pm The *Masquerade Fantasies* costume contest on the Ocean Key House Pier is open to walk-ons as well as serious costumers who've labored long for big prizes. Early birds get the few convenient seats.

11:00pm At nearby **Jimmy Buffet's Margaritaville**, chill with perfect margaritas and live entertainment. Jimmy might be there, but he'll be hard to spot among the masqueraders. (Hint: He's the guy who has lost his shaker of salt.)

Day 3. Sat.   Oct. 30, 1999
(Day 3. Saturday   October 28, 2000)

10:30am Once a bordello, **Blue Heaven** is now a backyard patio restaurant famous for generous breakfasts and quirky ambience. Yes, that *is* a rooster under your table.

Noon The **Conch Tour Train** takes you around the island. You'll learn about local history, architecture, vegetation, and more.

2:30pm Back in town, the *Duval Street Promenade* has begun. There's live entertainment as partyers in costume start arriving for the parade. At the Hilton Resort and Marina, get a temporary tattoo or have your body painted at the *Airbrush Artist Competition*.

3:30pm At the **801 Bourbon Bar**, the *Tea Dance* gets you mingling with that segment of the *Fantasy Fest* crowd that just can't wait to be outrageous.

5:00pm Put on your costume and get to **Alice's** on Duval for a preparade dinner. Sample the New World Fusion Confusion Cuisine, typified by dishes such as Mexican pot-stickers and Florida yellowtail over curried couscous. Huge windows offer views of ever-weirder and -wilder costumers.

7:00pm The *Fantasy Fest Parade* has begun! Don't worry if you're still dining—it'll take at least two more hours for the parade to travel the 12 blocks to the judge's reviewing stand near Alice's. After dinner, you'll encounter true oddities along some of the safest streets in the country. TV lights in the front of the Holiday Inn La Concha make it one of the best viewing locations.

11:00pm Duval will be packed until 1 a.m. For a change of scenery, head to the historic seaport for an icy beer at the definitively funky **Schooner Wharf Bar**. With live blues and Motown, it's the locally elected favorite bar in Key West and the perfect place to shed your costume and maybe jump into the harbor to cool off.

Alternatives

A short walk from Duval Street, the **Hyatt Key West** has a small beach along with first-class accommodations. The **Pier House Resort and Caribbean Spa** equips your stay with restaurants, bars, a spa, and the only downtown beach.

Cafe **Karumba** serves West Indies and Caribbean cuisine, such as curried *rotis* and jerk chicken, and its extensive rum bar makes daiquiris and mojitos from scratch. **La Trattoria** offers fine Italian dining with a fabulous *tiramisu*. **P.T.'s** sports bar and restaurant serves tasty ribs and sandwiches until late.

On *Fantasy Fest* Thursday, **Sloppy Joe's** annual toga party makes this live-music bar even wilder than usual. Try **Hog's Breath Saloon**'s house beer and fresh seafood from the raw bar, then check out live entertainment on the patio, which includes a homemade-bikini contest.

The Fun Also Rises

The Hot Sheet

HOTELS		ADDRESS	PH	FX	PRICE	RMS	BEST ROOMS
Hyatt Key West	Alt	601 Front St.	305-296-9900 800-233-1234	908-632-3025	$$$	120	Gulf vw
Ocean Key House Resort and Marina	★	0 Duval St.	305-296-7701 800-328-9815	305-292-7685	$$$$	95	All 900 sq ft suites, harbor front
Pier House Resort and Caribbean Spa	Alt	1 Duval St.	305-296-4600 800-327-8340	305-296-9085	$$$	142	Harbor front

RESTAURANTS	DAY	ADDRESS	PH	PRICE	REC	DRESS	FOOD
Alice's	3	1114 Duval St.	305-292-4888	$$	D	Local	Asian, South American
B.O.'s Fish Wagon	1	801 Caroline St.	305-294-9272	$	L/D	Local	Seafood
Bagatelle	2	115 Duval St.	305-296-6609	$$	D/L	Local	Caribbean
Blue Heaven	3	729 Thomas St.	305-296-8666	$	B/LD	Local	American
Cafe Karumba	Alt	1215 Duval St.	305-296-2644	$$	D	Local	West Indian, Caribbean
Camille's	2	703 1/2 Duval St.	305-296-4811	$	B/LD	Local	American
Flamingo Crossing	2	1105 Duval St.	305-296-6124	$	T	Local	Ice cream
Harbor View Cafe	1	see Pier House Resort	305-296-4600	$$	D/BL	Local	American
Mangoes	2	700 Duval St.	305-292-4606	$	L/D	Local	Continental
P.T.'s	Alt	920 Caroline St.	305-296-4245	$$	LD	Local	American
Pepe's Cafe	1	806 Caroline St.	305-294-7192	$	B/LD	Local	American
La Trattoria	Alt	524 Duval St.	305-296-1075	$$	D	Local	Italian

NIGHTLIFE	DAY	ADDRESS	PH	COVER	REC*	DRESS	MUSIC
801 Bourbon Bar	3	801 Duval St.	305-294-4737	None	S	Local	
Atlantic Shores Resort Pool Bar	2	510 South St.	305-296-2491	None	R(F)	Local	
Green Parrot Bar	1	601 Whitehead St.	305-294-6133	None	MP	Local	Rock, salsa, blues, swing
Hog's Breath Saloon	Alt	400 Front St.	305-292-2032	None	MP(F)	Local	Rock, pop
Jimmy Buffet's Margaritaville	2	500 Duval St.	305-292-1435	None	MP(F)	Local	Rock, blues
Schooner Wharf Bar	3	202 William St.	305-292-9520	None	MP(F)	Local	Blues, jazz, Motown
Sloppy Joe's	Alt	201 Duval St.	305-294-5717	$	MP(F)	Local	Country, rock

SIGHTS & ATTRACTIONS	DAY	ADDRESS	PH	ENTRY FEE
Conch Tour Train	3	303 Front St.	305-294-5161	$$
Fast Buck Freddie's	2	500 Duval St.	305-294-2007	None
Mallory Square Sunset Celebration	1	Mallory Sq.		None
The Mel Fisher Maritime Museum	2	200 Greene St.	305-294-2633	$
Sebago Catamaran	1	200 William St.	305-294-5687	$$$
Shipwreck Historium	2	1 Whitehead St.	305-292-8990	$
Chamber of Commerce		402 Wall St.	305-294-2587	

> ## Event & Ticket Info
>
> **Fantasy Fest**: Events are free. For a schedule of events, contact *Fantasy Fest Headquarters* (305-296-1817).

* M=Live music; P=Dancing (Party); R=Bar only; S=Show; (F)=Food served. For further explanation of codes, see page 14.

 NYC   Key West (EYW) <30 min./$5 No 76°/84° (24°/29°)

Guavaween

Origin: 1984   Event ★ ★ ★ ★ ★ City   **Attendance:** 100,000

One part Latin *carnaval*, a shot of costumed Halloween revelry, and a dash of Mardi Gras madness, ***Guavaween*** shakes up Tampa's Ybor City neighborhood. On the Saturday before Halloween, this intoxicating street party kicks off with the ***Mama Guava Stumble***—a parade of outlandish characters led by the mythical matriarch, Mama Guava. She delivers on her vow to take the "bore" out of "E-bore" City by inspiring extravagantly dressed party-goers to take over the town in an evening of live music, dancing, and fun.

Guavaween is a combination of *Halloween* and a tribute to Tampa's nickname, The Big Guava, which it got from the attempts of local pioneer Gavino Gutiérrez to cultivate the tropical fruit commercially. His enterprise failed, but a local newspaper columnist was able to plant the idea that if New York was The Big Apple, then Tampa must be The Big Guava. The Tampa area is as sun-drenched and zesty as a ripe guava, with a history that's as fascinating as the fruit is plump. From the Spanish explorers who founded it, to the pirates who once preyed upon ships in its bay, Tampa wears its past proudly.

In Spanish, *tampa* means "sticks of fire," and the city was once known as the Cigar Capital of the World. Ybor City is Tampa's oldest neighborhood, the former Spanish quarter and cigar-rolling section of town. Its enduring red-brick streets and century-old architecture give it a historic flavor. Nowadays, Ybor's old warehouses and cigar factories have been converted into nightclubs, galleries, and restaurants, making it Tampa's most happening area.

When you're not romping through the streets of Ybor City or exploring Tampa's revitalized downtown, you can cross the bay to enjoy the beaches and bars at the end of The Pier in St. Petersburg. Your three-day visit will provide just the right combination of relaxing days and wild costumed nights—and give you a whole new perspective on the not-so-humble guava.

Day-By-Day Plan For

Guavaween

Day 1. Thu. Oct. 28, 1999
(Day 1. Thursday   October 26, 2000)

9:00am Your three-day home on its own island in Tampa Bay, the four-star **Wyndham Harbour Island Hotel**, is centrally located—a mere 90-second People Mover monorail ride from downtown—and luxurious.

10:00am Make the scenic drive to historic Old Hyde Park Village. At one of **Joffrey's Coffee and Tea Co.** outdoor tables, order hot croissants stuffed with feta and spinach. Afterward, browse through the trendy stores and galleries in this renovated shopping district.

1:30pm Cruise over the Gandy Bridge into St. Petersburg for an afternoon of culture and calm amid quaint streets, many good art galleries, and lovely bay views. At the **Stone Soup Cafe**, join locals lunching on homemade soups, salads, and hearty sandwiches.

2:30pm Drive to the **Salvador Dali Museum** for a look at the world's largest private collection of the surrealist's work. On the 45-minute tour, pay attention to the similarities between the seascape images of Dali's native northern Spain and the pale-blue waters of Tampa Bay.

4:30pm Cha Cha Coconuts, on the St. Petersburg Pier, is part of a chain of tropical-themed bars. Order an afternoon cocktail or iced tea—it doesn't really matter since you're mostly here for terrific views of the bay and its gentle, sandy shores.

5:30pm When the sun merges with the water to the west, be perched on the Lower Gandy Bridge to take in St. Pete's best sunset views. The stunning light show might convince you to stay for dinner at **The Hurricane**, a typical beach-town seafood restaurant. If you do, there's also a disco and rooftop bar that make for a nice ending to the evening. Or ...

7:00pm Head back to Tampa for dinner at the chic **Mise en Place**. The duck salad with raspberry vinaigrette is the kind of delicacy that puts a restaurant on the culinary map. The chocolate-pecan-toffee mousse is equally irresistible. Top off the evening with a stop at its sophisticated jazz club, **442 at Mise en Place**.

Day 2. Fri. Oct. 29, 1999
(Day 2. Friday   October 27, 2000)

10:30am After breakfast, visit the **Tampa Museum of Art**. It has a prominent collection of antiquities and its Florida Gallery highlights Tampa's blossoming art scene. Or you could go to **The Henry B. Plant Museum**, where architecture and opulent furniture are the draw.

12:30pm Return to the Wyndham and enjoy great views and lunch in the upscale atmosphere of your hotel's **Harbourview Room**.

2:30pm Stroll three blocks up Channelside Drive to **The Florida Aquarium**, then wander around displays of thousands of native plants, animals, and sea creatures. The aquarium's 130,000-gallon saltwater habitat contains 20 species of fearsome sharks and friendly rays.

5:00pm After a rugged day of relaxing, close the afternoon with an even more relaxing swim in the Wyndham's heated pool.

8:00pm Cab to the **Columbia Restaurant** (be sure to make reservations well ahead of time). Established in 1905, it's Florida's oldest traditional Spanish and Cuban restaurant. Try the excellent paella and get a close-up view of the exuberant, authentic flamenco-dancing show, which features a flurry of foot stomping, hand clapping, and brightly colored costumes.

The Fun Also Rises

10:00pm When the rest of Tampa shuts down, Ybor City wakes up. Walk along Seventh Avenue, Ybor's hip main drag, where the brick streets are jammed with people—though not as many as there will be tomorrow night—weaving in and out of the clubs and bars that occupy some of the city's historic buildings. Sail through the early hours with a clean-cut crowd, drinks, and local and national bands at the smoky **Blues Ship Cafe**.

Day 3. Sat. Oct. 30, 1999
(Day 3. Saturday   October 28, 2000)

11:00am After a room-service breakfast, take a 30-minute drive to **Busch Gardens**, where you can experience the United States' closest thing to a genuine African safari. The extensive 300-acre theme park includes a world-class zoo of 2,800 animals. Your expedition starts at the Edge of Africa, which includes seven separate habitats for African animals.

1:00pm Wander to the Timbuktu section of the park for lunch at *Das Festhaus*, where you can get a decent cafeteria-style meal while listening to the oompah band in a cavernous hall.

2:30pm From the Sky Ride gondola, watch rhinos play in the African Veldt below. Move on to dolphin, bird, and ice shows before braving Montu, the world's tallest and longest inverted roller coaster, which makes six loops at 60 mph.

5:00pm At the Wyndham, don a *Guavaween* costume that flouts convention and breaks taboos. Since people-watching is the celebration's modus operandi, make sure to wear something—think of the wildest Halloween costume you'd ever wear—that allows you to see and be seen with equal ease. For the terminally bashful, participating as an observer only is also fine.

6:30pm Guarantee a good view of the *Mama Guava Stumble* parade of costumed revelers by arriving in Ybor City by 6 p.m., before the blocked-off streets become packed with party people. A good spot is on the balcony of one of the better clubs, **The Rubb**. Scary, sexy, humorous, political—a full spectrum of costumes colors Ybor. Anything goes on this high-energy night.

8:30pm Take a short walk away from *Guavaween's* swell of partyers for dinner at upscale **Bellini**. The menu provides a varied selection ranging from northern Italian dishes and brick-oven pizzas to filet mignon.

10:00pm *Guavaween* builds to its climax as multiple outdoor stages feature free concerts, transforming Ybor into a huge outdoor club. Sample from the wide selection of tap beers at the **Green Iguana Bar and Grill** or walk a few blocks off the main drag to dance at **Harpo's**. Head home knowing that next year's party is just 365 days away, and you'll probably need most of them to get all the guava madness out of your system.

Alternatives

It might seem strange to honor the 19th-century pirate Gaspar for a career of sinking ships and raiding Tampa Bay, but a pirate parade and series of outdoor concerts throughout town in February have made the *Gasparilla* festival Tampa's other famous event.

The **Hyatt Regency Tampa**, typically Hyatt, provides a convenient location in downtown Tampa. The 1920s-era **Don CeSar Beach Resort and Spa** is a luxurious beachfront resort and spa that offers a quiet alternative on the St. Pete side of the bay.

At **Bern's Steakhouse**, the 85,000-bottle wine cellar is the world's largest, and the steaks are good. The baby-back ribs are worth the 20-minute drive to **Louis Papa's Riverside** in the old fishing village of Tarpon Springs. You can also feast on other hearty dishes in a cute, down-home setting with a riverfront view.

The **Masquerade** draws a younger crowd, but it's the club that put Ybor City on the map of hip. Find your groove on one of the club's three dance floors.

The Hot Sheet

HOTELS		ADDRESS		PH	FX	PRICE	RMS	BEST ROOMS
Don CeSar Beach Resort and Spa	Alt	3400 Gulf Blvd.	(SP)	813-360-1881 800-282-1116	813-367-7597	$$$	275	Bayside city vw
Hyatt Regency Tampa	Alt	2 Tampa Center		813-225-1234 800-233-1234		$$	518	Regency club rm
Wyndham Harbour Island Hotel	★	1725 S. Harbour Island Blvd.		813-229-5000 800-996-3426	813-229-5022	$$	300	Harbour vw–even #s close to 30

RESTAURANTS	DAY	ADDRESS		PH	PRICE	REC	DRESS	FOOD
Bellini	3	2544 McMullen-Booth Rd.		813-724-5716	$$	D/L	Kazh	Italian
Bern's Steakhouse	Alt	1208 S. Howard Ave.		813-251-2421	$$	D	Yuppie	American
Columbia Restaurant	2	2117 E. 7th Ave.		813-248-4961	$$	D/L	Kazh	Spanish, Cuban
Harbourview Room	2	see the Wyndham hotel		813-229-5000	$$	L/BD	Kazh	American
The Hurricane	1	Golf Way at 9th Ave.	(SP)	813-360-9558	$$	D	Kazh	Seafood
Joffrey's Coffee and Tea Co.	1	1628 W. Snow Circle		813-251-3315	$	B/LD	Local	Pastries
Louis Papa's Riverside	Alt	10 W. Dodecanese Blvd.	(TS)	813-937-5101	$$	LD	Local	American
Mise en Place	1	442 Kennedy Blvd.		813-254-5373	$$	D/L	Kazh	New American
Stone Soup Cafe	1	4122 16th St.	(SP)	813-526-2975	$	L	Local	American

NIGHTLIFE	DAY	ADDRESS		PH	COVER	REC*	DRESS	MUSIC
442 at Mise en Place	1	see Mise en Place restaurant		813-254-5373		M	Kazh	Jazz
Blues Ship Cafe	2	1910 E. 7th Ave.		813-248-6097	$	MP	Local	Blues
Cha Cha Coconuts	1	800 2nd Ave. NE	(SP)	813-822-6655	None	M(F)	Local	Acoustic '70s rock
Green Iguana Bar and Grill	3	1708 7th Ave.		813-248-9555	None	R(F)	Local	
Harpo's	3	7th Ave. at 18th Ave.		813-248-4814	None	P	Local	Top 40
The Masquerade	Alt	1503 E. 7th Ave.		813-247-3319	$	P	Local	Hip-hop, alternative
The Rubb	3	1507 E. 7th Ave.		813-247-4225	$	MP	Local	Rock, reggae; swing

SIGHTS & ATTRACTIONS	DAY	ADDRESS		PH	ENTRY FEE
Busch Gardens	3	3000 E. Busch Blvd.		813-987-5082	$$$
The Florida Aquarium	2	701 Channelside Dr.		813-273-4020	$$
The Henry B. Plant Museum	2	401 W. Kennedy Blvd.		813-254-1891	$
Salvador Dali Museum	1	1000 3rd St. S	(SP)	813-823-3767	$
Tampa Museum of Art	2	600 N. Ashley Dr.		813-274-8130	$
Tampa/Hillsborough CVA		400 N. Tampa St.		813-223-1111	

Event & Ticket Info

Guavaween (Ybor City): Tickets ($8) are available in advance from *Ticketmaster* (813-287-8844), or can be purchased at the gate. The event never sells out. For more information, contact *CC Events Productions Inc.* (813-621-7121).

Alternative Event
Gasparilla: *Tampa/Hillsborough Convention and Visitors Association*, 813-223-1111

SP=Saint Petersburg; TS=Tarpon Springs

* M=Live music; P=Dancing (Party); R=Bar only; S=Show; (F)=Food served. For further explanation of codes, see page 14.

 NYC   Tampa (TPA) <30 min./$15 Yes   66°/84° (19°/29°)

The Fun Also Rises

Hookers' Ball/ Halloween

San Francisco, California, USA

Origin: 1978 | **Event** ★★★★★★★★★ **City** | **Attendance:** 50,000

The world's greatest *Halloween* party and the *Hookers' Halloween Ball* could only happen in San Francisco. Tens of thousands of the world's least inhibited partyers make Halloween the highlight of their year, dressing in outrageous costumes for the Castro street party (the Mutilated Mailman Who Met Cujo is a favorite) or paying to kiss the boot of a professional dominatrix at the *Hookers' Halloween Ball*. An array of nightclubs and the city's flourishing underground subculture round out a unique weekend of partying set against San Francisco's sinister mists, a golden October moon, and mournful groanings of foghorns off the bay.

The *Hookers' Halloween Ball*, an indoor event sponsored by the local prostitutes union (*really!*), attracts a large number of sex-industry workers, alternative types, curiosity-seekers, and open-minded partyers. With an attendance of 5,000, it's not a huge gathering, but as any of the pros here could tell you, it's not the size that counts—stamina and style are far more important. Everyone comes in costume, most are erotic, and a few revelers are a mere loincloth away from nudity. You can dance to local bands, go for verbal abuse or a beating in the dungeon room, or stop through the "carnival midway" to shop for bondage accessories.

At the *Halloween* street party in the Castro—homosexual center of the universe—you'll step into an outdoor cabaret theater. Halloween is San Francisco's Mardi Gras, and local eccentrics—gays and straights—make it crazy, bringing unequaled doses of drama and humor. You never know when you'll witness a stampede of "mad cows" or catch an all-male chorus dressed in Christmas lights and ostrich-feather minidresses, performing old Ziegfield Follies routines.

From food to feather fetishes, many trends have originated in the City by the Bay. While a visit to San Francisco's *Black and White Ball* provides a refined look at the city (see page 121), these three days emphasize San Francisco's multicultural and sometimes offbeat offerings. After all, it's the diversity of its people and the range of its offerings that make San Francisco one of the world's great and most visited cities.

Hookers' Ball/Halloween

Day 1. Fri. Oct. 29, 1999
(Day 1. Friday   October 27, 2000)

9:30am The chic, offbeat, original, and fun **Hotel Triton** is the perfect base for this weekend. With walking shoes on—it's a four-mile day—pass through Chinatown to nearby North Beach, the Italian district, for some of the world's best espresso drinks. Among many choices, **The Steps of Rome** is a good place to chat up local coffee types. Former beatnik hangout **Caffè Trieste** roasts its own coffee. Another '50s icon is **City Lights Bookstore**, which carries many works rejected by the publishing establishment.

11:00am Head north along Columbus, Grant, and/or Stockton streets to Washington Square Park, the heart of Little Italy. Hike up Telegraph Hill to take in some of the city's most photographed views from **Coit Tower**.

12:30pm Walk via the Greenwich and Filbert Steps down to and along Battery Street to **Yank Sing**. You could try an authentic Chinatown dive, but here you'll get the city's best dim sum in attractive surroundings.

3:00pm It's only a few blocks to Chinatown, the largest Chinese community outside of Asia. **Tien Hou Temple** and **Jeng Sen Temple** are worthy stops amid this excessively commercial district.

7:00pm Back in North Beach, enjoy a San Francisco institution, **Beach Blanket Babylon**, an outrageous cabaret show that helps confirm the city's offbeat reputation.

9:30pm South of Market Area (SOMA) attracts hip bar-hoppers who often start their evening with dinner at **Eleven**. The food and music is good, but the atmosphere is great—like being at a party.

11:30pm There are plenty of clubs—mostly catering to young people—within a short walk, but four long blocks away is Christy Turlington's **Up and Down Club**. There's a funky dance club upstairs and a more sophisticated jazz club on the street level.

Day 2. Sat. Oct. 30, 1999
(Day 2. Saturday   October 28, 2000)

10:00am Breakfast at **Café de la Presse**, next to the Triton, which has an international newsstand and tables out front.

11:00am Cab to Golden Gate Park and the **Asian Art Museum**, which has the largest collection of Asian art in the Western world. Stop at the **Japanese Tea Garden**, the oldest Japanese garden in the United States. Head east out of the park past bikers, skaters, runners, and walkers to the Haight-Ashbury district.

1:30pm In **Cha Cha Cha**'s tropical-fiesta atmosphere, piece together a *delicioso* lunch by sampling a variety of *tapas* (small plates).

3:00pm Though decidedly retail-oriented, the Haight is still hip. **Wasteland**, **The Aardvark's Odd Ark**, and **Piedmont Boutique** are sure bets for final touches on your costume. **Backseat Betty** carries "bad things for good girls and good things for bad girls." Return to your hotel and reflect on this: If you can remember the '60s, you probably weren't there.

8:00pm **Zuni Cafe** serves excellent nouveau-Mediterranean cuisine. One of the hottest restaurants in the city, it has a popular bar with live piano music, and you won't feel out of place in your costume.

10:00pm From 20-somethings to 70-somethings, guests at the *Hookers' Halloween Ball* check their inhibitions with their coats. Shop for a strop, G-spot T-shirt, or shiny new manacles. Booths hold representatives of adult publications, sex-education services, and alternative B&Bs (bed and bondages) where they don't do breakfast. At the boot-kissing booth, not only will unworthy you enjoy the privilege of planting one on Roxy's combat boots, you'll know that the $2 you pay for abuse goes to a charity fighting the maltreatment of your four-legged superiors. In the dungeon room, dominatrixes shackle, flog, and chastise all-too-willing volunteers. Whether you find this too much or too little, you can dance and people-watch for hours.

2:00am Several blocks away, the **Power Exchange Substation**—claiming to be San Francisco's only hetero sex club—accommodates lascivious tastes. There are safety rules, but once inside, just about anything goes. Rooms are rigged with bondage gear. Peepholes allow voyeurs to watch the action. Although "women, transsexuals, transvestites, and transgenders" are admitted free, only about a quarter of the patrons are hetero females.

Day 3. Sun. Oct. 31, 1999
(Day 3. Sunday   October 29, 2000)

9:30am The **Buena Vista Cafe** at Fisherman's Wharf claims to have introduced Irish coffee to the United States. It's also a fun place to have eggs and toast.

10:30am Walk along Fisherman's Wharf to the **Alcatraz** pier. Take in a wonderful ride on the bay, an interesting self-guided tour, and spectacular views of the city. (Tickets should be reserved a week in advance.)

1:30pm It's a short ride to **Greens** in Fort Mason. The Buddhist community's Zen Center operates this gourmet vegetarian restaurant. After lunch, visit the **Mexican Museum**'s changing exhibits of art and culture.

4:00pm Before returning to your hotel, relax and watch the kites at the Marina Green next door.

7:00pm Mecca's mingle-friendly bar is popular and its American-Mediterranean cuisine is superb. On Halloween, patrons show up in outrageous costumes then walk to Castro Street (avoiding traffic jams).

11:00pm The Castro is on fire! Especially from Market to 18th streets, revelers in homemade or cabaret-quality costumes dance, sing, and create as much mischief as possible. Beware the forest of human trees—you could be grabbed. Female impersonators dress as Valley girls or truck-stop waitresses. The ratio of voyeurs to participants varies, but everyone is giddy and one person's trick is another's treat at this Allhallow's Eve blast that could take place only in tolerant San Francisco. (In 2000, the Castro Halloween party takes place on Oct. 31, so you'll have to stay two more days to catch it.)

Alternatives

The famed *Exotic Erotic Ball* takes place the Saturday before Halloween weekend. *Exotic Erotic* draws 15,000 for the city's best and sexiest masquerade party. The entertainment features world-famous and local bands, Brazilian dancers, and circuslike acts with exotic-erotic twists.

The upscale **Pan Pacific**, downtown, is an attractive, comfortable modern hotel. **The Marriott at Fisherman's Wharf** is the high-end choice for that area. The **Harbor Court Hotel**, with bay views and refined English country-inn décor, puts you in SOMA.

223 Restaurant and Bar, near the Mecca and Zuni, has excellent food and a hopping crowd. On weekend nights, **Sol y Luna** is a good place for *tapas*. It converts to a fashionable Latin dance club after dinner hours. Try out star chef Reed Hearon's creations at either **Rose Pistola** (North Beach) or **Lulu** (SOMA).

The Hot Sheet

HOTELS		ADDRESS	PH	FX	PRICE	RMS	BEST ROOMS
Harbor Court Hotel	Alt	165 Steuart St.	415-882-1300 800-346-0555	415-777-5457	$$	177	Bay vw
Hotel Triton	★	342 Grant Ave.	415-394-0500 800-433-6611	415-394-0555	$$	140	Jr designer rms
The Marriott at Fisherman's Wharf	Alt	1250 Columbus Ave.	415-775-7555	415-474-2099	$$$	285	Junior suites
Pan Pacific	Alt	500 Post St.	415-771-8600 800-533-6465	415-398-0267	$$$$	330	Downtown SF vw

RESTAURANTS	DAY	ADDRESS	PH	PRICE	REC	DRESS	FOOD
2223 Restaurant and Bar	Alt	2223 Market St.	415-431-0692	$$	D	Kazh	American
Buena Vista Cafe	3	2765 Hyde St.	415-474-5044	$	B/L	Kazh	American breakfast
Café de la Presse	2	352 Grant Ave.	415-398-2680	$	B/LD	Local	American breakfast
Caffè Trieste	1	601 Vallejo St.	415-392-6739	$	B	Kazh	Pastries
Cha Cha Cha	2	1801 Haight St.	415-386-5758	$$	L/D	Local, Funky	Spanish, Cajun, Caribbean
Eleven	1	374 11th St.	415-431-3337	$$	D	Kazh, Local	Italian, American
Greens	3	Fort Mason Center, Bldg. A	415-771-6222	$$	L/D	Kazh, Local	Vegetarian
LuLu	Alt	816 Folsom St.	415-495-5775	$$	LD	Local	French Provençal
Mecca	3	2029 Market St.	415-621-7000	$$	D	Yuppie, Kazh	Mediterranean
Rose Pistola	Alt	532 Columbus Ave.	415-399-0499	$$	LD	Local	Seafood
Sol y Luna	Alt	475 Sacramento St.	415-296-8696	$$$	LD	Euro, Yuppie	Spanish, *tapas*
The Steps of Rome	1	348 Columbus Ave.	415-397-0435	$$	B/LD	Euro, Local	American breakfast
Yank Sing	1	427 Battery St.	415-781-1111	$$	L	Local	Dim sum
Zuni Cafe	2	1658 Market St.	415-552-2522	$$	D/L	Yuppie, Local	Mediterranean, Southwest

NIGHTLIFE	DAY	ADDRESS	PH	COVER	REC*	DRESS	MUSIC
Beach Blanket Babylon	1	678 Green St.	415-421-4222	$$$	S	Kazh	
Power Exchange Substation	2	86 Otis St.	415-974-1460	$	S	Local	
Up and Down Club	1	1151 Folsom St.	415-626-2388	$	P	Local	Hip-hop, jazz

SIGHTS & ATTRACTIONS	DAY	ADDRESS	PH	ENTRY FEE
Alcatraz	3	Pier 41	415-705-5555	$$
Asian Art Museum	2	75 Tea Garden Dr.	415-379-8800	$
Coit Tower	1	1 Telegraph Hill Blvd.	415-362-0808	$
Japanese Tea Garden	2	9th Ave. and Lincoln Blvd.	415-668-0909	$
Mexican Museum	3	Laguna St. and Marina Blvd. at the Fort Mason Center	415-441-0404	$

OTHER SIGHTS, SHOPS & SERVICES

	DAY	ADDRESS	PH	
The Aardvark's Odd Ark	2	1501 Haight St.	415-621-3141	None
Backseat Betty	2	1584 Haight St.	415-431-8393	None
City Lights Bookstore	1	261 Columbus Ave.	415-362-8193	None
Jeng Sen Temple	1	146 Waverly Pl.	415-397-2941	None
Piedmont Boutique	2	1452 Haight St.	415-864-8075	None
Tien Hou Temple	1	125 Waverly Pl.		None
Wasteland	2	1660 Haight St.	415-863-3150	None
San Francisco CVB		900 Market St.	415-391-2000	

Event & Ticket Info

Hookers' Halloween Ball (Venue to be confirmed): Tickets ($50) are usually available up to event time at the door, but you can buy them in advance through BASS Charge (800-225-2277) or Different Light Bookstore (415-431-0891).

Alternative Event
Exotic Erotic Ball: Exotic Erotic Ball Hotline, 415-567-2255

* M=Live music; P=Dancing (Party); R=Bar only; S=Show; (F)=Food served. For further explanation of codes, see page 14.

 NYC – 3   San Francisco (SFO) <30 min./$30 Yes/No   46°/69° (9°/21°)

December 1999

M T W T F S S
1 2 3 4 5
6 7 8 9 10 11 12
13 14 15 16 17 18 19
20 21 22 23 24 25 26
27 28 29 30 31

Houston/
Galveston,
Texas, USA

November/December 2000

M T W T F S S
27 28 29 30 1 2 3
4 5 6 7 8 9 10
11 12 13 14 15 16 17
18 19 20 21 22 23 24
25 26 27 28 29 30 31

Dickens on the Strand

Origin: 1974   Event ★ ★ ★ ★ ★ City   Attendance: 50,000

What do Charles Dickens and the Texas coast have in common? Not a thing, except for North America's largest Victorian Christmas celebration. Every year in the beachside city of Galveston, tens of thousands of revelers don period clothes and hoist cups of cheer to the literature and culture of 19th-century England.

What started as a potluck dinner to promote the city's historic venues has now become one of Texas' top winter events. Along with a day spent in search of the Ghost of Christmas Past, there are plenty of opportunities to enjoy Christmas present and future, thanks to a full schedule of attractions in nearby Houston. An array of nightclubs—with atmospheres ranging from spring break to elegant—round out the weekend of Texas partying.

Mention Galveston and Houston, the fourth-largest city in the United States, and two things come to mind: oil money and sandy beaches. Long the capital of the Texas oil "bidness," Houston, which earned the nickname Bayou City because it was founded near a creek (*bayou* is Southern for "creek"), is still dotted with high-dollar hangouts. The food scene is cosmopolitan, with a meaty Texas influence.

The choice of fun ranges from highbrow art museums and quiet botanical gardens to Texas-size nightclubs. December is a good time for a weekend that involves hopping into a car and driving from spot to spot—an activity best avoided during Houston's hellishly humid summers.

When you're ready for seaside fun, do what Houston's high rollers do: Head to Galveston Island, 50 miles to the southeast. In summer, all the fun takes place along its 32 miles of shoreline, but during winter, the party heads to the historic district of the city, The Strand.

The spirits of Oliver Twist, David Copperfield, and Queen Victoria come to this seaside party, where visitors are encouraged to take part in the period fun and dress the part as well. But whether you wear a cowboy hat, top hat, or no hat, you'll have a tough time topping this warm December weekend.

Dickens on the Strand

Day 1. Thu. Dec. 2, 1999
(Day 1. Thursday   November 30, 2000)

9:30am Check into the **Hyatt Regency Houston**—it's the city's largest hotel and has easy access to downtown attractions—and grab breakfast in the lobby cafe.

10:30am Walk downtown to get a sense of how oil money can be spent. Stop for a lofty perspective from the observation deck at **Chase Tower**.

Noon Lunch in the Montrose area, a funky neighborhood filling up with hip restaurants such as **Urbana**. The eclectic food is beautifully presented. If the weather cooperates, sit on the patio.

1:30pm View the **Menil Collection** of contemporary art, medieval pieces, and tribal artwork. The building itself is a work of art, designed by architect Renzo Piano of Italy. Nearby is the **Rothko Chapel**, which contains 14 site-specific paintings.

6:00pm For fine dining, try **Ruggles Grill**, which remains trendy, noisy, and hip.

7:30pm It's a holiday tradition and most fitting for this weekend—a production of Dickens' *A Christmas Carol*, performed by one of the nation's leading (and most underrated) theater companies, the **Alley Theater**. The theater itself is almost worth the price of admission.

10:00pm In the Theater District is the state's largest entertainment facility, **Bayou Place**. The $22 million nightclub-and-restaurant complex sprawls over 150,000 square feet. Stop by for a drink and sushi at **Sake**. It has a retro look and is the perfect place to end the day listening to Frank Sinatra. Or ...

11:00pm Stop at **Solero** for *tapas*, then head upstairs to its **Swank Lounge** for music and a nightcap.

Day 2. Fri. Dec. 3, 1999
(Day 2. Friday   December 1, 2000)

10:00am After breakfast in your hotel, choose one of two museums that are close to each other. The **Holocaust Museum Houston** was designed by the same person who created the one in Washington, DC, and it is a similarly moving exhibit. The **Museum of Fine Arts, Houston** has one of the nation's largest collections of art. It spans many centuries and cultures.

1:00pm Head to the Galleria area for a fine pan-American lunch at **Americas**. And although we don't usually recommend shopping, it is Christmas, and this is an amazing shopping center, so go to **theGalleria** to check out holiday decorations. This two-million-square-foot mall will be decked out with holiday decorations that include a Texas-size tree that rises from the middle of an ice-skating rink.

7:00pm Drive to dinner at **Maxim's**. Offerings here are pure gourmet: cream of lobster bisque, rack of lamb, chateaubriand, all enjoyed in one of four private dining rooms.

10:00pm Continue down Richmond Avenue. The hippest part of the thoroughfare is between the 5600 and 6500 blocks. Take your pick of bars featuring live rock, country, and blues. Check out **City Streets**, a "superclub" that's home to nightclubs for every interest: The Rose for country (all under a 35-foot replica of the Alamo); Blue Monkey for blues (guarded by a blue gorilla); the nautical-themed Atlantis for '70s and '80s hits; Cages for house music; and Stray Cats, a sing-along bar with dueling pianos.

12:30am For an upscale, late-night alternative, try **Sempers Supper Club** or **Elysee**. Both have dancing in a refined atmosphere.

Day 3. Sat. Dec. 4, 1999
(Day 3. Saturday December 2, 2000)

8:00am Enjoy a traditional Tex-Mex breakfast at the **Spanish Flower**, a star that stands out in a city that knows good south-of-the-border fare. Make sure to order extra tortillas—they come hot off the griddle.

9:00am Drive out to Clear Lake, about 20 minutes south of the city, for a look at the interactive visitor center for the **Space Center Houston**. This complex (created by Disney) brings the technology of space travel to a level that any visitor can enjoy. You can also eavesdrop on the crew of the space shuttle at Mission Status Center or take a behind-the-scenes tour.

1:00pm Continue driving south to Galveston. If you're staying over tonight, check into the European-style **Tremont House**, located in the heart of the festival action and within walking distance of most activities.

1:30pm Have some faire food and get in position for the **Queen's Parade**, led by a bagpipe band and the Queen's Guard of Beefeaters. The elegant procession of carriages and coaches is filled with men and women in Victorian finery and viewed by a heavily costumed crowd (there's free admission for those in period garb). The best viewing is from the second-floor balconies, but you'll have to quickly join the Galveston Historical Foundation to snag one of these aeries.

4:00pm Stroll The Strand, once called The Wall Street of the Southwest, to view the iron-front buildings that now house restaurants, pubs, and shops. Hear hand-bell choirs at Trafalgar Square, listen to carolers at Windsor Castle, and watch jugglers and magicians at Piccadilly Circus.

6:00pm When the last rays of sun fade, gas lanterns light up The Strand, marking the route of **Pickwick's Lanternlight Parade**. Costumed lantern-bearers escort parade wagons through streets in another salute to Christmas past.

7:30pm A short walk from the bustle brings you to **Fisherman's Wharf** for dinner—they serve delicious seafood with a view.

9:00pm Back in the thick of the party, choose from 27 draft beers at **Nina's Bourbon Street West** and enjoy local blues bands. Make a stop at **Yaga's Cafe & Bar** for live reggae music. Have a nightcap at **The Old Cellar Bar** and quietly reflect on Christmas past, present, and future.

Alternatives

Houston hosts a week-long shindig in September called *Houston Industries Power of Houston*. It includes downtown outdoor concerts, light shows, and food, wine, and beer tastings.

If you overnight in Galveston, have Sunday-morning tea at *1859 Ashton Villa*, an Italianate house and museum. You'll get typically British fare: fresh scones with marmalade, grilled tomatoes, and egg-and-cheese tarts. You can also enjoy the sounds of Christmas carols.

The **Hotel Galvez**, with a commanding view of the gulf, is a longtime Galveston favorite. In Houston, those looking for plenty of pampering will find it at the **Houstonian Hotel Club & Spa**, which has a full-service spa.

In Houston, you could try the ribs at **Goode Co. Barbecue** or have what many consider to be the finest meal in town at **Cafe Annie**. It's hard to choose among top-notch restaurants, but **La Griglia** is among the most hip in town. In Galveston, **Gaido's** serves up seafood fresh from the gulf. **The Wentletrap** offers an evening of fine dining at The Tremont, with esoteric favorites such as baked salmon Parmesan with gulf crab meat and lobster-brandy sauce or Hoisin pork tenderloin with Fuji-apple butter.

The **Houston Ballet** offers its version of *The Nutcracker* (see page 243) in the Wortham Center.

The Hot Sheet

HOTELS		ADDRESS	PH	FX	PRICE	RMS	BEST ROOMS
Hotel Galvez	Alt	2024 Seawall Blvd.	409-765-7721 800-996-3426	409-765-5623	$$	231	Gulf of Mexico vw
Houstonian Hotel Club & Spa	Alt	111 N. Post Oak Ln.	713-680-2626 800-231-2759	713-686-3701	$$$	291	
Hyatt Regency Houston	★	1200 Louisiana St.	713-654-1234 800-233-1234	713-658-8606	$$	963	City vw
The Tremont House	★	2300 Ships Mechanic Row	409-763-0300 800-874-2300	409-763-1539	$$	117	

RESTAURANTS	DAY	ADDRESS	PH	PRICE	REC	DRESS	FOOD
Americas	2	1800 Post Oak Rd.	713-961-1492	$$	L/D	Kazh	Southwestern
Cafe Annie	Alt	1728 Post Oak Rd.	713-840-1111	$$$	LD	Dressy	Continental, Southwestern
Fisherman's Wharf	3	Pier 22, Harborside Dr.	409-765-5708	$$$	D/L	Kazh	Seafood
Gaido's	Alt	3800 Seawall Blvd.	409-762-9625	$$	LD	Kazh	Seafood
Goode Co. Barbecue	Alt	5109 Kirby	713-522-2530	$	LD	Local	Barbecue
La Griglia	Alt	2002 W. Gray	713-526-4700	$$	LD	Dressy	Italian
Maxim's	2	3755 Richmond Ave.	713-864-8899	$$$	D/L	Dressy	French
Ruggles Grill	1	903 Westheimer Rd.	713-524-3839	$$$	D	Yuppie	American bistro, Southwestern
Sake	1	550 Texas Ave.	713-288-7253	$$	T/LD	Kazh	Japanese
Solero	1	910 Prairie St.	713-227-2665	$	T/LD	Local	*Tapas*
Spanish Flower	3	4701 N. Main St.	713-869-1706	$	B/LD	Local, Kazh	Mexican
Urbana	1	3407 Montrose	713-521-1086	$$	L/D	Kazh	Creole, Southwestern
The Wentletrap	Alt	2301 Strand	409-765-5545	$$$	LD	Dressy	Continental, French

NIGHTLIFE	DAY	ADDRESS	PH	COVER	REC*	DRESS	MUSIC
Alley Theater	1	615 Texas Ave.	713-228-8421	$$$	S	Kazh	
City Streets	2	5078 Richmond Ave.	713-840-8555	$	MP	Kazh	Rock, blues, country
Elysee	2	5055 Woodway	713-840-1115	$$	MP(F)	Dressy	Jazz
Houston Ballet	Alt	Wortham Center	800-828-2787	$$$	S	Kazh	
Nina's Bourbon Street West	3	215 22nd St.	409-762-8894	$	MP	Yuppie	R&B
The Old Cellar Bar	3	2013 Post Office St.	409-763-4477	None	R	Kazh	
Sempers Supper Club	2	2727 Crossview	713-782-6161	$	P(F)	Yuppie	International
Swank Lounge	1	see Solero restaurant	713-227-0459	$	P(F)	Local	'60s-'90s
Yaga's Cafe & Bar	3	2314 Strand	409-762-6676	$	MP	Kazh	Reggae

SIGHTS & ATTRACTIONS	DAY	ADDRESS	PH	ENTRY FEE
Chase Tower	1	600 Travis St.	713-228-8188	None
Holocaust Museum Houston	2	5401 Caroline St.	713-942-8000	None
Menil Collection	1	1515 Sul Ross	713-525-9400	None
Museum of Fine Arts, Houston	2	1001 Bissonnet St.	713-639-7300	$
Rothko Chapel	1	3900 Yupon	713-524-9839	None
Space Center Houston	3	1601 Nasa Rd. 1	800-972-0369	$$

OTHER SIGHTS, SHOPS & SERVICES

Bayou Place	1	520 Texas Ave.	713-230-1666	None
theGalleria	2	5075 Westheimer Rd.	713-621-1907	None
Greater Houston CVB		801 Congress	713-227-3100	

Event & Ticket Info

Dickens on the Strand (The Strand and 25th Street): Tickets ($8) are available at the gates. For information, contact *The Galveston Historical Foundation* (409-765-7834).

1859 Ashton Villa (2328 Broadway): Tickets ($14) for Morning Tea (breakfast) are available from *The Galveston Historical Foundation* (409-765-7834).

Alternative Event

Houston Industries Power of Houston: The Power Line, 713-684-6465

Houston—Area Code 713   Galveston—Area Code 409

* M=Live music; P=Dancing (Party); R=Bar only; S=Show; (F)=Food served. For further explanation of codes, see page 14.

 NYC –1   Houston Intercontinental (IAH) <60 min./$35
Hobby (HOU) <30 min./$20   Yes   43°/66° (6°/13°)

The Fun Also Rises

Christmas Nuts

Ask enough people what they do for fun during the holidays and you're likely to hear stories about dancing snowflakes, flying Christmas trees, and battles in which multiheaded mouse kings are felled by a girl's slipper. Maybe you dipped into the eggnog one time too many, but more likely, you'd be hearing a description of *The Nutcracker* ballet, the annual holiday-season drama that, for roughly two million fans each year, is as traditional as fruitcake and family gatherings.

The production that introduces many to classical dance, *The Nutcracker* is the most widely performed ballet in the world. Dance companies offer performances from Thanksgiving through New Year's, with several productions competing in large metropolitan areas. *The Nutcracker* is so beloved that it provides significant chunks of most ballet companies' budgets.

Based on the book *The Nutcracker and the Mouse King* (written by E.T.A. Hoffmann and revised by Alexandre Dumas), the legendary Marius Petipa, first ballet master to His Imperial Majesty, the Russian Tsar, created a detailed story and commissioned his friend, Peter Ilyich Tchaikovsky, to compose the music. Despite the weighty credentials of its writers, *The Nutcracker* was not well-received when it debuted in St. Petersburg in 1892.

But the show survived and, in 1944, the San Francisco Ballet brought *The Nutcracker* to the United States, offering its own choreography. It wasn't until 1954, however, that Americans fell in love with the production, when Russian George Balanchine created his signature full-length staging for the New York City Ballet. Now, many different versions are performed worldwide, including performances featuring the original choreography. In the United States, more than 550 dance companies perform *The Nutcracker*, with the biggest audiences in Boston and the most versions to choose from in the San Francisco Bay Area.

Attempts to widen audience appeal and translate the old-fashioned German setting into modern scenarios have produced increasingly novel adaptations. Ballet Arts Minnesota features rat armies on Rollerblades hurling cheese bombs. New Jersey's Suburban Dance Force cruises Clara, the heroine, through a Lemonade Sea to the classic surf-rock tune "Wipeout." The Pacific Northwest Ballet uses sets designed by off-the-wall children's author Maurice Sendak. The Baton Rouge Ballet Theatre sets its "Bayou Nutcracker" in the antebellum South, complete with plantations and a hot-air balloon grand entrance to the Land of Sweets. A "Southwest Nutcracker" in Tucson replaces Clara with Maria Martinez and includes Indian princesses and Clara's godfather dressed as Zorro. New York City's Mark Morris Dance Group throws the classical ballet out the window, but keeps the music in its "Hard Nut," replacing jetés and pliés with the frug, watusi, and hokey-pokey. Several companies, including Donald Byrd/The Group's "Harlem Nutcracker," translate the whole production to jazzy modern dance. San Francisco has the "Dance-Along Nutcracker," sponsored by the Lesbian/Gay Freedom Band—after some basic ballet instruction beforehand, sold-out performances feature hundreds of kids and adults, many in rented tutus, dancing to their own creative drummers, with some pas de deux looking suspiciously more like polkas.

Even without eccentric interpretation, the original *Nutcracker* is zany, with mouse-army battles and Clara arriving in fantasy lands riding sleighs, owls, and unicorns. No wonder that in the end she's surprised to wake up in her own bed. Was it real or all a dream? Clara's mother tells her, "If you love something very much it is always alive." The same sentiment can inarguably be applied to *The Nutcracker* ballet.

Las Vegas Rodeo
(National Finals Rodeo)

Origin: 1985	Event ★ ★ ★ ★ ★ ★ ★ City	Attendance: 140,000

What's riskier than wrestling a one-armed bandit in Glitter Gulch? If you're cinching up atop one of the world's meanest 2,000-pound bulls, *high steaks* takes on a whole new meaning. To an outsider, Las Vegas might seem incongruous with the down-and-dirty sport of rodeo, but this is big business Vegas style: The purse at the ***National Finals Rodeo (NFR)*** has grown from $500,500 in 1980 to more than $4 million in 1998.

The ***NFR*** features the cream of the crop from each year's Professional Rodeo Cowboys Association regular-season competitions. The top fifteen in each of the rodeo's seven main events—saddle-bronc riding, bull riding, bareback riding, calf roping, team roping, steer wrestling, and barrel racing—compete for prize money, sponsors, and glory.

The best cowboys and cowgirls travel thousands of miles to as many as 125 rodeos each year with the dream of driving their pickups down the Strip, past the lights, noise, and other hopefuls to the Thomas and Mack Center on the University of Nevada, Las Vegas campus. But the contestants aren't the only ones who find it a tough row to hoe to get to the ***Finals***. More than 170,000 tickets to the 10-performance event are sold each year, but the ***NFR*** is still one of the toughest tickets to come by in the sporting world. Thousands of fans travel to Las Vegas each December in the often-vain attempt to pick up scalped tickets.

Rodeo events are must-sees every night, but what goes on before and after is vintage Las Vegas, albeit with a kind of twang that speaks to the city's frontier roots. Las Vegas doesn't see this many cowboy hats in a year (for Vegas with a more Rat Pack feel, come for Super Bowl weekend, see page 51), and Western entertainment is found at almost every casino lounge and showroom. This weekend's standouts—Gold Coast, Sam's Town, and the ever-present Ricky and the Red Streaks at the Stardust—provide a look at an edgy, Western side of Vegas most people don't expect.

Las Vegas Rodeo

We've abandoned our itinerary formula for this chapter in favor of a more general overview of options built around the rodeo.

Hotel

If you're not dressed in Western attire, you might feel out of place at the **Gold Coast Hotel & Casino**, which caters to bull riders and buckle bunnies. As in most other casinos, the **NFR** is broadcast live and free on closed-circuit television. Other favorites are the **Binion's Horseshoe** hotel and **Sam's Town Hotel and Gambling Hall**. The only classy resort on the Strip that draws a large country contingent is the **MGM Grand**. The place is so big they could hold the rodeo in the center of the casino and no one would even notice.

Breakfast and lunch

Cheap eats are synonymous with Vegas. You won't have much farther to look for a bountiful breakfast than your hotel or casino's coffee shop. If you prefer your meals with all the excess this town is known for, line up for one of the huge buffets around town.

Area attractions

Las Vegas' main attraction is, of course, gambling. But this is the only week of the year when you can experience gambling as it might have been in the Old West, with lots of cowboy hats seated around blackjack tables waiting for the chance to cash in a winning hand with a big ol' "Yahoo!"

The **Fremont Street Experience** is a five-block electric canopy of twinkling Christmas lights suspended 90 feet above downtown Las Vegas. Live entertainment and more than two million light bulbs dazzle viewers.

If you're craving man-made wonder of a different type, make the short trip to the impressive **Hoover Dam**.

If you don't have the duds to do up the weekend right, do a little Western shopping at the NFR Cowboy Christmas Gift Show at Cashman Field Center. Remember this inviolable rodeo rule: No Gap jeans! Wranglers jeans and Justin boots are what you want.

Many Vegas hotels offer modern "visual attractions." At Sam's Town, it's the **Sunset Stampede**, an entertaining laser-and-water show.

Dinner

It's easy to eat cheap and big in Vegas—casinos don't mind losing money on food as long as customers walk across gaming floors to eat it. For down-home barbecue, many hotels feature cook-offs. **Mortoni's** in the Hard Rock Hotel offers high-quality Italian. New York, New York is worth a visit, not only for its awe-inspiring construction, but for the upscale **Gallagher's Steakhouse** and Italian restaurant, **Il Fornaio**, on its lower level.

Late-night entertainment

Lookin' for your next ex? **Dylan's Dance Hall & Saloon** is the place you might meet him or her. Big beers and lots of music act as aphrodisiacs during the **NFR**, or so the tall tale goes. Many of country music's biggest stars make a point to play to their fans during the **NFR**, so check local papers.

Other hot spots are the upstairs **Western Dance Hall** at Sam's Town and the downstairs hideaway with the postage-stamp-size dance floor at **Roxy's Saloon**. Nonstop action at **Rockabilly's** and the **Gold Coast Showroom**, converted during *Rodeo* to a huge Western dance hall, compete with the popular Ricky and the Red Streaks at the **Stardust Ballroom**. Ricky's raucous show, great dance music, and no dance floor make for quite a scene as hundreds of people end up dancing on the tables.

The Hot Sheet

HOTELS	ADDRESS	PH	FX	PRICE	RMS	BEST ROOMS
Binion's Horseshoe	128 E. Fremont St.	702-382-1600 800-237-6537	702-384-1574	$	360	Mtn vw
Gold Coast Hotel & Casino	4000 W. Flamingo Rd.	702-367-7111 888-402-6278	702-365-7505	$	740	Mtn vw
MGM Grand	3799 Las Vegas Blvd.	702-891-1111 800-929-1111	702-891-1030	$$	5,005	Grand Tower
Sam's Town Hotel and Gambling Hall	5111 Boulder Hwy.	702-456-7777 800-634-6371	702-454-8014	$	650	Park vw

RESTAURANTS	ADDRESS	PH	PRICE	REC	DRESS	FOOD
Gallagher's Steakhouse	3790 Las Vegas Blvd. S, New York New York hotel	702-740-6450	$$$	D	Kazh	Steakhouse
Il Fornaio	3790 Las Vegas Blvd. S, New York New York hotel	702-650-6500	$$	D	Kazh	Italian
Mortoni's	4455 S. Paradise Rd., Hard Rock Hotel	702-693-5047	$$$	D	Local	Italian

NIGHTLIFE	ADDRESS	PH	COVER	REC*	DRESS	MUSIC
Dylan's Dance Hall & Saloon	4660 Boulder Hwy.	702-451-4006	None	MP	Kazh	Country
Gold Coast Showroom	see Gold Coast Hotel	702-367-7111	$	MP	Kazh	Country
Rockabilly's	3785 Boulder Hwy.	702-641-5800	None	MP(F)	Kazh	Country
Roxy's Saloon	see Sam's Town Hotel	702-456-7777	None	MP	Kazh	Country, Top 40
Stardust Ballroom	3000 Las Vegas Blvd. S	702-732-6111	$	MP	Kazh	Country
The Western Dance Hall	see Sam's Town Hotel	702-456-7777	None	MP(F)	Kazh	Country

SIGHTS & ATTRACTIONS	ADDRESS	PH	ENTRY FEE
Fremont Street Experience	downtown, Fremont Street	702-678-5600	None
Hoover Dam	Hwy. 93, 36 miles SE of Las Vegas	702-294-3523	$
Sunset Stampede	see Sam's Town Hotel	702-456-7777	None
Las Vegas CVB	3150 Paradise Rd.	800-332-5333	

Event & Ticket Info

National Finals Rodeo (Thomas and Mack Center, UNLV, Tropicana Avenue at Swenson): Tickets ($27-$40) always sell out and are available only by lottery. About 200-500 SRO tickets are released the day of each rodeo. For ticket-lottery applications and information, contact *The Thomas and Mack Center Ticket Office* (702-895-3900) or *Las Vegas Events* (702-260-8605).

Downtown Hoedown & Downtown Rodeo Stampede: Fremont Street Experience, 702-678-5600

Benny Binion's NFR Bucking Horse and Bull Sale: The Thomas and Mack Center Ticket Office, 702-895-3900

Wrangler Tight Fittin' Jeans: (Holiday Inn Boardwalk Hotel & Casino, 3750 Las Vegas Blvd. S.): Free. Contact *Inventive Incentives* (888-321-7238)

Alternative Event

Miss Rodeo America Pageant: Miss Rodeo America Inc., 719-948-9206

Rodeo Rules

In addition to music, Las Vegas also hosts other rodeo events (see Event & Ticket info). For NFR action itself, don't plan any activities from about 6:45–9 p.m. nightly and for the final Sunday-afternoon competition. Here's a quick primer: Rodeos consist of two types of events. Bareback riding, saddle-bronc riding, and bull riding are the roughstock events. To qualify, cowboys have to stay on the bucking horse or bull for eight seconds. There are also timed events: calf roping, steer wrestling (also called the big-man's sport), and team roping. Ladies compete in barrel racing, where the line between human and animal blurs in a colorful display of teamwork and tight pants.

* M=Live music; P=Dancing (Party); R=Bar only; S=Show; (F)=Food served. For further explanation of codes, see page 14.

 NYC –3   McCarran (LAS) <30 min./$15   Yes   34°/57° (1°/14°)

December 1999

December 2000

New York, New York, USA

New Year's Eve New York

Origin: 1904	Event ★ ★ ★ ★ ★ ★ ★ ★ City	Attendance: 500,000

I f you like nothing better than a good party, there's really only one place to celebrate *New Year's Eve*: New York City's Times Square. With an overload of party opportunities, the world's tallest buildings, fastest pace, biggest business, and best of almost everything, anywhere, it's not surprising that New York hosts the biggest and most extravagant December 31 celebration on the planet.

I f you're ready to give up your seat on the couch come the end of the year, head for Times Square for the dropping of the famous ball (300 million will view the annual ritual on television). Don't want to stand in the cold with 500,000 of your closest and newest friends? Neither do we. Reserve a spot offering glamour, comfort, and a view at one of several hotels and restaurants on the square. Watch as the famous rhinestone ball begins its descent at 11:59 p.m., accompanied by 3,000 pounds of fluffy, floating confetti.

E ver since *The New York Times*, namesake of the square, sponsored the first ball lowering in 1907, the celebration has been a worldwide symbol of *New Year's Eve*. Now organized by the Times Square Business Improvement District, the festival includes strobe lights, pyrotechnics, and speeches, as well as the famous countdown to the new year and

the booming of fireworks going off in nearby Central Park. While the Times Square festivities are revving up, several other parties are already in full swing around the city, including First Night, a spinoff of the party that originated in Boston that features various events throughout the day and evening.

G ear up for the big night by exploring Manhattan Island, which stretches a narrow 22.7 miles between the East River and Hudson Bay, provides the backdrop for countless Hollywood movies, and is one of the most popular travel destinations in the world. Contrary to popular opinion, New York City sometimes does sleep, but it does so only grudgingly, and never before popping the corks on a few bottles of champagne.

New Year's Eve New York

At press time, details and prices for New Year's Eve 1999 events had not been determined. The only thing for certain is that New York will be a great place to be. Look for information on millennium events in our companion edition, The Fun Also Rises Travel Guide International, *as well as on our Web site.*

Day 1. Wed. Dec. 29, 1999
(Day 1. Friday   December 29, 2000)

8:00am A stroll through the **Royalton** hotel's block-long luxury-liner lobby prepares you for a three-day cruise through the greatest city on earth. The location is perfect, the service is impeccable, and the suites—ask for one with a circular bathtub—are gorgeous.

9:00am Start your visit to New York the way the ancestors of one out of four living Americans did—at **Ellis Island**. Cab to Battery Park at the tip of Manhattan and take the ferry. First stop is the **Statue of Liberty**. Unless you plan to climb the 354 steps for the 22-story view, it'll be a short visit to the ground-level museum before catching the ferry to Ellis Island. It takes about 90 minutes to tour the museum, which presents not only the history, but the fear, exhilaration, and hope associated with immigrating to the United States.

Noon Since you're in the neighborhood, stop at the **World Trade Center**. The incredible view from the 107th floor is augmented by interesting displays.

1:00pm Hail one of the 12,000 new and rejuvenated cabs that fill the city streets and head to Union Square. On Green Market days (Monday, Wednesday, Friday, and Saturday), sip hot cider and breathe in the scent of pine boughs before settling in for lunch at the **Union Square Cafe**. One of the most popular restaurants in New York, there's plenty to choose from on the American-with-hints-of-Italian menu and plenty to look at while you're deciding what to have.

3:00pm Long before the United Nations made the city its official headquarters in 1947, New York was an international city. But go to the **United Nations Headquarters** building for a fascinating tour of this landmark and a glimpse of the inner workings of the Security Council and General Assembly.

5:00pm It's a bit of a hike or a short cab ride back to your hotel for a well-earned break.

7:30pm Head downstairs to the hotel lobby's sunken bar for a warm-up drink or two. Celebrity sightings are not uncommon here. Make sure to check out the unusual restrooms, with fun-house-style mirrored walls and doors. Then go to the chic **44** restaurant for dinner.

10:00pm Make a foray to **The Four Seasons Hotel** bar after dinner, the classiest bar in New York. Just across from the 58th Street hotel entrance is a longtime hot spot, **Au Bar**. You'll know the place by the fleet of intimidating bouncers standing outside—it's a semiprivate club with a "guest list."

11:00pm Kick your heels over to **China Club** for house music and dancing. Immortalized by occasional *Saturday Night Live* skits, it's a loud, crowded place with lots of good-looking players. Proceed to **The Supper Club** for swing until your feet hurt—or 4 a.m., whichever comes first.

Day 2. Thu. Dec. 30, 1999
(Day 2. Saturday   December 30, 2000)

10:30am After waking up to the smell of fresh orchids and a room-service breakfast, walk nine blocks to the **Museum of Modern Art**. This airy, four-story museum showcases Van Gogh, Picasso, Andy Warhol, Jackson Pollack, Georgia O'Keeffe, and many others.

12:30pm In the middle of the winter wonderland at Rockefeller Center is an eight-stories-high Christmas tree that stands alongside an ice rink with skaters of all ages happily gliding around. The **Sea Grill** sits next to the ice and gives diners a fabulous view of the action. The fresh fish and American cuisine, open dining room, and service are all excellent. After sampling one of their killer desserts, rent a pair of skates and try taking a few graceful turns around the ice.

3:30pm Head back up Fifth Avenue toward 57th Street, where a giant snowflake graces the intersection. Christmas may be over, but there's still plenty of shopping (and, of course, gift exchanging) to do. Buy a packet of roasted chestnuts from a street vendor to keep you warm as you stroll down the avenue. 'Tis the season for decorations in the shop windows, and Tiffany & Co., Bergdorf Goodman, Steuben Glass, and Saks Fifth Avenue are but a few of the shopping experiences available. Explore St. Patrick's Cathedral along the way.

4:45pm Stop for tea at the elegant **New York Palace**, then walk back to the Royalton for a breather.

7:15pm For nighttime entertainment, head out for your pick of Broadway plays or choose from the offerings at the beautiful Lincoln Center, including the **New York City Ballet**'s *Nutcracker* (see page 243). Going to New York and not seeing a stage show is like going to Alaska and not seeing snow.

10:00pm Have a post-theater dinner at **Asia de Cuba**, the hottest restaurant in town. Inexpensive Cuban-Chinese eateries have long surprised visitors and been a staple of various New York neighborhoods, but Asia de Cuba elevates the unique cuisine to a more sophisticated level. Make a drink foray to the ultrachic **Morgans Bar** in the Morgans hotel.

12:30am Head to the **Tunnel** disco for dancing before calling it a night.

Day 3. Fri.   Dec. 31, 1999
(Day 3. Sunday   *December 31, 2000)*

9:30am If you get up early, head to Greenwich Village or farther south to SoHo. Both neighborhoods provide

wonderful walking opportunities. Make mental notes of funky spots you may want to check out later. Or walk ten blocks to the **Empire State Building**, the tallest building in the world when King Kong scaled it in 1933. Take the three elevators to the 102nd-floor observation deck for an unobstructed look over Central Park, Queens, New Jersey, and the twin towers of the World Trade Center.

11:30am No stay in New York would be complete without a visit to the **Carnegie Deli**. People come from all over the world to be served plenty of attitude with their scrambled eggs with lox and an onion bagel. Some of the wait staff seems as if they've been there since Moses (or at least Charlton Heston) parted the Red Sea. You could try one of their mile-high corned-beef sandwiches.

1:00pm After you've had your fill, get on your high horse —with a buggy attached. Pick from the lineup of horse-and-buggy duos at the south end of Central Park. Many are decorated in individual styles by their operators.

2:00pm The **Metropolitan Museum of Art** is practically a city in itself. Pick up a map at the information booth and choose from ancient Egypt, Asia, impressionists, 20th century, sculpture courts, or one of many other fascinating exhibit areas. You could spend an entire day here and not see the same thing twice.

4:30pm Buy a knish or a pretzel with mustard from one of the street carts in front of the museum. Walk down Madison Avenue, which in recent years has begun rivaling Fifth Avenue for shopping. You'll spot Barney's, Calvin Klein, Armani, and many other high-end shops.

7:00pm It's *New Year's Eve*! The party begins at Times Square. Give your black bow tie a tweak as you maneuver past the crowds that started assembling in the late afternoon. Head to the Renaissance Hotel for a spectacular party at *Foley's Fish House*, the upscale place to be. It's high above the crowds and has an awesome, unobstructed view of the *New Year's Eve* ball drop. Hang out at the bar before dining on very fresh fish. With room for only 80 folks, this classy, exclusive party is the gala of a lifetime. Dance to a jazz band and wait for the ball to drop. If you'd rather feel closer to the street-party atmosphere, trade the perfect view for more excitement at the nearby *Marriott Marquis*. It offers a bigger and rowdier party in two areas of the hotel. The views of Times Square are not as good, but you still get great city views and a feel of the energy circulating below.

11:45pm Watch as the excitement mounts in the square, and the mayor gets ready to drop the ball with practice countdowns and cheering from the parka-covered crowd. At 11:59 p.m., the ball begins its descent.

Midnight The glittering ball falls toward the heart of Times Square, 3,000 pounds of confetti float down on the heads of the party-goers below, the crowd erupts in cheers, and fireworks fills the skies.

12:30am The square clears out soon after the year commences, but there's no reason you have to go home yet. Unless, of course, you're planning to catch a quick flight to Nassau for Junkanoo, an event that begins the year with a 2 a.m. party (see *The Fun Also Rises Travel Guide International*). Whenever you do get to bed, dream about all the FUN the new year will bring!

Alternatives

Check the *First Night* New Year's Eve schedule. From ballroom dancing to ice-skating, this event is filled with fun activities all over Midtown Manhattan. Grand Central Station features various dancing exhibitions and events. In the evening, take a spin in the center of the station, where a dance band transforms the station into a grand ballroom with party-goers putting their ballroom-dancing lessons to good use.

Morgans hotel delivers modern comfort. Called the handsomest hotel in New York, it's located in Midtown Manhattan. The beautiful geometric patterns and décor will remind you of an Escher drawing. Every convenience is offered. Take advantage of the complimentary continental breakfast and afternoon tea. Morgans is also home to Morgans Bar and the spectacular Asia de Cuba restaurant. **The Four Seasons Hotel** is about as expensive as you can get, but it's elegant, chic, and the hotel of choice for many celebrities.

Le Cirque 2000 (formerly just Le Cirque) has a classic French kitchen that has been famous for years. Also on the list of trendy restaurants are **Patria** and **Indochine**. **Ferrier Bistro** has a small bar and restaurant, but it has the best recorded music in the city, along with good French-bistro fare.

Match Uptown has a lively bar scene along with a very good restaurant. In SoHo, the place to be is **Boom**, a restaurant with an active bar scene. If you go to Lincoln Center, a great stop for dinner afterward is **Iridium**—it has a jazz club downstairs. In Greenwich Village, try the new **Mercer Kitchen**. A hip dance club in the village is **Life, The Nightclub**.

You'll feel right at home in steel magnate Henry Clay Frick's old residence, which houses the **Frick Collection** of world-class European masterpiece portraits, antique furniture, and other valuable items he and his family collected throughout his lifetime.

Haven't had your fill of modern art? The **Solomon R. Guggenheim Museum** offers fantastic shows and art collections in a six-story spiral rotunda. If you can find time for the **American Museum of Natural History**—which displays more than 500,000 artifacts—must-sees include the History of Man exhibit, the replica of a life-sized blue whale hanging from the ceiling, dinosaur skeletons, and best of all, the Gem and Mineral Room where you can gawk at fallen meteors and glittering gems the size of a fist.

The Hot Sheet

HOTELS		ADDRESS	PH	FX	PRICE	RMS	BEST ROOMS
The Four Seasons Hotel	Alt	E. 57th St.	212-758-5700 800-332-3442	212-758-5711	$$$$+	370	Central Park vw
Morgans	Alt	235 Madison Ave.	212-686-0300 800-334-3408	212-779-8352	$$$	113	Madison Ave. vw
Royalton	★	44 W. 44th St.	212-869-4400 800-635-9013	212-869-8965	$$$$	168	Suites w/Japanese circular tubs

RESTAURANTS	DAY	ADDRESS	PH	PRICE	REC	DRESS	FOOD
44	1	44 W. 44th St.	212-944-8844	$$$$	D/BL	Dressy	American, continental
Asia de Cuba	2	237 Madison Ave.	212-726-7755	$$$$	D/L	Dressy	Latin, Asian fusion
Boom	Alt	152 Spring St.	212-431-3663	$$	LD	Kazh	Continental
Carnegie Deli	3	854 Seventh Ave.	212-757-2245	$$	B/LD	Kazh	Deli
Ferrier Bistro	Alt	29 E. 65th St.	212-772-9000	$$	LD	Kazh	French
Indochine	Alt	430 Lafayette St.	212-505-5111	$$$	D	Yuppie	French, Vietnamese
Iridium	Alt	48 W. 63rd St.	212-582-2121	$$	D	Kazh	American
Le Cirque 2000	Alt	455 Madison Ave.	212-303-7788	$$$$+	LD	Dressy	French
Match Uptown	Alt	33 E. 60th St.	212-906-9177	$$$	LD	Yuppie	Pan-Asian
Mercer Kitchen	Alt	99 Prince St.	212-966-5454	$$	LD	Kazh, Local	American
New York Palace	2	455 Madison Ave.	212-888-7000	$$	T	Kazh	Finger sandwiches
Patria	Alt	250 Park Ave. S	212-777-6211	$$$$+	LD	Dressy, Kazh	Latin
Sea Grill	2	19 W. 49th St.	212-332-7610	$$$	L/D	Dressy	Seafood
Union Square Cafe	1	21 E. 16th St.	212-243-4020	$$$$+	L/D	Dressy	American

NIGHTLIFE	DAY	ADDRESS	PH	COVER	REC*	DRESS	MUSIC
Au Bar	1	41 E. 58th St.	212-308-9455	$$$$+	P(F)	Euro	Disco
China Club	1	268 W. 47th St.	212-398-3800	$	MP	Kazh	Rock
The Four Seasons	1	99 E. 52nd St.	212-754-9494	None	R(F)	Dressy	
Life, The Nightclub	Alt	158 Bleeker St.	212-420-1999	$$	MP	Dressy, Kazh	R&B, progressive rock, funk
Morgans Bar	2	see Morgans hotel	212-726-7600	None	R(F)	Euro	
New York City Ballet	2	20 Lincoln Center	212-870-5570	$$$$+	S	Dressy	
The Supper Club	1	240 W. 47th St.	212-921-1940	$$	MP(F)	Dressy	Swing
Tunnel	2	220 Twelfth Ave.	212-695-4682	$$	P	Kazh	Contemporary

SIGHTS & ATTRACTIONS	DAY	ADDRESS	PH	ENTRY FEE
American Museum of Natural History	Alt	Central Park W at W. 79th St.	212-769-5100	$
Ellis Island Museum	1	Liberty Island	212-363-3200	$
Empire State Building	3	350 Sixth Ave.	212-736-3100	$
Frick Collection	Alt	1 E. 70th St.	212-288-0700	$
Metropolitan Museum of Art	3	Fifth Ave. at 82nd St.	212-535-7710	$
Museum of Modern Art	2	11 W. 53rd St.	212-708-9480	$$
Solomon R. Guggenheim Museum	Alt	1071 Fifth Ave.	212-423-3500	$$
Statue of Liberty	1	Liberty Island	212-363-3200	$
United Nations Headquarters	1	First Ave. betwn. 42nd and 48th sts.	212-963-7713	$
World Trade Center	1	1457 Broadway	212-323-2340	$$
New York City CVB		810 Seventh Ave.	212-484-1222	

Event & Ticket Info

New Year's Eve Times Square (Times Square, Broadway at 47th Street): For information, contact *Times Square Business Improvement District* (212-768-1560).

Foley's Fish House (Renaissance New York Hotel, 714 Seventh Ave.): Most recent information for the dinner ($550 per person) notes that this venue is sold out for New Year's Eve 1999. Contact *Foley's Fish House* (212-765-7676).

New York Marriot Marquis (1535 Broadway): Most recent information lists The View Lounge Party ($299 per couple) and two different dinner parties ($499 per couple) sold out for 1999. Contact the *New York Marriot Marquis* (212-704-8747).

Alternative Event
First Night: First Night Hotline, 212-922-9393

* M=Live music; P=Dancing (Party); R=Bar only; S=Show; (F)=Food served. For further explanation of codes, see page 14.

NYC   John F. Kennedy (JFK) <60 min./$40   La Guardia (LGA) <30 min./$30   No   30°/41° (-1°/5°)

State and Provincial Tourist Boards

United States and Canada

J ust in case you've been to all of the events in this book and still want to explore more of North America, here are some useful telephone numbers:

Alabama	800-252-2262	North Carolina	800-847-4862
Alaska	907-465-2010	North Dakota	800-437-2077
Arizona	800-842-8257	Ohio	800-282-5393
Arkansas	800-628-8725	Oklahoma	800-652-6552
California	800-862-2543	Oregon	800-547-7842
Colorado	303-892-1112	Pennsylvania	800-237-4363
Connecticut	800-282-6863	Rhode Island	800-556-2484
Delaware	800-441-8846	South Carolina	800-868-2492
Florida	888-735-2872	South Dakota	800-732-5682
Georgia	800-847-4842	Tennessee	615-741-2158
Hawaii	800-353-5846	Texas	800-888-8839
Idaho	800-635-7820	Utah	800-200-1160
Illinois	800-226-6632	Vermont	800-837-6668
Indiana	800-289-6646	Virginia	800-847-4882
Iowa	800-345-4692	Washington	800-544-1800
Kansas	800-252-6727	Washington, DC	202-789-7000
Kentucky	800-225-8747	West Virginia	800-225-5982
Louisiana	800-261-9144	Wisconsin	800-372-2737
Maine	800-533-9595	Wyoming	800-225-5996
Maryland	800-543-1036	Alberta	800-661-8888
Massachusetts	800-227-6277	British Columbia	800-663-6000
Michigan	800-543-2937	Manitoba	800-665-0040
Minnesota	800-657-3700	New Brunswick	800-561-0123
Mississippi	800-927-6378	Newfoundland	800-563-6353
Missouri	800-877-1234	Northwest Territories	800-661-0788
Montana	800-847-4868	Nova Scotia	800-565-0000
Nebraska	800-228-4307	Nunavut	800-491-7910
Nevada	800-237-0774	Ontario	800-668-2746
New Hampshire	603-271-2343	Prince Edward Island	800-463-4734
New Jersey	800-537-7397	Québec	800-363-7777
New Mexico	800-545-2040	Saskatchewan	800-667-7191
New York	800-225-5697	Yukon	403-667-5340

Junos

Alan Davis, Author

Alan is a needy person. He's spent his life taking on nearly impossible tasks in the hopes of gaining sympathy. Apparently it didn't work. But then what made him think that spending four years travelling to the world's most fun events is deserving of sympathy? Alan, an entrepreneur, philanthropist, publisher, and lecturer, began travelling professionally as a tour representative in 1967. This career path was interrupted by the pursuit of politically correct endeavors, but a fortune cookie set him back on the right path: "Preserve wild life—throw more parties."

Chuck Thompson, Editor

Alan Davis met Chuck Thompson while both were on assignment at Carnival in Trinidad. How Davis convinced Thompson to give up such extraordinary assignments to spend six months in front of a computer is a mystery for the ages, but great fortune for the readers of this book. Thompson is a contributing editor for *American Way* and *Escape* magazines. A senior travel editor for *American Way* magazine until 1997, he has worked on assignment for a variety of magazines in more than 15 countries.